Advances in Infancy Research

Volume 1

Contributors to This Volume

Marc H. Bornstein

Jerome S. Bruner

Jeffrey W. Fagen

Candice Feiring

Tiffany Field

Michael E. Lamb

Michael Lewis

Hanuš Papoušek

Mechthild Papoušek

Carolyn K. Rovee-Collier

ADVANCES IN INFANCY RESEARCH

VOLUME 1

editor
Lewis P. Lipsitt

Department of Psychology
and Child Study Center
Brown University
Providence, Rhode Island

associate editor
Carolyn K. Rovee-Collier

Department of Psychology
Rutgers University
New Brunswick, New Jersey

ABLEX Publishing Corporation

ISBN: 0-89391-045-7

ABLEX Publishing Corporation
355 Chestnut Street
Norwood, New Jersey 07648

Contents

Developing Trust and Perceived Effectance in Infancy
Michael E. Lamb

Direct and Indirect Interactions in Social Relationships
Michael Lewis and Candice Feiring

Musical Elements in the Infant's Vocalization: Their Significance for Communication, Cognition, and Creativity

Mechthild Papoušek and Hanuš Papoušek

The Retrieval of Memory in Early Infancy

Carolyn K. Rovee-Collier and Jeffrey W. Fagen

List of Contributors

(Numbers in parentheses indicate the pages on which the authors' contributions begin.)

Marc H. Bornstein: Department of Psychology, New York University, New York, New York 10003 (1)

Jerome S. Bruner: Harvard University, Cambridge, Massachusetts 02138 (41)

Jeffrey W. Fagen: Department of Psychology, Rutgers University, New Brunswick, New Jersey 08903 (225)

Candice Feiring: Educational Testing Service, Princeton, New Jersey 08540 (129)

Tiffany Field: Department of Pediatrics, Mailman Center for Child Development, University of Miami Medical School, Miami, Florida 33101 (57)

Michael E. Lamb: Departments of Psychology, Psychiatry, and Pediatrics, University of Utah, Salt Lake City, Utah 84122 (101)

Michael Lewis: Educational Testing Service, Princeton, New Jersey 08540 (129)

Hanuš Papoušek: Max-Planck-Institut Für Psychiatrie Klinik, Münich, Germany (163)

Mechthild Papoušek: Max-Planck-Institut Für Psychiatrie Klinik, Münich, Germany (163)

Carolyn K. Rovee-Collier: Department of Psychology, Rutgers University, New Brunswick, New Jersey 08903 (225)

PREFACE

This volume inaugurates a new series dedicated to the report of recent advances in infancy research. The need for the series has been apparent from the beginning of the publication of *Infant Behavior and Development,* the only English-language journal devoted exclusively to infancy research. With the publication of *Advances in Infancy Research,* this Publisher and this Editor have joined forces in a three-part publication effort including the aforementioned journal, the *Advances in Infancy Research* volumes, and a new series of monographs, called *Monographs on Infancy.* I am pleased to have Carolyn Kent Rovee-Collier joining me in the present endeavor as Associate Editor.

No other specialty within the field of child development has grown faster in recent years than that of infant behavior and development. We intend to provide in *Advances in Infancy Research* a forum for those who wish to write larger than journal-size and smaller than monograph-size. The middle-sized presentations which will find their way to this resource will be technical and scholarly articles. They will serve as primary references on authors' programmatic studies, critical collations of diverse data which yield to a common theme, and constructive attacks on old issues with new inputs.

We will invite presentations by scholars with exciting and innovative research programs relating to both human and animal infancy. Such an approach will not prevent the enlistment of seasoned authors with longstanding research programs, especially if we can persuade such authors to stand away from their accustomed vantage points and entertain new perspectives.

Although appearance in this series will be principally by invitation, in rare instances uninvited papers will be considered if submitted first in outline form. Whether invited or submitted, all papers will receive review by experts close to the area encompassed by the manuscript. It is our hope to guide authors to write *Advances* papers that will make substantive contributions for experts in the area and at the same time provide an overview of a critical topic in the field for readers whose own work is peripheral to the area covered.

The Editor acknowledges with gratitude the aid of his home institution, Brown University, which provided time and facilities toward the preparation of this volume. Much of the work on this first volume was carried out while the Editor was a Fellow of the Center for Advanced Study in the Behavioral Sciences at Stanford; we are indebted to the administration and staff of that wonderful place for facilitating this effort. I also wish to thank the following consultants for their editorial assistance: Eve V. Clark, Carol O. Eckerman, Robert N. Emde, Jerome Kagan, James Larimer, and Mark Liberman.

Finally it is with great pleasure that this volume is dedicated to Myrtle B. McGraw. Her contributions to the understanding of infant behavior and development are as much appreciated today as in their initial presentations. Myrtle McGraw has been a prolific researcher and writer in her own time. We can do no better than attempt to emulate her erudition and steadfast scholarship, her persistence in the presence of professional obstacles, her devotion to the developmental sciences, and her encouraging faith that advances in the field of infant development, and particularly brain-behavior relationships during that development, are the stuff of which maturity is made.

Lewis P. Lipsitt

DEDICATION

Myrtle B. McGraw, to whom we respectfully dedicate this first volume of *Advances in Infancy Research,* has been one of our finest pioneers in the study of infant behavior and development. She remains today a lively, inquisitive, avid aficionado of infancy research, of the literature on development, and of the people who are doing the research and writing about it.

It is fitting that a volume of this sort especially should be dedicated to Myrtle McGraw, for as one of the first developmental psychobiologists she concentrated much of her research effort on the understanding of *transitions in development.* Research *Advances* such as will be reported in these volumes are transitional episodes. They represent the achievement of a scholarly and intellectual plateau, at which authors may step back for a longer-range view of their past researches, the better to draw inferences and tentative conclusions from the results and history of their programmatic studies in order to see the future of the research area more clearly.

Myrtle McGraw has been a visionary, for in her scholarly orientation and research thrusts she swam, to an extent, against the tide. The waters in those early days of her work were safer for descriptive explorations, the documentation of changing behavior as a function of increasing age, the construction of norms from extensive *descriptive* studies, and the development of psychometric procedures based upon these norms. McGraw was more interested in the processes and mechanisms of behavior change than she was in the description and discussion of the developmental or behavioral status of children of different ages. She wanted to know how the brain worked and how the behavior reflected the mediating influence of the maturing brain. Her studies, like those reflected in her classic volumes, *Growth: A Study of Johnny and Jimmy* (N.Y.: Appleton-Century, 1935), and *The Neuromuscular Maturation of the Human Infant* (N.Y.: Columbia University Press, 1943), were about the influences of early experience on subsequent behavior, they were about the ontogeny of the brain, and the changing behavioral capacities which tissue change could permit, and they were about the behavior crises (she called them disorganizations and struggles) which the infant might endure even in the first year of life as brain-behavior *transitions* were transacted.

Myrtle McGraw is now at work on her reminiscences (she denies she is writing her autobiography), bound to be nuggets of reflection on her own early development, her mentors, her times (both good and hard), her legacy, and her uninterrupted devotion to the field of child development.

Professor McGraw was born August 1, 1899, "in the deep South." She earned her A.B. degree at Ohio Wesleyan in 1923, and her Master's and Ph.D. at Columbia University Teachers College (T.C.) in 1925 and 1931, respectively. A research assistant in the Institute for Child Development in 1928–1929, she held a Laura Spellman Rockefeller Fellowship in Child Development in 1927, and was a Psychology Intern at the Institute for Child Guidance in 1929. From 1930 to 1942 Dr. McGraw was associate director of the Normal Child Development Study at Babies Hospital, Columbia Presbyterian Medical Center. In 1942, Dr. McGraw says she became "a surburban mother and occasional teacher" at New York University and Adelphi University, whereafter, in 1953, she was appointed Professor of Psychology at Briarcliff College. She remained at Briarcliff until 1972, when she retired.

Dr. McGraw's publication history is impressive, before, during, and after her mothering days, and her thoughtful writings will generate further inquiry for years to come. With respect and affection we dedicate the first of this series to Myrtle McGraw. She will help this infant to endure, thrive, develop.

Foreword

CHALLENGES FOR STUDENTS OF INFANCY*

Myrtle B. McGraw

Two waves of concern about infancy and early childhood have hit the United States during this century. The first wave occurred during the 1920's and 1930's. We are in the midst of the second. A better appreciation of the current interest can be achieved if we take a glance at some of the parallelisms and divergences which characterized the earlier investigations.

For more than two thousand years, the infant had received scant attention by those engaged in intellectual inquiry (Aries, 1965; Sunley, 1968). What were the forces that triggered the arousal of researchers to the study of infancy in the 20th century? Certainly among the most influential forces was Darwin's Theory of Evolution. Darwin himself was among the first to conduct systematic observations of his own babies (Darwin, 1877). He was not concerned, however, with the nature of infancy or with the process of growth. Darwin's purpose was to accumulate evidence supporting his theory on the origin of the species. His identification of man with all other species provided the theoretical framework for that persuasive dichotomy, heredity *versus* environment. Darwin's theory paved the way for two significant assumptions: (1) that principles of behavior derived from investigations of animal subjects are applicable to the human; and (2) those traits present in the behavior of the newborn child can be ascribed to heredity, and those acquired subsequently are attributable to environmental influences.

The predominant investigators at the beginning of the century were drawn from that rising young academic discipline, Psychology. Those choosing animals as subjects focused their attention primarily on the phenomena of learning. They were of the opinion, apparently, that the "laws of learning" were universal, and that neither the age of their subjects nor the species was of prime importance. In fact, many of the animal researchers of that era never bothered to record the age of the rats whose trials and errors were being meticulously counted. They did not consider growth and development as

*Portions of this statement were published in *American Psychologist,* 1970, *25,* 754–756, and are reprinted here with permission of the American Psychological Association.

variables. Nevertheless, the principles of learning based upon laboratory studies of animals permeated pedagogical thinking and methods during the early decades of this century.

Although not the earliest to make objective observations of infants, John B. Watson was the first psychologist to subject newborn infants to what might be called scientific investigation. His purpose was not to study the process of growth and development. Rather, Watson sought to determine what specific traits, manifest in the newborn, were hereditary and presumably immutable. He found few. He thereupon became the archexponent for the environmentalist. From Pavlov's conditioning experiments with dogs, Watson captured a theoretical frame of reference appropriate for an explanation of complex human behavior. The theory was that if one could adequately control the environment of a growing child, one could, through the process of conditioning, mold that child according to one's choice. Clearly this theory put great responsibility upon adults responsible for child rearing.

After Watson left the academic laboratory and turned to advertising, he published for popular consumption (Watson, 1928). Perhaps Watson was the first scientific psychologist to invade popular journalism and to have a direct and immediate impact upon cultural practices in the bringing up of young children. Some of us still remember conscientious parents of the 1930's who would not dare pick up the crying infant; the child might become "conditioned" and cry in order to be picked up. Toilet training was to be started at about three weeks, and children should not be lifted off the potty until they performed, lest the conditioning process be interrupted. Feeding and sleeping were scheduled according to the clock, and parents were admonished not to cuddle or fondle infants lest they become too dependent upon parental attention.

In the laboratories the nature-nurture issue became a prime target for both animal and child investigators. The heredity versus environment controversy had them really locked into a conceptual bind. How to determine and to measure that which was innate and immutable, and distinguish this from what was acquired and was amenable to training? Aye, there was the rub!

Gesell challenged the rigid environmental view of Watson (Gesell and Thompson, 1929). Gesell contended that there was nothing one could do through training young infants to accelerate their development; one simply had to wait until the cells of the nervous system "ripened." Within this framework, Gesell introduced another dichotomy, that of maturation *versus* learning. Actually, this is closely related to the heredity-environment dichotomy, except that it does imply a kind of unfolding or delayed emergence of innate traits. In any event, it took some of the pressure off parents to start toilet training infants at three weeks, or to assume all the blame for their child's delayed or deviant behavior. On the other hand, another of Gesell's contributions to child development, for which he was most famous, would appear to be in contradiction to his maturation theory. It had a pernicious anxiety-arousal effect upon the parental public.

The use of intelligence tests with studies of school children had become accepted by psychologists as an effective means of measuring intellectual potential. The best known of these was Terman's Revision of the Binet which yielded an I.Q. (Intelligence Quotient). The I.Q. was the relation between mental and chronological age as reflected by the test scores. For some time it was taken for granted that the I.Q. reflected innate endowment. Gesell (1934) undertook to set up standardized tests for infants and for children below school age. What can one include in a behavioral test for infants? Only what the child is able to do, such as when he begins to sit, creep, walk, handle objects, and so on. On the basis of ratings on these tests, the child was given a Developmental Quotient (D.Q.), and its correlation with the I.Q. was heralded. While it was never stated categorically by Gesell or his coworkers, the general impression among the parental population was that the infant's D.Q. presaged the potential intellectual endowment. It became the vogue, especially among educated parents, to compare an infant's development against the Gesell norms. It is easy to see how these two contributions of Gesell would have anxiety-arousal qualities among parents. On the one hand, his maturation theory stated there was nothing one could do to accelerate an infant's development. On the other, the child's psychomotor achievements were presumed to forecast mental endowment.

This is not the proper occasion to take up a general discussion of the whole standardized testing movement and its effect upon American society in every facet. It should be pointed out, however, that every scientist longs for a good instrument of measure. The standardized test was the tool which the early developmental psychologists seized upon as a convenient instrument for measuring development. The essence of the standardized tests is that they are notations of achievement. They are like inventories of performances, milestones along the road. But they don't tell *how* the child got there! This focus upon achievements in the 1930's seems to have shunted the experimental psychologists away from the study of the *processes* of growth. It is rather interesting that in the first decades of the century, under the influence of G. Stanley Hall, students of child behavior were called "Genetic Psychologists." Then, as the measurement techniques gained precedence, they came to be known as "Child Psychologists." Within the profession child psychology was always a kind of stepchild of general and experimental psychology. Later, for some subtle reason, students of child development came to be called "Developmental Psychologists." But the Developmental Psychologists did not alter their methodologies or concepts appreciably from those that had been practiced earlier by the Child Psychologists. The child was compartmentalized, as the tables of contents of textbooks reveal. These categories went like this: infancy, preschool, middle years, puberty, and adolescence, or: motor development, language development, emotional development, personality development, and so on. None of these categories is adequate to reflect the process of growth, the phenomenon of constant change, and the interaction of one system with another. Perhaps one reason these aspects of growth and development were not given due recognition by the early experimentalist was that there was no easy method for measuring a constantly changing phenomenon. We should have a specialty called "Growth Scientist."

Research psychologists were not the only ones who called attention to the significance of infancy and early childhood. Nor were they the only ones who contributed to the cultural thinking and practices with regard to child rearing. Perhaps the greatest, certainly the most pervasive, impact upon the culture came from psychoanalytic theories. Freud's ascription of adult neurosis to early childhood experiences lifted somewhat the behavioristic pressure for achievement and placed the emphasis upon personality adjustment, and particularly upon child-parent relationships. It cannot be said, however, the psychoanalytical theories and practices restored parental confidence. It is true that the Victorian taboos over infantile psychosexual behavior such as thumb sucking and masturbatory activities were removed and parents were admonished to give love to their child. Parental love became something of a panacea. Parents were warned of the dangers of rejection or overprotection of the child. In practice these warnings were often confusing. Was a mother overtly demonstrating love in order to cover up her basic feelings of child rejection? Certainly during this century a great body of factual data about child development has accumulated and a plethora of concepts and theories have become a part of the cultural milieu. Yet we still have a generation of uncertain, anxiety-ridden parents.

THE CURRENT FOCUS ON EARLY CHILDHOOD

It is not possible to pinpoint any particular ideologies or theories which have given rise to the present interest in early childhood development. The forces were many; they were complex and intertwined. Sputnik shocked the nation out of a state of educational complacency. The disparity of educational opportunities and achievements of children from differing socioeconomic and ethnic groups was brought to light. It was suggested that children from less favorable environments entered school with their educational handicaps already established. To alleviate this situation, the federal government set up Head Start programs. The outcome of the Head Start programs has led to the claim that even the prekindergarten period is too late. Education begins in the cradle.

Clearly the goal of this current wave of concern is to develop the optimum potential of all children. The prevailing notion is that these goals can be achieved by manipulation of the environment in which the child lives. To some extent these ideas are reinforced by experiments on the effects of "sensory deprivation," "prolonged isolation," and the comparative effects of "enriched and impoverished" environments. Such studies have been conducted on animals, children, and adults. Once again, the emphasis seems to be shifting to the environmental side of the continuum, but it is not locked in with the old heredity-environment dichotomy. It is generally recognized now that nature-nurture are interdependent forces and to try to separate them clouds inquiry. A few studies (McGraw, 1935; Moore, 1960; Fowler, 1962) have demonstrated that the performances of the young, in some specific activities, can be advanced beyond normal expectancy. But we have not as yet learned how to develop to the maximum the potential of all growing children.

CHALLENGE FOR THE RESEARCHERS
OF GROWTH

Contemporary Growth Scientists are the legatees of a vast body of concepts, theories, and research strategies inherited from the "psychological establishment." Of course, the Growth Scientists will be drawn from many disciplines and from diverse areas of psychology including Developmental Psychology. Already it is apparent that some dyed-in-the-wool experimentalists are selecting the human infant in preference to animals for special investigations. The challenge for all the students of growth, regardless of their scientific expertise and theoretical orientation, is to scan the legacy of knowledge and skills, and to have the courage to rule out those theories and techniques which are not applicable to the study of complex, ever-changing phenomena relating to the growth and development of organisms. Many experimentalists fail to consider that their own preconceptions may operate as uncontrolled variables within a particular situation.

Will the experimentalist, skillful in the manipulation of the variables and instruments of measurement, be able to recognize that the way the infant is held or positioned may also be a factor in the results obtained? Will the examiner be so focused on toddlers' responses to the items set before them that it goes undetected that the child's wiggling and climbing off the chair and running toward the door is his way of saying that there is pressure on his bladder? Will researchers trained to use the I.Q. be able to devise strategies to evaluate a multiplicity of systems constantly in flux, each system influencing another and in different degrees? All growth and development is not in the form of accretion. The Growth Scientists will need to design methods which reveal the rises and falls, the pulsations and rhythms manifest in the growth of a given function. An understanding of these pulsations and rhythms may become promising guidelines for the development of optimum potentials of the growing child. There is evidence that many current investigators (see Endler, Boulter, and Osser, 1968) are alert to the problem and that is the first step to improving methodologies.

THE CHALLENGE OF CULTURAL ACCEPTANCE
OF SCIENTIFIC THEORIES

In the past it has been traditional for scientists, especially those dealing with basic sciences, to be removed from the applied implications of their findings. They were searching for fundamental truths, and whatever society did with them was none of their concern. On the other hand, many atomic physicists have voiced a sense of responsibility for the way society makes use of their knowledge. During this century, we have been able to see how many psychological theories have been applied and misapplied in the matter of child rearing and education. If the periods of infancy and the early years are as important for total development as generally contended, it is reasonable to expect the behavioral scientists to take some responsibility for the way in which their thoughts and theories are adopted into the cultural patterns of child management. Just how this can be done is not clear because it has never been systematically undertaken by any scientific discipline. The general public has faith in science and the mass media, and is quick to announce that science has proved one thing or another. Sometimes the misapplication of a theory may be ascribed to the use of a particular word, perhaps a word that was originally drawn from another discipline.

Let us consider for a moment some current thoughts which have the potential for creating parental anxiety. Take the question of "critical periods" as applied to learning. The concept was first used by embryologists. It was reinforced by Lorenz's (1935) study of imprinting. Recently it has been emphasized in connection with the studies of effects of an impoverished environment. It has been asserted that if the impoverishment occurs at critical periods, then the damage done may be irreversible (Bowlby, 1969). Back in 1935 (McGraw, 1935), the writer applied the term "critical period" to the acquisition of motor skills during infancy. If the agreed meaning of the term "critical periods" carries the idea that whatever is attained in development or learning *must* be achieved during a specified period, then the term should not be applied to normal behavioral growth. In the aforementioned instance, it was intended to signify that there are *opportune* times when specific activities can most economically be learned. If that opportune time is missed, then the methods of instruction should be altered for later learning of the same function. It is the irreversibility of damage done which adds emotion and fear to the "critical period" concept.

The amount of emphasis attached to certain concepts can also distort their meaning when adopted into the culture. Take, for example, the current emphasis on cognition. No investigator would contend that cognition operates independently of other aspects of learning. Yet merely because it is the focus of investigative activity, cognition, like the old notion of personality adjustment, is a kind of umbrella for other goals. Expose the child to the right knowledge, in the right way, and at the right time, and the job would be well done.

Perhaps most urgently of all, Growth Scientists need to review the accepted principles of learning as they have been articulated and generally accepted. These learning principles were determined largely by animal studies in laboratory situations and studies of children in the classroom. There is every reason to suspect that they are not applicable to the process of growth taking place during infancy and the early years. There is pressing need for totally new guidelines for the benefit of those persons responsible for the management and socialization of the child from birth to three years. The most dominant force is change, change in the organism and change in behavior from day to day. Consistency in parental management doesn't mean setting up a pattern or rule and sticking to it. It means dealing with a child in a manner consistent with the individual's developmental changes. To do this effectively requires knowledge, sensitivity, intuition and flexibility. So the challenge is to orient mothers and teachers toward the concept of change, not toward stability in the ordinary sense. Parents should be taught to observe, to scan, and to detect the non-verbal as well as verbal signals of child growth, and to design methods of instruction accordingly.

The United States may well be at the threshold of institutional reorganization for the care and education of the young. To help children develop will require new knowledge and special preparation on the part of those responsible for them. They need to be knowledgeable, but also intuitive and observant. Child care specialists and parents will require preparation quite unlike that offered to elementary school teachers or even mothers of today.

The Growth Scientists are challenged to provide a theoretical frame of reference for the education of infants and young children. They are advised also, to take account of the way in which their theories and pronouncements are adopted into the culture so that the growing child of today can confidently meet the social changes of the 21st century.

REFERENCES

Aries, P. *Centuries of childhood.* New York: Vintage Books (Random House). 1965.

Bowlby, J. *Attachment and loss* (Vol. 1): *Attachment.* London: Hogarth (New York: Basic Books) 1969.

Darwin, C. Biographical sketch of an infant. *Mind,* 1877, *2,* 285–294.

Endler, N. S., Boulter, L. R., and Osser, H. *Contemporary issues in developmental psychology.* New York: Holt, Rinehart, and Winston, 1968.

Fowler, W. Teaching a two-year-old to read. *Genetic Psychology Monographs,* 1962, *66,* 181–283.

Gesell, A. *Infant behavior: Its genesis and growth.* New York: McGraw Hill, 1934.

Gesell, A. and Thompson, H. Learning and growth in identical twins. *Genetic Psychology Monographs,* 1929, *24,* 3–212.

Lorenz, K. Der kumpan in der Umwelt des Vogels. Der Artgenosse als auslosendes Moment sozialer Verhaltungsweisein, *Journal of Ornithology,* 1935, *83,* 137–213.

McGraw, M. B. *Growth: A study of Johnny and Jimmy.* New York: Appleton-Century, 1935.

Moore, O. K. *Automated responsive environments.* Hamden, Ct.: Basic Education, Inc., 1960 (a film).

Sunley, R. Early nineteenth century literature on child rearing. In D. Evans Ellis (Ed.), *Readings in behavior and development.* New York: Holt, Rinehart, and Winston, 1968.

Watson, J. B. *The psychological care of infant and child.* New York: W. W. Norton, 1928.

PSYCHOLOGICAL STUDIES OF COLOR PERCEPTION IN HUMAN INFANTS: HABITUATION, DISCRIMINATION AND CATEGORIZATION, RECOGNITION, AND CONCEPTUALIZATION

Marc H. Bornstein

NEW YORK UNIVERSITY

Advances in Infancy
Research, Vol. I

I. INTRODUCTION

This chapter is concerned with some of the ways in which young human infants perceive color. Described are investigations of color perception, rather than of chromatic sensation. The developmental study of *chromatic sensation* tends to be quantitative and is concerned with sensory questions such as, When does the human infant begin to see color? The developmental study of *color perception* tends to be qualitative and is concerned with perceptual or cognitive questions such as, Do infants remember simple and complex colors equally well? In just the last few years research has advanced considerably in many areas of sensory psychophysics so that today we have a substantially better understanding than before of the nature of sensory abilities and functions near the beginning of life (see, for example, Cohen & Salapatek, 1975, or Salapatek & Cohen, 1982). One area in which especially rapid advances have been made is chromatic vision. Research activity between 1975 and 1980 has shown that after approximately three or four months postnatal, human beings are probably *seeing* color in a normal, trichromatic fashion and in a way that will remain essentially stable until old age (Bornstein, 1978; Bornstein & Teller, 1982). The principal aims of this *Advances* chapter are to look at issues related to the infant's *perceiving* color and to compare and contrast infant color perception with that of adults.

II. TWO LEGITIMATE QUESTIONS

It is legitimate to ask two basic questions at the outset of a chapter concerned with infant color perception. First, Why study color perception? And, second, Why study the early development of color perception in infants?

The first question engenders a quite succinct reply: Color is a significant source of information about the environment. Aside from its terrific aesthetic value for primates, which itself is significant since aesthetics has direct implications in eliciting and maintaining visual attention, color is nearly ubiquitous in the environment. Most natural or man-made objects in the world are colored. Further, color serves several basic psychological functions: Color aids in the visual differentiation of surfaces, it helps to mediate object recognition, and it facilitates visual search. In this sense, color is a highly important perceptual attribute of things. Thus, it is hardly surprising that surveys of the human factors literature indicate that we locate objects in visual space more readily and accurately on the basis of our knowledge of their color than on the basis of alternative visual cues such as size or shape (e.g., Christ, 1975).

Why, second, an infant-developmental view? Vision, in general, seems to be especially important in infancy; it is a principal information-gathering mode, and color is, as I have suggested, a significant source of information about the environment. For infants and very young children, color may be an especially salient perceptual cue (e.g., Dodd & Lewis, 1969; Lewis & Baumel, 1970; Young-Browne, Rosenfeld, & Horowitz, 1977). Further, it may be valuable to study color perception in infancy for its contribution to our understanding normative perceptual processes at an early stage of development, that is, to know the quality, limits, and functions of this kind of perception (among others) early in life. In turn, the study of perception in infancy permits critical developmental comparisons; in this way, for example, immature perception can be compared or contrasted with mature perception.

For these reasons, and probably for many others, there has been a sustained scientific interest in the development of both chromatic sensation and color perception (see Bornstein, 1978, for a recent historical review). Significantly, that history began over a century ago with the benchmark publication of Charles Darwin's (1877) biographical sketch of son Doddy. Darwin wondered whether and when his infant child could see colors; these are, as I have suggested, sensory and quantitative questions. The topics in this chapter, written a century later, address questions on the perceptual and qualitative side.

III. SENSATION VERSUS PERCEPTION

In color, the study of sensation is separable from the study of perception. Yet, at the same time the study of sensation is integral to the study of perception. Is this a paradox? I think not. Psychologists who investigate *color sensation* tend to be psychophysiologists and psychophysicists interested in topics related, on the one hand, to retinal anatomy, central mechanisms of neuronal processing of color, etc., and, on the other, to spectral luminosity, the mathematical theory of color vision, etc. Knowledge about these topics is independent of much of the subject matter that occupies psychologists who investigate *color perception*. Preference, discrimination, organization, and memory exemplify issues with which perceptual and cognitive psychologists are concerned. However, in color, the investigation of perceptual questions is not independent of the investigation of sensory ones; at minimum, data about sensory function are crucial to structuring perceptual experiments. The best example of this asymmetry is represented in the knotty (and historical) problem of the brightness-hue confound in color. This problem is neatly summarized in the following question: If the infant prefers, discriminates, groups, or remembers particular colors, is she doing so on the basis of their hue or on the basis of their brightness? In changing colors, the variables of hue and brightness can be confounded, and it is incumbent on the perceptual psychologist to separate the two in order to come to firm conclusions about the perception of either one alone. Such a separation (for example, in the control of brightness cues) depends, however, on information garnered from studies of sensory function, in specific of spectral sensitivity and brightness discrimination. In this way, progress in understanding perception depends asymmetrically on progress in understanding sensation.

Two interrelated assumptions that are born of the foregoing considerations underpin and motivate the research into perceptual processes reported here. The first is that perceptual studies in infancy that have involved color heretofore have usually failed to examine colors under sufficiently specified or controlled conditions so that, for example, investigators could say exactly which wavelengths at what luminances were shown or could point with relative certainty to hue, rather than, say, to brightness, as the effective independent variable. Corollarily, hue has only infrequently been treated as a single dimension in infant studies of color perception in the past. The second assumption motivating this research is that the sensory study of chromatic vision in infancy has presently advanced to the point where, really for the first time, perceptual studies of color (at least in older infants) have been able to proceed on reasonably informed sensory grounds.

This chapter presents the results of a series of recent studies that have investigated questions related to the infant's perception of color. These experiments were conducted with specified stimuli under appropriately controlled conditions so that they speak to issues in color perception in a new, informed way; further, color is applied to a wide variety of issues in separate spheres of perceptual development.

IV. SOME STUDIES OF COLOR PERCEPTION IN INFANTS

The seven sections that follow look at a set of specific issues in how color is perceived near the beginning of life. These include the differential perception of simple versus complex colors by infants; the status of color in the component-compound-configuration question in infant perception; the infant's perception of hue qualities in the spectrum; the infant's ability to discriminate within and between hues; whether the "discrepancy principle" applies in the domain of color; the infant's differential recognition of simple and complex colors; and, the early development of a concept of color by babies. Some of these issues are unique to color perception; or, using color makes a unique contribution to the perceptual issue. Each section briefly considers research related to a particular area of infant perception and then focuses around one or two new experiments; the data on a given subject are not yet complete in some cases. In the spirit of an *Advances* series, these discussions are often speculative; sometimes they are intentionally provocative.

By themselves, both the study of color and the study of infancy are modestly esoteric and technical topics. For this reason, it may be helpful to review, if only briefly, the basic methods by which these specific studies of infant color perception have progressed.

A Note on Methods.

Typically these infant studies are conducted on term, healthy babies on or about their four-month birthday. This is the reference group to which proper generalization could be made. No infants with any familial history of color-vision deficiency are included. Experimental groups are usually constructed of equal numbers of boys and girls; groups typically total approximately 10; and these groups are always constructed by a random assignment of subjects.

The infant sits in a standard infant chair facing a matte-white stimulus panel; chromatic stimuli are exposed through a central window in the panel. A view of the infant's face and a signal lamp light (above and behind the baby) that indicates exposure of a stimulus are televised over one monitor to an experimenter behind the stimulus panel and over a second monitor to an observer. This video signal is also recorded to be scored at a later time.

Chromatic stimuli in these experiments consist of glossy-collection Munsell Hues of blue (dominant wavelengths: 470 nm, 475 nm, 476 nm, and 477 nm), blue-green (490 nm and 491 nm), green (504 nm and 507 nm), green-yellow (565 nm and 567 nm), yellow (581 nm and 583 nm), yellow-red (599 nm and 603 nm), red (493c), and purple (551c and 552c). Color is a tridimensional stimulus domain comprised of variations in hue, brightness, and saturation. (The latter two are Value and Chroma in Munsell terms.) Although brightness and saturation might vary with experimental requirements, in general hue is the principal subject of study *passim,* and in these experiments stimuli are equated for Value (usually at 5/) and Chroma (/2 or /10). In research that is to involve hue perception, brightness differences must be controlled. Because of recent advances in the psychophysics of infant color perception, our understanding how to control brightness has greatly increased. For example, we know that the young infant's spectral sensitivity is on a par with that of the young adult (e.g., Bornstein & Teller, 1982), that the infant's discrimination of achromatic stimuli falls to chance at adult brightness matches (Peeples & Teller, 1975), and that the infant's successive discrimination of brightness is quite poor next to his simultaneous discrimination of brightness or his successive discrimination of hue (Kessen & Bornstein, 1978). Bornstein and Teller (1982) fully discuss the rationales, methods, and adequacy of the experimental control of variables like brightness in infant color research. The studies reported in this chapter rely on recent developments in our understanding of chromatic vision in infants in that the colors used are equated for brightness by adult spectral sensitivity coefficients—in the Munsell system, the equation for Value and Chroma is by adult judgments—and the discriminations tested are typically successive. Both tactics significantly diminish the role of brightness vis-à-vis hue as a compelling factor in the results.

Munsell colors are uniform to standardization if the illuminant used in their display approximates C.I.E. Illuminant 'C' (6700° K) under which they are originally calibrated. Color samples used in these studies are flooded from overhead with light of an appropriate color temperature (6500° K). The luminance of the colors is 51.3 cd/m^2, and ambient light in the infant observation room is 30 fL. Stimulus size for the infant usually approximates $12° \times 17°$.

Infant's looking to hundredths of a second is judged from video-tape records of the baby's face and eyes by scorers unaware of which stimuli were presented or in which experimental group the infant participated. Interscorer reliabilities in judging the attention of infants are always high ($rs > .90$).

Analysis of these perception studies has never shown that the infant's sex is a meaningful or significant factor. Accordingly, results here are always reported with data from boys and girls pooled.

A. Colors: Simple Versus Complex

Although physically continuous, the natural spectrum appears to adults as divided into four prominent regions represented by psychological qualities of hue commonly called *blue, green, yellow,* and *red.* Most colors have more than one hue quality in them, however. Within a color region, the green for example, those toward the short-wavelength end are increasingly bluish, whereas those toward the long-wavelength end are increasingly yellowish. Away from its boundaries—between blue and green and between green and yellow—and toward the center of the green region, a narrow band of wavelengths appears minimally bluish or yellowish. They are purer green and are in a sense psychologically simple. Colors that approximate a boundary between hues represent increasingly equal contributions of two hue qualities and hence are psychologically more complex. In brief, the extent of domination of one hue quality in a color helps to determine the relative psychological status of the color as "simple" or "complex."

Psychological complexity may have implications for cognitive processing of colors. Adults learn and identify simple colors faster than complex ones (Beare, 1963; Heider, 1972; Rosch, 1978). For example, in three experiments, Bornstein and Monroe (1980) recently found that, *ceteribus paribus,* adults will name and classify simple colors (centers of color categories) more rapidly than complex (boundary) ones.

Human infants, like adults, have given evidence that they, too, perceive qualitative regions or hue categories in the spectrum; that is, babies respond to wavelength variation within a limited spectral region as if they perceive the region to be dominated by one perceptual quality (Bornstein, Kessen, &

Weiskopf, 1976). Therefore, it seems reasonable to suggest that infants might find certain chromatic stimuli—those where a single hue quality predominates—relatively simple perceptually or cognitively, whereas they might find other chromatic stimuli—those at hue interstices where two qualities are seen—relatively more complex. Do infants perceive colors as simple or complex? This question was answered by observing the effect of stimulus repetition on infant habituation.

Habituation of visual attention in infants is believed to reflect (at least in part) the infant's acquisition of information about the stimulus (see Cohen, DeLoache, & Strauss, 1979; Cohen & Gelber, 1975). Predictably, repetition of a simple stimulus accelerates habituation, whereas the re-presentation of a complex stimulus relatively retards habituation. Thus, Caron and Caron (1968) found that within a fixed amount of time infants habituated most to repetition of a simple 2 X 2 checkerboard, less to one 12 X 12, and least to one 24 X 24. Likewise, Cohen (1969, Experiment II) found that the repetition of stimulus trials consisting of high degrees of change (lights moving over four or 16 positions) slowed habituation in infants relative to trials with a lower degree of change. And, recently, Bornstein, Ferdinandsen, and Gross (1981) have found that infants habituated faster and more to vertically symmetrical (i.e., redundant) patterns than to asymmetrical ones constructed of the same elements. The influence of stimulus complexity on habituation rate is so clear and consistent that Jeffrey and Cohen (1971, p. 89) have observed that:

> Experiments demonstrating reasonably clear cases of habituation...have tended to use simple geometric forms. On the other hand, those revealing little habituation or habituation in only a few of their infants...have used more complex photographs or three-dimensional stimuli.

On the basis of these findings, habituation rates to the repetition of different chromatic stimuli were observed in the present study in an effort to assess the infant's perception of the relative complexity of colors.

In this study, infants were habituated with four different chromatic stimuli: one each selected within the hue categories blue and red—both of these were presumed to be simple—and one each selected from regions of transition between infant hue categories, blue-green and yellow-red—they were presumed to be more complex. Habituation consisted of 12 10-sec presentations of the same color, and subsequently rates of habituation in the four groups were compared. All infants declined during habituation, and extra-experimental pretest and posttest trials with a neutral pattern confirmed that this decline reflected the children's waning interest in the habituation stimulus, rather than sensory adaptation, general fatigue, or other change in state.

The influence of stimulus complexity on habituation rate was examined quantitatively in the following way. Total looking times for six successive pairs of habituation trials for each child were determined, and linear regression functions were fit to each child's data by the method of least squares. A slope of the decrement in looking for each child was thus obtained. Subsequently, average slopes were calculated within groups and compared across groups.

Rates of habituation among the four groups differed ($p < .01$), as shown by analysis of variance, however the slopes for the two groups that saw simple colors (blue and red) did not differ, nor did the slopes for the two groups that saw complex colors (blue-green and yellow-red). The main difference emerged when the slopes for the pooled simple groups were compared to those for the pooled complex groups: Habituation to the simple colors resulted in a predictably and significantly ($p < .05$) steeper mean slope (−.75) than habituation to the complex colors (−.54). (The consistency of this result across individual children was supported by nonparametric analysis.)

First looks on each trial followed a similar pattern; the correlation *(r)* between slopes for first and total looking was .66.

Figure 1 shows the results of this slope analysis: Infants habituate to colors dominated by a single hue quality faster than to colors constituted of two equal hue qualities.[1] Other studies, reviewed above, have shown that complexity of visual patterns and the duration of infant attention are related. At minimum, the results of this study generalize the relationship between stimulus complexity and habituation beyond form to color.

Why do infants habituate to simpler colors more quickly? Or alternatively, why does chromatic complexity tend to hold the infant's attention? One possibility is that infants find complex colors more visually pleasing. To assess this possibility, preference, defined in terms of initial looking at the simple and complex colors, was analyzed. Analysis of variance showed that there were no reliable differences in looking on the initial pair of trials among the four groups. (If anything, infants tended to find the simple colors more pleasing initially.) In short, rates of habituation to these simple and complex colors were not differentially influenced by preference.[2]

---

[1]Organisms other than man which see color also seem to partition the spectrum into categories of hue, e.g., honey bees (von Frish, 1964), pigeons (Wright & Cumming, 1971, Experiments I and II), and monkeys (Sandell, Gross, & Bornstein, 1979). Does the behavior of these animals indicate that they too perceive different spectral wavelengths as psychologically simple or complex? Wright and Cumming (1971, Experiment III) found evidence for such differential perception in pigeons: Birds showed "much slower" acquisition of matching-to-sample with wavelengths selected from boundary or transition regions between pigeon "hues" than with wavelengths centrally located within pigeon "hues".

[2]Individual preference was related to rate of habituation across infants. A strong negative correlation emerged between the slope of habituation and the amount of initial looking, $r(38) = -.53, p < .001$. In other words, infants who looked more initially tended to be those who habituated faster.

On the general issue of preference, Bornstein (1975) found that infants tend to prefer simple hues to complex ones when the stimuli are monochromatic. The broad-band nature of the stimuli used in the present experiments apparently weakens this effect.

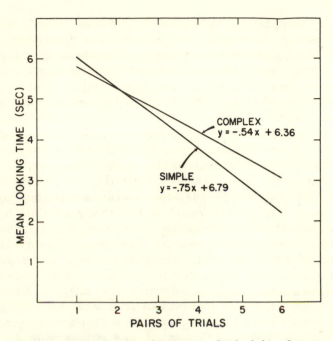

Fig. 1. *Habituation functions (mean least squares fit) for babies shown psychologically simple and complex colors.*

A second possibility is that colors toward the middle of the spectrum, like blue-green and yellow-red, would (for some reason) lead to slower habituation than colors at the ends of the spectrum, like blue and red. (Unfortunately, the complexity dimension is confounded with stimulus location in the spectrum in this experiment.) There is no *a priori* reason to expect this to be so since, for example, the colors were equated in saturation, which varies with spectral location. Nor was there any reason based on physical characteristics of the stimuli. Moreover, data from a different study help to reject this explanation. In that study (Bornstein et al., 1976, Study 1), babies in 14 different groups were habituated with a wide variety of monochromatic colors. Across groups, slope of habituation varied with proximity of the habituation wavelength to the center of a color category regardless of its location in the spectrum. As here, the closer the wavelength is to the center of a hue category—that is, the psychologically simpler the stimulus is—the steeper the slope (Bornstein, 1978, p. 157, n. 6).

An infant's attention is maintained in the presence of two-hued colors more than one-hued ones, and this pattern of attention does not reflect initial preference or other structural aspects of the stimulus. It is possible, alternatively, that two-hued colors maintain attention because they may be more difficult for infants to assimilate: That is, slower habituation to blue-green than to blue, for example, may reflect the fact that blue-green is more complex for infants than is blue; apparently, it is for adults (see above). Young infants, like adults, seem to see the physical spectrum as divided into "categories" dominated by single hue qualities. It may be therefore that colors falling toward the centers of hue categories are simple for infants, in the sense that they are assimilated quickly to structures extant in infant perception; combinations of colors fall at the interstices between categories and are perceived as complex.

At this juncture a subsidiary question related to these perceptual processes arises. What is the perception of chromatic stimuli at the boundary between two categories, e.g., blue and green, like for infants? Do they perceive such a mix as the sum of two independent components (i.e., blue plus green), or do they perceive the mixture as a single color configuration (i.e., blue-green)? If babies categorize blue-green alternately as blue then green, this alternation could be expected to slow habituation in the same way that the actual temporal alternation between two different hues does (Bornstein et al., 1976, Study 2; see also Section IV-D.) If, alternatively, babies see blue-green as a color configuration, they might find the configuration more difficult to assimilate than a simpler basic hue for which their "categorical" perception provides a handy template. Either interpretation leads one to expect slow habituation—a conclusion which points to an explanatory poverty of habituation data by themselves. Post-habituation test data help to distinguish these alternative interpretations; they are assessed in the next section.

In summary, the rate of habituation of infant attention to different stimuli can tell us something about the infant's perception of their complexity. In this experiment, infants habituated faster to some colors, which for adults are single hues, than to others, viz. two-hue complexes. This finding suggests that infants, too, perceive that some colors in the visual spectrum yield predominately a single, perhaps simpler percept, whereas others give rise to multiple, and hence more complex perceptions.

B. Components, Compounds, Configurations, and Colors

Visual stimuli are complex in that they are compounded of and analyzable into multiple elements, features, or simpler components; at the same time, stimuli form configurations, or unified integrated wholes. A *component* is an element; a *compound* is the sum of those elements; and a *configuration* is the Gestalt of the elements. Components and compounds are physical entities, whereas configurations are psychological. When a baby looks at a complex visual stimulus, what does she see (and take away with her)? Some of the individual components? The compound? The stimulus configuration? The answer to this question is far from straightforward, since the literature suggests that the infant's mental or chronological status, the complexity and integrity of the stimulus, the domain from which it is selected, as well as the experimenter's method of asking the question interact to produce different results. Though studies of the component-compound-configuration question in perceptual development are relatively few in number, Cohen (Cohen et al., 1979; Cohen & Gelber, 1975) has characterized a trend in infant perception, suggesting that infants younger than five months encode and remember stimuli in terms of their component elements, whereas older infants, children, and adults encode and remember components *and* the configuration.

Cohen's conclusion rests on data such as the following. Certainly infants younger than five months encode components since they are sensitive to component changes in a stimulus. For example, infants will dishabituate when either the inner circle or outer square of a circle-in-a-square configuration is changed to a triangle (Milewski, 1976). Further, four-month infants habituated to a red circle and a green triangle on alternating trials recover to a blue square or yellow dumbbell (novel compounds) but not to a red circle or a green triangle (the original stimuli) or, interestingly, to a red triangle or a green circle (novel compounds of the original components); that is, young babies seem to habituate to and recover on the basis of separable components rather than a configuration (Cohen, 1979, cited in Cohen et al., 1979). Between four months and five months, infants switch from responding to a visual compound solely on an analytical basis of "heterogeneous summation" by adding sensitivity to the configuration; that is, they begin to perceive in a synthetic Gestalt mode. Conditioned to turn their heads in the presence of a compound (circle, cross, and two dots), 8- to 16-week-olds extinguish with the same frequency of head turns in the presence of the compound as in the presence of the components, whereas 20-week-olds turn more for the configuration than for the sum of its components (Bower, 1966). Finally, five-month infants who are familiarized with a red diamond show a novelty response to a green square relative to either a green diamond or a red square—indicating greater sensitivity to change in both color and form than in either alone. Further, they show novelty preferences for a red square or a green diamond when paired with the familiarization compound (the red diamond)—indicating that they are sensitive, respectively, to component form or color changes. However, "the presence of the familiar compound on test yielded even greater novelty preferences, indicating attention to a compound dimension as well as to the specific components.... Attention to form and to color and to the compound dimension is highly developed by 22 weeks" (Fagan, 1977, p. 351).

Studies of component-configuration differentiation, such as these, have typically used multidimensional stimuli, e.g., a red circle. However, on the basis of data forthcoming from such studies it is difficult to decide whether the child has shown a discriminative response to the "configuration" change because it is a configuration change per se or because the child's individual responses to change in two perceptually separate component dimensions summate. The fact that most studies cannot distinguish between these alternatives has lead to Cohen's developmental hypothesis and, unfortunately, to theoretical confusion.

The perceptual structure of colors permits us to approach the component-compound-configuration question in a manner that circumvents difficulties associated with multidimensional stimuli. Colors, as we have seen, can be arrayed along a continuum of simplicity from "unique" (e.g., a green with *no* blue or yellow in it—Boynton, 1975) through greater mixes of hue neighbors (e.g., bluish-green) to hue mixtures of balanced, subjective equality between components (e.g., blue-green). Do infants see and code a color that is equally blue and green as a configuration, i.e., a blue-green, or as the compound of independent components, i.e., a blue and a green? Operationally, would infants habituated to a color mixture dishabituate or would they generalize habitation to a test stimulus that was a component of the mixture?

The following experiment helps to answer this question and begins to address the component-compound-configuration problem generally using color. Two groups of infants were habituated on 12 trials to color mixtures, one to blue-green, and the other to yellow-red. Both groups habituated significantly ($ps < .001$) and did so at similar rates. Following habituation, the babies were tested with one component of the mixture, blue for the blue-green group and red for the yellow-red group. Infants in both groups discriminated hue components from compound colors of which they were a part: The group habituated to blue-green dishabituated to blue, and the group habituated to yellow-red dishabituated to red ($ps < .01$). If infants perceived a complex color (blue-green) as compounded of individual hues (blue and green), rather than as a single configuration (blue-green), habituation to the compound might have resulted in generalization to one or both of its components. The results of the present study indicate that it did not. Similarly, Adkinson and Berg (1976) found that four-day-old neonates dishabituate to blue (472 nm) from blue-green (496 nm). Further, Kessen and Bornstein (1978) found that four-month infants dishabituate to *both* components (blue and green) after habituation to a compound (blue-green). (In a similar vein, Cohen, Gelber, & Lazar, 1971, found that infants who were habituated to colored forms dishabituated to change of either component.) Thus, the possible interpretation that habituation to a compound actually consists of habituation to one component and not to the other is discouraged. It is possible alternatively that habituation is to both individual components and that recovery is not to the presence of one but to the absence of the other; this interpretation is unlikely, too, since habituation to both components, not the configuration, implies habituation to the two individually and should still result in generalization to either one alone. The data from this study argue that even though complex colors may consist of two simpler hues they are perceived early in infancy as complex color configurations with their own integrity; configural habituation (to blue-green) does not necessarily imply construction of any mental representation of component(s) (blue and/or green).

Going back to the habituation problem (Section IV-A), we can see that the habituation and test data together reinforce the idea that a color compound (e.g., blue-green) is perceived as a complex configuration. For infants, therefore, it may very well be that increased information in cognitively more challenging spatial or chromatic structures retards habituation.

These color data stand in contradistinction to a strict developmental hypothesis (outlined earlier) that compound stimuli are encoded and remembered by infants five months and younger exclusively in terms of their components. The study of color in this connection shows either that color is special, or that infants at four months are on the cusp of a developmental change, or that domain and development interact. In any event, for the younger infant some compound stimuli may be configurations and qualitatively different from their constituent components. This conclusion is based on limited sampling in the domain of color; however, some further support for a revisionist view comes from olfaction. Some time ago, Engen and Lipsitt (1965, Experiment 2, reported by Kaye in Reese & Lipsitt, 1970) showed that two-day-olds who were habituated to a compound of heptanol (16.7%), amyl acetate (33.3%), and diluent (50%) dishabituated to components of the compound when they were presented singly. Heptanol and amyl acetate are different from each other in quality, and adults independently scaled the components in this mixture as equally intense. Like compound colors, compound odors may not be perceived by young infants as the simple sum of their components, but perhaps as Gestalt-like configurations, qualitatively different from their components.[3]

In summary, babies who are habituated to a stimulus compounded of two simple hues dishabituate to presentation of one (or both) component(s) alone. This result suggests that babies see a complex color as a configuration and not simply as the sum of individual components of the configuration.

C. Perception of Hue Qualities in the Spectrum

Light varies in a number of ways, such as intensity and wavelength. The intensity scale is a continuum, and physical changes in intensity afford continuous psychological changes in brightness. The wavelength spectrum is also a continuum, and variation in wavelength leads to a continuous variation in hue. However, brightness and hue differ in that hue changes have distinctive perceptual qualities to them. Indeed, for adult observers

---

[3]The complexity of this story is influenced by many variables. For example, hamsters which learn to avoid a taste mixture generalize to individual components of the mixture; thus, under some circumstances, taste mixtures may bear similarity to their components (Nowlis, 1978).

qualitative differences among hues are the spectrum's salient characteristic. (Excellent early examples are Aristotle's discussion of the rainbow, in Ross, 1913, and Newton's, 1671–1672, original description of the prismatic dispersion of sunlight.) Are the qualities that adults see in the spectrum, the hues, salient early in life?

Consider discriminations among different chromatic stimuli. Green (e.g., 504 nm) and red (e.g., 660 nm) are qualitatively distinct from blue (e.g., 476 nm), however red is farther from blue than is green on the wavelength scale (as it is around the hue circle in a two-dimensional color space—Boynton, 1975). Thus, discrimination among chromatic stimuli—qua *wavelengths*—could be motivated by physical distances among them. The farther apart two wavelengths are quantitatively, the greater their mutual discriminability or perceptual distinctiveness. Alternatively, discrimination among chromatic stimuli—qua *hues*—could be motivated by qualitative differences. In this sense the basic hues are equally discriminable or different from one another. Figure 2 compares these two possible patterns of discrimination graphically. In the one case (A), both middle and long wavelengths are discriminated from short wavelengths, but more distant long wavelengths provoke a greater discrimination response. In the alternative case (B), both green and red are discriminated from blue, but the two provoke essentially equivalent discrimination responses.

Previous studies have suggested that infants may perceive some differences among wavelengths in terms of hue qualities. For example, Bornstein et al.

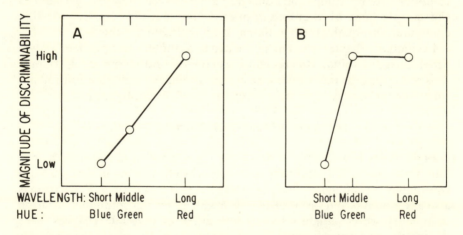

Fig. 2.   *Two possible patterns of discriminability among physically different, psychologically simple hues. In both cases, short-wavelength blue is the standard against which comparison is made. A: Response magnitude is a monotonic (and linear) function of the degree of physical change from the standard stimulus. B: Response magnitude is a simple function of psychological change from the standard stimulus. (See the text.)*

(1976) habituated infants to light of a given wavelength and later tested them with the same light and with two new lights whose wavelengths differed from the habituation light by equal physical amounts. Babies tended to dishabituate to the new test lights differentially: They generalized habituation to a new light if it was (for adults) predominantly the same hue as the habituation light, but they dishabituated to a light of a different hue.

To ascertain whether babies perceive other differences among different hues in this way, infants in two groups were habituated to light of one hue and later tested for their discrimination of lights of two different hues. The new lights were unequally different from the habituation stimulus in wavelength, but for adults the two new lights were equivalently different from the habituation stimulus in hue. In the experiment, babies in one group were habituated over 12 10-sec trials to blue; those in another to red. Both groups habituated significantly ($ps < .001$) and did so in similar ways. Following habituation, both groups of babies were tested with blue, green, and red. Thus, one test hue *retested* babies with the habituation stimulus, and the two other test hues were novel (one, the green, was *common* to both groups; for both, the remaining test hue was *different* from the habituation stimulus). Each baby saw a different random order of the three test stimuli followed by its counterbalanced order. (The two groups are comparable since for babies habituated to blue or to red the test red or blue are equally distant, and in each group the green was equally novel as well as closer to the habituation stimulus than was the other test stimulus.) All trials lasted 10 seconds.

Looking in the test was analyzed by comparing the means of the last two habituation trials, the retest trials, the common (green) test trials, and the remaining different test trials. An analysis of variance comparing groups and trials showed only a main effect of trials ($p < .001$). Both groups followed the same pattern, and the means for the two groups combined are plotted in Figure 3. Parametric analysis showed that babies looked equally at the end of habituation and on the retest; they increased looking significantly from the end of habituation to the common and different stimuli ($ps < .001$ and .05, respectively); but they looked between the two novel colors equally. (Babies also looked longer at the two novel test colors than at the retest, $p < .01$; such a comparison is fairly conservative since the retest trials appeared randomly in the test phase and regression effects on looking times over the course of testing are to be expected.) Nonparametric analyses exactly mirror the parametric ones and show the consistency of these results across infants. In general, the results follow pattern B of Figure 2 and indicate that (in addition to recognizing the habituation hue) infants give an equivalent discrimination response to change among simple hues independent of the actual hues involved.

This study suggests that young infants are sensitive to qualities of hue in the spectrum since they dishabituated equally to stimulus changes which were qualitatively equivalent (for adults) but which were quantitatively unequal. In

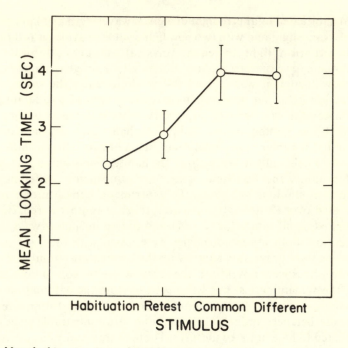

Fig. 3.   Mean looking time (in sec ± S.E.M.) at the end of habituation and in the test series, including the retest, the common, and the different trials. These are combined-groups data.

interpreting this result, however, one must be sensitive to both floor and ceiling effects. The findings probably do not reflect a ceiling effect on looking since the babies looked at the novel test stimuli only 40% of the time the stimuli were available. Nor are the findings likely to reflect a floor effect, in the sense that any or all dishabituations are quantal and equivalent, since under other circumstances infants dishabituate to chromatic change in the degree to which they perceive a new stimulus to be different from an habituation stimulus (see Section IV-D).

The present findings are further supported by a reinterpretation of results of Fagan (1974). Fagan found that four-month infants prefer hetero-chromatic to homochromatic checkerboards. If infants discriminate hues in a "qualitative" manner, red-green and red-blue checkerboards should receive equal attention but more, say, than red-orange; this prediction is borne out by Fagan's data. Thus, infants not only see categories of hue in the spectrum (Bornstein et al., 1976), they seem to respond to change or difference among hues in an appropriately qualitative manner.

This is not an expected result. Stimulus generalization, for example, would predict that the more distant from one another two stimuli lie on a continuous dimension, the greater their mutual discriminability should be. The result is not unique, however. Beside wavelength, certain other dimensions, notably voice-onset time (VOT) in audition, are perceived to vary qualitatively against change that is quantitative: For adults (e.g., Liberman, Cooper, Shankweiler, & Studdert-Kennedy, 1967) and infants alike (e.g., Eimas, Siqueland, Jusczyk, & Vigorito, 1971), sufficient change along the VOT continuum engenders qualitative discriminations among "categories" of voicing contrasts. Eimas (1975) has elaborated on the infant's qualitative perception of change across perceptual boundaries between juxtaposed phoneme categories. Like the quantal perceptions provoked by hue changes to green or to red from blue found here, Eimas (1975) found that changes of 20, 60, or 100 msec in VOT yield discrimination responses of equal magnitude in infants so long as each change crosses the boundary to a new perceptual category. The infant's modes of perceiving "hues" and "phonemes" are similar in many ways (Bornstein, 1979); the qualitative nature of discriminability among perceptual categories is one.

In summary, babies who are habituated with light of one hue and then tested with two novel lights equally different from the habituation light in hue but unequally different from the habituation hue in wavelength dishabituate significantly and equivalently to the two novel hues. This finding supports the claim that infants see qualitative variation along a dimension of sensation that adults mark by similar qualitative differences.

D. Quantitative Discrimination within and between Hue Categories

As Boynton (1978, pp. 188–190) has correctly observed, our understanding of color perception lies both in our understanding of color *classification* and in our understanding of color *discrimination*. The first kind of perception is qualitative, and the second is quantitative; the two coexist in an imperfectly reciprocal way. Both qualitative and quantitative perceptions contribute to the infant's perceptual understanding of the world.

The infant's qualitative perception of colors was discussed in Section IV-C. Like adults, infants give evidence that they see regions of the wavelength spectrum to be dominated by single qualities of hue. For example, Study 1 of Bornstein et al. (1976) showed that infants who were habituated to a stimulus of one hue, say a blue of 480 nm, generalized to another stimulus of the same hue, a blue of 450 nm, but dishabituated to a third stimulus of a different hue, say a green of 510 nm. Study 2 in the same report showed that habituation to re-presentation of one wavelength from a single hue category (blue of 480 nm) and habituation to the quasi-random alternation of two wavelengths (450 nm–480 nm) from the same hue category (blue) were equally rapid and that both were faster than habituation to the alternation of two wavelengths (480 nm–510 nm) from different hue categories (blue and green).

In the absence of understanding that wavelength generalization and discrimination are not perfectly correlated or that the time error in a successive task reduces discriminative acumen, these results alone could imply that infants cannot discriminate 450 nm from 480 nm. But, wavelengths in spectral categories are not identical; most *are* discriminable from one another. Though two blues are discriminable, however, their effective (perceptual) difference may be small, smaller than the difference, say, between blue and green. These considerations lead directly to the following question: Is discrimination within hue categories less, equally, or more acute than discrimination across categories?

It is possible to use habituation to study this quantitative aspect of color perception in infants. Habituation rate is sensitive to stimulus complexity or heterogeneity (or, at least, it is sensitive to the infant's perception of stimulus complexity or heterogeneity). A distinction may be drawn between "spatial" heterogeneity, i.e., the degree of complexity within a stimulus, and "temporal" heterogeneity, i.e., the degree of interstimulus variation over trials. This distinction notwithstanding, there is good evidence that heterogeneity of stimulation (over trials as well as within a trial) maintains looking behavior in infants more than does stimulus homogeneity. The classic study was conducted by Fantz (1964). He showed pairs of magazine advertisements to infants. On 10 successive one-minute exposures, one of the two patterns remained constant, while the other varied from trial to trial. Infants older than two months declined in looking at the constant stimulus, but maintained (indeed increased) looking at the changing pattern. Other studies have confirmed that trial-to-trial variation of geometric forms (Bornstein, Gross, & Wolf, 1978; Caron & Caron, 1968, 1969) or faces (Cornell, 1974) slows the course of habituation relative to re-presentation of the same stimulus.

The infant's discrimination of colors within and between categories of hue was approached here by comparing rates of habituation in three groups. One group was shown the same chromatic stimulus (a blue of 476 nm) on every trial. (A trial consisted of the duration of the infant's first look.) Another group was shown a variety of six chromatic stimuli selected within the boundaries of the infant's blue category as determined in Bornstein et al. (1976); they were 455 nm, 470 nm, 476 nm, 480 nm, 484 nm, and 490 nm. If wavelengths in a category were indiscriminable for infants, these two groups ought to habituate (i.e., reach a criterion decrement from initial looking) equally quickly; if the wavelengths are only similar, habituation to variety ought to be somewhat slower than habituation to identity. Figure 4 shows that infants reached a fixed habituation criterion with repetition of a single blue (1.4 pairs of trials) significantly faster ($p < .01$) than they reached the same criterion with the multiple blue series (3.5 pairs of trials).

The infant's ability to discriminate within a hue category has not proved to be as good as his ability to discriminate between or among hue categories.

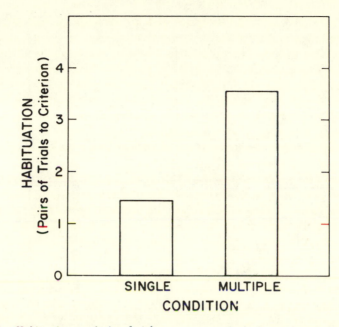

Fig. 4.   Habituation rate (pairs of trials to a constant criterion) to re-presentation of the same chromatic stimulus (single condition) and to presentation of a series of different chromatic stimuli from the same hue category (multiple condition).

Data of Fagan (1974) and of Bornstein et al. (1976) have previously suggested this. A third group of infants in the present study was shown a variety of hues (blues, greens, yellows, and reds); they took twice as long to habituate (7.4 pairs of trials) as did infants shown variety within a hue (3.5 pairs).

In summary, the sensitivity that habituation shows to stimulus variation permits assessment of the infant's differentiation of variation *within* a hue category—where it exists but is small—as well as of variation *among* hues—where it is larger.

E.   The Discrepancy Principle and Color

Dishabituation to stimulus change following habituation of visual attention has been widely and correctly taken to indicate discrimination (e.g., Cohen et al., 1979; Kessen, Haith, & Salapatek, 1970). Since habituation is believed to involve construction of some mental representation or schema of the stimulus (e.g., Cohen & Gelber, 1975; Jeffrey & Cohen, 1971; Olson, 1976), stimuli presented for discrimination after habituation must be compared with that mental representation. Theory suggests that when input and schema match, further looking is inhibited; when a mismatch occurs,

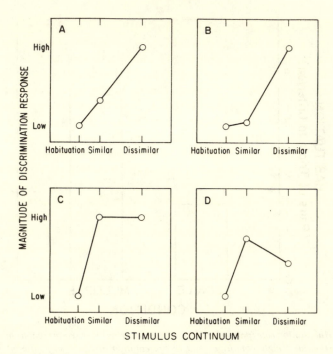

Fig. 5. *Four logical patterns of the baby's discriminative response to novel stimuli of differing psychological similarity from a habituation stimulus. A: Response magnitude is a monotonic (and linear) function of the degree of difference of the test stimuli from the habituation stimulus B: Response magnitude is related to the degree of difference among test and habituation stimuli; habituation generalizes to the similar stimulus but not to the dissimilar one. C: Response magnitude is a function of simple difference among test and habituation stimuli; discriminable stimuli elicit equivalent amounts of dishabituation. D: Response magnitude is a nonmonotonic function of the discrepancy of test stimuli from the habituation stimulus; similar stimuli elicit more dishabituation than do dissimilar stimuli. (See the text.) (Positions of the similar and dissimilar stimuli have been scaled arbitrarily so that the dissimilar stimulus is displaced three times the distance from the habituation stimulus as the similar stimulus. This is a general relation meant to be independent of any particular stimulus dimension.)*

expectancy is violated, and attention is re-elicited. A basic question therefore arises: What degree of stimulus change is necessary to recapture infant attention?

Logically, four patterns of discriminative behavior are plausible vis-à-vis two degrees of stimulus change, that is, first, change between a habituation stimulus and a stimulus that is *similar* to the habituation stimulus and, second, change between a habituation stimulus and one *dissimilar* to it. These patterns are shown in Figure 5. (Certainly, more than two degrees of change would yield additional information.)

One intuitively appealing relationship states that a high correlation exists between the degree of stimulus change and the degree of response change; that is, the greater the physical discrepancy between a new stimulus and the habituation stimulus, the greater the response to the new stimulus. In its strongest form, this relationship would follow a linear, monotonic pattern shown graphically in Figure 5A. Obviously, magnitude of the discrimination response need not be linearly ordered. (Indeed, in practice it would be difficult to differentiate between linear-monotonic and simply monotonic relationships; clearly, both spacing of stimuli along the abscissa and the units in which the dependent variable—usually attention—is measured along the ordinate will influence the final form of the functional relationship between the two.) Pattern A represents an extension of stimulus-generalization theory and has been the preferred or implicit prediction of many investigators of infant discrimination (e.g., Caron, Caron, Caldwell, & Weiss, 1973; Cohen & Gelber, 1975; Jeffrey & Cohen, 1971; Kessen et al., 1970). A second possible relationship exists. If one of two test stimuli closely resembles the habituation stimulus psychologically, generalization of habituation to the similar stimulus would likely result. Such a pattern is shown graphically in Figure 5B. This pattern shows a clear disruption of the linear (or even monotonic) relationship illustrated in Figure 5A; here, one would expect little or no behavioral change to the similar stimulus but a large change to the dissimilar one. Third, dishabituation might be "all-or-none," where any discriminable changes in stimulation recruit roughly equivalent degrees of interest regardless of the physical or psychological distance between habituation and test stimuli. This pattern is shown in Figure 5C. (This pattern of results, based on change among different hues, was seen in Section IV-C.) Finally, a less intuitive though frequently found relationship, deriving originally from Wundt (see Berlyne, 1960, p. 201), is shown in Figure 5D. Here response magnitude is a nonmonotonic function of the degree of dissimilarity between the test and habituation stimuli. According to this view, attention following habituation will be an inverted-U function of discrepancy between novel and familiar stimuli because a moderate difference between the test stimulus and the mental representation of the habituation stimulus may excite further exploration, whereas a stimulus that is too novel cannot be related to the mental representation that is available (e.g., Dember & Earl, 1957; Kagan, 1971; McCall, 1971).

The discrepancy between views A and D notwithstanding, most data in the infant literature provide evidence for one or the other. On the one hand, Cohen et al. (1971), Cornell (1975), Saayman, Ames, and Moffett (1964), and Welch (1974) have argued for a linear or, at least, monotonic relation between the degree of novelty and the degree of evoked attention in infants following habituation. On the other hand, McCall and Melson (1969), Zelazo, Hopkins, Jacobson, and Kagan (1973), and McCall, Kennedy, and Appelbaum (1977) have argued for the curvilinear relation. (An important consideration brought by Zelazo et al. to bear on this debate is that initial recovery may be a linear or monotonic function of discrepancy whereas recovery sustained over time may be curvilinear; see also Hopkins, Zelazo, Jacobson, & Kagan, 1976.)

Among the several issues that becloud interpretation of tests of the infant's discriminative behavior following habituation, inadequate stimulus selection is prominent (Thomas, 1971). Many studies have varied patterns multidimensionally. As a consequence, it is difficult to specify variables or the degree of "discrepancy" (especially for infants). When, for example, Zelazo et al. (1973) asked adults to rate relative discrepancy among four comparison stimuli in their experiment, 27 percent of observers actually ranked among the least discrepant the stimulus which the experimenters themselves designated to be most discrepant from their standard. In many previous experiments, the lack of any suitable metric of form (Zusne, 1970) has obfuscated stimulus control and disallowed clear *a priori* rationale for stimulus selection. Appropriate tests of discrimination call for variation of stimulation along a single dimension. Assessments with color can be of value because the wavelength continuum constitutes such a dimension.

Which function (A-D) does color discrimination follow? To answer this question, stimulus change in two degrees—to stimuli similar to and dissimilar from the habituation stimulus—was explored in two separate groups. In this experiment, infants in one group were habituated over 12 trials to blue-green, and infants in a second group were habituated to yellow-red. Both groups habituated significantly (*ps* < .001) and did so at similar rates. Following habituation, babies in both groups were tested with blue and red. One test hue was psychologically *similar* to the habituation color: blue for the blue-green group and red for the yellow-red group. The other test hue was psychologically *dissimilar* from the habituation color: red for the blue-green group and blue for the yellow-red group. Each test hue appeared twice and in counterbalanced order; half of the babies in each group saw blue first, the other half saw red first. Again, trials lasted 10 seconds.

Looking in the test was analyzed by comparing the means of the last two habituation trials, the similar test trials, and the dissimilar test trials; the similar and dissimilar trials were also compared to each other. An analysis of variance comparing groups and trials showed only a main effect of trials (*p* < .001). Both groups followed the same pattern, and the means for the two groups combined are plotted in Figure 6. Further parametric analysis showed that babies increased looking significantly from the end of habituation to both the similar stimulus (*p* < .01) and the dissimilar stimulus (*p* < .001); but that they dishabituated more to the dissimilar stimulus than to the similar one (*p* < .01). Nonparametric analyses exactly mirror the parametric ones and show the consistency of the results across infants (disallowing the interpretation that some infants were dishabituating equally to both stimuli and others dishabituating only to the dissimilar stimulus).

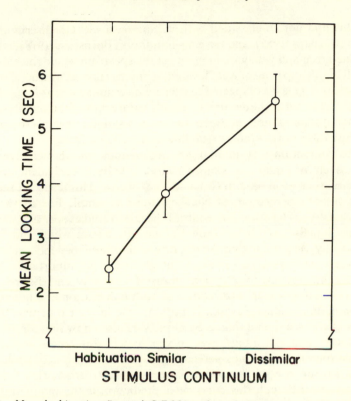

Fig. 6. Mean looking time (in sec ± S.E.M.) at the end of habituation and to similar and dissimilar changes in test stimuli. These are combined-groups data. (Abscissa spacing as in Figure 5.)

In general, the results of this experiment follow pattern A of Figure 5. They indicate that infants distinguish both similar and dissimilar colors from a habituation color and that infants show a monotonic (and perhaps linear) degree of discrimination response from habituation to similar and to dissimilar stimuli. (Since spacing on the abscissa is essentially arbitrary, there is no basis on which to choose linearity over simple monotonicity.) This pattern of results is the one predicted by stimulus-generalization theory.

The results obtained overall failed to support patterns B or C from Figure 5. However, stimulus selection is a key consideration in both. If the similar stimulus were indiscriminable or barely discriminable from the habituation stimulus or were, for some reason, co-classified with it by the baby (as exemplified in Bornstein et al., 1976), pattern B would result. The fact that degree of recovery is a monotonic (and linear) function of novelty, therefore, suggests that the test stimuli are *in situ* discriminable from the habituation stimulus and not co-classified with it. Since wavelength discrimination in adults (Graham, 1965), and perhaps in infants (Bornstein, 1978), is finest in the blue-green and yellow-red regions of the spectrum where the habituation stimuli in this experiment were located, stimulus change in either direction in almost any degree was expected to excite a discrimination, as it did. Further, the babies looked at the dissimilar stimulus more than at the similar one; their unequal dishabituation between the two disallows the interpretation of dishabituation to the similar stimulus as a ceiling effect.

If dishabituation was quantal, i.e., all-or-none, or were changes to two qualitatively or equally dissimilar stimuli involved, equivalent degrees of dishabituation, as in pattern C, could be expected. This result is exemplified in the infant's perception of change from one simple hue to two others (Section IV-C). The different results of these two studies speak to the issue of whether infants have a threshold for novelty above which they respond equivalently. Apparently, not all discriminable stimuli beyond a certain level of novelty are responded to equivalently.[4] This is an important distinction that has implications for the perception of similarity and dissimilarity by infants, and it shows that the choice of both habituation and test stimuli in discrimination studies plays an important role in their outcome. Together results of this study and that in Section IV-C also show that, depending on habituation and test alternatives, psychological differences can outweigh physical ones in the infant's perception of color.

Nowhere do the data support pattern D in Figure 5, the discrepancy principle, even though this curvilinear prediction is the major rival to the stimulus-generalization prediction. However, two arguments must be considered before concluding that the curvilinear hypothesis is not applicable to these data. First, as Hopkins et al. (1976) have suggested, short-term attention in infants frequently follows the linear prediction, while long-term attention may follow the curvilinear prediction. The data here are reported for rather short-term discriminations—test followed habituation immediately—and hence might be expected to conform to the generalization prediction. Second, finding a "discrepancy" result may depend on employing a degree of stimulus change not reached with the stimuli included in this study. True "discrepancy" might require finding a more dissimilar stimulus selected from the same dimension as the habituation stimulus— seemingly not possible with qualitatively different colors—or employing stimulation from another dimension entirely. (A face was shown at the conclusion of this study; it is extradimensional to color but engaged more looking. Faces may be special stimuli, however.) When attention is a monotonic function of discrepancy, as here, the curvilinear prediction may

---

[4]Blue and blue-green are different (Sections IV-B, E) but not as different, apparently, as are blue and red (Section IV-C).

not apply, or stimulation may not have been sufficiently dissimilar to reveal the entire curvilinear function.

In summary, colors which may be dissimilar from an infant's newly-formed mental representation of a reference color will hold the infant's attention even longer than colors which are also discriminable from but are more similar to the reference color. This is at least true in short-term tests. A very different relationship holds when the dissimilar colors are equally dissimilar from the reference color.

F. Recognition Memory and Chromatic Complexity

Beyond the bare fact of memory in infancy—now amply demonstrated (see, e.g., Cohen & Gelber, 1975)—a variety of questions related to the parameters of infant memory arises. These questions concern study time, stimulus class and complexity, durability of memory, the effects of interference, and their interaction. A substantial literature in infant pattern vision already speaks to several of these questions. One general question is: To what extent are results true of patterns generalizable to color?

Other, more specific questions arise, too. For example, are stimuli that differ in psychological complexity equally durable in infants' memory? Color is potentially a valuable domain in which to explore such questions about the quality of recognition memory in infancy since the specification of complexity in form perception is an unresolved issue (see Zusne, 1970). In color, on the one hand, all wavelengths are equivalent in physical terms; on the other, physiological, psychological, linguistic, comparative, and developmental data converge to suggest that some regions of the spectrum are psychologically simpler, more salient, and more readily categorized than are other spectral regions (see Bornstein, 1973, 1975).

The literature on recognition memory for color per se, or on the effects of study time, stimulus class or complexity, durability, or interference is rather meagre. Holding size, shape, and contour constant, Schaffer and Parry (1969, 1970), Cohen et al. (1971), Bornstein (1976), and Fagan (1977) have all found that young infants, who were habituated to one color, discriminate a change in color, rudimentary evidence that babies must hold in memory information about the habituation color per se. Fagan (1977) studied the effects of familiarization time on five-month infants' recognition of colors versus simple geometric forms: "... given the stimuli employed, less study time was required prior to recognition when color served as the relevant component dimension than when attention to form was required as a source of recognition" (p. 371). Several investigators have studied duration of color memory. Pancratz and Cohen (1970) found that infants failed to recognize a color after a five-minute delay; Strauss and Cohen (1980) found that five-month infants could recognize the form and color of a pattern both after 15 minutes, but had forgotten the color at a 24-hour test. Finally, Bornstein (1976) studied the effects of delay and interference on the four-month infant's color memory. In that study, recognition of a habituation color resisted three minutes of retroactive interference from stimulation on the same dimension (another color) or very different dimensions (mother's face and voice).

An extreme way to test recognition memory for stimulus parameters like complexity may be to assess memory following a delay or interference. (Note that the two are confounded: Is there ever delay without some kind of interference?) Studies of the effects of interference on infant recognition memory for dimensions other than color suggest that minimal interference does not disrupt recognition (e.g., Caron & Caron, 1968, 1969; Gelber, 1972, cited in Cohen & Gelber, 1975; Martin, 1975) as much as extensive interference does (DeLoache, 1976), and that interference that is perceptually different from the to-be-remembered material is less disruptive (Fagan, 1971) than is perceptually similar interference (DeLoache, 1976; Fagan, 1973). In the present experiment, the relative strength of infant recognition memory for simple and complex colors was assessed following interference on the same dimension as the habituation stimulus.

Four groups of infants participated in a study that followed a habituation-interference-retest design. Habituation consisted of 12 exposures of the same color. Two groups were habituated with psychologically simple colors, blue and red respectively, and two with complex colors, blue-green and yellow-red respectively. Interference consisted of eight exposures (each of four colors was shown twice); pairs of simple and complex groups were matched for interference. The retest consisted of two exposures of the original habituation stimulus intermixed with two exposures of an achromatic, control pattern (a face). Exposures lasted 10 seconds.

Infants in all four groups habituated significantly ($ps < .001$) and did so at similar rates. The four groups showed no systematic differences when compared on initial looking (the mean of the first two trials) or on final looking (the mean of trials 11 and 12), though as discussed above (Section IV-A) babies shown simple colors habituate more quickly than do babies shown complex colors. Further, the babies in these four groups did not differ in the amount of time they looked at the interference stimuli interpolated between habituation and the recognition memory test.

The main focus of the study was on the retest. Following habituation, a low level of looking at the original stimulus is presumed to indicate "recognition", and recovery of looking to a habituation stimulus is presumed to indicate lack of recognition or "forgetting". The two groups shown the simple hues, blue and red, looked equal amounts on the retest trials; likewise, the two groups shown the complex colors, blue-green and yellow-red, looked equivalent amounts of time on the retest. Figure 7 shows the pattern of infant looking on the last two habituation trials, on the memory retest trials, and to the facial pattern for the combined simple and combined complex groups. An

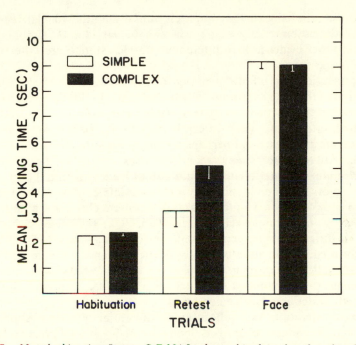

Fig. 7. *Mean looking time (in sec—S.E.M.) for the combined simple and combined complex color groups at the end of habituation, in recognition memory (retest), and at a control pattern (a face).*

analysis of variance that compared these combined groups over trials showed a highly significant main effect for trials ($p < .001$) as well as a significant groups by trials interaction ($p < .02$). (The main effect for groups was not significant.) Post-hoc tests identified the source of the interaction. Infants shown simple and complex colors looked equally on the last two habituation trials and on the two control test trials, however babies looked significantly longer at the complex colors than at the simple ones on the recognition memory retest ($p < .05$). Indeed, from their low level of looking on the last two habituation trials, only the infants who saw the complex colors showed a significant ($p < .001$) recovery on the retest.[5] (The original habituation stimulus also appeared in the sequence of "interference" trials in each group;

[5]An alternative analysis is to obviate real time and pin each child's recovery to looking at some common neutral stimulus. One index—unity minus the proportion of looking on the retest trials to looking at the face—accomplishes this inter-infant equation. Babies in the two groups that saw psychologically simple colors did not differ on this index, nor did babies in the two groups that saw complex colors. When indices for the simple (X = 0.65) and complex (X = 0.44) groups were compared, however, the difference between the two was significant ($p < .02$), indicating that even when the babies were equated for level of looking they showed a greater recovery to complex colors than to simple ones.

on these trials, the babies in the complex groups dishabituated relative to their last two habituation trials, $p < .02$, whereas the babies in the simple groups did not, further evidence that differently complex stimuli are differentially durable in memory.)

The conclusion that infants' memory for psychologically simpler colors is more durable than their memory for psychologically complex ones must be tempered by the particulars of this study. For example, the fact that variegated interference was interposed between habituation and the recognition test suggests that perhaps retroactive interference magnified the retention difference for simple versus complex colors. In the absence of (similar? uniform?) interference, would babies have differentially forgotten complex colors? Further, in this study, only two simple colors were compared with two complex ones. Though infants prefer monochromatic blue and red to blue-green and yellow-red (Bornstein, 1975, 1978), the babies in this study showed no differential preference among the four broad-band Munsell colors that were used. To separate conclusively the influence of preference from stimulus simplicity on memory, memory for a nonpreferred simple color (e.g., green) ought to be compared with that for a preferred complex color (e.g., yellow-red) under comparable conditions.

These considerations aside, the infants' differential recovery to simple and complex colors cannot be ascribed to any initial differential preference. Nor was there a between-groups difference in the final level of habituation, another factor thought to influence recovery from habituation (cf. Caron, Caron, Minichiello, Weiss, & Friedman, 1977). Nor was interference between groups unequal. Nor could the interference colors differentially "prompt" remembering, since simple and complex colors are "configurations" (Section IV-B) of independent status. Nor were there differences in state among the groups; babies in the simple and complex groups looked the same amounts on the last habituation pair and on the control trials. Rather, greater recovery to more complex colors may best be ascribable to poorer recognition memory for stimuli of greater complexity.

In summary, infants, who showed equal preference initially, habituated to the same criterion, received equivalent interference, and gave no indication of a differential state change, still recognized psychologically simple chromatic stimuli better than complex ones as evidenced by their maintained habituation to simple colors, but not to complex colors, following habituation and interference.

G.   "Perceptual" and "Conceptual" Classifications of Color

According to classical (Aristotelian) opinion, conceptual behavior is expressed when novel, discriminable stimuli are treated equivalently to or categorized with members of an extant class. James (1980, p. 463) argued that in conception, "all that is required is that [organisms] should recognize the same experience again," and even though modern language has changed contemporary authorities, such as Bourne (1966, p. 1), describe conceptual behavior is essentially the same way: "... a concept exists whenever two or more distinguishable objects or events have been grouped or classified together and set apart from other objects on the basis of some common feature or property characteristic of each."

Further, Bruner, Goodnow, and Austin (1956) and Neisser (1967) have distinguished "perceptual" from "conceptual" levels of classification. Perceptual classification seems to entail immediate, almost sensory identification of an object or attribute, whereas conceptual classification seems to reside in experience or judgment. Thus, according to Neisser (1967, p. 95), "there is an unmistakable difference between 'seeing' that two things look similar and 'judging' that they belong to the same category."

Bornstein (1981) has recently reviewed the literature on perceptual classification in infants. Babies have been shown to group or treat equivalently discriminable colors (Bornstein et al., 1976), mirror-image patterns (Bornstein et al., 1978), views of the same cube (Day & MacKenzie, 1973), VOTs (Eimas, 1975), rise times (Jusczyk, Rosner, Cutting, Foard, & Smith, 1977), and even select chemical stimuli (Jacobs, Smutz, & Du Bose, 1977; Lipsitt, 1977; Steiner, 1977). In an example referred to earlier, Bornstein et al. (1976) showed that babies who were habituated to one hue (e.g., blue) would generalize habituation to a different novel blue, but not to a novel hue (e.g., green).

Conceptual classification has been studied in infants less frequently. Yet, when babies generalize habituation to novel, discriminable instances of a class of discriminable, perceptually dissimilar stimuli to which they have been habituated they can then, according to accepted definition, be said to have formed and utilized a concept. For example, Cohen (1977) and Fagan (1979) have found that infants who are familiarized with a related set of faces or poses of faces of different people will generalize to a novel face or pose from the same set. Can infants likewise acquire a general concept of color?

Basically, two experiments are required to answer this question. One is to show that babies can discriminate among colors, and the other is to show that with special experience babies will classify those discriminable colors together. These two experiments are reported here. In essence, habituation experience was varied to look more closely at perceptual and conceptual classification of color in infants. Both experiments followed the same general design that deviated somewhat from previous studies in this series. The experiments consisted of two experimental phases, habituation and test; trials lasted the duration of the infant's first unrestricted look (prior to statistical analysis looking times were log transformed); looking was monitored over successive *pairs* of trials, and habituation was determined as a percentage (criterion $\leq 50\%$) of an infant's looking on a baseline pair of trials; a pair of post-criterion trials served to stabilize habituation; and, finally, the test with novel colors always immediately followed habituation.

The first experiment examined infants' discrimination of colors. Infants were habituated to blue and then tested, in a counterbalanced design, with green and red. Finally, the babies were retested with the original blue.

Babies declined in looking significantly ($p < .001$) to re-presentation of the habituation stimulus. Further, the duration of the infants' looking on the criterion and post-criterion pairs of trials did not differ, indicating that habituation was stable.

An analysis of variance that included the habituation criterion, post-criterion, and test trials showed a significant main effect of trials ($p < .001$). Newman-Keuls analysis revealed that the amount of looking at green and red reliably exceeded looking at blue on the criterion pair ($p < .01$ in both comparisons) and on the post-criterion pair ($p < .05$ and $< .01$, respectively), that the babies gave the criterion and post-criterion pairs of trials equal attention, and that the babies showed no difference in the amount they looked at green and at red. A similar analysis failed to yield any differences among the criterion, post-criterion, and retest of blue.

Three aspects of these data warrant discussion. First and most pertinently, babies who habituated to one hue dishabituate to different hues. The data clearly confirm that infants discriminate among hues, now shown in a variety of studies. Second, babies who are habituated to blue dishabituate equally to green, which borders on blue, and to red, which is more distant from blue than is green. That babies dishabituated equally replicates the results reported in Section IV-C showing that infant discrimination among simple hues is in some sense qualitative. Third, babies who are habituated to blue recognize it and, within limits, their recognition memory for a simple hue is immune to retroactive interference from other hues. The data therefore also replicate the memory results introduced in Section IV-F.

Babies in the first experiment gave basic evidence that they discriminate among hues. The second experiment was designed to test whether young infants have or can acquire a more general concept of color. To ascertain this, babies were habituated to a variety of colors and tested subsequently with a novel color. Infants' habituation to the color series would index formation of the concept of color, while generalization to a novel color would index the infants' utilization of the concept.

Colors used in this study ran the full gamut of the spectrum, including blue, blue-green, green, green-yellow, yellow, yellow-red, red, and red-blue (or purple); they were shown at each of two saturation levels. A baby was habituated to three simple hues (e.g., blue, green, and yellow) and to two mixtures of each and was then tested twice with the fourth remaining simple hue (e.g., red) and a neutral, control pattern. (Note that no color that contained the test hue—if red then yellow-red, red, or purple—ever appeared during the habituation sequence.) Half the babies saw the novel hue intermixed with the test pattern; the other half, in perhaps a purer test of the hypothesis, saw the novel color twice and then the control pattern twice.

Babies declined in looking significantly ($p < .001$) during habituation. Further, babies looked equivalently between criterion and suppression pairs of trials; again, habituation was stable.

Figure 8 shows the main results of the second study: Babies generalized habituation to the novel color and dishabituated to the control pattern. An analysis of variance that included the criterion, post-criterion, and test stimuli showed a significant main effect of trials ($p < .001$). Newman-Keuls analysis revealed that looking at the control pattern differed from looking at the criterion, post-criterion, and novel colors ($p < .01$ in each comparison), but that looking on the novel-color trials did not significantly differ from looking on the criterion or post-criterion trials, which did not differ from each other. Nonparametric analysis established the stability of this result: The same number of babies increased from habituation to test as decreased.

In order to insure that babies generalized habituation within a class and dishabituated to a new class rather than just a new stimulus or a different member of a similar class, an additional six babies were habituated to a variety of colors and then shown two novel colors, one of which appeared in a different shape. (On this additional test, the novel color was covered with a

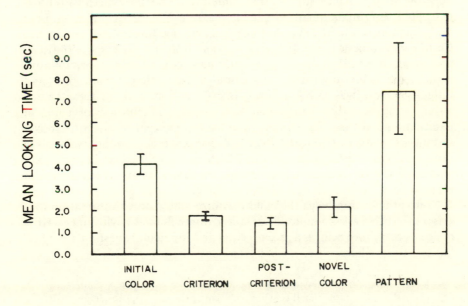

Fig. 8. Mean looking time (in sec ± S.E.M.) at the beginning of habituation (initial color trials), at criterion and at post-criterion, on novel color test trials, and to a control pattern.

matte-white mask that occluded all but a 12° central circular area of the color.) An analysis that included this test, the criterion and post-criterion pairs, the two novel color trials, and the control stimulus again showed a significant effect of trials ($p < .01$), and Newman-Keuls analysis revealed that looking at the control pattern was greater than looking at any of the colors ($p < .01$ in each comparison), but that there were no differences in looking on the color trials. In short, babies again generalized habituation across colors, but a change in the shape of the novel color was not sufficient to elicit dishabituation.

The results of the second and auxiliary experiments demonstrate that infants will habituate to a variety of colors indicating that they can form a general concept of color. When babies are tested with a novel color, they generalize habituation suggesting that they can utilize the concept.

Habituation in the first experiment may represent formation of a simple percept through repeated exposure to the same stimulus. In the second experiment, habituation more closely approximates formation of a more general concept through multiple exposure to a variety of discriminable, perceptually dissimilar stimuli from the same domain.[6] Bruner et al. (1956) have argued that perceptual and conceptual behaviors of this sort rest on similar processes. In a circumscribed way, the data from these two experiments with babies support that contention. The first experiment shows perceptual discrimination of color in infants; results of the second experiment build on those of the first and show generalization within a stimulus domain. Certainly the infants in the second experiment were not just responding to all colors as identical since they discriminate color. Moreover, in both experiments babies discriminated a stimulus class different from color, and fatigue or state was never a factor in habituation. Rather, these results strongly indicate that babies can form a general concept of color in habituation and that they are able to utilize the concept to categorize novel instances of the class (Bourne, 1966). The results of the second study resemble those of other investigations (cited earlier) that have used similar multiple-example habituation techniques to assess the formation of other concepts in infants.

Conceptualization helps the child organize and process information that arises in an otherwise complex, diverse, and unpredictable environment. How concepts come into being is a preeminently developmental question, though it has most often been posed by philosophers:

> Now, I would fain know at what time it is men are employed in [abstracting notions]..., and furnishing themselves with those necessary helps for discourse. It cannot be when they are grown up, for then it seems they are not conscious of any such

---

[6]"Percepts" seem to be more easily constructed during habituation than "concepts" (as in Section IV-D). Here, infants took almost three times as many trials to reach a criterion with a heterogeneous variety of colors than with simple repetition.

painstaking; it remains therefore to be the business of their childhood. (Berkeley, 1874, pp. 182–183)

These results suggest that further investigation of the relationship between the characteristics of a stimulus class and the ontogeny of concept formation and utilization may represent a meaningful direction for the study of cognitive development in early infancy.

In summary, one experiment showed that babies would habituate to a single hue and discriminate novel hues, and a second experiment showed that babies would habituate to a variety of colors and, if shown a novel color subsequently, would generalize habituation to the novel color. Together, the two experiments suggest that infants can discriminate among colors and also form and utilize concepts about them.

V. DISCUSSION AND CONCLUSIONS

Although study of the ontogeny of color perception in infancy has an old and venerable history, only relatively recently have sufficient progress in understanding infant sensory capacity and persistent attention to psychophysical control permitted a refreshed (and hopefully advanced) look at the subject. The main purpose of the studies collected here is to survey from this modern perspective several applications and extensions of color to some current topics in perceptual research with infants. This chapter shows that such applications and extensions can be of interest for a variety of reasons. At minimum, these studies provide new data on rich and varied aspects of color perception in infants. Further, they give good evidence that color, as a domain of investigation, can play an important role in the growth of our understanding of infant vision, for itself and in comparison with mature perception. Color, too, can be used profitably as an alternative domain to pattern in the exploration of more general problems and questions about early perception. Indeed, the use of patterns is often not optimal for critical tests of perceptual hypotheses since a persistent problem in pattern research is that there is no metric of form.

The experiments presented in this chapter speak additionally to several more broadly conceived issues in the study of infant sensation, perception, and cognition. Four of these warrant further consideration: They are motivation in infant looking, the interpretation of habituation in infants, the physiological and cognitive determinants of attention in infants, and developmental continuity and change in human perception and cognition of color.

From these studies it is obvious that the cognitive status of chromatic stimuli in infant perception varies, a fact that calls for some reconsideration of the infant's motives to look initially or to continue to look at colors. In a previous study (Bornstein, 1975), I found that four-month-olds tend generally to pay more attention to simple colors (when they are monochromatic) than to complex colors. The babies' looking in that situation was short-term and can best be interpreted in terms of preference since adult ratings of the pleasantness of the same colors paralleled the infants' fixations. However, this interpretation may apply only to an infant's initial looking or looking over relatively short, fixed periods (say 10 or 15 sec); the same interpretation may not apply to experience that is extended or repeated beyond initial exposure of a stimulus. Over a longer term, the infant's difficulty in processing or categorizing a stimulus may crucially recruit more attention to it. Complex colors, for example the boundaries between hues, are not easily categorized, and they may maintain infant attention over longer periods (exposures in the habituation study in Section IV-A were 2 minutes in duration). Perhaps complex stimuli hold the infants' attention longer as "cognitive" rather than "affective" motives for looking come into play. The temporal distribution of infant visual attention thus suggests a two-process model of visual control, wherein short-term looking may be interpreted as "affectively" motivated, and long-term looking as "cognitively" motivated. This view is consonant with other contemporary models of the differential control of infant short- and long-term attention (e.g., Cohen, 1973; Fagan, 1977; Jeffrey, 1976; Zelazo et al., 1973).

The experiments presented in this chapter also speak to important methodological issues in the study of infant perception since they reinforce the notion that how one interprets habituation and test results depends in large degree on the nature of stimulus variation in habituation and which test alternatives are available to infants. Previously, Fagan (1976), using the paired-familiarization method, found that discrimination among seven-month-olds must be interpreted in light of the way the habituation question is asked. In his study, infants who were familiarized with one face discriminated another face in preference to the original, but those who were familiarized with one male face discriminated a female face in preference to yet a different male face; or, infants who were familiarized with one pose of a face discriminated another pose of the same face in preference to the original pose, but those who were familiarized with one pose of a face discriminated another face in preference to a different pose of the original face. Over all these conditions, babies showed sensitivity to a particular face, to male qualities of a face, to a particular pose, and to generalized poses depending on familiarization and test alternatives. As far as early chromatic information processing is concerned, the results of the several experiments reported here suggest that infants can not only tell colors apart qualitatively and discriminate among them, but they can abstract chromatic aspects from the perceptual environment. These considerations ought to provoke investigators of infant perception to more circumscribed interpretations of habituation results.

When sophisticated perceptions occur near the beginning of life and are so orderly, they yearn for explanation either in terms of the density of early, selective experience or in terms of extant physiological substrates. For several phenomena discussed here—habituation, discrimination, memory, and psychological complexity—there exist potential neurological bases. For example, in experiments of Monnier, Boehmer, and Scholer (1976), rabbits were habituated to one wavelength and then shown a wavelength of a complementary color or, after a delay, they were shown the habituation color again, both in attempts to elicit dishabituation. The measures in this study were not behavioral, however, but neurophysiological, and they included amplitude of the evoked potential at four principal sites along the visual pathway, the retina, optic tract, lateral geniculate body, and visual cortex. In these experiments, amplitude of the evoked potential habituated at the geniculate and cortex only, and following a change in color or a delay, amplitude dishabituated only at the cortex. Thus, habituation of color seems to have an identifiable neurological correlate that is central in origin.

There are possible physiological determinants in man that could underlie differences in the infant's behavioral attitude to psychologically simple and complex colors too. For example De Valois (1973; De Valois & De Valois, 1975) identified classes of neural cells along the retinogeniculostriate pathway that are selectively sensitive to wavelengths in the blue-, green-, yellow-, and red-appearing regions of the spectrum. The wavelengths that mark maximal sensitivity of these electrophysiological classes stand in close correspondence to the dominant wavelengths of simple colors used in the studies reported here. As a consequence of the match between wavelength stimuli used here and the neural processes they typically excite, encodability and the level of processing in memory afforded simple colors may be facile and deeper automatically than that afforded complex colors, given equal exposure or familiarization. It follows from this psychobiological perspective that simple chromatic stimuli may naturally have a differential advantage in processing and retention.

An alternative, related cognitive explanation for this differential may be the relative information loads carried by psychologically simple versus complex colors. Babies habituate faster to psychologically simpler colors than to more complex ones, and they seem to perceive complex colors as configurations rather than as the simple sum of discriminable components. It would seem reasonable to conclude that the reduced level of information in simpler colors not only means that they can be assimilated faster and easier but that they can be remembered better.

The differential sensitivity infants display to complexity of chromatic stimuli is directly germane to the study of sensation and perception, but it is also pertinent to the study of cognitive development more broadly conceived. It may be interesting, as a final consideration, to ask whether the facile encodability and enhanced durability in memory of psychologically simple chromatic structures relative to complex ones in infants have identifiable correlates in later cognition. Following Berlin and Kay's (1969) discovery that certain colors are universally "focal" in human color naming and universally exemplary of color concepts, Rosch (1973) confirmed the psychological salience and "prototypical" status of focal colors in experimental cross-cultural and developmental studies. Making developmental comparisons, for example, she found that three- to four-year-old children preferentially attend to focal colors, more accurately match them, and, like Berlin and Kay's adults, more frequently choose them as representative of basic color names (Heider, 1971). Making cross-cultural comparisons, she found that American and Dugum Dani (a Stone Age people from New Guinea) more readily name focal colors and more accurately recall them from both short- and long-term memory (Heider, 1972). The significance of the infant's general preference for simple colors and their facilitation in infant information processing and memory may foretell the advantage these structures hold generally in attention, learning, and memory in childhood and adulthood (Berlin & Kay, 1969; Bornstein, 1975, 1978; Heider, 1971, 1972; Odom, 1972; Odom & Guzman, 1972; Rosch, 1973; Seitz & Weir, 1971; Suchman & Trabasso, 1966; Trabasso, Stave, & Eichberg, 1969).

The topics discussed in this chapter focus mainly on the baby's perception of color, but they span the range of infant perception, from attention to cognition. Color is fascinating to young children; at least adults (including myself) tend to think that it is. Perhaps this is why adults saturate the child's world with color. Andrew Lang's (1889 *ff*) renowned 12-volume collection of children's fairy tales attests to this fact. He titled them *The Blue, Brown, Crimson, Green, Grey, Lilac, Olive, Orange, Pink, Red, Violet,* and *Yellow Fairy Books.*

ACKNOWLEDGMENTS

This research and preparation of this chapter were partially supported by The Spencer Foundation, the National Institutes of Mental Health, and a Biomedical Sciences Research Grant to Princeton University. I am grateful to Helen G. Bornstein, Victoria Seitz, and an anonymous reviewer for comments on earlier versions of this chapter, to Kay Ferdinandsen for assistance in data collection and analysis, and to Arlene Kronewitter and Mary Ann Opperman for aid in preparing the manuscript. Request reprints from the author, Department of Psychology, New York University, 6 Washington Place, New York, N.Y. 10003.

REFERENCES

Adkinson, C. D., & Berg, W. K. Cardiac deceleration in newborns: Habituation, dishabituation, and offset responses. *Journal of Experimental Child Psychology,* 1976, **21**, 46–60.

Beare, A. C. Color-name as a function of wave-length. *American Journal of Psychology,* 1963, **76,** 248–256.

Berkeley, G. *A treatise concerning the principles of human knowledge.* Philadelphia: Lippincott, 1874.

Berlin, B., & Kay, P. *Basic color terms: Their universality and evolution.* Berkeley: University of California Press, 1969.

Berlyne, D. E. *Conflict, arousal, and curiosity.* New York: McGraw-Hill, 1960.

Bornstein, M. H. Color vision and color naming: A psychophysiological hypothesis of cultural difference. *Psychological Bulletin,* 1973, **80,** 257–285.

Bornstein, M. H. Qualities of color vision in infancy. *Journal of Experimental Child Psychology,* 1975, **19,** 401–419.

Bornstein, M. H. Infants' recognition memory for hue. *Developmental Psychology,* 1976, **12,** 185–191.

Bornstein, M. H. Chromatic vision in infancy. In H. W. Reese & L. P. Lipsitt (Eds.), *Advances in child development and behavior* (Vol. 12). New York: Academic Press, 1978.

Bornstein, M. H. Perceptual development: Stability and change in feature perception. In M. H. Bornstein & W. Kessen (Eds.), *Psychological development from infancy.* Hillsdale, N.J.: Erlbaum, 1979.

Bornstein, M. H. Two kinds of perceptual organization near the beginning of life. In W. A. Collins (Ed.), *Minnesota symposia on child psychology* (Vol. 14). Hillsdale, N.J.: Erlbaum, 1981.

Bornstein, M. H., Ferdinandsen, K., & Gross, C. G. The perception of symmetry in infancy. *Developmental Psychology,* 1981, **17,** 82–86.

Bornstein, M. H., Gross, C. G., & Wolf, J. Z. Perceptual similarity of mirror images in infancy. *Cognition,* 1978, **6,** 89–116.

Bornstein, M. H., Kessen, W., & Weiskopf, S. Color vision and hue categorization in young human infants. *Journal of Experimental Psychology: Human Perception and Performance,* 1976, **2,** 115–129.

Bornstein, M. H., & Monroe, M. D. Chromatic information processing: Rate depends on stimulus location in the category and psychological complexity. *Psychological Research,* 1980, **42,** 213–225.

Bornstein, M. H., & Teller, D. Y. Color vision. In P. Salapatek and L. B. Cohen (Eds.), *Handbook of infant perception.* New York: Academic Press, 1982.

Bourne, L. E. *Human conceptual behavior.* Boston: Allyn and Bacon, 1966.

Bower, T. G. R. Heterogeneous summation in human infants. *Animal Behaviour,* 1966, **14,** 395–398.

Boynton, R. M. Color, hue, and wavelength. In E. C. Carterette & M. P. Friedman (Eds.), *Handbook of perception* (Vol. 5). New York: Academic Press, 1975.

Boynton, R. M. Color in contour and object perception. In E. C. Carterette & M. P. Friedman (Eds.), *Handbook of perception* (Vol. 8). New York: Academic Press, 1978.

Bruner, J. S., Goodnow, J. J., & Austin, G. A. *A study of thinking.* New York: Wiley, 1956.

Caron, A. J., Caron, R. F., Caldwell, R. A., & Weiss, S. J. Infant perception of the structural properties of the face. *Developmental Psychology,* 1973, **9,** 385–399.

Caron, A. J., Caron, R. F., Minichiello, M. D., Weiss, S. J., & Friedman, S. L. Constraints on the use of the familiarization-novelty method in the assessment of infant discrimination. *Child Development,* 1977, **48,** 747–762.

Caron, R. F., & Caron, A. J. The effects of repeated exposure and stimulus complexity on visual fixation in infants. *Psychonomic Science,* 1968, **10,** 207–208.

Caron, R. F., & Caron, A. J. Degree of stimulus complexity and habituation of visual fixation in infants. *Psychonomic Science,* 1969, **14,** 78–79.

Christ, R. E. Review and analysis of color coding research for visual displays. *Human Factors,* 1975, **17,** 542–570.

Cohen, L. B. Observing responses, visual preferences, and habituation to visual stimuli in infants. *Journal of Experimental Child Psychology,* 1969, **7,** 419–433.

Cohen, L. B. A two process model of infant visual attention. *Merrill-Palmer Quarterly,* 1973, **19,** 157–180.

Cohen, L. B. *Concept acquisition in the human infant.* Paper presented at the meeting of the Society for Research in Child Development, New Orleans, 1977.

Cohen, L. B., De Loache, J. S., & Strauss, M. S. Infant visual perception. In J. Osofsky (Ed.), *Handbook of infancy.* New York: Wiley, 1979.

Cohen, L. B., & Gelber, E. R. Infant visual memory. In L. Cohen & P. Salapatek (Eds.). *Infant perception: From sensation to cognition* (Vol. 1). New York: Academic Press, 1975.

Cohen, L. B., Gelber, E. R., & Lazar, M. A. Infant habituation and generalization to differing degrees of stimulus novelty. *Journal of Experimental Child Psychology,* 1971, **11,** 379–389.

Cohen, L. B., & Salapatek, P. (Eds.), *Infant perception: From sensation to cognition.* New York: Academic Press, 1975.

Cornell, E. H. Infants' discrimination of photographs of faces following redundant presentations. *Journal of Experimental Child Psychology,* 1974, **18,** 98–106.

Cornell, E. H. Infants' visual attention to pattern arrangement and orientation. *Child Development,* 1975, **46,** 229–232.

Day, R. H., & McKenzie, B. E. Perceptual shape constancy in early infancy. *Perception,* 1973, **2,** 315–320.

Darwin, C. H. [A biographical sketch of a young child.] *Kosmos,* 1877, **1,** 367–376.

DeLoache, J. S. Rate of habituation and visual memory in infants. *Child Development,* 1976, **47,** 145–154.

Dember, W. N., & Earl, R. W. Analysis of exploratory, manipulatory, and curiosity behaviors. *Psychological Review,* 1957, **64,** 91–96.

De Valois, R. L. Central mechanisms of color vision. In R. Jung (Ed.), *Central processing of visual information* (Vol. 7/3A of *Handbook of sensory physiology*). New York: Springer-Verlag, 1973.

De Valois, R. L., & De Valois, K. K. Neural coding of color. In E. C. Carterette & M. P. Friedman (Eds.), *Handbook of perception* (Vol. 5). New York: Academic Press, 1975.

Dodd, C., & Lewis, M. The magnitude of the orienting response in children as a function of changes in color and contour. *Journal of Experimental Child Psychology,* 1969, **8,** 296–305.

Eimas, P. D. Speech perception in early infancy. In L. B. Cohen & P. Salapatek (Eds.), *Infant perception: From sensation to cognition* (Vol. 2). New York: Academic Press, 1975.

Eimas, P. D., Siqueland, E. R., Jusczyk, P., & Vigorito, J. Speech perception in infants. *Science,* 1971, **171,** 303–306.

Fagan, J. F. Infants' recognition memory for a series of visual stimuli. *Journal of Experimental Child Psychology,* 1971, **11,** 244–250.

Fagan, J. F. Infants' delayed recognition memory and forgetting. *Journal of Experimental Child Psychology,* 1973, **16,** 424–450.

Fagan, J. F. Infant color perception. *Science,* 1974, **183,** 973–975.

Fagan J. F. Infants' recognition of invariant features of faces. *Child Development,* 1976, **47,** 627–638.

Fagan, J. F. An attention model of infant recognition. *Child Development,* 1977, **48,** 345–359.

Fagan, J. F. The origins of facial pattern recognition. In M. H. Bornstein & W. Kessen (Eds.), *Psychological development from infancy.* Hillsdale, N.J.: Erlbaum, 1979.

Fantz, R. L. Visual experience in infants: Decreased attention to familiar patterns relative to novel ones. *Science,* 1964, **146,** 668–670.

Garner, W. R. *The processing of information and structure.* New York: Wiley, 1974.

Graham, C. H. (Ed.). *Vision and visual perception.* New York: Wiley, 1965.

Heider, E. R. "Focal" color areas and the devleopment of color names. *Developmental Psychology,* 1971, **4,** 447–455.

Heider, E. R. Universals in color naming and memory. *Journal of Experimental Psychology,* 1972, **93,** 10–20.

Hopkins, J. R., Zelazo, P. R., Jacobson, S. W., & Kagan, J. Infant reactivity to stimulus-schema discrepancy. *Genetic Psychology Monographs,* 1976, **93,** 27–62.

Jacobs, H. L., Smutz, E. R., & DuBose, C. N. Comparative observations on the ontogeny of taste preference. In J. M. Weiffenbach (Ed.), *Taste and development.* Bethesda, Md.: DHEW, 1977.

James, W. *The principles of psychology.* New York: Henry Holt, 1890.

Jeffrey, W. E. Habituation as a mechanism of perceptual development. In T. J. Tighe & R. N. Leaton (Eds.), *Habituation.* Hillsdale, N.J.: Erlbaum, 1976.

Jeffrey, W. E., & Cohen, L. B. Habituation in the human infant. In H. Reese (Ed.), *Advances in child development and behavior* (Vol. 6). New York: Academic Press, 1971.

Jusczyk, P. W., Rosner, B. S., Cutting, J. E., Foard, C. F., & Smith, L. B. Categorical perception of nonspeech sounds by 2-month-old infants. *Perception & Psychophysics,* 1977, **21,** 50–54.

Kagan, J. *Change and continuity in infancy.* New York: Wiley, 1971.

Kessen, W., Haith, M. M., & Salapatek, P. H. Human infancy: A bibliography and guide. In P. Mussen (Ed.), *Carmichael's manual of child psychology.* New York: Wiley, 1970.

Kessen, W., Haith, M. M., & Salapatek, P. H. Human infancy: A bibliography and guide. In P. H. Mussen (Ed.), *Carmichael's manual of child psychology.* New York: Wiley, 1970.

Lang, A. (Ed.). *The blue, brown, crimson, green, grey, lilac, olive, orange, pink, red, violet, and yellow fairy book.* London: Longmans, Green, and Co., 1889 ff.

Lewis, M., & Baumel, M. H. A study in the ordering of attention. *Perceptual and Motor Skills,* 1970, **31,** 979–990.

Liberman, A. M., Cooper, F. S., Shankweiler, D. P., & Studdert-Kennedy, M. Perception of the speech code. *Psychological Review,* 1967, **74,** 431–461.

Lipsitt, L. P. Taste in human neonates: Its effects on sucking and heart rate. In J. M. Weiffenbach (Ed.), *Taste and development.* Bethesda, Md.: DHEW, 1977.

Martin, R. M. Effects of familiar and complex stimuli on infant attention. *Developmental Psychology,* 1975, **11,** 178–185.

McCall, R. B. Attention in the infant: Avenue to the study of cognitive development. In D. N. Walcher & D. L. Peters (Eds.), *Early childhood: The development of self-regulatory mechanisms.* New York: Academic Press, 1971.

McCall, R. B., Kennedy, C. B., & Appelbaum, M. I. Magnitude of discrepancy and the distribution of attention in infants. *Child Development,* 1977, **48,** 772–785.

McCall, R. B., & Melson, W. H. Attention in infants as a function of magnitude of discrepancy and habituation rate. *Psychonomic Science,* 1969, **17,** 317–319.

Milewski, A. E. Infants' discrimination of internal and external pattern elements. *Journal of Experimental Child Psychology,* 1976, **22,** 229–246.

Monnier, M., Boehmer,, A., & Scholer, A. Early habituation, dishabituation and generalization induced in the visual centres by colour stimuli. *Vision Research,* 1976, **16,** 1497–1504.

Neisser, U. *Cognitive psychology.* New York: Appleton-Century-Crofts, 1967.

Newton, I. New theory about light and colors. *Philosophical Transactions of the Royal Society,* 1671–1672, **80,** 3075–3087.

Nowlis, G. H. *Quality coding in the rodent gustatory system: A labeled line system?* Paper presented at the Rockefeller University, New York, February, 1978.

Odom, R. D. Effects of perceptual salience on the recall of relevant and incidental dimensional values: A developmental study. *Journal of Experimental Psychology,* 1972, **92,** 285–291.

Odom, R. D., & Guzman, R. D. Development of hierarchies of dimensional salience. *Developmental Psychology,* 1972, **6,** 271–287.

Olson, G. M. An information processing analysis of visual memory and habituation in infants. In T. J. Tighe & R. N. Leaton (Eds.), *Habituation: Perspectives from child development, animal behavior, and neurophysiology.* Hillsdale, N.J.: Erlbaum, 1976.

Pancratz, C. N., & Cohen, L. B. Recovery of habituation in infants. *Journal of Experimental Child Psychology,* 1970, **9**, 208–216.

Peeples, D. R., & Teller, D. Y. Color vision and brightness discrimination in two-month-old human infants. *Science,* 1975, **189**, 1102–1103.

Peeples, D. R., & Teller, D. Y. White-adapted photopic spectral sensitivity in human infants. *Vision Research,* 1978, **18**, 49–53.

Reese, H. W., & Lipsitt, L. P. *Experimental child psychology.* New York: Academic Press, 1970.

Rosch, E. H. Natural categories. *Cognitive Psychology,* 1973, **4**, 328–350.

Rosch, E. Human categorization. In N. Warren (Ed.), *Studies in cross-cultural psychology* (Vol. 1). London: Academic Press, 1978.

Ross, W. D. (Ed.). *The works of Aristotle* (Vol. 6). De Coloribus. (T. Loveday & E. S. Forster, trans.). Oxford: The Clarendon Press, 1913.

Saayman, G., Ames, E. W., & Moffett, A. Response to novelty as an indicator of visual discrimination in the human infant. *Journal of Experimental Child Psychology,* 1964, **1**, 189–198.

Salapatek, P., & Cohen, L. B. (Eds.). *Handbook of infant perception.* New York: Academic Press, 1982.

Sandell, J. H., Gross, C. G., & Bornstein, M. H. Color categories in Macaques. *Journal of Comparative and Physiological Psychology,* 1979, **93**, 626–635.

Schaffer, H. R., & Parry, M. H. Perceptual-motor behaviour in infancy as a function of age and stimulus familiarity. *British Journal of Psychology,* 1969, **60**, 1–9.

Schaffer, H. R., & Parry, M. H. The effects of short-term familiarization on infants' perceptual-motor co-ordination in a simultaneous discrimination situation. *British Journal of Psychology,* 1970, **61**, 559–569.

Seitz, V., & Weir, M. W. Strength of dimensional preferences as a predictor of nursery-school children's performance on a concept-shift task. *Journal of Experimental Child Psychology,* 1971, **12**, 370–386.

Steiner, J. E. Facial expressions of the neonate infant indicating the hedonics of food-related chemical stimuli. In J. W. Weiffenbach (Ed.), *Taste and development.* Bethesda, Md.: DHEW, 1977.

Strauss, M. & Cohen, L. B. *Infant immediate and delayed memory for perceptual dimensions.* Paper presented at the International Conference of Infant Studies, New Haven, Conn., April, 1980.

Suchman, R. G., & Trabasso, T. Color and form preference in young children. *Journal of Experimental Child Psychology,* 1966, **3**, 177–187.

Thomas, H. Discrepancy hypothesis: Methodological and theoretical considerations. *Psychological Review,* 1971, **78**, 249–259.

Trabasso, T., Stave, M., & Eichberg, R. Attribute preference and discrimination shifts in young children. *Journal of Experimental Child Psychology,* 1969, **8**, 195–209.

von Frisch, K. *Bees: Their vision, chemical senses, and language.* Ithaca, N.Y.: Cornell University Press, 1964.

Welch, M. J. Infants' visual attention to varying degrees of novelty. *Child Development,* 1974, **45**, 344–350.

Young-Browne, G., Rosenfeld, H. M., & Horowitz, F. D. Infant discrimination of facial expressions. *Child Development,* 1977, **48**, 555–562.

Zelazo, P. R., Hopkins, J. R., Jacobson, S., & Kagan, J. Psychological reactivity to discrepant events: Support for the curvilinear hypothesis. *Cognition,* 1973, **2**, 385–393.

Zusne, L. *Visual perception of form.* New York: Academic Press, 1970.

INTENTION IN THE STRUCTURE OF ACTION AND INTERACTION*

Jerome S. Bruner

HARVARD UNIVERSITY

I. INTRODUCTION

What I shall take for granted at the outset (and develop later) is that most of what we speak of in common sense terms as human action is steered by intentions of the following kind and in the following way. An intention is present when an individual operates persistently toward achieving an end state, chooses among alternative means and/or routes to achieve that end state, persists in deploying means and corrects the deployment of means to get closer to the end state, and finally ceases the line of activity when specifiable features of the state are achieved. The elements of the cycle, then, comprise aim, option of means, persistence and correction, and a terminal stop order.

*This is an expansion of a paper presented at a meeting on the "Organization of Action," Maison des Sciences de l'Homme, Paris, 12 January 1979. I am particularly grateful for the assistance of Virginia Sherwood.

Advances in Infancy
Research, Vol. I

The cycle is, of course, much like a TOTE unit (Miller, Galanter, & Pribram, 1960). There are several unspecified features present in this type of cycle. The principal one has to do with the nature of feedback and correction. In the nature of things, feedback in such an action cycle is always context-dependent: It is computed by reference to the feed-forward signal inherent in the action aim of the organism. A correction procedure involves a re-deployment of means whose objective is to minimize the discrepancy between one's present position and what had been anticipated as the position appropriate to achieving the sought-after end state. We shall later refer to the restricted contexts in which such cycles occur as *formats*.

There is another matter hidden in my description that wants to be made explicit. It is not necessary that, in such intended human action, the actor be able to account for or be conscious of the nature of his intentions. Much of intentional action takes place below the threshold of reportable awareness. Driving a motorcar whilst conversing with a friend provides a familiar case. But I would want to emphasize that a special status inheres in those intentional acts that *are* reportable and conscious. The distinction is important not only in the ethical sense intended by such concepts as "responsibility", but also from the point of view of how conscious reportability extends the range of corrections accessible to the actor. Perhaps it does so by making conscious intentions more combinable through the use of language. I need to mention this rather banal point for reasons that are obvious. I shall be discussing the support of intentional action in the relation that develops between infant and mother and it matters mightily when and how the child achieves reportable awareness of what he is trying to do. Not only will I claim that action in fact has such an intentional quality, but that it is perceived by others with whom we are interacting to have such a quality. Not *all* behavior is seen as steered by intentions. Some actions are seen as *caused* by events, regardless of what the actor "intended". The response of others to action is strongly affected by whether it is seen as caused or intended. If it is seen or interpreted as the latter, it will be more often subject to correction of a kind not usually given to action perceived as caused. This is illustrated by reference to Anscombe's two sentence types, the one depicting caused behavior, the other intended action:

I am going to be sick.
I am going to cross the street.

In the latter case, a beholder may reply, "Watch out for traffic," which would be an inappropriate mode of responding to the former. There are, as we shall also see, different conditions placed on actions and behaviors (if I may use these terms for intended and caused acts). Intended actions are judged in terms of preparatory, essential, sincerity, and felicity conditions; caused

behaviors are not (Searle, 1969). This is true both of overt action and of speech acts.

Another preliminary remark. It has to do with the graininess of the theory of action I am presenting, its decomposability into elementary units. We know that intentional acts can become constituents of, serve as means subroutines in, other intentional acts. Intentions are obviously nesting and nestable or, in a technical sense, have the property of iterativeness and recursivity. In some systems of intentional behaviour, like speaking a natural language, there are discernible, analyzable levels that go to make up a communicative act—say an utterance. These have the property that they cannot be understood from bottom up, but are amenable to interpretation only from the top down. When we say that distinctive features are the constitutents *en pacquet* of phonemes, and that phonemes and their allophonic slippages are constituents of morphemes, that morphemes somehow fill the grammatical slots of a sentence, etc., we imply top-down determination. Each level below is constrained by the level above in a fashion that makes it extraordinarily difficult to describe how language is produced or even comprehended. Language is a very special case in the sense that the design features of the system are in many ways quite unlike any other system of intentional action known in the biological world (and I do not mean to exclude the social world by using the term "biological"). Yet, for any system of action—from skilled motor activity to such highly symbolic, rule-governed activities as flirtation or stock brokering—there is a possible description of the manner in which constituents are composed into higher-level action structures. And the crucial point is that it is the task of anybody learning to carry out skilled, intentional action to figure out the rules of composition (and decomposition) of the system.

This is not to say that caused behavior is not hierarchial, decomposable, and recomposable. Rather, it is to underline the fact that the formation and transformation of intentional actions are subject to different types of control. We can change the procedure by which we greet others by the more or less immediate incorporation of feedback. "Knowing about" converts into "knowing how" in intentional action more directly than in the case of caused behavior. Where seemingly intentional actions are not subject to such direct conversion of knowledge into action, we begin looking for causes.

This brings me to the final preliminary remark I must make. It is quite the most typical thing about the actions of our species that in the course of growth our intentions outstrip our capacities for fulfilling them or, indeed, even for recognizing fully what they are about. The young infant will typically reveal a situation-related restlessness, a general activation before he is able fully to recognize means to an end, and indeed there is a body of data in the field of motivation that suggests that, under such conditions of activation, it may be necessary for the immature organism to learn what the end state is that terminates the diffuse intentionality (if I may use such a bizarre phrase as a synonym for activation). It certainly becomes necessary for him to learn how to deploy the means for achieving the desired end state. It is characteristic of organisms like man, with a conspicuously helpless immaturity, that they cannot operate to achieve their goals (or to learn them, for that matter) by trial-and-error behavior, and they do not have enough of a wired-in repertoire of try-out routines to guide them much in such trial and error. In consequence, they are dependent, like no species yet ever evolved, upon a tutoring relationship with adults who can help them learn to carry out their intended actions directed to goals. It is quite obvious that something of this order occurs in language acquisition and in other forms of social skill learning. It is equally obvious that such also occurs when one observes the child learning to cope with the world of objects during the first two years of life. Or if it is not immediately obvious, I hope I will be able to make it so shortly.

Now it will seem to some readers that the distinction we have introduced between intentional action and caused behavior is not unlike that between an operant and a respondent. Is intentional action (as here intended!) the same as operant conditioning? Professor Skinner remarks:

> Statements which use such words as 'incentive' or 'purpose' are usually reducible to statements about operant conditioning, and only a slight change is required to bring them within the framework of a natural science. Instead of saying that a man behaves because of the consequences which *are* to follow his behavior, we simply say that he behaves because of the consequences which *have* followed similar behavior in the past. This is, of course, the Law of Effect or operant conditioning. (1953)

Skinner talks about operant conditioning thusly:

> An operant is an identifiable part of behavior of which it may be said, not that no stimulus can be found which will elicit it (there may be a respondent the response of which has the same topography), but that no correlated stimulus can be detected upon occasions when it is observed to occur. It is studied as an event appearing spontaneously with a given frequency. (1938)

> The change in frequency . . . (of the operant) . . . is the process of *operant conditioning*. (p. 66, 1953).

> It is not correct to say that operant reinforcement 'strengthens' the response which precedes it. The response has already occurred and cannot be changed. What is changed is the future probability of responses in the same *class*. It is the operant as a class of behavior, rather than the response as a particular instance, which is conditioned. (p. 87, 1953).

There is one crucial difference between Skinner's account and mine—as well as some critical ones that stem from it. I would argue that intentional acts do indeed occur because of the consequences the actor forsees—even if other consequences may follow. This requires that a theory of intentional action contain a central place for a representation of the world in terms of its means-ends possibilities. Indeed, reinforcement of other people's acts depends upon whether or not we see them deploying means and ends with foresight, anticipation, ingenuity, etc. Most human behavior, including the behavior of infants, is judged and rewarded not by the delivery of food pellets but by how their behavior is seen by others. All of which is not to say that behavior change is not sensitive to the consequences that follow it. It plainly is. But one of the things that changes as a result of consequences is the anticipation of future consequence. We know from the studies of Tversky & Kahneman (1978) that hypotheses about consequences rarely follow the pattern proscribed by operant conditioning functions. To rule out the role of anticipation based on the complex processing of past experience in the forming and transforming of behavior is to rule out much that is interestingly human about human behavior—especially its problem-solving character.

Is intentional action, then, like trial-and-error behavior? I confess that since the celebrated Krechevsky-Spence controversy on "hypothesis versus chance" in discrimination learning I have found the distinction rather meaningless. How long a string of left-turning responses do you need to call the behavior a hypothesis? How many wrong consequences does a randomly-generated "trial" require in order for it to be suppressed? Tolman was fond of describing behavior as "docile," subject to easy correction. Yet much problem solving guided by conscious and reportable hypotheses is rigid by virtue of the problem solver's tendency to "write off" or "explain away" unfavorable consequences as atypical or special in one way or another. I believe one can sail in cleaner air by taking one position or another—that behavior of a certain description is guided by hypotheses or intentions, *or* that it is guided by "trial-and-error" built on the summating of past encounters. In what follows, I shall unabashedly take the former position, knowing that the data will one day decide.

II.   ON INTERACTION

Now, a little reflection upon the interesting problems raised in the introduction makes it plain that for a state of transaction between infant and adult to prevail, adults must have a representation in their heads about the nature of human development. That is to say, to take the case of language, the adult, in order to help the child to his goals of linguistic mastery, must not only know what constitutes human mastery, but also must have a developmental theory of the performance of the child *en route* to that final state. I have already commented on the centrality of the concept of intention in adults' theories of children's behavior and will return to it again. If there is anything to the doctrine of an inbuilt, if not innate, Language Acquisition Device, LAD (Chomsky, 1965), for young children faced with the flow of the language about them, in my view there must be something comparable in the adult that deserves the title Language Assistance Service (LAS). In this veiw as well, the acquisition of langauge is a dialogue between the child's acquisition device and the adult's assistance service, between LAD and LAS. Certainly the findings of Shatz & Gelman (1973) on four-year-olds being able to talk appropriately in "Baby Talk" register to two-year-olds suggest that the adult assistance service opens its doors to potential clients at a very tender age indeed. And the past several years of research on mother-infant linguistic interaction points to the fact that there is an enormous amount of fine tuning in the mother's responses to the child's talk (or his very effort to talk) that could not have got there simply by virtue of the mother's having been exposed to other babies or having read John Lyons on Noam Chomsky (1970).

With respect to helping the child manipulate the world of objects, there is a comparable problem. David Wood and his co-workers (Wood, Bruner, & Ross, 1976) have explored what mothers do when helping their child to do things like drinking from a cup or putting together an interlocking set of blocks. The mother's performance is an interesting and uncanny set of maneuvers on the theme we have been exploring. She is obviously operating on a very intricate and subtle and updatable theory of the child's performance. Let me specify some of the maneuvers Wood, Ross and I observed in a study of a tutor teaching three- to five-year-olds how to assemble a set of interlocking blocks to make a pyramid.

A. *Modelling.* The mother typically models not only the final pyramid by constructing it slowly and with conspicuous marking, but also the subassemblies that she recognizes the child will need to create the constituents. She does this only after she has achieved the child's concentrated attention.

B. *Cueing.* Once the child has achieved a means-end routine or subroutine of any kind, she cues him with respect to the opportunities for using it so that it may reach successful conclusion.

C. *Scaffolding.* She systematically reduces the number of degrees of freedom that must be controlled by the child in carrying out parts of the task—as in helping him guide blocks into place when he is attempting to put them into the assembly. She also, by way of attentional scaffolding, protects him from distraction by limiting the site in which the task occurs, and by ritualizing it. I shall talk of this shortly in the context of language acquisition as "format construction," as a means of limiting the complexity of tasks to situations where the child is able to carry out tasks and to evaluate feedback off his own bat.

D. *Raising the ante.* It is characteristic of most mothers we have observed that once the child has mastered one component of the task, they find ways of challenging him to incorporate it into a more complex routine for achieving a more remote end. It may often have the nature of teasing rather than teaching (challenging the child, as one mother put it, to "make the ultimate effort").

But its function is certainly benign and it is a feature of variation in mother-infant interaction that saves the child from being bored out of action by a series of confirming reinforcements when he already knows that he already knows.

E. *Instruction.* And the final irony: When the child already knows how to do it *and* can indeed *account for* what he's doing, at that stage the mother starts using verbal instruction seriously and successfully. Verbal instruction appears only when the child is able to encode his acts in joint reference with the interlocutor, his mother. The signal for its use is the child's ability to say *that* he is doing something (in reply to "What are you doing?") and can begin to give a *reason* for doing it. Instruction is a conspicuous adjunct of metacognition.

The conclusion to which I am forced is that the mother is operating as if the child had intentions in mind, as if he were trying to deploy means to its realization, as if he were out to correct errors, as if he had a finished task in mind—but that he is not quite able to put it all together in a fashion to suit him or his mother. She imposes regularity and constraint on the task, takes account of his channel capacity for information processing, and keeps him activated by managing to keep full effectance just out of reach. I can come to one of two conclusions. Either the mother is a victim of common sense and does not really understand action, else she would put her charge into a Skinner box and devise a schedule of reinforcement for his operant responses. Or, she is behaving appropriately toward an immature member of the species who does in fact operate along the lines of intentional action I originally proposed.

Now language acquisition. This is not the occasion to go deeply into the question of the functions that language fulfills and the means whereby conventionalized devices or procedures are developed and used for their fulfillment. I do not want to be engaged directly in this issue at this point, it is enough to say that something of the order of speech act theory and the Gricean cycle (Grice, 1957) plus some set of controlling maxims to regulate presuppositions are for me an essential aspect of any linguistic theory and particularly of one that hopes to make contact with work on acquisition. What I would like to do is take first the case of the child learning to label, and then to move on to the child mastering requestive forms, as illustrations of my points. The account parallels what I have said about acquiring manipulative skills.

III. LABELLING

Consider an infant learning to label objects. Anat Ninio and I (Ninio & Bruner, 1978) observed Richard in his home every two weeks from his eighth month until he was two years old, videotaping his actions so that we could study them later. We visited when he and his mother had their regular play time. It is naturalistic observation in a familiar setting. In the instance we shall discuss, he and his mother are "reading" pictures in a book and Richard is learning how to "label" them. Before this kind of learning begins, certain things already have been established. Richard has mastered pointing as a pure indicating act, marking by pointing to unusual or unexpected objects rather than things wanted immediately. He has also picked up the "semanticity hypothesis"—that sounds refer in some singular way to objects or events. Richard and his mother, moreover, have long since established well-regulated turn-taking routines, which probably were developing as early as his third or fourth month (Stern, 1977). And finally, Richard has learned that books are to be looked at, not eaten or torn—that objects depicted are to be responded to in a particular way and that vocalizations occur in a privileged position in dialogue.

Videotapes obtained in such settings are difficult and time-consuming to analyze. Analysis requires manageable and reliable coding systems to extract and transcribe richly complex behavior in terms of useful categories. Let me note in passing that the category system employed in studies of early language and speech act acquisition are in no sense theoretically neutral. I doubt there can be such categories in the study of behavior. If one chooses to define the category system in "centimeters-grams-seconds," the classical c.g.s. system of "objective psychology," the linguistic nature of what is observed will slip through the coarse net. Our technique of analysis was based quite straightforwardly on a transactional model in which we sought for regularities in the sequence of linguistic and gestural exchanges between mother and child. In such analysis, the objective is to discover interactional structures—much as in any form of linguistic analysis that uses discourse as its data base. The data base is the number of episodes of "reading," carefully defined in terms of starting and terminating conditions. These in turn can be divided into turns and rounds (Garvey, 1974) and various forms of matching responses between mother and child. There is nothing particularly new about such analysis. The only cautionary note is that it must be sensitive to the linguistic aspects of exchanges, and that will inevitably lock one into a theory of language. The reader is referred to the Ninio & Bruner paper for the details of the analysis.

As for the mother's role in "book reading," she (like all mothers we have observed) drastically limits her speech in the format and maintains a steady regularity. In her dialogues with Richard in "bookreading" she uses four utterance types in her speech and in a strikingly fixed order. First, to get his attention, she says "Look". Second, with a distinctly rising inflection, she asks "What's that?" Third, she gives the picture a label, "It's an X." And finally, in response to his actions, she says "That's right." Each of these utterance types is highly contingent on Richard's behavior. She only says "What's that?" when he has responded to "Look" and only labels when he has given some responsive gesture or vocalization to "What's that?"

In each case, a single verbal token accounts for from nearly half to more than 90 percent of the utterance types. The way Richard's mother uses the four speech constituents is closely linked to what her son says or does, as noted. When she varies her response, it is with good reason. Thus, if *he* initiates a cycle by pointing and vocalizing, then *she* responds invariably and at the appropriate point in the cycle rather than at the beginning.

Her fine tuning is fine indeed. For example, if after her query Richard labels the picture correctly, she will virtually always skip the label and jump to the response "Yes." Like the other mothers we have studied, she is following ordinary polite rules for adult dialogue.

As Roger Brown has described the baby talk of adults, it appears to be an imitative version of how babies talk. Brown (1977) says: "Babies already talk like babies, so what is the earthly use of parents doing the same? Surely it is a parent's job to teach the adult language" (p. 10). He resolves the dilemma by noting, "What I think adults are chiefly trying to do, when they use [baby talk] with children, is to communicate, to understand and to be understood, to keep two minds focussed on the same topic" (p. 12). Although I agree with Brown, I would like to point out that the content and intonation of the talk is baby talk, but the dialogue pattern is adult.

To ensure that two minds are indeed focused on a common topic, the mother develops a technique for showing her baby what feature a label refers to by making 90 percent of her labels refer to whole objects. Since half of the remainder of her speech is made up of proper names that also stand for the whole, she seems to create few difficulties, supposing that the child also responds to whole objects and not to their features.

The mother's (often quite unconscious) approach is exquisitely tuned. When the child responds to her "Look!" by looking, she follows immediately with a query. When the child responds to the query with a gesture or a smile, she supplies a label. But as soon as the child shows the ability to vocalize in a way that might indicate a label, she raises the ante. She withholds the label and repeats the query until the child vocalizes, and then she gives the label if the child does not have it fully or correctly.

Later, when the child has learned to respond with shorter vocalizations that correspond to words, she no longer accepts an indifferent vocalization. When the child begins producing a recognizable, constant label for an object, she holds out for it. Finally, the child produces appropriate words at the appropriate place in the dialogue. Even then the mother remains tuned to the developing pattern, helping her child recognize labels and make them increasingly accurate. For example, she develops two ways of asking, "What's that?" One, with a falling intonation, inquires about those words for which she believes her child already knows the label, the other, with a rising intonation, marks words that are new.*

Even in the simple labelling game, mother and child are well into making the distinction between the given and the new. It is of more than passing interest that the old or established labels are the ones around which the mother will shortly be elaborating comments and questions for new information:

> Mother: What's that? [with falling intonation]
> Child: Fishy.
> Mother: Yes, and see him swimming?

After the mother assumes her child has acquired a particular label, she generally drops the attention-getting "Look!" when they turn to the routine. In these petty particulars of langauge, the mother gives useful cues about the structure of her native tongue. She provides cues based not simply on her knowledge of the langauge but also on her continually changing knowledge of the child's ability to grasp particular distinctions, forms or rules. The child is sensitized to certain constraints in the structure of their dialogue and does not seem to be directly imitating her. I say this because there is not much difference in the likelihood of a child's repeating a label after hearing it, whether the mother has imitated the child's label, simply said "Yes," or only laughed approvingly. In each case, the child repeats the label about half the time, about the same rate as with *no* reply from the mother. Moreover, the child is eight times more likely to produce a label in response to "What's that?" than to the mother's uttering the label.

I do not mean to claim that children cannot or do not use imitation in acquiring language. Language must be partly based on imitation, but though the child may be imitating another, langauge learning involves solving problems by communicating in a dialogue. The child seems to be trying to get through to the mother just as hard as she is trying to reach her child.

Dialogue occurs in a context. When children first learn to communicate, it is always in highly concrete situations, as when mother or child calls attention to an object, asking for the aid or participation of the other. Formally conceived, the format of communication involves an intention, a set of

*Much of what we have observed in labelling exchanges involves what Cohen (1972) calls "attention-getting" and "attention-holding." I mention this here not so much to relate our observations to his findings as to point to the risk of over-extending them. In fact, where language is concerned, the attention of the speaker must be drawn to structural features of the situation—either dialogic context or the general semantic context in which speech is occurring. For attention to be usefully directed in language acquisition, it must be guided by structural, attention-*holding* features of the situation. It is the distinction drawn by Vygotsky (following Pavlov) to the First and the Second Signalling Systems. Unless attention comes to be controlled by the latter, it cannot guide the child to inspect the linguistic regularities being created in the exchange.

procedures, and a goal. In this sense, the formats of language acquisition are much like the tasks described by Wood, Bruner & Ross (1976).

IV. REQUESTING

A second major function of speech is requesting something of another person. Roy, Ratner, and I (Bruner, Roy, & Ratner, in press) have been studying its development during the first two years of life. Requesting requires an indication that you want *something* and *what* it is you want. In the earliest procedures used by children it is difficult to separate the two. First the child vocalizes with a characteristic intonation pattern while reaching eagerly for the desired nearby object—which is most often held by the mother. As in virtually all early exchanges, it is the mother's task to interpret, and she works at it in a surprisingly subtle way. During our analyses of Richard when he was from eight to 24 months old and Jonathan when he was eight to 18 months old, we noticed that their mothers frequently seemed to be teasing them or withholding obviously desired objects. Closer inspection indicated that it was not teasing at all. They were trying to get the infants to reach for what they wanted and to "say something" (as one mother urged her son), pressing them to make their intentions clearer. When the two children requested nearby objects, the mothers were more likely to ask, "Do you really want it?" than, "Do you want the X?" The mother's first step is pragmatic, to get the child to signal that he wants the object.

Children make three types of requests, reflecting increasing sophistication in matters that have nothing to do with language. The first kind that emerges is directed at obtaining nearby, visible objects; this later expands to include distant or absent objects where the contextual understanding of words like *you/me, this/that* and *here/there* is crucial. The second kind of request is directed at obtaining support for an action that is already in progress, and the third kind is used to persuade the mother to share some activity or experience.

When children first begin to request objects, they typically direct their attention and their reach entirely toward the object, opening and closing their fists, accompanied by a "standard," stereotyped call with characteristic intonation pattern. As this request expands, between 10 and 15 months, an observer immediately notes two changes. In reaching for distant objects, a child no longer looks solely at the desired object, but shifts his glance back and forth between the object and his mother. His call pattern also changes. It becomes more prolonged, or its rise and fall in intonation is repeated, and it is more insistent.

When consistent word forms appeared, they were initially idiosyncratic labels for objects, gradually becoming standard nouns that indicated the desired objects. The children also began initiating and ending their requests with smiles. The development of this pattern is paced by the child's knowledge, which is shared with the mother, of where things are located and of her willingness to fetch them if properly asked. Once the child begins requesting distant and absent objects, the mother has an opportunity to require that the desired object be specified; her emphasis shifts from the pragmatic to the referential. Other conditions begin to be imposed; the request, for example, must be "legitimate" and "appropriate," the object essential, "timetable" conditions must be honoured—and when the request is not granted, the child is expected to understand and accept the mother's verbal reasons.

Requests for joint activity contrast with object requests. I think they can be called precursors to invitation. They amount to the child asking the adult to share in an activity or an experience—to look out of the window into the garden together, to play Ride-a-Cock-Horse, to read together. They are the most playlike form of request, and in consequence they generate a considerable amount of language of considerable complexity. It is in this format that the issues of agency and share (or turn) emerge and produce important linguistic changes. Most of these requests are for activities that are quite ritualized and predictable. There tend to be rounds and turns, and no specific outcome is required. The activity itself is rewarding. In this setting the child first deals with share and turn by adopting such forms of linguistic marking as *more* and *again*. These appear during joint role enactment and migrate rapidly into formats involving requests for distant objects.

It is also in joint role enactment that the baby's first consistent words appear and, beginning at 18 months, word combinations begin to explode. *More x* (with a noun) appears, and also combinations like *down slide, Mummy ride, Mummy read, Eileen do*. Indeed, it is in these settings that full-blown ingratiatives appear in appropriate positions, as in prefacing a request with *nice Mummy*. Ingratiatives serve to assure that the other continues to act as a means to the achievement of intention.

After the children were 17 months old, the mothers we studied began to demand that they adhere more strictly to turn taking and role respecting. The demand can be made most easily when they are doing something together, for that is where the conditions for sharing are most clearly defined and least likely, since playful, to overstrain the child's capacity to wait for a turn. But the sharp increase in agency as a topic in their dialogue reflects as well the emergence of a difference in their wishes. The mother may want the child to execute the act requested of her, and the child may have views contrary to his mother's about agency. In addition, the child's requests for support more often lead to negotiation between the pair than is the case when the clarity of the roles in their joint activity makes acceptance and refusal easier. A recurrent trend in development during the child's first year is the shifting of agency in all manner of exchanges from mother to infant. Even at nine to 12 months, Richard gradually began taking the lead in give-and-take games (Bruner, 1978), and peekaboo games follow a similar pattern (Ratner & Bruner, 1978). In bookreading too, Richard's transition was quite rapid. Role shifting is very much part of the child's sense of script, and I believe it is typical of the kind of "real world" experience that makes it so astonishingly easy for children to master soon afterwards the deictic shifts, those contextual changes in the meaning of words that are essential to understanding the language. The prelinguistic communicative framework established in their dialogue by mother and child provides the setting for the child's acquisition of this language function. His problem solving in acquiring the deictic function is a *social* task: to find the procedure that will produce results, just as his prelinguistic communicative effort produced results, and the results needed can be interpreted in relation to role interactions.

The last type of request, the request for supportive action, has a very special property. It is tightly bound to the nature of the action in which the child is involved. To ask others for help in support of their own actions, children need at least two forms of knowledge. One of them represents the course of action and involves a goal and a set of means for getting to it. The second requirement is some grasp of what has been called the arguments of action (Parisi & Antinucci, 1976): who does it, with what instrument, at what place, to whom, on what object, etc. Once children have mastered these, they have a rudimentary understanding of the concepts that will later be encountered in case grammar (cf. Fillmore, 1968).

The degree to which a child comes to understand the structure of tasks is the degree to which his requests for support in carrying them out become more differentiated. These requests do not appear with any marked frequency until he is 17 or 18 months old and consist of bringing the "work" or the "action" or the entire task to an adult: a music box to be rewound, or two objects that have to be joined together. In time, a child is able to do better than that. He may bring a tool to an adult or direct the adult's hand or pat the goal (the chair on which he wants up). He is selecting and highlighting relevant features of the action, though not in a fashion that depends on what the adult is doing. Finally at about the age of two, with the development of adequate words to refer to particular aspects of the action, the child enters a new phase: He requests action by guiding it successively. The pacemaker of the verbal output is progress in the task itself.

Let me give an instance of this successive guidance system. Richard, it transpires, wishes to persuade his mother to open a cupboard so that he can get something out; she is seated (and very pregnant). Successively, he makes the following requests:

> Mummy, Mummy; Mummy come... Up, up; up... Cupboard... Up cupboard, up cupboard, up cupboard: up... Get up... Cupboard, cupboard... Cupboard-up, cupboard-up, cupboard-up... Telephone... Mummy... Mummy get out telephone.

His mother objects and asks him what it is he wants after each of the first two requests. She is trying to get him to set forth his request in some "readable" order before she starts to respond—to give a reason in terms of the goal of the action. Richard, meanwhile, achieves something approaching a request in sentence form by organizing his successive utterances in a fashion that seems to be guided by his conception of the needed steps in the action. The initial grammar of the long string of task-related requests is, then, a kind of temporal grammar based on an understanding not only of the actions required, but also of the order in which these actions must be executed. This bit of child language is an interpersonal script based on a young child's knowledge of what is needed to reach the goal in the real world; it is the intentional matrix in which language develops.

Requesting, I think, serves as an ideal model for what we have been discussing as our general theme. Its very form in language and in the context of its appropriacy depends upon the formulating and the transmitting of intentions and, by its very nature, it forces what at the outset I referred to as explicit, reportable intentions. It is no curiosa that the mother, before the lesson of request is over, insists that the child, almost like a student of the philosophical Miss Anscombe (1957), should make clear (or be prepared, at least, to make clear) what it is that he has in mind in launching on a line of behavior that requires that another enter in to help change his state of the world, to paraphrase Hintikka (1974).

V.   CONCLUDING COMMENT

One final point. Intentions involving more than a single person in their execution are the stuff of which social life is composed. Social psychologists refer to their being brought together as a negotiatory process. It is indeed negotiatory, but the negotiation requires a context or format or, as some prefer, a scenario, in order for the two or more sets of intentions to be meshed smoothly. Much of earlier developmental psychology stressed that children were egocentric, and by implication could not enter into scenarios in a way that made it possible for them to see the role of the other. When one observes the conversation of four-year-olds (as Nelson & Gruendel [1977] have), it becomes clear that much of what has been taken for egocentrism is simply a failure on the part of the child to grasp the nature of the scenario. They report that four-year-olds who may show egocentrism in the standard, adultocentric tasks used in Geneva can nonetheless bring off dialogues over a toy telephone as follows:

Gay: Hi.
Dan: Hi.

Gay: How are you?
Dan: Fine.
Gay: Who am I speaking to?
Dan: Daniel. This is your Daddy. I need to speak to you.
Gay: All right.
Dan: When I come home tonight we're gonna have...peanut butter and jelly sandwich...uh...at dinner time.
Gay: Uhmmm. Where're we going at dinner time?
Dan: Nowhere, but we're just gonna have dinner at 11 o'clock.
Gay: Well, I made a plan of going out tonight.
Dan: Well, that's what we're gonna do.
Gay: We're going out.
Dan: The plan, it's gonna be, that's gonna be, we're going to MacDonald's.
Gay: Yeah, we're going to McDonald's. And ah, ah, ah, what they have for dinner tonight is hamburger.
Dan: Hamburger is coming. O.K. Well, goodbye.
Gay: Bye.

To return to my preliminary remarks, there are three alternative views that can be entertained as to why we ever considered that the organization of action was other than I have described it here. One is that at the "natural" or biological level, the "machine language" of the system is in fact as it has been described by exponents of a model of "trial-and-error-cum-reinforcement." I think it can be said that the arguments of von Holst & Mittelstaedt (1950) and of Miller, Galanter, & Pribram (1960) score strongly against this view by demonstrating that at the molecular level as well there must be something "intentional" present that makes possible the generating of a subsequent correction term. The second view is that the socialization process "shapes" human action into its highly intentional form. This is doubtless true, in the sense that ever higher-level intentional systems are called for by adults in their interaction with children. Nonetheless, what is most crucial is that human young have the capacity to respond to such "goading" by adults in the society. The third view holds that intentional activity in man is "required" by the nature of the "social-technical" system into which man enters. The social-technical system of human society can be conceived of as a treasury of "prosthetic devices" in the form of means for achieving ends. The evolution of the species is such as to have shaped man's action patterns into an ever more intention-directed, means-sensitive, corrective form. It is likely that older views of action result from a spirit of reductionism that believed the "true" nature of man could best be explained by using a phylogenetically primitive model that ignored man's evolution into a tool and symbol user.

Let me end where I started. The evidence of child-adult interaction argues strongly, I claim, that human behavior is organized under the control of intentions in fact and as perceived. The child-rearing folk wisdom of the species rearing young for participation in human culture reflects that organization. I think that psychology should follow suit!

REFERENCES

Anscombe, G. E. M. *Intention.* Oxford: Blackwell, 1957.

Bernstein, N. A. *The coordination and regulation of movement.* London: Pergamon, 1967.

Brown, R. Introduction to C. E. Snow & C. A. Ferguson (Eds.), *Talking to children: Language input and acquisition.* Cambridge: Cambridge University Press, 1977.

Bruner, J. S. Learning how to do things with words. In J. Bruner & A. Garton (Eds.), *Human development,* Wolfson Lectures 1976. Oxford: Oxford University Press, 1978.

Bruner, J., Roy, C., & Ratner, N. The beginnings of request. In K. E. Nelson (Ed.), *Children's language,* Vol. 3. New York: Gardner Press, in press.

Chomsky, N. *Aspects of the theory of syntax.* Cambridge, Mass. M.I.T. Press, 1965.

Cohen, L. Attention-getting and attention-holding processes of infant visual preferences. *Child Development,* 1972, **43**, 869–879.

Fillmore, C. J. The case for case. In E. Bach & R. Harms (Eds.), *Universals in linguistic theory.* New York: Holt, Rinehart & Winston, 1968.

Garvey, C. Some properties of social play. *Merrill-Palmer Quarterly,* 1974, **20**, 163–180.

Grice, H. P. Meaning. *Philosophical Review,* 1957, **66**, 377–388.

Hintikka, J. Questions about questions. In M. K. Munitz & P. K. Unger (Eds.), *Semantics and philosophy.* New York: New York University Press, 1974.

Lyons, J. *Chomsky.* London: Fontana (Modern Masters), 1970.

Miller, G. A., Galanter, E., & Pribram, K. H. *Plans and the structure of behavior.* New York: Holt, 1960.

Nelson, K. & Gruendel, J. At morning it's lunch time: A scriptal view of children's dialogue. Paper presented at the Conference on Dialogue, Language Development and Dialectical Research, University of Michigan, Ann Arbor, December 1977.

Ninio, A. & Bruner, J. S. The achievement and antecedents of labelling. *Journal of Child Language.* 1978, **5**(1) 1–15.

Parisi, D. & Antinucci, F. *Essentials of grammar.* New York & London: Academic Press, 1976.

Ratner, N. K. & Bruner, J. S. Games, social exchange and the acquisition of language. *Journal of Child Language,* 1978, **5**, 391–401.

Searle, J. *Speech acts.* Cambridge: Cambridge University Press, 1969.

Shatz, M., & Gelman, R. The development of communication skills: Modifications in the speech of young children as a function of listener. *Monographs of the Society for Research in Child Development,* 1973, **38**(5), No. 152.

Stern, D. *The first relationship: Infant and mother.* London: Fontana/Open Books, 1977.

Skinner, B. F. *The behavior of organisms.* New York: Appleton-Century-Crofts, 1938.

Skinner, B. F. *Science and human behavior.* New York: Macmillan, 1953.

Tversky, A. & Kahneman, D. Causal schemata in judgments under uncertainty. In M. Fishbein (Ed.), *Progress in social psychology.* Hillsdale, N.J.: Lawrence Erlbaum, 1978.

von Holst, E. & Mittelstaedt, H. Das reafferenzprinzip. *Naturwissenschaften,* 1950, **37**, 464–476.

Wood, D., Bruner, J. S., & Ross, G. The role of tutoring in problem solving. *Journal of Child Psychology & Psychiatry,* 1976, **17**, 89–100.

INFANT AROUSAL ATTENTION AND AFFECT DURING EARLY INTERACTIONS

Tiffany Field

MAILMAN CENTER FOR CHILD DEVELOPMENT
UNIVERSITY OF MIAMI MEDICAL SCHOOL

Advances in Infancy
Research, Vol. I

I. AROUSAL, ATTENTION, AND AFFECT
DURING EARLY INTERACTIONS:
AN INTEGRATIVE MODEL

Early interpersonal relations are the foundation for social development. Since early interaction behaviors appear to relate to later social development (Bakeman & Brown, 1980; Sigman & Parmelee, 1980), to later cognitive development (Cohen & Beckwith, 1979; Ramey, Farran, & Campbell, 1979), and to language behaviors (Field, 1979b), a number of early intervention programs have attempted to facilitate early interactions (e.g., Bromwich & Parmelee, 1979; Field, Widmayer, Stringer, & Ignatoff, 1980; Kogan, 1980). Arousal, attention, and affect are important components of early interactions.

The problem with many early interaction studies is that they fail to consider arousal, attention and affect (or any two of these processes) simultaneously. Behavioral and psychophysiological data on early interactions reveal a need for an integrative model to explain the multivariate relationships among arousal, attention, and affect. This chapter summarizes some of those data and suggests an integrative model for arousal, attention and affect during the social interactions of both normal and high-risk infants. The model may facilitate future investigations of these relationships and intervention strategies for their improvement of early interactions of high-risk infants.

Figure 1 presents the basic model:

1. Attentiveness and positive affect during early interactions occur within a range or band of activation which has as its lower limit an attention threshold and as its upper limit an aversion threshold. The activation band for normal infants is depicted by the dotted lines in Fig. 1. The lower limit reflects a threshold for accepting or attending to stimulation and the upper limit a threshold for rejecting or averting stimulation.
2. The upper and lower thresholds of the activation band shift and the band width varies as a function of the infant's rest activity/arousal cycles.
3. An intrinsic curvilinear relationship between stimulation and arousal/ attention/affect processes suggests that only moderate stimulation (be that quantitatively moderate or moderately discrepant stimulation) would fall

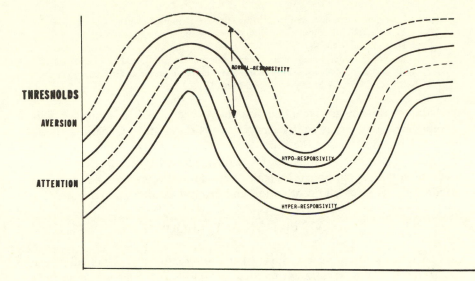

REST-ACTIVITY/AROUSAL CYCLES

Fig. 1. Proposed "optimal activation band."

within the activation band. As the thresholds of the band shift, the relative discrepancy or amount of stimulation perceived by the infant may also shift.

4. Within the activation band positive affect may occur and vary in form and energy (e.g., from smiling to laughing) as a function of the combined arousal level, stimulation properties, and attentive/affective response energy.

5. Moderate levels of positive affect serve to modulate arousal and sustain attention.

6. If and when stimulation and/or affective responsivity exceed moderate levels, the upper limit of the activation band is approached, at which point the infant will manifest an inattentive response (e.g., gaze aversion). If that limit or threshold is exceeded, an aversive reaction or negative affect (e.g., fussing or crying) will occur.

7. As the infant develops, arousal cycles may lengthen and the proposed activation band may widen as manifested by longer periods of attentiveness and more modulated affective responses.

8. The activation band width and thresholds vary as a function of individual differences.

9. The activation band may be narrower and the arousal cycles shorter in infants experiencing developmental delays or deficits (be they perceptual, motor, cognitive, or physiological delays or deficits). More specifically, as depicted in Fig. 1, there may be a narrower band for hypo-responsive infants (e.g., preterm, Down syndrome, and autistic infants) which may be delimited by a higher-than-normal attention threshold and a lower-than-normal aversion threshold. Similarly, there may be a narrower band for hyper-responsive infants (e.g., post-term, hyperactive, and autistic infants). In contrast to the posited activation band of hypo-responsive infants, the band of hyper-responsive infants may be delimited by both lower attention and lower aversion thresholds;

10. This model can be tested by shifting stimulus parameters in the range of the hypothesized thresholds and simultaneously monitoring behaviors such as gaze, facial expressions, vocal expressions, and body movements and physiological responses such as heart rate and respiration. These measures could then be analyzed using spectral analyses techniques (e.g., Gottman, 1979; Porges, Bohrer, Cheung, Drasgow, McCabe, & Karen, 1979).

Although this integrative model has not yet been assessed, a number of its components are suggested by early interaction studies. Generally, these studies have investigated the infant's attentiveness or the infant's affective behavior and its relationship to arousal based on behavioral and, occasionally, psychophysiological data. The studies can be grouped accordingly as research on attention and arousal or affect and arousal.

II. ATTENTION AND AROUSAL

The infant's attentiveness during early interactions has typically been measured by the behaviors gazing at or gazing away from a social partner. Several have suggested that in addition to regulating perceptual input, gaze behavior serves to regulate internal physiological state or arousal (Stechler & Carpenter, 1967; Stern, 1974). These researchers claim that the infant can reduce his or her state of arousal by turning away from a stimulus that is too intense, too complicated, or too discrepant from an internal model. Similarly, turning away from a redundant and boring stimulus to seek a new stimulus can increase the infant's state of arousal. Gaze aversion in normal (Field, 1977, 1979b; Stern, 1974) and autistic infants (Hutt & Ounsted, 1966) has been interpreted as an attempt to control stimulation and modulate internal state or arousal within a given range.

In the absence of independent measures of state or arousal, either behavioral or psychophysiological measures, this interpretation is speculative. The circularity of ascribing both the manifestation and control of arousal level to gaze behavior is problematic. In addition, since gaze aversion can be interpreted as both stimulus-seeking and stimulus-blocking behavior, the use of gaze behavior, without the simultaneous recording of other measures (e.g., a heart rate index of attention/arousal), contributes to ambiguity. Despite these shortcomings, some suggestive observations have derived from early interaction studies in which visual attention has been the variable of interest.

A. Gaze Behavior, an Underlying Physiological
Rhythm and Regulatory Background
for Affective Behavior

In most studies of visual attention mean gaze duration, number of visual fixations or percentage of stimulus presentation time the infant gazes at the stimulus have been measured. Rarely are all three reported together, and almost no attention has been paid to the parameters of gazing away from the stimulus or the relationship between gazing-at and gazing-away. Stern (1974), who considers gaze behavior as the "regulatory background for affective behaviors" during early interactions, measured the distributions of frequencies and durations of gazing-at and gazing-away behavior, as well as the contingency of infant and mother gaze during early–face-to-face interactions. The data on frequency and duration of gaze suggested an alternating rhythm of gazing-at and gazing-away. This characteristic alternation of gazing-at and gazing-away from the mother or other social partner differs dramatically from the more prolonged visual fixations of objects (Brazelton, Koslowski, & Main, 1974; Field, 1979c). Across all mother–infant interactions of the Stern study the median gaze-to-gaze interval showed no significant correlation with the percentage of infant gazing time at mother. The distribution of gaze-to-gaze intervals remained stable and did not appear to reflect changes in the infant's visual interest, suggesting that gaze-to-gaze intervals may be a manifestation of an underlying physiological rhythm. However, separate distributions of gazes-at and gazes-away shifted reciprocally as a function of the infant's interest in the mother's stimulation. Thus, Stern (1974) concluded that gaze initiation and termination are a function not only of the stimulation associated with the interactions but also of the infant's internal state. Both the infant, by his on–off visual behavior, and the mother, by constantly altering her behavior in response to changes in the infant's visual attention and state, appeared to contribute to the regulation of infant state or arousal.

Brazelton and his colleagues (Brazelton et al., 1974) view the mother's sensitivity to her infant's on–off visual signals and her alteration of behavior according to these as her most important function during early interactions. In the Brazelton et al. (1974) study the intensity, frequency, and sequence of mother and infant interaction behaviors such as vocalizing, smiling, and touching were plotted as a function of the infant's looking and looking away periods during early face-to-face interactions. Although there were individual differences, mothers generally emitted shorter, fewer, and less intense behaviors during their infants' looking-away periods. Brazelton et al. (1974) suggested that the infant uses these periods of looking-away "as if he were attempting to reduce the intensity of the interaction, to recover from the excitement it engenders in him, and to digest what he has taken in during the interaction. These, perhaps, represent a necessary recovery phase in maintaining homeostasis at a time in infancy when constant stimulation without relief could overwhelm the baby's immature systems" (p. 59).

Stern (1974) provides a description of a typical infant–mother face-to-face interaction in which gaze averting is also interpreted as the infant's attempt to process information and modulate arousal. "It consists of the infant looking at the mother, smiling, vocalizing, and showing other signs of mounting arousal and positive affect, including increasing motor activity. As the intensity of his state increases, he begins to show signs of displeasure, momentary sobering, a fleeting grimace, interspersed with the smiling. The intensity of arousal continues to build until he suddenly averts gaze sharply with a quick but not extensive head turn which keeps the mother's face in good peripheral view, while his level of 'excitement' clearly declines. He then returns gaze, bursting into a smile, and the level of arousal and affect build again. He again averts gaze, and so on. The infant gives the clear impression of modulating his states of arousal and affect within certain limits by regulating the amount of perceptual input" (p. 209).

To what degree the infant's on–off visual behavior or gazing-at, gazing-away during early interactions is an underlying rhythm reflecting internal state and to what degree that behavior is responsive to the stimulation provided is indeterminate. Continuous gaze behavior data of the type presented by Stern (1974) and by Brazelton et al. (1974) might be subjected to spectral and cross-spectral analytic methods as described by Gottman (1979) and Porges et al. (1979) to detect cyclicity, cross-cyclicity, and lead-lag relationships between the gaze behavior of the infant and the activity of the mother. Spectral analysis might reveal the degree to which there is an inherent cyclicity to the gaze behavior, while cross-spectral analyses, identifying phase relationships between the two series of data, would yield cross-correlations between the two series and information about the lead-lag relationships or the degree to which one series (gaze behavior of infant or activity of mother) is leading the other. Analyses of this kind may also provide information on why the infant initiates gazes at the moment he does and terminates gazes at the moment he does, a question asked by a number of interaction researchers (Brazelton et al., 1974; Field, 1979c; Stern, 1974).

B.   Gaze Behavior
and the Discrepancy Hypothesis

Interaction gaze behavior has also been discussed in the context of the discrepancy hypothesis by Stern (1974) and others (Stechler & Carpenter, 1967). According to the discrepancy hypothesis (Hunt, 1965; Kagan, 1971), attention is elicited when stimulation is discrepant from schema available to the infant. The relationship between discrepancy and attention is assumed to be curvilinear with moderately discrepant stimuli producing the greatest attention. Visual habituation or diminished gaze is assumed to relate to the formation of an internal model. As the internal model is formed, the stimulus becomes progressively less discrepant relative to the internal model, and visual attention decreases.

In the Stern (1974) study already described, mothers were noted to frequently exaggerate their facial and vocal behaviors and at other times to exhibit a restricted or unimaginative repertoire of behaviors. Both of these occasions were characterized by infant gaze aversion, as if the mother's behavior as a stimulus event had exceeded or fallen below an optimal range of discrepancy.

Analogous to experiments on visual habituation in which a novel stimulus is presented after response decrement to the repeated presentation of the initial stimulus, the mother is described as continuously varying her behavior as the infant appears to lose interest. Although Stern (1974) does not provide data to support the discrepancy and habituation phenomena during early interactions, he makes the following claim: "When an entire play session is analyzed to show overall response decrement to the mother's face, however, none is found. This does not mean that the phenomenon does not occur for short runs within the interaction. Our impression is that such runs do occur but are washed out by the mother rapidly responding to any response decrement by recorrecting the stimulus level of her behavior" (p. 207).

Another problem with invoking an habituation process to explain the infant's gaze-averting periods during early interactions is that the infant does not look bored, nor does he appear to be seeking new stimulation during these periods. There is none of the fixed, intense attention typically directed toward a new object (Brazelton et al., 1974) as he averts gaze and looks toward something else.

Unfortunately, quantitative assessments of the infants' attention as a function of the discrepancy of maternal behaviors and the infants' gaze averting as a function of an habituation process have not been made during early interactions, perhaps because of the rapidity with which interaction events occur and the complexity of measuring these. Some have suggested that simultaneous physiological measures and a larger, more precise descriptive body of kinesics coordinated with the measurement of visual behavior might be applied to early interactions to test the discrepancy and habituation hypotheses.

C.   Gaze Aversion as "Cutoff" Behavior

The discrepancy hypothesis explanation for gaze behavior has been rejected by some as untenable and circular (Srouf, Waters, & Matas, 1974). Sroufe and his colleagues point out that in a number of their studies the same stimulus occasioned a number of different responses depending on the context. The context investigated by Sroufe and his colleagues included the home-laboratory setting, mother–stranger interaction partner and familiarization time with the stranger. The paradigm was a stranger approach to the infant and a mother's masked-face approach. Wariness or gaze aversion was coded and heart rate monitored. Although behavior ratings did not differ as a function of these contexts there was significantly greater heart rate acceleration during the stranger approach and in the laboratory situation. In addition, more wariness was shown toward the stranger following a brief familiarization period (30 sec) than a longer period (3 min). Sroufe et al. (1974) suggest that these studies show that "... the same 'stimulus' event can occasion the entire range of affective response, depending on context. It is difficult to imagine that mother-with-mask becomes more or less discrepant from an internal model depending on the setting ... or that an approaching stranger becomes less discrepant as laboratory familiarization time increases. Explanations based on amount of discrepancy, although always possible, become increasingly post hoc and cumbersome as such findings continue to emerge." (p. 60).

Sroufe and his colleagues (e.g., Sroufe & Waters, 1977), advance instead the notion that gaze aversion serves a "coping function" to enable "assimilation of novel events" (p. 8). In a stranger-approach study, Waters et al. (1975) reported a temporal relationship between heart rate acceleration, gaze aversion and subsequent heart rate recovery with heart rate acceleration occurring prior to gaze aversion. The case was then made that "... this aversive reaction served a coping function for the infant. By temporarily blocking off contact with the approaching stranger, in a manner analogous to the 'cutoff' behaviors of birds and other animals in conflict (Chance, 1962), the infant modulates arousal and prevents a disorganizing all-or-none response (here, crying). The modulating effect on arousal enables the infant to re-engage the stranger, preserving the strong tendency to approach and assimilate novel experiences" (p. 8). This interpretation is supported by the observation that those infants who averted gaze tended to engage the stranger more readily on subsequent stranger approach episodes whereas those who cried showed heart rate acceleration and crying earlier in the second episode of stranger approach.

It is reasonable to expect that Stern might view an infant's gaze alternation as variable responsivity to discrepancy changes in a mother's stimulation, whereas Sroufe and colleagues might view gaze aversion, in their more stressful stranger situations, as "cutoff" behavior or a coping function. The interaction situation recorded by Stern and the stranger approach by Sroufe are very different contexts in which the infant's gaze behavior is occurring (nonstressful and stressful situations respectively) which would reasonably lead to these different interpretations.

D. Gaze Aversion for Information Processing and Arousal Modulation

Still another interpretation related to each of the previously discussed hypotheses is that the infant looks away from his or her interaction partner to process information and modulate arousal associated with the interaction stimulation. This hypothesis derives from our early interaction studies in which heart rate was monitored. Directional heart rate changes were similar to those reported by Waters et al. (1975): There is a pre-gaze aversion heart rate acceleration, perhaps reflecting heightened arousal or an aversive response to "too much stimulation" provided by the mother or other interaction partner. Following gaze aversion, there is heart rate deceleration (Field, 1981). The possibility arises that just as orienting to an external stimulus may be represented by cardiac deceleration, the cardiac decelerations following gaze aversion may reflect "processing" of the preceding stimulation. The infant may turn away from stimulation as the information approaches an "overload," because he requires the gaze aversion to modulate arousal and process the stimulation without distraction or further input.

Borrowing from an adult model presented by Kendon (1967) the adult speaker more frequently looks away from the listener than the listener from the speaker, because he has more information to process—namely the planning for what he will say as well as the feedback from his listener, which can interfere or distract him from planning his next words; thus, we are positing a model similar to that of Sroufe and Waters (1977), namely that the infant gaze averts to modulate arousal (to prevent a disorganizing all-or-none response) and to process the information associated with the previously received stimulation (to assimilate the novel events).

The measure of stimulation we have used in early interactions is the percentage of interaction time that the mother provides discrete stimulation (verbal and tactile stimulation) and, for response measures, the infant's heart rate and gazing at or away from mother. In one series of studies we monitored infant behavior and heart rate during spontaneous face-to-face interactions with various interaction partners, including father, mother, preschool-age sibling, and infant peer, and situations in which the infant was faced toward a mirror or an infant-size raggedy ann doll. In a second series we attempted to manipulate the amount of stimulation provided the infant by giving interaction instructions to the interaction partner (the mother) and by animating the doll. In all these we monitored the infant's visual attentiveness and associated arousal levels (manifested by heart rate) to better understand the relationships between infant gaze behavior and arousal levels. The basic model assessed was a curvilinear relationship between amount of stimulation and infant attentiveness/arousal, with the attention behavior conforming to an inverted U function and the heart rate behavior to a U function (Field, 1980a).

In all these studies the infant is positioned in an infant seat, face-to-face with the interaction partner or object. One video camera is focused on the infant, the other on the partner. Their two pictures are fed through a digital timer and a split screen generator into a single videotape recorder. The resulting split screen image provides a frontal view of the partner and infant, each on one side of the image, along with a digital time display along the base of the image. Heart rate of the infant is recorded via telemetry, and the audiotape of the heart rate record is synchronized with the video by placing a signal spike on the audiotape at second 0 of the videotape. For all of these studies normal and high-risk (preterm and/or post-term) infants were observed. The infants were about 3–4 months of age, with the preterm and post-term infants being 3–4 months corrected age.

In the first series of studies (Field, 1981b), the infant was videotaped in a spontaneous face-to-face interaction with various interaction partners including mother, father, preschool age sibling, and infant peer (either a stranger peer or twin peer in the case of twins). Also in this series, infants were seated facing a mirror or an infant size raggedy ann doll. Although the planned duration of each interaction situation was 3 min, these were occasionally shorter due to infant state changes. Thus, the measures of interaction partner activity (vocalization and touching) and infant gaze aversion were converted to proportion of interaction time these behaviors occurred.

The data for partner activity and infant gaze aversion as a function of the different partners are illustrated in Fig. 2. As can be seen, father activity was greater than mother activity which, in turn, was greater than sibling and peer activity. Infant gaze aversion was approximately equivalent in father, sibling, and peer interaction situations which, in turn, was greater than in the mother interaction situation. Preterm infants manifested more gaze aversion than term infants in all situations, although the interaction partner's activity did not differ for preterm and term infants except in the mother situation in which mothers of preterm infants were more active. Comparisons across these situations suggest that in the high activity (father) and low activity (preschool

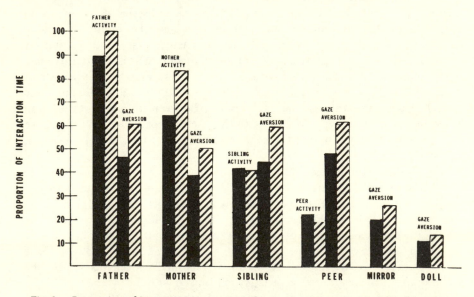

Fig. 2.   *Proportion of interaction time term and preterm infants spend looking at various social stimuli. (■ term infants, ▨ preterm infants).*

sibling and peer) situations there is more infant gaze aversion than in a moderate activity situation (interaction with the mother). These comparisons suggest a curvilinear relationship between activity level of interaction partner and gaze aversion of the infant, with high or low levels of activity being associated with high levels of gaze aversion.

The very low levels of infant gaze aversion during the raggedy ann doll situation reflect a different kind of gaze behavior of the infant (more prolonged gaze) occurring in situations where there is virtual inactivity of a social object. These differences between gaze behavior during interaction with animate and inanimate social objects have also been reported by Brazelton et al. (1974). The slightly higher levels of gaze aversion activity during the mirror than during the doll situation may relate to the infant himself providing, via his mirror image, more animate stimulation. It is interesting that in these less stimulating or less animate situations there are no differences in the amount of gaze aversion of term and preterm infants. During the more animated situations preterm infants may require more looking away time due to less developed information processing or arousal modulation abilities.

In another study (Field, 1979c) we attempted to manipulate the amount of stimulation provided the infant by giving instructions to the mother prior to the interaction and by automating the raggedy ann doll. In this study the amount of stimulation provided the infant was varied in increasing order of stimulation from (1) a suspended, infant-sized raggedy ann doll, to (2) a head-nodding, talking raggedy ann doll, to (3) an imitative mother (less stimulating than normal as her behaviors were restricted to simple imitations of her infant's behaviors), to (4) a "normal" acting, spontaneous mother. Heart rate was measured due to its posited association with attentional behaviors, i.e., attentiveness or an orienting response is reportedly accompanied by heart rate deceleration while a defensive reaction or aversive response is paralleled by heart rate acceleration (Graham & Clifton, 1966; Sokolov, 1953). Because of the rapidity with which behaviors and their associated heart rate responses occur during early interactions and because heart rate requires time to return to baseline, the frequent sampling of heart rate might be confounded by directional heart rate changes which are merely a return to baseline. Therefore, we analyzed tonic heart rate (heart rate change from averaged baseline heart rate to heart rate averaged over 3-minute segments) rather than phasic or directional heart rate change. The interactions of both term and preterm infants were recorded.

The results of this study showed a progressive increase in gazing time to the lesser animated "social faces" (see Fig. 3) and a parallel decrease in tonic heart rate by both groups of infants. With increasing amounts of stimulation there appeared to be less visual attentiveness to the faces and an accompanying elevation in tonic heart rate. In addition, there was less visual attentiveness and more elevated heart rate in the preterm infants (except during the

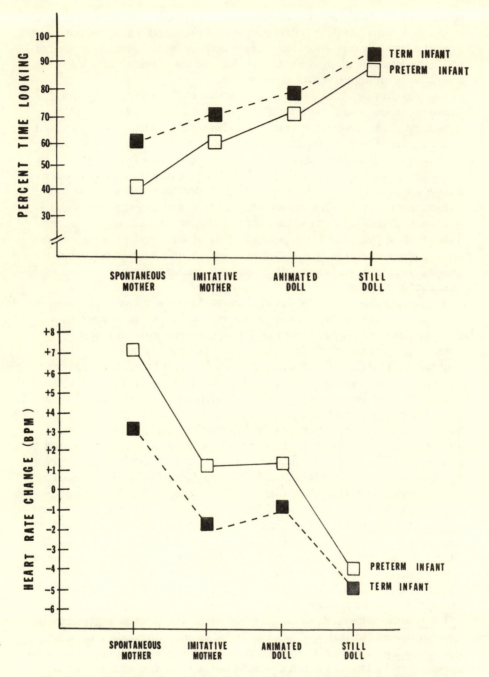

Fig. 3. Percent looking time and mean heart rate change from baseline activity to the various animated and inanimate situations.

inanimate doll situation), suggesting that the preterm infants were perhaps more highly "aroused" and less able to sustain visual attentiveness to the more animated faces than the term infants at equivalent postconceptional or maturational ages. All infants may have required more looking away time during the animated face situations to process the greater amount of information contained in those and to regulate the greater arousal potentiated by the more animated stimuli. Preterm infants may have spent more looking away time than term infants because of less developed arousal modulation abilities and/or information processing skills.

In another study in this series (Field, 1977, 1979b) mothers were given instructions prior to face-to-face interactions which effectively (1) increased the amunt of stimulation provided for the infant by asking the mother to keep her infant's attention or (2) decreased the amount of stimulation by asking the mother to imitate her infant's behaviors. These two interaction situations were then compared with a spontaneous "normally behaving" mother interaction situation. All three situations were counterbalanced to control for potential shifts in infant arousal levels. The amount of stimulation the mother provided was measured, as was the infant's gaze behavior and heart rate during these situations. Infant visual behavior and tonic heart rate (change from resting heart rate to heart rate averaged over the interaction situation) were analyzed. In this study, term infants, preterm, and post-term infants were compared.

Briefly, the results suggested that as the amount of stimulation lessened from the attention-getting to the normal to the imitative situation, infant gaze-at-mother increased, and tonic heart rate levels diminished for all three groups of infants. Attentiveness and arousal levels, therefore, appeared to be optimal during the less stimulating, imitative situation. Infant gaze as a function of amounts of maternal activity is depicted in Fig. 4 and the tonic heart rate in Fig. 5. An interesting observation relating to changes in arousal level was that infants who experienced the attention-getting (or highly stimulating) situation first showed elevated heart rate levels and more gaze aversion in the subsequent imitation (or less stimulating) situation. Those who experienced the more optimal stimulation situation (imitation) first sustained more gazing at mother with associated lower levels of heart rate during the more stimulating attention-getting situation. But, their mothers, apparently having noted the affects of imitation, were using imitation as an attention getting device.

There was more gaze aversion in the post-term infant group and even more gaze aversion in the preterm infant group with correspondingly more elevated tonic heart rate levels in the post-term infant group and the highest levels of heart rate in the preterm infant group. Both of thse groups may have been more aroused and less attentive, and perhaps less able to process the stimulation or modulate arousal associated with the stimulation provided, thus requiring more looking away periods than the groups of term infants.

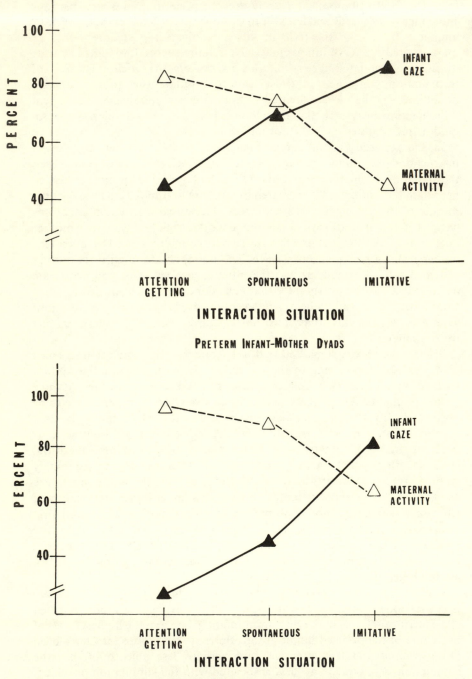

Fig. 4. *Percent of interaction time featuring infant gaze and maternal activity during attention-getting, spontaneous, and imitative interaction situations.*

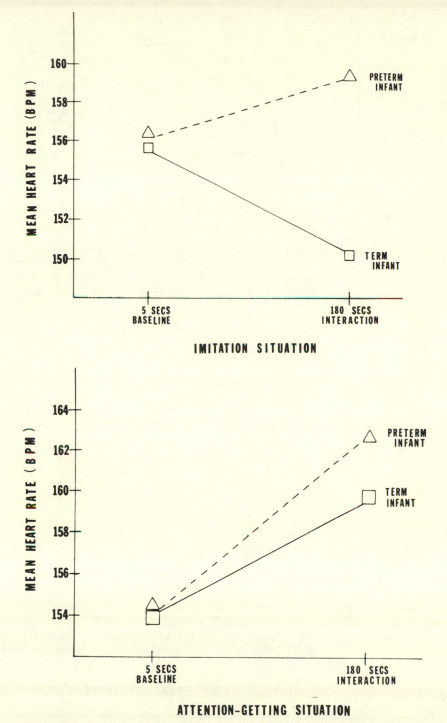

Fig. 5.   Mean heart rate during baseline and interaction situations (imitation and attention-getting).

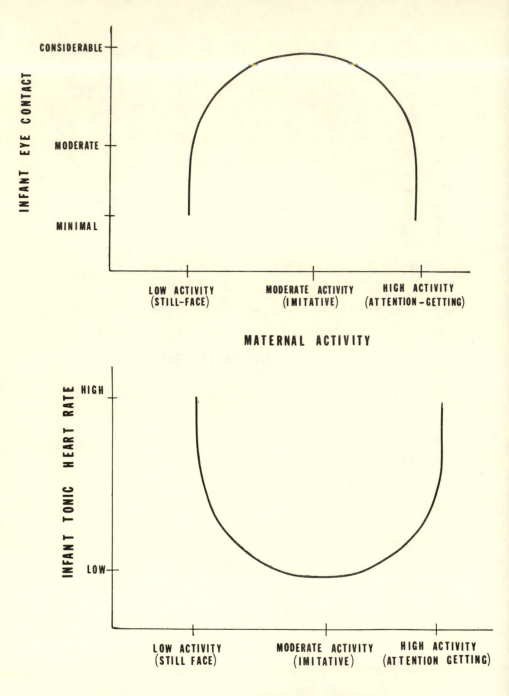

Fig. 6. *Hypothetical relationship between maternal activity and infant eye contact and maternal activity and infant heart rate during still-face, imitative; and attention-getting interaction situations.*

In a subsequent study (Field, 1981a) attention-getting, imitative, and still-faced mother situations were compared. The latter is a situation in which the mother is asked to remain still faced and silent (Tronick et al., 1978). These situations, as in the first study, were counterbalanced to control for any shifts in infant arousal level. In this study the postulated curvilinear relationships emerged with gaze behavior following an inverted U-shaped function and heartrate a U-shaped function as shown in Fig. 6; that is, moderate amounts of maternal stimulation (imitation) were associated with optimal infant gaze behavior and lower tonic heart rate levels.

Since a number of researchers of infant attention and heart rate have suggested that infant heart rate may be artifactually elevated by movement (Campos, Emde, Gaensbauer, & Henderson, 1975; Obrist, Webb, Sutterer, & Howard, 1970; Waters, Matas, & Sroufe, 1975), i.e., that the physical movement of gaze aversion might artifactually elevate heart rate, an analysis of phasic or stimulus-locked heart rate was performed. Gaze aversion episodes were selected from the videotapes, which were time-locked to heart rate records, with a minimal interval of 30 sec interspersing selected gaze averting behaviors. What emerged from this analysis was that heart rate acceleration preceded the physical gaze aversion behavior (see Fig. 7)

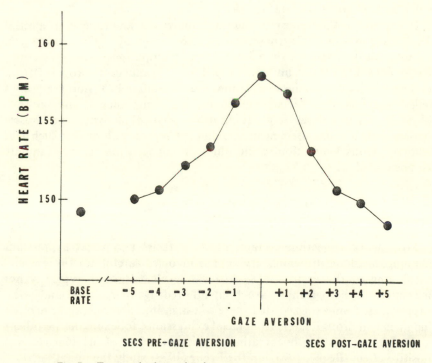

Fig. 7.   *Temporal relationship between gaze aversion and heart rate.*

suggesting that the infants' arousal level may have contributed to heart rate acceleration preceding gaze aversions rather than that gaze aversion movement artifactually elevated heart rate (Field, 1981a). Similar pregaze aversion heart rate accelerations have also been reported by Sroufe and his colleagues (Waters et al., 1975).

One of the problems with interpreting a high-arousal–gaze aversion relationship from pregaze aversion heart rate in these studies is that other behaviors were not analyzed. For example, a possible pregaze aversion grimace may have contributed to heart rate acceleration, again following the suggestion that heart rate may be an artifact of movement (Campos et al., 1975; Obrist et al., 1970; Waters et al., 1975). Changes in muscle tension have been reported to dramatically affect heart rate (Obrist et al., 1970). However, as Sroufe and Waters (1977) have noted, "this relationship between respiration, muscle tension and heart rate need not reduce the value of heart rate as a dependent variable as long as its relationship to independent variables is lawful. If heart rate reliably decelerates during attention and accelerates during stress, whether such changes are mediated by muscle tension is irrelevant to psychological interpretations in most cases. That is, the question of whether heart rate is instrumental in the deployment of attention or in response to intense stimulation is generally secondary to its value as a reliable correlate" (p. 19).

In any case, with on-line computer technology and new time series spectral analyses programs (Gottman, 1979), Porges et al. 1979) which can simultaneously assess the shared variance of multiple measures, interactions could be analyzed for multiple measures of stimulation provided (e.g., maternal vocal and tactile stimulation) multiple infant behavioral responses (e.g., gaze behavior, facial expressions, body movements) and multiple physiological responses (e.g., respiration, physical activity, and muscle tension) which might affect heart rate. In the temporary absence of such data analyses, arousal–attention relationships during early interactions can only be postulated.

III. AFFECT AND AROUSAL

Most work concerning infant affect or facial and vocal expressions (smiling, laughing, frowning, crying) has involved careful descriptions and cataloging of the expressions. Arousal levels, although typically not measured physiologically, have been inferred again by facial and vocal expressions. Some suggest that there is a high interobserver agreement on judgments of arousal levels from facial expressions, for example, a mother's and other adult's independent rating of their perceptions of an infant's level of positive affect (Beebe, 1973). In the Beebe (1973) study the infant's actions were coded in fine detail and the changes in the infant's repertoire occurring at the time the mother judged changes in positive affect were determined. Agreement was reportedly high (95 percent) that the infant's mouth opening, head raising, and gazing-at-the-adult behaviors were associated with the adults' judgment of an increase in positive arousal, but arousal was inferred.

A.   Arousal Levels Inferred From
Facial and Vocal Expressions

Several researchers have recorded second-by-second changes in affective behavior and inferred arousal changes by the behavior (Als, Tronick, & Brazelton, 1979; Brazelton et al., 1974; Tronick, Als, & Brazelton, 1979) or by the accompanying heart rate (Lewis, Brooks, & Haviland, 1978; Vaughn & Sroufe, 1979). For example, Brazelton et al. (1974), in the mother–infant face-to-face interaction study already described, mapped infant affective behaviors during the infants' looking and looking away periods, inferring arousal changes from the affective and attentive behaviors. Affective behaviors of the mother were superimposed on the infants' looking/looking away periods to provide a picture of the synchrony between infant and maternal behaviors during their early interactions. Although these graphed cycles of attention and affect appeared to suggest synchronous and asynchronous cycles, analytic techniques were not used to assess the coupling of these.

Als et al. (1979) also conducted microanalyses of the affective and attentive behaviors occurring during mother–infant face-to-face interactions. These behaviors were then clustered into "monadic phases" of disengagement, orienting, and engagement, and then "messages" (continue, modify, or stop) as well as affective levels (positive, neutral, and negative) were inferred from these phases. These phases were plotted as square waves denoting positive and negative affect shifts. Although this is a parsimonious way of reducing and summarizing continuous behavioral data, and although the positive/negative affective quality of the interactions can be meaningfully represented in this form, the precise and subtle shifts in behavior are lost. In addition, once again, without independent validating measures of arousal such as EKG, EMG, or respiration, only inferential statements about "heightened" or "dampened" arousal levels can be made.

In a similar treatment of interaction data, Tronick et al. (1979) assigned scaled scores to the positive and negative affect behaviors of both infant and mother and then calculated the synchrony (coupling or interlocking) of these affective cycles by performing running correlations of the scaled scores of infant and mother affect. Although this too may be a parsimonious way to summarize the data, the specific affective displays and gaze behaviors as well as their relationships are again lost using this scaling technique. As Gottman

(1979) has suggested, time series spectral and cross-spectral analyses might be more appropriate techniques to determine the cyclicity and coupling of affective behaviors during early interactions. Since continuous, real time data on multiple variables can now be coded, for example, by using electronic recording devices such as the datamyte and analyzed via time series, spectral analyses techniques, the precise affective displays, attentive behaviors, and their temporal features can be preserved and analyzed for relationships.

A.   Arousal Levels Inferred From Emotional Expressions and Heart Rate

More precise shifts in infant arousal and affect have been monitored to more precise changes in stimulation by Lewis et al. (1978) and by Sroufe and his colleagues (Vaughn & Sroufe, 1979; Waters et al., 1975). However, all of these studies were conducted in less "naturalistic," more stressful situations—namely a stranger's approach to the infant.

In a chapter appropriately entitled "Hearts and Faces," Lewis et al. (1978) videotaped facial expressions and monitored heart rate of the infant as a stranger approached and departed. The most consistent finding was that heart rate deceleration accompanied an attentive face. However, there was no relationship between "wary" faces and heart rate acceleration. Although the photographed faces published in their chapter appear to be more attentive than wary looking, Lewis et al. labelled these faces "wary" and suggested that the failure to find a concomitant heart rate acceleration may be due to their being no consistent relationship between facial expression and heart rate. Alternatively, they suggested that "the lack of response specificity that Lacey et al. (1963) reported for the ANS may also apply to the ANS and other systems such as facial expression." Finally, Lewis et al. suggested "there is always the possibility that a more careful measurement procedure would reveal a relationship."

Although Lewis et al. (1978) convincingly attempt to "throw out infant heart rate with the baby's bath water," they posited the following model of synchrony to explain their results. "In any response-producing situation, there is a competitive system: response synchrony or covariation for more efficient behavior and response asynchrony for the termination of ongoing behavior. In situations where the need to act predominates—in cases of extreme stress or where efficient processing is necessary—more responses may covary...For everyday situations with lower or little arousal, response sets are more likely not to covary...Very frightened infants, left alone without their mothers and being approached by a stranger in a strange manner, are in a high state of arousal; facial expression, motoric activity and heart rate are more likely to show a high correspondence. When the infant's mother is physically close, an approaching stranger is less arousing and therefore causes less covariation" (p. 117).

Infants approached by a stranger in the Waters et al. (1975) study did show cardiac accelerations according to "wary" expressions. These discrepant findings may relate to the aversiveness of the situation, since in the Lewis et al. (1978) study the stranger approach was a very brief period and the mother was present, whereas in the Waters et al. (1975) study the infant was left alone with the stranger. Although Waters et al. (1975) provide limited information on the time locking of the heart rate and facial expression data and the beat-to-beat heart rate changes, there appeared to be a temporal relationship between heart rate and gaze aversion, with gaze aversion typically occurring just prior to the peak of a strong heart rate acceleration quickly followed by heart rate recovery and renewed looking at the approaching stranger.

A more precise relationship between heart rate and affective behavior is presented by Vaughn & Sroufe (1979). In their study the temporal relationship between heart rate acceleration and crying was examined during a peek-a-boo game in which the mother's appearance from behind a screen was alternated with a stranger's appearance, both the mother and stranger wearing masks. Pre-crying heart rate in beats-per-minute suggested that the heart rate acceleration began well before the onset of crying, suggesting that the acceleration is not merely a by-product or measurement artifact of crying. The accelerations were above and beyond a return to baseline following orienting.

C. Sroufe's "Tension Release" Model of Affect

In addition to mapping temporal relationships between heart rate and negative affective responses such as gaze aversion and crying, Sroufe and his colleagues have investigated the relationships between heart rate and positive affective responses such as smiling and laughter. Using the masked approach of mother and stranger (Sroufe, Waters, & Matas, 1974), Sroufe et al. describe the following sequence of behaviors: When the infant is presented with a masked adult, there is orienting, behavior fixation and pronounced heart rate deceleration. When the mother is approaching there is positive affect with continuing deceleration up to the point of smiling and laughter. Following the latter there is dramatic acceleration reportedly due to muscular activity. When the stranger approaches there is negative affect and acceleration (following the deceleration of orienting) which becomes even more pronounced with crying.

A schematic of the heart rate data during this procedure appears in Fig. 8, adapted from Sroufe & Waters (1976). Their interpretation of this sequence is as follows: "The initial phase appears to be an affectively neutral period of appraisal. During this period of orienting and behavior fixation the processing of stimulus content calls for a degree of effort on the part of the infant ('tension' develops). The period of appraisal can be followed either by crying or the motor response of turning away (both with the autonomic

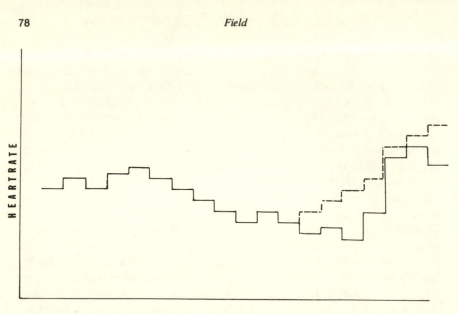

Fig. 8.   A schematic of the heart rate data during positive (—) and negative (---) affective displays. (Adapted from Sroufe & Waters, 1976.)

discharge implied in tachycardia) or by smiling. Thus, smiling is part of a mechanism for tension release following behavior fixation which, unlike crying, enables continued engagement of the novel situation, ultimately promoting assimilation" (p. 9).

Thus, in Sroufe's model, gaze aversion, smiling, and laughter are seen as a "tension release" following appraisal and assimilation of stimulation. These affective behaviors serve as "coping functions" for the infant to "modulate arousal and prevent a disorganizing all-or-none response such as crying." In a laughter study in which a range of sensory games (loud sounds, loss of balance, peek-a-boo, looming approach, and masked approach) were played with the infant, smiling and laughter alternated (Sroufe & Wunsch, 1972). About this study Sroufe and Waters (1976) noted that laughter built reliably from smiling on early trials and faded again to smiling on later trials. "Effortful assimilation" was implicated in "recognitory smiles," faster effortful assimilation, and therefore a "steeper tension fluctuation" or an "arousal jag," was implicated in laughter. Although Sroufe attributes a significant amount of these affective displays to "tension release" following the infant's "assimilation" (a relatively unmeasurable variable), he does acknowledge that context, salience, and background activity or stimulation strongly determine whether positive affect (smiling or laughter) or negative affect (wariness or crying) occurs.

Sroufe's (1979) model is schematically illustrated in a number of papers as an excitation-relaxation cycle, showing a hypothetical threshold and

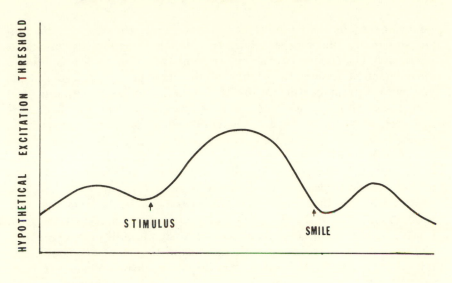

Fig. 9. *A schematic of Sroufe's tension-release hypothesis. (Adapted from Sroufe & Waters, 1976.)*

relationship to overt behaviors (see Fig. 9). Some suggested problems with his model as depicted in the schematic are that: (1) the underlying process of successful assimilation or failure to assimilate is not operationally defined nor would it be easily operationalized. Data illustrations of "assimilation" are not provided by Sroufe; (2) the hypothetical threshold is a very narrow, straight line band which might more appropriately be illustrated as a shifting hypothetical threshold as a function of organismic and context variables; and (3) positive affect (for example, smiles) appears to occur at the lowest ebb of the relaxation component of the cycle, suggesting that smiling follows tension release rather than provides the tension release as described in the presentation of his affect data. Although Sroufe's model provides an organizing framework for much of the stranger-approach data, and his measurement of affect and its temporal relationship to heart rate provide an experimental model for early interaction research, studies involving interactions suggest more complex models and more complex measurement/analyses problems.

   The utility of Sroufe's model is currently being assessed by Fogel and his colleagues (Fogel, Diamond, Langhorst, & Demos, 1980) during early interactions, using the Tronick et al. (1978) still-face paradigm. Fogel et al. (1980) record a spontaneous face-to-face interaction between infant and mother; the mother then leaves and in that interim the infant's behavior alone is recorded. The mother returns and, following the infant's first look or following the infant's first smile, the mother ceases all behavior, as in the still-face situation. Following the still-face situation there is another spontaneous interaction. Each infant was randomly assigned to one of two groups prior to the interaction session. In the first group the experimenter signaled the mother to perform the still face after the infant first looked at the mother and in the second group after the infant's first smile. The first look was hypothesized to represent increasing tension while the decreasing part of the tension function was presumed to be expressed by smiling. In this way, Fogel et al. (1980) are assessing Sroufe's tension-release model, hypothesizing that if the mother's incongruous still face is presented following a smile (the posited "tension release"), the infant will show fewer gaze averting and distress behaviors than if her still face follows a gaze by the infant (which in Sroufe's model is on the ascending limb of an excitation/relaxation cycle). Fogel et al confirm this hypothesis. There was significantly more gaze avoid, distressed brow, and crying behavior during the spontaneous situation subsequent to the still face situation in the group where mothers performed the still face after the infants' first look. Thus, if infants experienced this interaction perturbation (still face) when first looking at the mother (as tension is presumably increasing) as opposed to first smiling at the mother (post-tension release) they show more distress behaviors in the subsequent spontaneous interaction. Using the same paradigm we have provided conformatory heart rate data on these relationships (Adler-Stoller & Field, 1980).

The recording of multiple affective and physiological responses during these situations might more precisely tap the affective and physiological relationships on this posited excitation/relaxation cycle. The complexity of relating multivariate behavioral and psychophysiological data derived from early interactions to models such as the excitation/relaxation cycle is further compounded by having to integrate data on organismic variables such as rest/activity cycles as well as individual differences.

IV.   INFANT STATE, AGE, AND INDIVIDUAL DIFFERENCES

Variability in attention, affective behaviors, and arousal during early interactions is considerable. Although rarely considered by early interaction researchers, individual differences and organismic variables such as infant state and developmental change may contribute to the variability reported. For example, the study of Fogel et al. (1980) just described yielded marked individual differences in gaze avoid behavior. Two subjects showed markedly divergent behaviors from their groups (the first look and first smile groups). For the first look group the trend for the group was an increase in gaze avoid during the still-face and subsequent spontaneous interaction, starting from initially low gaze avoidance during the spontaneous interaction prior to the still-face situation. The divergent subject showed the opposite pattern: She gaze avoided during the spontaneous interaction and looked more frequently at the mother during the still-face and subsequent spontaneous interaction.

The amount of gaze avoid behavior for the first smile group remained fairly constant over the three conditions (spontaneous, still face, resumption of spontaneous interactions), but the divergent subject showed a markedly different pattern. Like the divergent subject of the first look group, this infant spent the majority of his time in gaze avoid during both the initial and resumed spontaneous interactions, but showed zero gaze avoidance during the still-face.

Of these individual differences, Fogel et al. (1980) suggest: "These infants seem consistent with the model proposed by Field (1979c) of an infant who has immature sensory processing capacities and is therefore overstimulated by his mother's attempts to get him to attend to her. Such infants cope with these stresses by continuing to look away from the mother. As soon as one can get the mother to reduce her rate of activity, which is what happens in the still-face condition, the infant will turn to look at her and will apparently take advantage of this opportunity to watch his mother without interference. We reviewed the videotapes for these two subjects and found that they were both somewhat fussy during the normal interaction. Their mothers were extremely active while the infants were fussy and avoidant, but they did not seem overly intrusive compared to the other mothers in the sample. It is hard to determine, lacking background information, whether the avoidance was a result of the mother's behavior, the immaturity of the infant's sensory processing capacities, or whether the increased gazing during the still-face period was simply a matter of chance" (p. 20).

As Fogel et al. suggest, these divergent subjects may represent individual differences in sensory processing capacities due to immaturity, inasmuch as they were two of the youngest subjects (8 months as opposed to a mean of 10 months). Alternatively, their divergent behavior may have reflected differences in state as manifested by their unusual fussiness. Although individual differences, state, and age variables are important factors, they are rarely considered in the investigation of attention, affect, and arousal during early interactions. Presumably these factors would affect attention and aversion thresholds and relative width of the postulated activation band during interactions.

A. Infant State

Among the state cycles thought to affect the infant's arousal level and thereby his or her attention and affective responsivity to stimulation during early interactions are rest/activity cycles and feeding cycles. Despite the paucity of parametric studies systematically recording responses to stimulation during various states, the state variable has been implicated in the high subject loss in infant research and in the discrepant findings on infant attention processes (Clifton & Nelson, 1976). Although infant researchers now attempt to study their subjects in an optimal state, continuous monitoring of state occurs only rarely. Most of the infant studies in which state has been continuously monitored were conducted during sleep. For example, Wolff (1966), using auditory and tactile stimuli, noted that the infants' receptivity and responsivity to stimulation varied considerably as a function of whether the infant was in irregular or regular sleep. A mild auditory stimulus elicited a smile during irregular sleep but a startle during regular sleep; a drowsy infant responded with either a smile or a startle when a moving object was suddenly introduced into his visual field. Rose et al. (Rose, Schmidt, & Bridger, 1978), on the other hand, found no differences in infants' responses to tactile stimulation across these sleep states, but rather noted that time elapsed from sleep onset had a decidedly strong influence on infant responsivity to tactile stimulation. Time elapsed from onset of wakefulness might similarly affect the responsiveness of infants during their wakeful interactions.

One of the few examples of continuous state monitoring during wakefulness is the Brazelton neonatal behavioral assessment scale (Brazelton, 1973). However, these state recordings are only used for an evaluation of the infant's predominant state and his or her state lability. The infant's attentive and affective responsivity to the stimulation are not assessed as a function of the state of the infant during the delivery of stimulation. Yet thresholds and responsivity to auditory and visual stimuli probably vary as a function of the infant being in drowsiness, quiet alert, or active alert. Similarly, thresholds and responses to aversive reflex maneuvers likely vary as a function of the infant being in an active alert or crying state—all acceptable states for the administration of these Brazelton items.

An example of the variability of attentive and affective behaviors across a narrow range of wakefulness, for example in a quiet alert or an active alert state, is provided by a study on the spontaneous toy play of an infant at intervals across a four month period of infancy (4 to 8 months of age) (Fischer, 1973). During quiet alert states the infant manifested a greater number and more prolonged periods of visual attentiveness to toys than she did during quiet active states. During the latter state the infant emitted many more positive as well as negative affective responses, for example, smiling, laughing, fussing, and crying. Over each of forty-eight 1-hour videotaped spontaneous play periods there were alternating periods of rest (attentive)/activity (affective) cycles which approximated a 1 to 2 ratio of the infant's spontaneous play time, suggesting a vacillation of state and attentive/affective activity.

The Fogel et al. (1980) study just described suggests that attentive and affective responses also vary as a function of the infant having received stimulation (the violation of expectancy, still face) immediately following an attentive or an affective response during which the infant's state or "level of tension" differed. Sroufe and Wunsch (1972) similarly note that a social stimulus such as a looming game (where a mother's head looms into her infant's stomach saying "Ah Boom") on one trial will elicit laughter whereas on a subsequent trial will elicit crying, suggesting variability in infant state or "level of tension" during these two same-stimulus episodes.

Infants are also noted to differentially respond to stimulation as a function of where they are on the feeding cycle. Pomerleau-Malcuit & Clifton (1973), for example, provided vestibular stimulation (rocking) to neonates during a pre- and post-prandial state and noted more positive responses to vestibular stimulation post-feeding. More prolonged periods of attentiveness to toys were also noted during a post than a pre-prandial period in the Fischer (1973) study.

Thus, although thresholds and responsiveness to stimulation appear to vary as a function of rest/activity and feeding cycles, and although investigators attempt to assess infants during optimal phases on those cycles, the infant's state is rarely monitored throughout an interaction. One of the problems of continuous monitoring relates to the ambiguity of wakeful state definitions. Whereas sleep states have been carefully defined by a number of investigators (Parmelee & Stern, 1972; Sterman & Hoppenbrouwers, 1971; Thoman, 1975), similar definitions have not been published on wakeful states. Many of the attentive and affective behaviors recorded during early interactions are the very descriptors used to define wakeful states—for example, brightening, widening, and focusing of the eyes. In addition, because interaction stimulation and responses occur with such rapidity, the effect of state on attentive and affective behavior is confounded by the intensity and frequency of the stimulation. At the very least, however, a baseline recording of infant state prior to an interaction might be used as a covariate in our analyses of attentive and affective behaviors during early interactions.

B. Age of Infant

Attentive and affective behaviors during early interactions are noted to vary by age of infant, with more prolonged periods of attentiveness and more rigorous affective responses occurring in older infants, except during occasional stages when the infant appears to become less interested in face-to-face interactions and more interested in manipulating objects (Trevarthen, 1974).

Among the many variables which may contribute to age changes in attention and affect during interactions are changes in wakeful activity, state regulation, arousal modulation, sensory thresholds, and information processing skills. Infants' wakeful activities were monitored, for example, by

Dittrichova & Lapackova (1964) across the first 6 months of life. The mean percentage of wakefulness time quadrupled (10 to 47 percent) as did the mean percentage of wakeful activity, for example, babbling (0 to 44 percent), whereas crying diminished from 12 to 2 percent.

Sensory thresholds reputedly decrease with development in all sensory modalities as measured by behavioral or autonomic responses. In the tacile modality, for example, Lipsitt and Levy (1960) noted an increasing sensitivity to electrotactile stimulation over the first 4 days of life. Lipsitt and his colleagues (Lipsitt, Engen, & Kaye, 1963) also noted dramatic developmental changes in the olfactory threshold over the first 4 days of life. Infants were administered a chemical in an ascending order of percent concentration of the solution. The infants' threshold decreased from a 60 percent to a 15 percent solution over the first 4 days.

Also during the first 4 days, Bartoshuk (1962) demonstrated that heart rate acceleration to sound increased reliably with age. Berg (1975) showed greater heart rate decelerations to 2-sec bursts of 70 dB white noise in 10-month-old than 4-month-old infants and greater acceleration to 2 sec bursts of 90 dB white noise again in the 10-month-old infants. Thus, there is some evidence of developmental changes in sensory thresholds when unidimensional stimuli are presented. Presumably these developmental shifts would also appear for the thresholds to multidimensional stimuli occurring, for example, during early interactions.

Age changes in affective displays and their relationship to shifting thresholds have been suggested by some investigators (Emde et al., 1978; Sroufe & Waters, 1976). Wolff (1963), in tracing the ontogeny of the smile, notes that the very earliest waking smiles are elicited by low-level tactile and kinesthetic stimulation (e.g., light touches on sensitivie areas, blowing on the skin, gentle jogging). These are low-intensity responses to mild stimulation and typically occur following feeding. By the second week, auditory stimulation, especially a high-pitched voice, is the most effective elicitor of the smile. By the third week of life, the first alert smile occurs, invoking more focused attention, a brightening of the eyes, and the mouth pulled into a grin. At this time a nodding head accompanying vocal stimulation is more effective than the voice alone. During the fourth week pat-a-cake (three vigorous bounces of the hands) which had not elicited any smiling at 3 weeks becomes the most effective stimulus and remains the most effective stimulus across the first 3 months, producing smiling even in fussy infants.

Sroufe and Waters (1976) describe the same progression of smiling from a low level response to an active response elicited by low to moderate level to moderately intense stimulation over the first four weeks. A similar ontogeny of laughter has been traced by Sroufe and Wunsch (1972) in response to various games played by mothers, including peek-a-boo, the looming game, masked approach, lipsmacking, etc. During the fourth to sixth months vigorous multimodal tactile and auditory stimulations elicit laughter. The laughter response to this vigorous stimulation (which previously caused crying) is immediate. After 6 months tactile and auditory stimulations become less effective elicitors than social and visual stimulation. In these situations the mother introduces an age-appropriate game. The infant visually attends to her, smiles, vocalizes, and occasionally laughs, appearing to hover within a very narrow range just around an upper threshold. The games are repeatedly played and varied by the mother, [e.g., varying in discrepancy and intensity of facial and vocal displays as if "facilitating the progressive extension of the infants' optimal range of pleasurable arousal and affect" (Stern, 1974, p. 207)].

It is interesting that the games mothers spontaneously play with their young infants during early interactions are the same games which Sroufe and Wunsch (1972) noted to be effective elicitors of smiling and laughter (Field, 1979a; Gustafson, Green, & West, 1979). For example, mothers of 4-month-olds in the Field (1979a) study played I'm-gonna-get-you and pat-a-cake (more rigorous tactile, kinesthetic games) more frequently than peek-a-boo (a visual, social game) during their spontaneous interactions, probably because their infants smiled and laughed more frequently and more vigorously with these. These data suggest that with increasing age there is a decreasing sensory threshold, an increasing defensive threshold and a correspondingly wider band of optimal activation.

Although most of the changes in behavioral and cardiac responses to stimulation have been cited as developmental shifts in sensory thresholds, simultaneous developments in spontaneous behavioral and cardiac activity may also explain the differences noted. For example, increases in affective responses and in spontaneous affective displays have been noted in a longitudinal study of face-to-face interaction from 6 to 26 weeks by Kaye and Fogel (1980). Six-week-old infants rarely emitted spontaneous smiles and vocalizations, although they responded to their mother's smiles, vocalizations, or facial exaggerations with a corresponding smile or vocalization about 20 percent of the time. By 26 weeks the infants were just as likely to respond to their mothers as to initiate a smile or vocalization. Thus, the degree to which variables such as state and age affect the sensory or effector side of the organism is indeterminate.

C. Individual Differences

A number of years ago, Lipsitt et al. (1963) suggested that assessments of sensory thresholds might be used to tap individual differences. Since that time, however, very few studies have attempted to tap individual differences in sensory thresholds. Furthermore, whereas individual variability of arousal levels, attentive, and affective responses during early interactions is considerable, individual differences are rarely described.

In an attempt to determine whether there are individual differences in neonates' intensity of response to various stimuli and whether these differences are stable, Birns (1965) repeatedly administered different stimuli (a soft tone, a loud tone, a cold disc, and a pacifier) to infants during the first 5 days of life. Ratings were made on an intensity continuum including inhibitory responses, no response and positive response. Individual differences among infants were found, and these differences showed significant day-to-day stability. Most infants could be characterized as being either slightly, moderately, or intensely responsive to stimuli, regardless of the modality or the nature of the stimulus. Frank and Cranbury (1975), on the other hand, noted marked variability across modalities in response to startle-like stimuli, with some infants startling to noise and not to light, whereas others startled to light and not to noise, thereby exhibiting "real personality differences" (p. 717) from the first days of life.

Considerable individual variability in responsiveness to social stimuli has also been noted at the neonatal period by Brazelton neonatal scale examiners (c.f. Sameroff, 1980). For older infants, graphic depictions of variable attentive and affective responses during early interactions can be seen in the behavior cycles drawn for five different infants and their mothers by Brazelton et al. (1974) and for twin infants and the same mothers by Stern (1971). These are rare examples of the presentation of individual data. Individual data are unfortunately frequently buried in group difference data.

In summary, the role that these variables play in early interaction research is unclear. Some studies have alluded to the necessity of the infant being in an alert state for an interaction to be "synchronous" or "harmonious" (Brazelton, Kolowski, & Main, 1974; Field, 1977, 1978). Others refer to the varying ability of adults in helping infants modulate arousal levels and maintain alert states (Sander, 1970; Thoman, 1975) or to the increasing duration of interactions as infants mature and come to modulate their activity rhythms and arousal levels (Brazelton et al., 1974). Although researchers have suggested that such organismic variables and varying arousal levels contribute to differences in the attentive and affective behaviors observed during early interactions, behavioral and psychophysiological measures of state changes or arousal levels have not been monitored during these interactions. In the absence of continuous behavioral state recording and independent psychophysiological measures of arousal levels, the effects of organismic variables on early interactions remain speculative. The paucity of longitudinal studies on early interactions leaves us with little data on developmentals shifts in interaction behaviors, and the frequent averaging of individual data for group data presentations limits our knowledge of individual variability.

V. AROUSAL, ATTENTION, AND AFFECT
OF HIGH-RISK INFANTS

The effects of infant state, age, and individual differences on attentive and affective responsivity during early interactions are often more apparent in comparisons between normal and high-risk infants. High-risk infants frequently appear less developed, less able to modulate state, and dramatically different as individuals from their normal peers. Recent volumes by Field et al. (Field, Goldberg, Stern, & Sostek, 1980; Field, Sostek, Goldberg, & Shuman, 1979) include a number of studies conducted on the early interactions of high-risk infants, including preterm, post-term, autistic, and Down syndrome infants. The studies of these infants highlight a number of disturbances in arousal, attention, and affective processes during early interactions. All of these infants appear to conform to one of two extremes on a continuum of being either hypo-aroused/hypo-responsive (Preterm, Down syndrome, or autistic infants) or hyper-aroused/hyper-responsive (post-term, autistic, and hyper-active infants) during early interactions.

A. Hypo-Responsive Preterm, Hyper-Responsive
Post-Term Infants: Sokolov's Model
of Orienting and Defensive Responses

Exemplary of these two extremes are the preterm infant and the post-term infant. At birth and during early infancy the preterm infant has been described by many as being hypotonic (or floppy) and slow to respond, with weak responses to stimulation (Brown & Bakeman, 1979; DiVitto & Goldberg, 1979; Field, 1977; Field et al., 1978). The post-term infant, on the other hand, is hypertonic, extremely irritable, not easily consoled, and hyper-responsive to stimulation (Field et al., 1978).

The Brazelton neonatal behavioral assessments of these infants at birth (Brazelton, 1973) yield the following general response profiles. For interactive processes the preterm infants are rarely alert and often fail to respond to, track, or localize visual and auditory stimulation. On motor and reflex items they show weak reflexes, limited muscle tonus, and weak responses to passive stimulation. They are rarely irritable and often do not respond to aversive stimuli. Post-term infants respond aversively with crying to many types of stimulation and are difficult to console. Motorically they are hyper-responsive to reflex maneuvers and appear to be hypertonic (Field et al., 1978).

Neonatal habituation studies by our group (Field, Dempsey, Hatch, Ting, & Clifton, 1979) and by Rose et al. (Rose, Schmidt, & Bridger, 1976) compared the behavioral and cardiac responses of term and preterm infants to repeated stimulation. In the Rose et al. study (1976), the preterm infants showed only weak behavioral responses, whereas the term infants showed heart rate acceleration and limb movements which habituated over trials. In the Field et al. (1979) study a series of trials of a more intense tactile stimulus and two 90 dB auditory stimuli were presented. The preterm infants showed heart rate acceleration and behavioral responding to these stimuli. The data from the two studies combined suggest that the sensory thresholds of the preterm infants are higher than those of the term infants.

These findings are supported by a more recent study by Tronick and Clifton (in preparation) in which the preterm infant as compared to the term infant was behaviorally and autonomically less responsive to a 75 dB rattle sound, more reactive to a 90 dB rattle sound, and more easily disorganized by shorter interstimulus intervals. Additionally, the preterm infant showed an inability to habituate these stimuli.

These studies suggest that higher intensity auditory and tactile stimuli were required to elicit behavioral and cardiac responses. In addition, once these responses were elicited, the preterm infants continued to respond, or did not show habituation of their responses.

During early interactions the preterm infant appears passive and unresponsive, and the post-term infant appears to resist interaction stimulation by squirming and crying activity (Field, 1977). The mothers of these infants often accelerate their activity in response to the unresponsiveness of their infants, as if "working harder" to elicit responses. These attempts are counterproductive since they result in more gaze aversion and fussiness of their infants (Field, 1977). In an already described interaction study (see page 14 and Fig. 4 and 5) the mothers of preterm and post-term infants were stimulating their infants (verbally or tactilely) a greater percentage of time than were the mothers of term infants, and the preterm and post-term infants gaze averted and were fussy a greater percentage of the interaction time. Although the amount of gaze aversion and fussing was reduced during the interaction situation in which the mother was less active (imitation situation), their gaze aversion activity was still higher than that of term infants, and tonic heart rate levels of both groups were correspondingly higher. Only during the interaction situation with an inanimate raggedy ann doll were the visual attention and tonic heart rate levels of the preterm infants equivalent to those of the term infants (study described on page 13, Fig. 3). Without the animated doll situation, in which the preterm infants did gaze avert more often and show higher tonic heart rate than term infants, we might have attributed the preterm infants' excessive gaze aversion to the seemingly excessive stimulation provided by their mothers.

Combined, these studies suggest that the preterm infants' thresholds to stimulation may be higher. Once their thresholds are exceeded, they may experience more difficulty modulating the arousal and processing the information contained in the stimulation. This is manifested by their failure to habituate and by their long periods of gaze aversion (which we have suggested may function as periods of arousal modulation and information processing). In addition, the excessive gaze aversion and elevated heart rate during interactions suggest that the range of optimal arousal (and therefore optimal stimulation) may be more restricted for these infants. The threshold for attentive or orienting responses may be higher whereas the upper threshold for an aversive/defensive reaction may be lower, resulting in gaze aversion and elevated heart rate of the infant when a level not far above the attention threshold is exceeded. As a result, the mother or other interaction partner may have a very narrow range within which to provide stimulation and expect optimal responsivity. Similarly, although the post-term infant may have absolutely lower attention/orienting and aversion/defensive thresholds, his optimal range or activation band (as labelled in our model in Fig. 1) may also be restricted.

These data might be interpreted using Sokolov's (1963) model of orienting and defensive responses. According to his model there are three zones; a zone below a sensory threshold, a zone between a sensory threshold and a defensive threshold, and a zone above the defensive threshold. In the zone below the sensory threshold the infant does not respond to stimulation because his receptors or processing abilities are not adequate—either due to immaturity or pathology. Above the sensory threshold is a zone of orienting or attentional responses. The infant's receptors and processing abilities are adequate to respond discretely to stimulation which exceeds the sensory threshold but falls below the defensive threshold. In the zone above the defensive threshold the infant's responses are defensive (e.g., startle reflexes) and disorganized (crying and motoric disorganization). The stimulation may be excessively intense, overwhelming the infant's receptors, or the infant may already be processing information at full capacity and is unable to process more input. Using Sokolov's model we might interpret preterm and post-term infants as having other-than-normal sensory and defensive thresholds and narrower zones between these thresholds.

B. Hypo- and Hyper-Aroused Autistic Infants

The data on the thresholds of autistic infants are complex, with some suggesting that thresholds are lower and others suggesting that they are higher (Hutt & Hutt, 1968; Ornitz & Ritvo, 1968). Additionally, autistic infants have been characterized as hyper- or hypo-aroused leading to the postulation of two separate groups by Ornitz and Ritvo (1968). Studies by Sroufe and his colleagues (Sroufe & Morris, 1973; Sroufe, Steucher, & Stutzer, 1973) suggest two very different constellations of behaviors in autistic children and two correspondingly different tonic heart rate levels.

Hyperactivity and negativistic behavior in one group was associated with unusually high tonic heart rate levels, whereas passivity in the other group was paralleled by unusually low tonic heart rate levels. With successful treatment (e.g., imitation training) the hypo-aroused children exhibited a significant increase in tonic heart rate level, whereas the hyper-aroused showed a significant decrease.

Films of early interactions featuring infants who were later diagnosed autistic were studied by Massie (1980) and Kubicek (1980) and reported in Field et al. (1980). The films of these infants featured the classic interaction aversion behaviors including back arching, squirming, limb flapping, head aversion, and gaze averting behaviors, suggesting active avoidance of social interaction at a very early stage in infancy. The films also featured intrusive behaviors of the adult attempting to interact with these infants.

Sroufe et al. (1973) report heart rate acceleration responses of the autistic child during interaction avoidant behaviors. Further support for both the hypoarousal and hyper-arousal hypotheses of autism is provided by the heart rate correlates of the stereotypic finger flicking in these children (Sroufe et al., 1973). Just prior to the onset of finger flicking, heart rate began to accelerate, whether the child was observed during bed rest when heart rate was initially low and stable or during stress when heart rate was elevated. Heart rate peaked after the onset of this behavior and returned to base levels following offset (Sroufe et al., 1973). Thus, finger flicking may serve as an arousal-modulating behavior much as gaze aversion has been described as an arousal-modulating behavior during the early interactions of autistic infants. Microanalyses of their interactions suggest that these behaviors also serve as turn-taking cues during the joint activities of autistic children, the cues or behaviors of others being monitored with peripheral vision (Martini, 1980).

C. Hypo-Affective Down Syndrome Infants

Still another group whose early interactions appear disturbed are Down syndrome infants. The early affective or emotional expressions of these infants appear to be muted. For example, crying is less intense and social smiling less frequent, less intense, and less engaging (Emde, Katz, & Thorpe, 1978). Parents describe these infants as having "lonely," "mad," or "scared" expressions. The Down syndrome infant, like the preterm infant, is noted to be "floppy" or hypotonic with some irregular muscle tone in some muscle groups and less motor activity or cycling of the limbs. The social smile of the Down syndrome infant is slow to develop and deviant by its dampened intensity (upturned mouth, but minimal movement of the eyes), and the infant engages in minimal eye contact (Emde et al., 1978).

Using laughter-evoking stimulation games (peek-a-boo, looming face, etc.) with Down syndrome infants, these infants were noted to lag considerably behind normal infants in the onset of laughter (Cicchetti & Sroufe, 1978), and their laughter was rare. Latencies to smile and laugh were longer, and the infants often smiled to stimuli which typically induced laughter in normal infants. The most markedly hypotonic infants in the sample did not laugh at all to these items during the first year. Cicchetti and Sroufe (1978) refer to an arousal modulation problem of these infants, suggesting that the hypo-responsivity, low reactivity to stress and rare heart rate acceleration activity of these infants may indicate a sympathetic nervous system problem or an immature adrenal system, namely an abnormality in catecholamine metabolism reflected by significantly low dopamine-beta-hydroxylase in the blood and less epinephrine in the urine (Alexrod, 1974; Keele et al., 1969).

In relation to the affect model of Sroufe (as previously described) Cicchetti and Sroufe (1978) suggest that these infants are unable to process the incongruity of stimulation with sufficient speed to produce the "tension jag" required for laughter. These observations, coupled with the long latencies to cry and to cease crying during fearful situations, suggest that the Down syndrome infant is not readily highly aroused, and when highly aroused, does not readily recover.

Early interaction studies by our group (Field, 1980b) and by Jones (1980) depict these infants as having flattened affect with minimal smiling, laughter, crying, and eye contact. Mothers report that they do not feel their Down syndrome infants really see or hear them when they are interacting. Like the preterm infant, the Down infant may have a higher threshold to stimulation (attention threshold) and a lower threshold for defensive reactions or aversive responses resulting in a very narrow band for optimal stimulation and responsivity.

Thus, despite considerable individual differences, the preterm, post-term, autistic, and Down syndrome infants exhbit hypo- and hyper- extremes in arousal, attention, and affect processes during early interactions.

VI. AN OPTIMAL ACTIVATION BAND
HYPOTHESIS

The hypotheses and data on arousal, attention, and affect processes during early interactions, then, suggest the need for an integrative model which might orient future investigations of these relationships. The focus on only one or two of these processes at a time, points to a number of questions which seemingly can only be answered by focussing on all three processes. With the use of multiple behavioral and psychophysiological measures and multivariate analysis techniques, the temporal relationships of the precisely defined arousal, attention, and affective behaviors might be identified.

The model suggested to us, by a review of the data on early interactions of normal and high-risk infants and by the models of Sokolov (1963) and by Sroufe (1979), is an optimal activation band model. This model, depicted in Fig. 1, will be briefly outlined again here with some supporting data examples taken from the literature just reviewed.

Briefly, the model posits the following: Attentiveness and positive affect occur within a range or band of activation which has as its lower limit an attention threshold and as its upper limit an aversion threshold. The activation band for normal infants is depicted by the dotted line in Fig. 1. The lower limit reflects a threshold for accepting or attending to stimulation and the upper limit a threshold for rejecting or averting stimulation. Examples of supportive data are the gaze behavior and affect responses from (1) the laughter stimulus situation (Sroufe & Wunsch, 1972) showing no response, smiling, then laughter and finally gaze aversion and crying as the laughing stimulus parameters are changed; (2) the stranger approach situation data showing attentive responses and heart rate decelerations when the stranger is at a distance and gaze aversion, and heart rate accelerations as the stranger approaches (Waters et al., 1975) and (3) the change from attentive, positive affect and low tonic heart rate to gaze aversion, fussiness, and elevated tonic heart rate as the mother's amount of stimulation is increased from a spontaneous to an attention-getting interaction situation (Field, 1979b).

Second, the upper and lower thresholds of the activation band shift and the band width varies as a function of the infant's rest–activity/arousal cycles. Evidence for this proposition comes from (1) differential responding (laughing or crying) to the same stimulus depending on state and context variables (Sroufe & Waters, 1976); and (2) greater attentiveness to stimulation during rest component and greater affective responses to same stimulation during activity component of rest/activity cycle (Fischer, 1973).

Third, an intrinsic curvilinear relationship between stimulation and arousal/attention/affect processes suggest that only moderate stimulation (be that quantitatively moderate or moderately discrepant stimulation) would fall within the activation band. As the thresholds of the band shift, the relative discrepancy or amount of stimulation perceived by the infant may also shift. An example of supporting data for this relationship during early interactions comes from our manipulation of maternal activity. Maternal stimulation in the low activity still-face vs. the moderate activity spontaneous-face versus the high activity attention-getting situations, conforms to an inverted U, as does infant attention (gaze behavior) and affective responsivity (smiling). Tonic heart rate conforms to a curvilinear U function with elevated levels during still-face and attention-getting interaction situations and lower levels during spontaneous and imitative situations (see Fig. 6).

Within the activation band positive affect may occur and vary in form and energy (for example, from smiling to laughing) as a function of the combined arousal level, stimulation properties, and attentive/affective response energy. An example of this is the infant frequently moving from smiling to laughing and back to smiling across laughter stimulus trials. This behavior variation is associated with variable arousal levels (as manifested by increasing tonic heart rate levels from smiling to laughing), decreasing attentiveness from smiling to laughing, and a stimulus intensity increase required to evoke laughing as opposed to smiling. These stimulus and response variations are reported for mother–infant gameplaying by Field (1979a), Sroufe and Wunsch (1972), and Stern (1974).

Moderate levels of positive affect serve to modulate arousal and sustain attention. Smiling, a more moderate level of positive affect than laughing appears to modulate arousal (tonic heart rate levels are lower for smiling than laughing) and to sustain attention (eyes are more often open and mutual eye contact more frequent during smiling than laughing) (Sroufe et al., 1974). If and when stimulation and/or affective responsivity exceeds moderate levels, the upper limit of the activation band is approached, at which point the infant will manifest an inattentive or gaze averting response in order to modulate arousal and process information contained in that stimulation. If that limit or threshold is exceeded, an aversive reaction or negative affect (e.g., fussing or crying) will occur. The need to modulate arousal as the aversive threshold is approach is reflected by heart rate accelerations just prior to gaze aversion (Field, 1981a; Waters et al., 1975) and heart rate accelerations just prior to crying (Vaughn & Sroufe, 1979). Evidence for processing information during gaze aversion is provided by heart rate decelerations just after gaze aversion and prior to return of gaze (Field, 1981a). If stimulation continues and, particularly if it intensifies or accelerates during infant gaze aversion, the infant will fuss, and with further increases will cry (Brazelton et al., 1974; Field, 1980a; Stern, 1974).

The activation band may be narrower and the arousal cycles shorter in infants experiencing developmental delays or deficits (be they perceptual, motor, cognitive or physiological delays or deficits). More specifically, as depicted in Fig. 1, there may be a narrower band for hyper-responsive infants (e.g., preterm, Down syndrome, and autistic infants), which may be delimited by a higher-than-normal attention threshold and a lower-than-normal aversion threshold. Similarly, there may be a narrower band for hyper-responsive ifnants (e.g., post-term, hyperactive, and autistic infants). In contrast to the posited activation band of hypo-responsive infants, the band of hyper-responsive infants may be delimited by both lower attention and lower aversion thresholds. It is not clear whether these narrower-than-normal bands and their higher- or lower-than-normal level thresholds may relate to developmental delays and/or deficits in arousal modulation and/or information processing abilities. As already elaborated in Section V, data on hypo-responsive preterm infants (Field, 1979a), hypo-aroused autistic infants (Sroufe et al., 1973), and hypo-affective Down syndrome infants (Cicchetti &

Sroufe, 1978; Emde et al., 1978) suggest that they may have higher sensory or attention thresholds and lower defensive or aversion thresholds, and thus, narrower activation bands. Narrower bands, but absolutely lower-than-normal sensory and defensive thresholds, may characterize the hyper-aroused, autistic, and hyper-responsive post-term infant (Field et al., 1978).

As the infant develops, arousal cycleds may lengthen and the proposed activation band may widen as manifested by longer periods of attentiveness and more modulated affective responses. A number of studies have documented longer cycles of wakefulness and attentiveness as the infant matures (Dittrichova & Lapackova, 1964), lower response thresholds for all sensory modalities (Bartoshuk, 1962; Berg, 1975; Lipsitt & Levy, 1960; Lispitt et al., 1963), as well as modulated affective responses (Sroufe, 1979) and more sophisticated information processing (Clifton & Nelson, 1976). During early interactions, the same stimuli (intense auditory and tactile stimulation) which elicited crying during the first few months will elicit laughing at 5–6 months (Sroufe & Waters, 1976).

This model can be tested by shifting stimulus parameters on the range of the hypothesized thresholds and monitoring operationally defined, observable behaviors (e.g., gaze, facial expressions, vocal expressions, and body movements) and physiological behaviors (e.g., heart rate, respiration, and muscle tension). Multivariate measures such as these can now be simultaneously monitored and analyzed with more sophisticated measurement tools (e.g., the datamyte and telemetry) and more developed data analyses technique (e.g., time series spectral analysis described by Gottman, 1979, and Porges et al., 1979).

This model could be assessed during early interaction studies in which the following might be varied: (1) interaction situation—controlled and naturalistic situations; (2) stimulus parameters–frequency, intensity, complexity, and discrepancy of stimulation varied in the range of predicted upper and lower activation band thresholds to determine band width and variability; (3) state/arousal cycles of the infant; (4) types of infants including normal, hypo-responsive (preterm, Down syndrome, and autistic infants), and hyper-responsive (post-term, hyperactive, and autistic) infants. Behavioral measures including visual attention (gaze), facial expressions (Smiling, frowning), vocal expressions (laughing, crying), and body movement (head, limb and trunk movements) could be videotaped and coded via an electronic datamyte recorder to preserve the frequency, duration, and sequence of behaviors. Simultaneously, heart rate (EKG), respiration (chest bellows), limb movement (activity bracelet), and trunk movement (stabilimeter) could be monitored without much discomfort to the infant. These measures could then be time locked to the videotaped/datamyte coded behavioral record. The relationships of these measures could be assessed using a regression analysis model, and their coupling or shared variance could be assessed via time series spectal analyses. If the posited model is supported by the data, it might suggest intervention strategies for the early interactions of high-risk infants.

VII.   SUMMARY

Arousal, attention, and affect are important components of early interactions. An integrative approach to the study of these processes is critical to understanding their relationships. However, these are rarely studied together in the context of early interactions.

Studies on attention and arousal during early interactions suggest that the infant alternately gazes toward and away from his or her social partner. Gazing away or gaze aversion is considered a stimulation cut-off behavior which typically occurs as the infant experiences an information overload and/or heightened arousal level. During gaze aversion, information processing and arousal modulation are thought to occur. Temporal relationships between heart rate and gaze aversion support this notion; for example, elevated heart rate prior to gaze aversion may reflect increasing arousal associated with an information overload, whereas heart rate deceleration occurring during the gaze aversion may reflect information processing. In addition, data are reported which suggest a curvilinear relationship between infant gaze aversion and the amount of stimulation during interactions and between heart rate levels and stimulation; with high and low stimulation interactions being characterized by excessive gaze aversion and elevated heart rate.

Affective behaviors such as smiling and laughing, fussing and crying occur against a background of alternating gaze and gaze aversion. Positive affective behaviors are viewed by some investigators as the infant's tension release, or those behaviors which enable the infant to maintain attentiveness without experiencing the disorganizing effects of heightened arousal levels. Without the arousal modulation of affective behaviors the infant may show excessive gaze aversion; without periods of gaze aversion for information processing and arousal modulation the infant may experience disorganization manifested by negative affect, such as crying. These postulated relationships are supported by cardiac activity data showing heart rate deceleration prior to smiling and heart rate acceleration prior to crying.

Factors which appear to influence arousal, attention and affect during interactions are the infants' state and age. Depending on the state and age of an infant, he or she will respond differently to the same stimulus. A looming play face, for example, will elicit laughing at one moment and crying at another moment. The same stimulus will evoke crying in a young infant and laughter in a slightly older infant. Thresholds for attending to and for averting stimulation as well as the range between them, within which the infant attentively and affectivley responds, appear to vary by state and by age. Considerable variability on these also occur across individuals and across groups of infants.

High-risk infants, for example, appear to have higher or lower thresholds, and a narrower range of responsivity. For example, preterm and Down syndrome infants appear to have higher thresholds and post-term and autistic infants lower thresholds. Their narrower range of responsivity may contribute to the excessive gaze aversion and elevated heart rate noted in these groups. In turn, these may affect their information processing and arousal modulation abilities.

An integrative model is proposed for organizing these arousal, attention, and affect data and for guiding further studies of these processes during early interactions. Assessments of this model will require simultaneous monitoring of multiple behavioral and psychophysiological measures and more sophisticated analyses of their temporal relationships.

Early researchers have debated the "lumping" of behaviors versus the "untangling" of behaviors, or macroanalyses vs. microanalyses (Cairns, 1979; Lamb, Suomi, & Stephenson, 1979). Microanalyses have yielded reams of data and some loss of perspective. Macroanalyses have failed to answer questions such as the functional significance of gaze aversion, smiling, or laughter. With more sophisticated instrumentation, statistical and computer technology, the microanalysis task has been simplified. As the relationships between real-time behavioral and psychophysiological data emerge from this multivariate complex, so might the perspective.

REFERENCES

Adler-Stoller, S. & Field, T. Alteration of mother and infant behavior and heart rate during a still-face perturbation of face-to-face interaction. Unpublished manuscript, U. Miami, 1980.

Als, H., Tronick, E. & Brazelton, T. B. Analysis of face-to-face interactions in infant-adult dyads. In M. Lamb, S. Suomi, & G. R. Stephenson (Eds.), *Social interaction analysis*, Wisconsin: University of Wisconsin Press, 1979.

Axelrod, J. Neurotransmitters. *Scientific American*, 1974, **230**, 58–71.

Bakeman, R., & Brown, J. Early interaction: Consequences for social and mental development at three years. *Child Development*, 1980, **51**, 437–447.

Bartoshuk, A. K. Response decrement with repeated elicitation of human neonatal cardiac acceleration to sound. *Journal of Comparative and Physiological Psychology*, 1962, **55**, 9–13.

Beebe, B. A. Ontogeny of positive affect in the third and fourth months of the life of one infant. Unpublished doctoral dissertation, Columbia University, 1973.

Berg, K. Cardiac components of defense responses in infants Psychophysiology, 1975, **12**, 224.

Birns, B. Individual differences in human neonates' responses to stimuluation. *Child Development*, 1965, **36**, 249–256.

Brazelton, T. B. *Neonatal Behavioral Assessment Scale.* London: Spastics International Medial Publications, 1973.

Brazelton, T. B., Koslowski, B., & Main, M. The origins of reciprocity: The early mother-infant interaction. In M. Lewis & L. A. Rosenblum (Eds.), *The effect of the infant on its caregiver.* New York: Wiley, 1974.

Bromwich, R., & Parmelee, A. An intervention program for preterm infants. In T. Field, A. Sostek, S. Goldberg, & H. H. Shuman (Eds.), *Infants born at risk.* New York: Spectrum, 1979.

Brown, J. V., & Bakeman, R. Relationships of human mothers with their infants during the first year of life: Effect of prematurity. In R. W. Bell & W. P. Smotherman (Eds.), *Maternal influences and early behavior.* New York: Spectrum, 1979.

Cairns, R. B. (Ed.), *The analysis of social interactions.* Hillsdale, N.J.: Lawrence Erlbaum Associates, 1979.

Campos, J., Emde, R., Gaensbauer, T., & Henderson, C. Cardiac and behavioral interrelationships in the reactions of infants to strangers. *Developmental Psychology,* 1975, **11,** 589-601.

Chance, M. R.A. An interpretation of some agonistic postures: The role of "cutoff" acts and postures. *Symposium of the Zoological Society of London,* 1962, **8,** 71-89.

Cicchetti, D. & Sroufe, L. A. An organizational view of affect: Illustration from the study of Down's syndrome infants. In M. Lewis & L. A. Rosenblum (Eds.), *The development of affect, Vol. 1.* New York: Plenum, 1978.

Clifton, R. K., & Nelson, M. Developmental study of habituation in infants: The importance of a paradigm, resposne system and state of the organism. In T. Tighe & R. Leaton (Eds.), *Habituation: Neurological, comparative and developmental approaches.* Hillsdale, N.J.: Lawrence Erlbaum, 1976.

Cohen, S. E., & Beckwith, L. Preterm infant interaction with the caregiver in the first year of life and competence at age two. *Child Development,* 1979, **50,**767-776.

Dittrichova, J. & Lapackova, V. Development of the waking state in young infants. *Child Development,* 1964, **35,** 265-270.

DiVitto, B. & Goldberg, S. The effects of newborn medical status on early parent-infant interaction. In T. Field, A. Sostek, S. Goldberg, & H. H. Shuman (Eds.), *Infants born at risk.* New York: Spectrum, 1979.

Emde, R., Katz, E., & Thorpe, J. Emotional expression in infancy: II. Early Deviations in Down's syndrome. In M. Lewis & L. A. Rosenblum (Eds.), *The Development of Affect, Vol. 1.* New York: Plenum Press, 1978.

Field, T. Effects of early separation, interaction deficits and experimental manipulations on infant-mother face-to-face interaction. *Child Development,* 1977, **48,** 763-771.

Field, T. The three Rs of infant-adult interactions: Rhythms, repertoires and responsivity. *Journal of Pediatric Psychology,* 1978, **3,** 131-136.

Field, T. Games parents play with normal and high-risk infants. *Child Psychiatry and Human Development,* 1979, **10,** 41-48. (a)

Field, T. Interaction patterns of high-risk and normal infants. In T. Field, A. Sostek, S. Goldberg, & H. H. Shuman (Eds.), *Infants born at risk.* New York: Spectrum, 1979. (b)

Field, T. Visual and cardiac responses to animate and inanimate faces by young term and preterm infants. *Child Development,* 1979, **50,** 188-194. (c)

Field, T. Interactions of high-risk infants: Quantitative and qualitative differences. In D. Sawin R. C. Hawkins, 1. O. Walker & J. H. Peniticuff (Eds.), *Current perspectives on psychosocial risks during pregnancy and early infancy.* New York: Brummer/Mazel, 1980. (a)

Field, T. Peer interactions of high-risk infants and children. In T. Field, S. Goldberg, D. Stern, & A. Sostek (Eds.), *Interactions of high-risk infants and children.* New York: Academic Press, 1980. (b)

Field, T. Infant gaze aversion and heart rate during face-to-face interactions. *Infant behavior and development,* 1981 (a)

Field, T., Dempsey, J., Ting, G., Hatch, J., & Clifton, R. Cardiac and behavioral responses to repeated tactile and auditory stimulation by preterm and full-term infants during the neonatal period. *Developmental Psychology,* 1979, **15,** 406–416.

Field, T., Goldberg, S., Stern, D., & Sostek, A. (Eds.), *High-risk infants and chldren: Adult and peer interactions.* New York: Academic Press, 1980.

Field, T., Hallock, N., Ting, E., Dempsey, J., Babiri, C., & Shuman, H. H. A first year follow-up of high-risk infants: Formulating a cumulative risk index. *Child Development,* 1978, **49,** 119–131.

Field, T., Sostek, A., Goldberg, S. & Shuman, H. H. (Eds.), *Infants born at risk.* New York: Spectrum, 1979.

Field, T., Widmayer, S., Stringer, S., & Ignatoff, E. Teenage, lower class black mothers and their preterm infants: An intervention and developmental follow-up. *Child Development.* 1980, **51,** 426–436.

Fischer, T. Rhythms of infant play. Unpublished master's thesis, Tufts University, 1973.

Fogel, A. Personal communication, 1980.

Fogel, A., Diamond, G. R., Langhorst, B. H., & Demos, V. Affective and cognitive aspects of the two-month-old's participation in face-to-face interaction with its mother. In E. Tronick (Ed.), *Joint regulation of behavior.* New York: Cambridge University Press, 1980.

Frank, U. A., & Cranbury, P. F. The development of individuality in neonates. *Journal of the Medical Society of New Jersey,* 1975, **72,** 717–720.

Gottman, J. M. Detecting cyclicity in social interaction. *Psychological Bulletin,* 1979, **86,** 338–348.

Graham, F. K., & Clifton, R. K. Heart rate cahnge as a component of the orienting response. *Psychological Bulletin,* 1966, **65,** 305–320.

Gustafson, G. E., Green, J. A., & West, M. J. The infant's changing role in mother–infant games: The growth of social skills. *Infant Behavior and Development,* 1979, **2,** 301–308.

Hunt, J. McV. Intrinsic motivation and its role in psychological development. *Nebraska Symposium on Motivation,* 1965.

Hutt, S. J., & Hutt, C. Stereotypy, arousal and autism. *Human Development,* 1968, **11,** 277–286.

Hutt, C. & Ounsted, C. The biological significance of gaze aversion with particular reference to the syndrome of infantile autism. *Behavioral Science,* 1966, **11,** 346–356.

Jones, O. Mother–child communications in very young Down's syndrome and normal children. In T. Field, S. Goldberg, D. Stern, & A. Sostek (Eds.), *High-risk infants and chlidren: Adult and peer interactions.* New York: Academic Press, 1980.

Kagan, J. *Change and continuity in infancy.* New York: Wiley, 1971.

Kaye, K., & Fogel, A. The temporal structure of face-to-face communication between mothers and infants. *Developmental psychology,* 1980, **16,** 454–464.

Keele, D. K., Richards, C., Brown, J., & Marshall, J. Catecholomine metabolism in Down's syndrome. *American Journal of Mental Deficiency,* 1969, *74,* 125–129.

Kendon, A. Some functions of gaze-direction in social interaction. *Acta Psychologica,* 1967, **26,** 22–63.

Kubicek, L. Mother interactions of twins: An autistic and non-autistic twin. In T. Field, S. Goldberg, D. Stern, & A. Sostek, (Eds.), *High-risk infants and children: Adult and peer interactions.* New York: Academic Press, 1980.

Lacey, J. T., Kagan, J., Lacey, B. C., & Moss, H. A. The visceral level: Situational determinants and behavioral correlates of autonomic response patterns. In P. H. Knapp (Ed.), *Expressions of the emotions in man.* New York: International Universities Press, 1963.

Lamb, M. E., Suomi, S. J., & Stephenson, G. R. (Eds.), *Social interaction analysis.* Madison, Wisc.: The University of Wisconsin Press, 1979.

Lewis, M., Brooks, J., & Haviland, J. Hearts and faces: A study in the measurement of emotion. In M. Lewis & L. A. Rosenblum (Eds.), *The development of affect, Vol. 1.* New York: Plenum Press, 1978.

Lipsitt, L. P., Engen, T., & Kaye, H. Developmental changes in the olfactory threshold of the neonate. *Child Development,2* 1963, **34,** 371–376.

Lipsitt, L. P. & Levy, N. Electro-tactual threshold in the neonate. *American Journal of Psychology,* 1960, **73,** 630–632.

Martini, M. Structures of interaction between two autistic chldren. In T. Field, S. Goldberg, D. Stern, & A. Sostek, (Eds.), *High-risk infants and chldren: Adult and peer interactions.* New York: Academic Press, 1980.

Massie, H. N. Pathologic interactions in infancy. In T. Field, S. Goldberg, D. Stern, & A. Sostek (Eds.), *High-risk infants and children: Adult and peer interactions.* New York: Academic Press, 1980.

Obrist, P. A. Webb, P. A. Sutterer, J. R., & Howard, J. L. Cardiac deceleration and reaction time: An evaluation of two hypotheses. *Psychophysiology,* 1970, **6,** 695–706.

Ornitz, E. M. & Ritvo, E. R. Perceptual inconstancy in early infantile autism. *Archives of General Psychiatry,* 1968, **18,** 78–98.

Parmelee, A. H., & Stern, E. Development of states in infants. In C. Clemente, D. P. Purpura, & F. G. Mayer (Eds.), *Sleep and the maturing nervous system.* New York: Academic Press, 1972.

Pomerleau-Malcuit, A., & Clifton, R. K. Neonatal heart rate response to tactile, auditory, and vestibular stimulation in different states. *Chld Development,* 1973, **44,** 485–496.

Porges, S. W., Bohrer, R. E., Cheung, M. N., Drasgow, F., McCabe, P., & Keren, G. A new time-series statistic for detecting rhythmic co-occurrence in the frequency domain: The weighted coherence and its application to psychophysiological research. Unpublished manuscript, University of Illinois, 1979.

Ramey, C. T., Farran, D. C., & Campbell, F. A. Predicting I.Q. from mother–infant interactions. *Child Development,* 1979, **50,** 804–814.

Rose, S. A., Schmidt, K., & Bridger, W. M. Cardiac and behavioral responsivity to tactile stimulation in premature and full-term infants. *Developmental Psychology,* 1976, **12,** 311–320.

Rose, S., Schmidt, K., & Bridger, W. H. Changes in tactile responsivity during sleep in the human newborn infant. *Developmental Psychology,* 1978, **14,** 163–172.

Sameroff, A. J. (Ed.) Organization and stability of newborn behavior: A commentary on the Brazelton Neonatal Behavior Assessment Scale. *Monographs of the Society for Research in Child Development,* 1978, **43,** 177.

Sander, L. W. The longitudinal course of early mother–child interaction: Cross-case comparison in a sample of mother–child pairs. In B. M. Foss (Ed.), *Determinants of infant behavior IV.* New York: Academic Press, 1970.

Sigman, M., & Parmelee, A. Longitudinal evaluation of the preterm infant. In T. Field, A. Sostek, S. Goldberg, & H. H. Shuman (Eds.), *Infants born at risk.* New York: Spectrum, 1979.

Sokolov, E. N. *Perception and the conditioned reflex.* New York: Macmillan, 1963.

Sroufe, L. A. Socioemotional development. In J. D. Osofsky (Ed.), *Handbook of infant development.* New York: Wiley, 1979.

Sroufe, L. A., & Morris, D. L. Respiratory-cardiac relationships in children. *Psychophysiology,* 1973, **10,** 377–382.

Sroufe, L. A., Steucher, H. U., & Stutzer, W. The functional significance of autistic behaviors for the psychotic child. *Journal of Abnormal Child Psychology,* 1973, **1,** 3, 225–240.

Sroufe, L. A., & Waters, E. The ontogenesis of smiling and laughter: A perspective on the organization of development in infancy. *Psychological Review,* 1976, **83,** 3, 173–189.

Sroufe, L. A., & Waters, E. Heart rate as a convergent measure in clinical and developmental research. *Merrill-Palmer Quarterly,* 977, **23,** 2, 3–25.

Sroufe, L. A., Waters, E., & Matas, L. Contextual determinants of infant affective response. In M. Lewis & L. Rosenblum (Eds.), *The origins of behavior, Vol. 2: Fear.* New York: Wiley, 1974.

Sroufe, L. A., & Wunsch, J. P. The development of laughter in the first year of life. *Child Development,* 1972, **43,** 1326-1344.

Stechler, G., & Carpenter, G. A viewpoint on early affective development. In J. Hellmuth (Ed.), *The exceptional infant, Vol. 1.* Seattle: Special Child Publications, 1967.

Sternman, M. B., & Hoppenbrouwers, T. The development of sleep-waking and rest-activity patterns from fetus to adult in man. In M. Sterman, D. McGinty, & A. M. Adinolfi (Eds.), *Brain Development and Behavior.* New York: Academic Press, 1971.

Stern, D. N. A micro-analysis of mother–infant interaction: Behavior regulating social contact between a mother and her 3½ month-old twins. *Journal of American Academy of Child Psychiatry,* 1971, **10,** 501-517.

Stern, D. N. Mother and infant at play. In M. Lewis & J. Rosenblum (Eds.), *The effect of the infant on its caregiver.* New York: Wiley, 1974.

Thoman, E. B. Early development of sleeping behaviors in infants. In N. R. Ellis (Ed.), *Abberant development in infancy: Human and animal studies.* New York: Wiley & Sons, 1975.

Trevarthen, C. Conversations with a two-month-old. *New Scientist,* 1974, **2,** 230-233.

Tronick, E., Als, H., Adamson, L., Wise, S., & Brazelton, T. B. The infant's response to entrapment between contradictory messages in face-to-face interaction. *Journal of Child Psychiatry,* 1978, **17,** 1-13.

Tronick, E., Als, H. & Brazelton, T. B. Monadic Phases: A structural descriptive analysis of infant-mother face-to-face interaction. *Merrill-Palmer Quarterly,* 1979, **26,** 3-24.

Tronick, E., & Clifton, R. Habituation of auditory stimuli by preterm infants, in preparation.

Vaughn, B., & Sroufe, L. A. The temporal relationship between infant and heart rate acceleration and crying in an aversive situation. *Child Development,* 1979, **50,** 565-567.

Waters, E., Matas, L., & Sroufe, L. A. Infants' reactions to an approaching stranger: Description, validation and functional significance of wariness. *Child Development,* 1975, **46,** 348-356.

Wolff, P. M. Observations on the early development of smiling. In B. M. Foss (Ed.), *Determinants of infant behavior II.* London: Methuen, 1963.

Wolff, P. M. Causes, controls & organization of behavior. *Psychology Issues,* 1966, **5,** Monograph no. 17.

DEVELOPING TRUST AND PERCEIVED EFFECTANCE IN INFANCY

Michael E. Lamb

UNIVERSITY OF UTAH

Advances in Infancy
Research, Vol. I

I. INTRODUCTION

Research conducted over the last two decades has demonstrated that newborn infants have unexpectedly well-developed perceptual capacities, and that most of the deficiencies in perceptual functioning that normal neonates share disappear over the first months of postnatal life (Bornstein, 1979; Cohen & Salapatek, 1975a, 1975b; Eisenberg, 1976, 1979). The young infant also manifests attentional and exploratory strategies that maximize the ability to learn about objects in the environment (e.g., Haith, 1979), and Piaget (1952, 1954), among others, has documented the processes through which an understanding of objects and their properties is acquired.

In this essay, I discuss one aspect of this fascinating theme, focusing on the infant's dawning understanding of the behavior of social objects (people). Compared with inanimate objects, people have several rather unique properties, and an understanding of their propensities, I propose, has major implications for early social and personality development. It is my contention that, from social interaction in the first half-year of life, the infant develops: 1) a conception of itself as an effective, competent, organism, and 2) a conception of the reliability or trustworthiness of significant adults. These two emergent conceptions may be of greater significance, as far as students of social development are concerned, than any other attainments or events occurring during infancy. An analysis of the processes involved demands that we discard traditional boundaries between aspects of social, cognitive, perceptual, psychophysiological, and memorial development and recognize the essential unity and coherence of developmental processes. Additional discussions on this topic have recently appeared in Lamb and Sherrod (1981).

The crux of my argument is that conceptions of both personal effectance and the reliability of specific people depend upon an awareness on the part of the infant that its signals or behaviors predictably elicit responses from those people. The development of trust requires that: 1) there are predictable associations between at least some infant and adult behaviors; 2) the infant be aware of these associations; and 3) the infant recognize that specific people are consistently responsible for the predictable responses to its behavior. Conceptions of personal effectance, by contrast, do not depend on an ability to recognize the mediation of specific individuals. Indeed this conception need not grow out of interactions with people rather than objects, although I believe that it invariably does simply because people mediate more predictable and salient associations in the early months than objects do. Another important difference between trust and perceived effectance is that the hedonic quality of the adult's response is crucial to the development of trustful relationships but may not be significant in the development of perceived effectance. This makes it particularly important to distinguish between trust and perceived effectance in research on individual differences in early social development.

The next two sections of this chapter comprise a discussion of the infant's emergent capacity both to learn and remember associations between its actions and environmental events and to recognize specific individuals. In Section IV, I consider the social interactions which seem most likely to facilitate the infant's recognition of associations between its own social behaviors and the responses of adults. In the fifth section, I discuss the affective consequences of early social expectations and in the final substantive section, I discuss the origins and implications of individual differences in perceived effectance and interpersonal trust.

II. LEARNING CAPACITIES OF HUMAN INFANTS

There has long been considerable controversy about the ability or inability of neonates and young infants to learn and remember simple associations. In an early review, Dorothy Marquis (1931) concluded that newborns could indeed be conditioned, although she noted methodological problems with much of the relevant research. Forty years later, Sameroff (1971) reached a rather different conclusion, arguing not simply that neonatal conditioning *had* not been demonstrated but that it *could* not be demonstrated. More specifically, he argued that classical conditioning could not occur in the first three postnatal weeks because

> there must be a differentiation of the schema systems related to both the US [unconditioned stimulus] and CS [conditioned stimulus]. For distance receptors, this development seems to take about 3 weeks, after which the infant begins to be able to coordinate his differentiated perceptual response systems with other sensory-motor schemas such as sucking or head turning. (Sameroff, 1971, p. 10)

Operant conditioning which occurred neonatally, Sameroff continued, was usually shortlived, without any transfer of training to the next session. Criticizing one widely-cited demonstration of neonatal learning (Lipsitt, Kaye, & Bosack, 1966), Sameroff argued that no "true" learning was involved (Sameroff & Cavanaugh, 1979). Defending this claim, Sameroff and Cavanaugh reasoned that since the behavior and reward (sucking for a liquid food reward) naturally go together, true learning was not necessary for newborns to make this association. The fact that they "learned" the association in only one trial was cited as further evidence that "learning" was not involved.[1]

---

[1]Whether or not biologically prepared associations are involved, one trial learning has been known to psychologists for years. Skinner (1932) discussed this phenomenon in one of his early papers and had little difficulty in describing it as learning. In Skinner's view, the rapid learning of the association was due to the careful elimination of distractions (i.e. other responses and stimuli which might be associated with a reinforcer) that might retard the association between a behavior (e.g. lever pressing) and a reward.

Other researchers have taken issue with Sameroff's conclusions. After reviewing the literature, for example, Rovee-Collier and Lipsitt (1981) concluded that the "inhibitory and conditioning deficiencies which have previously been attributed to immaturity may simply reflect the nature of the conditioning task in relation to the organism's capabilities, the evolutionary significance of the experimental problem, and the extent to which the context within which the task is presented acts as a "setting event" ". Instead of arguing, as Sameroff does, that true learning is not involved when associations are facilitated by biological preparedness, other students of learning have argued with increasing persuasiveness that a great deal of the learning that occurs throughout the animal kingdom is facilitated by biological preparedness (Hinde & Stevenson-Hinde, 1973; Seligman, 1970). Many associations are of such adaptive significance (i.e., they confer survival or reproductive advantage) that they are readily established with only a small number of pairings. Rudy and Cheatle (1977) and Smith and Spear (1978), for example, have shown that infant animals learn to avoid poisons or noxiously flavored foodstuffs after only one trial, even when the odor or taste cue, the poison, and the nausea are widely separated in time; it is clearly adaptive to learn such associations rapidly. Analogously, there are constraints on learning, such that certain associations are hard—if not impossible—to learn even after an extensive number of pairings. That infants appear to learn rapidly to suck for food rewards may be taken as evidence, then, of a well-prepared learned association. Inborn factors *facilitate* learning.

Rovee-Collier has also written extensively about the difficulties experienced by researchers in demonstrating conditioned associations in early infancy (Rovee-Collier & Gekoski, 1979; Rovee-Collier & Lipsitt, 1981). She has drawn extensively upon studies of animal learning and behavior in arguing that failures to demonstrate learned associations in infancy result in part from a failure to consider "the economics" of infant learning and behavior. In organisms of all ages and species, she argues, the benefits gained from learning an association must (over time) exceed the costs or else it would not be profitable to learn the association. Likewise, the cost of performing the operant response must be less than the value of the reward or else the infant would not perform it thus making it impossible to determine whether the association has been learned. The energy balance between costs and benefits is especially critical for very young human infants because they have little excess energy to waste in unprofitable behaviors.

The concepts of preparedness and cost-benefit analysis are extremely pertinent to discussions of learning in early infancy. Many of the apparent failures to demonstrate learning occurred when researchers implicitly assumed that, if learning were possible, it should be possible to teach associations between any two stimuli or between any stimulus (reward) and any response (operant). Thus, for example, several researchers tried unsuccessfully to condition foot withdrawal elicited by electric shocks to auditory stimuli (see Bijou & Baer, 1965, for a review). Incorrect assumptions led researchers to employ inappropriate test situations in their attempts to assess the conditionability of young infants.

Two investigators of infant learning and memory provide the most informative evidence about the emergent ability of young infants to remember learned operant responses. Working in Czeckoslovakia with a group of infants who, along with their mothers, remained residents of a research facility throughout the first few months of life, Papoušek (1961; Papoušek & Bernstein, 1969) studied changes over time in learning and memory. Papoušek showed that learned behavioral modifications did occur during the neonatal period, although the learning was unstable and the infants forgot the learned response by the next of the daily test sessions. During the second month of life, however, infants remembered how to perform from one day to the next and it then became possible to teach new responses. Infants who had learned to turn to the left upon hearing a buzzer, for example, could now be taught to turn right instead. The capacity to remember learned responses emerged at about the same age regardless of how many training sessions the infants had experienced previously, suggesting to Papoušek that a certain degree of neural maturation was a prerequisite for long term learning and memory. Papoušek's data suggest that appreciable memory of the association between the infant's behavior and specific environmental consequences cannot occur before the second month of life. This estimate may be conservative, however: Papoušek provided infants with only ten training trials each day as he wished to study developmental changes in the process of conditioning rather than how early learning was possible.

A series of studies by Rovee-Collier and her colleagues (Davis & Rovee-Collier, 1979; Rovee & Fagen, 1976; Sullivan, Rovee-Collier, & Tynes, 1979) provide equivalently important information about memory for associations between infant behavior and environmental consequences. By two to three months of age, infants could remember learned responses (to jiggle their legs in order to produce movement of a suspended mobile) for at least 6 to 14 days. Furthermore, when infants were briefly reminded of the association (i.e., mobile was jiggled over their heads), three-month-olds remembered the operant responses they learned four weeks earlier (Rovee-Collier, Sullivan, Enright, Lucas, & Fagen, 1980). Finally, in a provocative study, Little (1973) reported that some 20-day-old infants remembered a classically conditioned response 10 days after the training session.

For our purposes, arguments about when infants can first learn and remember are not crucial. The dispute between Sameroff (e.g., 1971) and Rovee-Collier (e.g., Rovee-Collier & Lipsitt, 1981) concerns the infant's capacity to establish associations through classical conditioning; all agree that newborns are amenable to operant conditioning and there is no disagreement about the learning capacities of infants older than one month of age.

Regardless of when 'true' learning first takes place, it is clear that infants are capable of learning and remembering somewhat arbitrary associations between their own behavior and environmental consequences by the second month of life. Furthermore, individual infants in the studies of Little (1973) and, more recently, of Thoman, Korner, and Beason-Williams (1977) remembered associations much earlier than this. Thoman et al.'s study is especially interesting because it suggests that when the association to be learned is potentially adaptive and is not costly, inter-session retention is possible even in newborns. In this study, a woman's voice was repeatedly played when crying neonates were picked up for soothing. (As I shall note presently, holding is the most effective means of soothing infants.) After repeated pairings of the voice and the hold, the voice alone acquired some capacity to soothe the crying infants whereas when voice and hold had not been paired, the voice did not have soothing properties. Since no other researchers have demonstrated such impressive associative learning and long-term retention in infants as young as this, the finding is sufficiently important to demand independent replication particularly since a close inspection of the data reveals that the effect, though statistically significant, was rather modest.

III. RECOGNITION

The concept of perceived effectance demands only that the infant develop a generalized expectancy that its actions can elicit environmental reactions. By contrast, the concept of trust in others demands not only such an expectation but also the realization that specific individuals consistently mediate important consequences. This means that the recognition of people is an essential prerequisite for the development of trust in others.

Unfortunately, although many researchers have ostensibly studied recognition, the evidence is inconclusive. Some researchers have reported that within the first month of life, infants can distinguish specific perceptual characteristics of their mothers from the characteristics of others (Macfarlane, 1975; Carpenter, 1973, 1974). This evidence is controversial (Maurer & Salapatek, 1976; Haith, Bergman, & Moore, 1977), however, and in any event, *discrimination* of mother's smell or face from another's does not amount to *recognition* of mother. This criticism cannot be leveled at two provocative studies reporting that three-week-old (Mills & Melhuish, 1974) and three-day-old (DeCasper & Fifer, 1980) infants sucked more to produce their mothers' voices than strangers' voices.

When preferential looking is the dependent measure, there is some evidence of discrimination between one and three months when multimodal cues are available (e.g., voice and face) but not when unimodal information alone is provided (Bigelow, 1977). After three months, discrimination on the basis of visual (Bigelow, 1977: three months; Sherrod, 1979: five months) or auditory (Brown, 1979: 4 months) information alone is possible. Olson (1981) concluded that recognition becomes possible somewhere between three and five months, but this is a very conservative estimate since Olson explicitly emphasized evidence of unimodal (visual) recognition in reaching his conclusion. In the real world, of course, infants have available multimodal cues that can be used in recognizing their parents. By 3½ months of age, for example, infants look at their mothers when their voices are heard and at their fathers when their voices are heard (Spelke & Owsley, 1979) suggesting that multimodal recognition is possible before this (younger infants were not tested). In the absence of methodologically sound studies that compare infants' responses to ecologically-valid, multimodal representations of people, we cannot say when recognition first becomes possible. It is certainly possible by the second or third months of life, by which time infants are clearly capable of learning and remembering simple associations.

IV. THE SIGNIFICANCE OF THE DISTRESS-RELIEF SEQUENCE

Thoman et al. (1977) were successful in demonstrating conditioned associations in neonates, I believe, because they studied learning in the most propitious circumstances. In this section, I attempt to explain why I consider responses to infant distress so important, and why I believe the earliest social expectations and self concepts develop out of distress-relief sequences. My arguments are based on five propositions: 1) the distress-relief sequence is perhaps the most predictable naturally-occurring association of infant behavior and environmental reactions; 2) the ratio between baseline and conditional probabilities are most propitious in the distress-relief sequence; 3) it is an economical, or cost-effective, association for an infant to learn; 4) the events to be associated are highly salient to young infants; 5) it provides the infant with multiple perceptual cues at a time when it is maximally capable of taking in this information.

A-1. Predictability

The predictability of the distress-relief sequence depends on preeminent response tendencies in both infants and adults that appear to have a biological basis. When adults hear a crying baby, they experience an autonomic arousal and a mixture of aversion and empathy that together activate the adult to initiate an attempt to stop the infant's cry (Frodi, Lamb, Leavitt, & Donovan,

1978; Frodi, Lamb, Leavitt, Donovan, Neff, & Sherry, 1978; Murray, 1979). The infant cry has imperative characteristics ensuring that it is more likely to be perceived and responded to than any other social behavior or signal. The most common response to a crying baby is to pick it up and hold it to the shoulder, perhaps speaking soothingly at the same time (Bell & Ainsworth, 1972). Experimental studies conducted by Korner and her colleagues (Korner & Grobstein, 1966; Korner & Thoman, 1970, 1972) show that the most effective way of soothing a distressed infant is to pick it up. (If the infant is hungry, of course, it is usually picked up to be fed; the pick-up itself may bring partial or temporary quieting even before the nipple is offered.) Thus the sequence is a very predictable one: The distressed infant cries; its cry typically elicits a response which usually includes picking it up. This usually quiets the infant, terminating the cry. No other social interaction in infancy is quite as predictable or occurs quite so frequently.

Much has been written recently about face-to-face interaction between parents and infants, with a view to demonstrating the infant's awareness of the rules of reciprocal turn-taking (e.g., Brazelton, Yogman, Tronick, & Als, 1979; Als, Tronick, & Brazelton, 1979; Stern, 1977; Strain & Vietze, 1975). Scrutiny of these data, however, reveals that reciprocal turn-taking is not characteristic of face-to-face interaction—simultaneous coaction is more common (Strain & Vietze, 1975; Vietze, Strain, & Falsey, 1975; Stern, 1977). Even when turn-taking occurs, furthermore, the specific behaviors (of both adult and infant) are extremely varied. Thus, for example, the adult may respond to one or a combination of the infant's smiles, vocalizations, stares, reaches, or leg movements with a smile, vocalization, touch, look, playface expression, or a combination of these. Unlike the distress-relief sequence, which is highly standardized, face-to-face interaction is not consistent, or frequent enough for infants to learn about the predictability of social responses to their behavior. The probable preeminence of the distress-relief sequence is also suggested by research in other cultures. In many other cultures, for example, young infants are carried almost constantly in slings that afford little opportunity for face-to-face interaction with mothers, yet assure prompt responses to the infants' cries (e.g., Goldberg, 1972, 1977; Konner, 1972, 1977; Brazelton, 1977).

A-2. Conditional and Baseline Probabilities

In a recent essay, Watson (1979) discussed another set of conditions affecting the perception of contingency. He argued that the perception of contingency depends not simply on the probability that stimulus and response are actually associated, but on the extent to which the conditional probabilities differ from the baseline probabilities. Consequently, the perception of contingency is facilitated when the response and its consequence or associate initially occur relatively rarely.

Watson's conclusion is important, because it adds circumstantial support to the claim here regarding the special importance of the distress-relief sequence. First, relative to other potential communicative behaviors such as smiling, vocalizing, and gazing, infant distress is fairly infrequent, and it becomes less frequent with age, whereas these other social behaviors occur more commonly with age (Moss, 1967). Likewise, relative to other infant-related adult actions, picking up and holding the infant to the shoulder is fairly uncommon. Second, social behaviors such as smiling, vocalizing, and gazing are much more likely to occur independent of eliciting or responsive bids from the partner (i.e., noncontingently) than are distress and relief behaviors. Third, the variety of events eliciting these behaviors is far greater than is the variety of events eliciting pick-up and soothing, and these positive social behaviors are much more interchangeable. Thus the ratio of baseline to conditional probabilities is far greater for behaviors in the distress-relief sequence than it is for other social behaviors. These facts maximize the salience of distress-relief events in the perception of social contingencies and thus in the development of social and self expectations.

A-3. Cost-Effectiveness

Crying is a metabolically costly behavior for infants to perform, and consequently it is advantageous to cease crying rapidly. The cessation of crying, therefore, is a cost-effective behavior, and it is economical to learn the association between the termination of crying and the approach/pick up of the adult simply because the one accompanies the termination of a very costly activity. Rovee-Collier and Lipsitt (1981) point out that it is easiest to condition low energy responses in very young infants: High energy responses (like foot-kicking) can only be conditioned later. What could involve less energy expenditure than the termination of a costly behavior? The key association in the distress-relief sequence, I believe, is that involving the termination of crying; the onset of the cry may be attributed to a variety of endogenous or exogenous events, and it is not until later (when the infant's energy/economy balance is less precarious, amongst other things) that the infant *begins* to cry intentionally.

A-4. Salience of the Events

During the first two months of life, the infant has a somewhat limited capacity to modulate its own states—particularly distress states (Emde & Robinson, 1979; Berg & Berg, 1979). As a result, there occur frequent and irregular changes from one state to another; the infant is sometimes incapable of initiating the response that would prevent the disequilibrium or permit the reattainment of an equilibrium state. Instead, the infant is often dependent on exogenous intervention—notably by its caretaker(s)—for reequilibration and state modulation. The caretaker's response to infant distress is an important component of state modulation, since it constitutes the most effective means of restoring the young infant from the somewhat disorganized state of distress to the organized state of quiet alertness. It seems reasonable to propose that the two states themselves (distress and quiet alertness) are by their very nature, more salient and memorable for young infants (and indeed for adults!) than are states such as drowsiness or sleep. Similarly, one would expect the alert infant to be especially capable of noting the medium (pick up and hold by the caretaker) accounting for the transition from one state to the other. Certainly, no other social or nonsocial interactions in the early months of life involve events that are as salient or as likely to be noticed, and this should increase the likelihood of associations being learned and remembered.

A-5. The Implications of Quiet Alertness

As noted earlier, when an adult picks up a crying infant and holds it to the shoulder, the infant is likely to cease crying and assume a state of quiet alertness (Korner & Thoman, 1970, 1972). In this temporary state of alertness, the infant is maximally capable of taking in perceptual information; it is more attentive in this state than in any other (Berg & Berg, 1979; Wolff, 1966). During those seconds, it is thus most likely to learn about (and remember) the rich variety of perceptual information presented by the caretaker who is the most salient and proximal aspect of the environment. His/her proximity and behavior assure the infant exposure to the visual, auditory, olfactory, and tactile cues that characterize her/him. There is a considerable amount of evidence that social stimuli have a special ability to attract the attention of infants (Sherrod, 1981).

As far as the infant's social development is concerned, this has two important consequences. First, the repeated co-occurrence of the multimodal perceptual characteristics of the caretaker facilitates the development of a multimodal concept of the caretaker—something that seems to occur gradually over the first few months of life (Spelke & Cortelyou, 1981)—and contributes to its developing capacity to recognize specific people. In partial replication of an earlier study by Aronson and Rosenbloom (1971), for example, McGurk and Lewis (1974) found that four- and seven-month-olds, but not one-month-olds, were disconcerted when the source of the mother's voice was experimentally displaced from the locus of her face. This indicated that the older infants expected the facial movements and sounds to be coordinated, whereas the one-month-olds did not. Second, the characteristics of the caretaker are repeatedly associated in the distress-relief sequence with the termination of a negative state and the onset of a pleasurable event: relief of distress and the transition to quiet alertness, respectively. Both the regularity and the pleasureable affect are important, for they facilitate the development of social expectations (i.e., expectations regarding the predictable responsiveness of specific people) and the development of positive emotional relationships.

B.   Research on Distress-Relief-Contingencies

In addition to the experimental research by Thoman et al. (1977), there have been only two studies of distress-relief contingencies and their consequences. In a longitudinal study, Bell and Ainsworth (1972) found that the more promptly mothers responded to their infants' cries in the first three months of life, the less those infants cried later in the year. Infants whose mothers responded contingently switched from crying to more mature means of communication. By the end of the year, these infants also appeared to have the greatest confidence in their mothers' accessibility (see below). Unfortunately, these mothers responded promptly to various infant signals, not just cries, so we cannot determine how important the responsiveness to cries was.

In a smaller longitudinal study, Gekoski (1974) later showed that some two-month-olds ceased crying in anticipation of a caretaker's interventions, perhaps because they heard their approaching footsteps or saw them approaching. The number of infants exhibiting this anticipatory quieting increased linearly to 92 percent at six months of age. Gekoski suggested that these infants were developing expectations that their mothers would approach, pick them up, and soothe them. This was a small study, however, and there remains a clear need for further attempts to verify whether social expectations are indeed involved and when these expectations are established. Unfortunately, the study does not indicate precisely when the infants ceased crying, and what (if anything) they did instead.

C.   From Distress-Relief to Other Contexts

For several reasons, therefore, the distress-relief sequence provides the likeliest context for the infant to learn about the relationship between its behavior and the responses of others. Interestingly, the importance of the distress-relief sequence was recognized by Rousseau (1762) two centuries ago, although recent discussions have emphasized other social—interaction sequences (e.g., Stern, 1977). Like many conditioned associations, the association between distress and its relief by the caretaker may exist without the organism either being aware of it or expecting the caretaker's response. I suggest, however, that some time after the distress-relief associations have been learned, the infant becomes aware of the associations, and thus comes to *expect* a social response to its distress. It is quite likely that the infant does not initially recognize the importance of the exogenous mediation in relieving its distress and producing quiet alertness; this would be consistent with Piaget's (1952, 1954) descriptions of the neonate's egocentric interpretation of events. In fact, theoretical and empirical considerations suggest that awareness of operant contingencies and expectations of environmental responses to individual behavior do not emerge before the second quarter year of life (see below).

Quite possibly, the infant acquires through distress-relief experiences little more than the crudest awareness of the contingent relationship between its own behavior and environmental responses to it. As a result, one should observe evidence of personal effectance before conceptions regarding others' reliability or responsiveness develop. As noted below, the appreciation of control in one context motivates attempts to control other environmental events. Consequently, we would expect infants to start searching for contingencies involving their behavior in other social and nonsocial contexts once expectations have developed out of the distress-relief contingencies. As the infant's capacity to recognize specific adults develops, furthermore, the adults' responsiveness to other signals will surely affect the infant's expectations regarding their behavior. Thus the adult's responsiveness in a variety of contexts is likely to determine the infant's expectations of him/her. However, it may be easier for researchers to study the infant's expectations in distress-relief situations simply because the units of meaningful behavior are clearer here than they are in other social situations (e.g., face-to-face interaction).

Even if I am correct in proposing that social expectations and perceived self-effectance are first developed in the course of the repetitive distress sequences, they are also evident in other social situations from the second quarter year of life. Although more quantification and methodological detail would be desirable, Tronick, Als, Adamson, Wise, and Brazelton (1978) and Fogel, Diamond, Langhorst, and Demos (1979) have described infant responses suggestive of social expectations. These investigators reported that when an adult stared impassively at an infant instead of behaving in his/her typical sociable fashion, the infant appeared surprised. It would be interesting to determine both how early this surprise occurs (since this would suggest that the infant's expectations were violated), and also how early the infant responds to the adult's unresponsiveness with repeated, accentuated, solicitations in an apparent attempt to draw the adult into interaction since this would show the infant behaving intentionally. Expectations and intentions should not develop simultaneously since they involve different cognitive capacities. According to Piaget (1952), infants become able to distinguish between means and ends between 6 and 8 months of age, and this differentiation makes intentional behavior possible. Despite their very different approach, McCall and his colleagues (1979a, 1979b; McCall, Eichorn, & Hogarty, 1977) have also argued that the third quarter-year is when the capacity to discriminate between means and ends emerges.

There is no evidence currently available concerning the first occurrence of intentional social behavior: This constitutes a serious gap in our knowledge of early social development. There are, however, several indications that a change in the nature of adult-infant relations occurs between 6 and 9 months, when the ability to distinguish between means and ends makes it possible for infants to act so as to elicit specific responses from adults. In 1968, Escalona commented on the emergence in the third quarter year of life of persistent efforts to elicit social responses. Sander (1962) defined this as a phase in which active and intentional social bids first occurred, and Sroufe and Wunsch (1972) reported that infants began at this age to laugh in anticipation of the adults' social behavior.

D. Summary

In sum, although the documentation remains disconcertingly poor, we can perceive three major phases in the development of social cognition. In the first quarter year, the infant learns the associations between its own behavior and that of caretaking adults. By the beginning of the second quarter year, it has developed expectations that the adults will respond in predictable ways. In the third quarter year, finally, it begins to behave intentionally -- emitting social bids in order to elicit adult responses. Conceptions of personal effectance require an awareness only *that* environmental consequences to one's actions are predictable; conceptions of others' reliability demand also that one recognize the regular mediation of specific people and so are unlikely to occur until a little later. I have argued that conceptions of personal effectance and the earliest social expectations develop out of the interactions centered around the distress-relief sequence, but these expectations may provide "hypotheses" which babies then test in social interactions that do not involve cries and adults' responses to them. Thus we see social expectations emerging in various social contexts such as face-to-face interaction. If intentional behavior does not emerge until social expectations have been established for several months in various social contexts, then I would expect intentional cries to emerge at roughly the same time as intentional behavior in other (non-distress) social contexts.

V. AFFECTIVE CONSEQUENCES OF SOCIAL EXPECTATIONS

Having developed expectations regarding predictable responses to its behaviors, the infant proceeds to two crucial conclusions: about itself and about its caretakers. About itself, it develops an elementary and fundamental self concept—a conception of itself as a competent or effective organism that has some control over its environment. About its caretakers, it develops conceptions of their reliability and predictability: conceptions that underlie a basic sense of trust in or mistrust of others. Let me consider each of these concepts in turn.

A.   Perceived Effectance and Effectance Motivation

During the last dozen years, several psychologists have discussed the developmental significance of experience with contingent or controllable stimulation (e.g., Abramson, Seligman, & Teasdale, 1978; Lewis & Goldberg, 1969; Watson, 1979; Seligman, 1975; Suomi, 1981; Lamb, 1981). There is a remarkable consensus that experience with contingent stimulation leads infants to develop a conception of their control over the environment, and that this in turn has motivational consequences—leading to further efforts to master or exert control over the environment. Exactly why the perception of contingency should be motivating is less often discussed. White (1959), in his seminal review, argued that humans found perceived control inherently rewarding, and Watson (1979) likewise implied that the perception of contingency is rewarding. Skinner (1953) proposed that organisms found it inherently rewarding to receive environmental feedback and "make the world behave." Thus in Papoušek's (Papoušek & Papoušek, 1975) investigations, infants were observed to continue their operant responding even though they were already sated and rejected the milk "reward."

Rotter (1954, 1966) was one of the first contemporary psychologists to discuss the motivational consequences of perceived control, which he viewed as a joint consequence of 1) the effectiveness of the operant in securing reinforcement and 2) the value of the reinforcement to the individual. Seligman and his colleagues (Seligman, Maier, & Solomon, 1971) showed that after brief experience with uncontrollable punishment, animals ceased *attempting* to control the punishment—failing to avoid it even when that was possible. This is referred to as learned helplessness—a condition whose negative motivational implications are (presumably) analogous to the positive motivating consequences of experience with contingent (controllable) events. Seligman (1975) later proposed that prolonged exposure to noncontingent stimulation in infancy and early childhood would have serious developmental consequences, impairing the ability to recognize contingencies, and making the child less motivated to initiate behavior and engage in activities that might lead to the discovery of new contingencies between its own behavior and environmental consequences.

An early study on the effects of experience with predictable social stimuli was reported by Lewis and Goldberg (1969) who found that the more responsive mothers were to the vocalizations and cries of their three-month-old infants, the more rapidly the infants learned in an habituation task. A recent intervention study by Riksen-Walraven (1978) confirmed the importance of parental responsiveness for the development of effectance ("self-efficacy"). Pretest data revealed significant correlations between a measure of parental responsiveness and two measures of the infant's exploratory behavior at nine months. Further, Riksen-Walraven found that the infants who reached the criterion for contingency learning had more responsive caretakers than those who did not. A three-month long intervention designed to increase the parents' responsiveness significantly improved both exploratory behavior and contingency learning, whereas a program that just affected the *amount* of parental stimulation did not influence either. In other words, the responsiveness of the parent affected the infants' behavior, apparently via an effect on the infants' effectance motivation.

Although his studies concern control over nonsocial contingencies, the research conducted by Watson and his colleagues is pertinent to this discussion (Watson, 1966, 1971, 1979; Watson & Ramey, 1972). As one would predict from the brief review provided earlier, Watson found that four-month-olds readily learned to perform operant responses (leg movements) associated with interesting consequences (movements of a mobile). More impressive is that fact that the infants appeared to enjoy controlling the environmental events: They smiled more when they controlled the movement of mobiles over their cribs than they did when the mobiles' movements occurred spontaneously and unpredictably (i.e., not under their control). Experience with contingency made infants more attentive and responsive in other learning situations (Watson, 1966). These findings suggested that four-month-olds can become aware of the contingencies between the mobiles' movements and their own actions and that infants enjoy their potency or control. In one study, Watson (1972) reported that the enjoyment of control was evident in infants as young as two months of age.

That infants develop a sense of perceived effectance from their experiences with controllable stimulation is suggested by several recent studies. Finkelstein and Ramey (1977) showed that 6- to 10-month-old infants who had experience with response-contingent (i.e., controllable) stimulation learned new operant responses more rapidly than infants who did not have this prior experience. Later, Ramey and Finkelstein (1978) showed that this was also true of three-month-olds. Unexpectedly, however, Ramey and Finkelstein (1978) found that prior experience with noncontingent stimulation also facilitated the infants' learning, suggesting that prior experiences of control over stimulation did not affect later acquisition in three-month-olds. Watson (1979) similarly reported that reliable generalization was not obtained with infants younger than four months of age. Papoušek (1961) found that operant learning became robust in the third month of life, but he was concerned only with conditionability, not with the infant's perception of effectance, which is likely to occur later in development.

The fourth month thus seems to mark a turning point not in conditionability, but in the infant's understanding of the conditioning experience and its awareness of its potency over the environment. When younger infants appear to recognize control (e.g., Watson, 1972) it may be situationally-bound: the infants enjoy control of a specific environmental event (e.g., the movements of a mobile) but do not generalize the perception of control to other contexts. The generalized notion, which constitutes the perception of personal effectance, is not evident before the second quarter year of life. This transition is appropriately coincident with the beginning of the stage of secondary circular reactions in Piaget's (1954) ontogenetic scheme—a stage marked by the emergent capacity to repeat activities in order to recreate interesting events in the environment. Unfortunately, both the theoretical predictions and the empirical evidence concern infant control over nonsocial stimuli: we can only surmise that infants become aware of their control over social stimuli at about the same age. Gekoski's data, however, suggest that at least some infants may develop social expectations substantially earlier than this (Gekoski, 1974). We do not know whether expectations about people in general and expectations about specific individuals develop simultaneously or asynchronously.

B. Interpersonal Trust

Aside from a wealth of clinical reports (e.g., Erikson, 1950), evidence that trust in the caretaker develops as a consequence of the caretaker's consistent responsiveness is available only from Ainsworth's longitudinal study (Ainsworth, Bell, & Stayton, 1974; Ainsworth, Blehar, Waters, & Wall, 1978). In this study, Ainsworth related information about early maternal responsiveness to the infants' behavior in the standardized "Strange Situation" around one year of age. This procedure was designed to observe how infants organize their attachment behaviors around attachment figures when distressed. Special emphasis was placed on the infant's behavior upon reunion with the adult from whom it had been separated briefly. Most infants attempted to interact with the adult upon reunion; usually they approached and sought contact with the adult, although some were content to interact at a distance. These infants, deemed "securely attached" by Ainsworth, were those whose mothers were promptly and appropriately responsive from early in the infants' lives. Other infants responded to reunion by avoiding, rather than seeking, interaction; they looked or moved away, turned their backs, and/or ignored the adults' solicitations. These "avoidant" infants had mothers who were earlier deemed insensitive; not only did they fail to respond more frequently than the mothers of the secure infants, but when they did respond, they often behaved negatively. They displayed, and admitted, aversion to physical contact with their infants, and so their attempts at soothing were abbreviated and inept. A third group of ("resistant") infants mingled proximity/contact seeking bids with angry rejecting behavior; their mothers, in turn, had been inconsistently and unpredictably responsive in earlier interactions.

Since the Strange Situation procedure was described (Ainsworth & Wittig, 1969) it has been studied quite extensively. Two findings are especially pertinent here. First, barring the environmental and social instability that appears to occur quite frequently (Thompson, Lamb & Estes, in preparation, Vaughn, Egeland, Sroufe, & Waters 1979), there appears to be remarkable stability over time in the way infants behave toward specific attachment figures in the Strange Situation (Connell, 1976; Waters, 1978). Second, the patterns of behavior are specific to the individual: When the same infants are observed with different attachment figures, their behavior often differs (Lamb, 1978). Presumably, the way the infant behaves toward any attachment figure depends on the way that person has behaved toward the infant.

As Ainsworth (1977) has hinted, one can view infant behavior in the Strange Situation as a manifestation of the infant's implicit expectations about the adult's behavior. The securely attached infant, for example, can explore away from the adult and actively seeks interaction upon reunion, presumably because it trusts or expects that the adult will be accessible and appropriately responsive. These expectations are reasonable and likely consequences of the adult's earlier behavior. By contrast, the avoidant baby expects the adult to respond aversively and so seeks to avoid interaction. The angry/resistant infant is uncertain about the adult's likely behavior because of the adult's earlier inconsistency.

The distinction between the two patterns of insecure attachment is crucial. Avoidant infants apparently have parents who are *predictably aversive,* whereas the angry/resistant infants have parents whose behavior is unpredictable. Following the line of reasoning outlined in this chapter, one would expect the avoidant infants to have higher perceived effectance than the angry-resistant infants. However, since the mothers of avoidant infants respond to them less predictably (i.e., are less contingently responsive) than the mothers of securely-attached infants, their infants should have lower perceived effectance than the securely attached infants. This underscores the importance of distinguishing between these two patterns of insecure attachment: While both avoidant and rejecting infants lack trust in their attachment figures, avoidant infants have developed some notion of their own effectance, while rejecting infants lack perceived effectance as well as trust.

The suggestion that the adult's pattern of response to the infant's early signals predicts the infant's later behavior in the Strange Situation confirms that the infant's expectations are involved. Unfortunately, it is not clear that the adult's responsiveness to distress cues is crucial, both because adults who are responsive to cries tend to be responsive to other cues as well and because the Strange Situation assessment occurs many months after the earliest expectations are developed. In order to assess the importance of adult responsiveness in the distress-relief sequence, one would need to assess individual differences in infant's expectations in the second quarter year of life, rather than at the end of the first year. It would also be revealing to determine, in a longitudinal study, how much and why these early expectations change over time, or whether the adult's later behavior simply reinforces the expectations established early in the infant's life. Certainly, responsiveness to distress is not necessarily involved in establishing expectations of specific people, since infants develop distinctive patterns of behavior with their fathers (Lamb, 1978) even when the fathers seldom participate in distress-relief sequences.

There are other reasons for caution before accepting this interpretation. First, evidence concerning the relationship between early maternal behavior and later infant behavior in the Strange Situation comes from one intensive but small longitudinal study with only 23 subjects (Ainsworth et al., 1974). Second, the patterns of behavior observed in the Strange Situation do not always correspond to contemporaneous behavior at home: Indeed, infants sometimes behave very differently in the two situations (Ainsworth et al., 1972). If enduring, transsituational expectations regarding an individual are involved, infants should not behave differently in familiar and unfamiliar environs. However, if the adults' behavior differed predictably in different contexts, one would expect infants to develop situation-specific expectations. Evidently, there is a need for considerably more research in this area.

VI.   PREDICTIVE VALIDITY
OF STRANGE SITUATION BEHAVIOR

Thus far, the Strange Situation has been used as a means of exploring individual differences in infant-parent relationships and in the infants' concepts regarding the adults' reliability and predictability (i.e., trust). Researchers have not focused explicitly on perceived effectance. However, since infants' conceptions of others (trust) and of self (perceived effectance) are in part consequences of similar infant-parent interactions, it should be possible to score the infant's behavior in the Strange Situation (e.g., attempts to explore or master the environment) in such a way as to examine individual differences in behavior relevant to perceived effectance. The two dimensions (trust and perceived effectance) should be highly correlated for securely-attached and resistant infants but not for avoidant infants. Indeed, when exploring the predictive validity of behavior in the Strange Situation, researchers have recorded later behaviors that seem related to the perceived effectance dimension as well as behaviors indicating a generalization of conceptions about trustworthiness to people other than caretakers.

As far as the generalization of conceptions regarding people's trustworthiness is concerned, the evidence is substantial. Main (1973) reported that securely-attached one-year-olds were more cooperative with an adult playmate and a Bayley tester 8½ months later than were avoidant or angry/resistant infants who were, respectively, avoidant and resistant with the unfamiliar adults. Thompson and Lamb (in preparation) found the greatest sociability among 12- and 19-month-olds who fell in one of the secure attachment subgroups, and the least sociability among those who were characteristically avoidant or resistant. Lieberman (1977), Waters, Wippman, and Sroufe (1979), and Pastor (1980) found that securely-attached children were more socially competent in interaction with preschool-aged peers; Easterbrooks and Lamb (1979) found that individual differences within the secure attachment category were related to differences in initial sociability with infant peers.

As for evidence of individual differences in perceived effectance, the case is less clear because the construct has seldom been the explicit focus of research. Matas, Arend, and Sroufe (1978) reported that securely-attached infants were later more persistent, self-reliant, and enthusiastic in problem-solving situations than insecurely-attached infants were, but the differences were not impressive, perhaps because the researchers failed to distinguish between the two groups of insecurely-attached infants. Standardized measures and systematic ratings (Block & Block, 1980) by observers familiar with the children indicated that securely-attached infants displayed greater ego-resiliency and ego control as preschoolers (Arend, Gove, & Sroufe, 1980). Again, however, the two groups of insecurely-attached infants were not distinguished, and the constructs investigated seem related to both trust and perceived effectance. Less ambiguous was a recent report by Tracy, Farish, and Bretherton (1980) who found no differences in exploratory behavior between avoidant and securely-attached infants, although both groups were distinguished from the angry-resistant infants. Harmon and his colleagues (1979) reported that avoidant infants scored as highly on measures of mastery motivation and exploration as securely-attached infants, although the avoidant infants performed more poorly on the Bayley scales. (Harmon et al. did not use the Strange Situation procedure to classify infants, however.)

Although the studies by Watson, Ramey, and their collaborators involved "perceived effectance" as developed in brief training sessions rather than over months of social interaction, they did confirm that experience with predictability or control became translated into a generalized conception of individual effectance. An extensive body of research and speculation concerning effectance motivation, learned helplessness, and locus of control attests to the developmental significance of this construct (Dweck, 1978; Harter, 1978; Lefcourt, 1976; Phares, 1976; Seligman, 1975)—a construct which I believe has its roots in the early interactions between infants and caretakers.

VII. A RESEARCH AGENDA

The interpretation of early social development presented here demands that students of infant social development pay much greater attention to research on infant learning and cognitive development than has traditionally been the case. It implies that the artificial distinctions between aspects of social, cognitive, perceptual, memorial, and psychophysiological development must be set aside (see also Lamb & Sherrod, 1981; Schaffer, 1979). Quite apart from the heuristic significance of this synthesis, the specific speculations presented here raise several questions for future investigations.

First, experimental and naturalistic observational research is needed to determine both how early infant social expectations are evident and whether these are evident in distress-relief contexts earlier than in other social interactions. It is also important to determine whether there are individual differences in the onset and nature of these expectations and whether these are lawfully related to variations in the caretakers' behavior. Other research is needed to determine whether individual differences in caretakers' response patterns predict individual differences in infants' perceived effectance and related constructs such as conditionability.

A component analysis of the prerequisites for the development of social expectations and intentions (see Sections II, III, IV-C, IV-D) suggests that there should be an orderly ontogenetic sequence of the following sort. First, infants might enjoy control in specific, narrowly defined contexts, beginning as early as the first quarter year of life. Second, between 3 and 6 months, there should be evidence of generalization of this awareness, as a conception of personal effectance is established. Third, again in the second quarter year of life, recognition of specific people should permit the development of trust in these individuals. Finally, this trust should be generalized to other people, probably between 8 and 12 months of age. There is little evidence concerning this developmental sequence, and careful research efforts are needed.

Certain of the questions raised by the interpretations offered in this chapter cannot ethically be answered by research on human parents and infants, but experimental research using animal models would be revealing. One basic question concerns the long-term significance of the infant's earliest social and personal concepts. Are they both equivalently resistant to modification unless the adult's behavior changes markedly and dramatically? Vaughn et al.'s (1980) and Thompson et al.'s (in preparation) data are relevant here: When the stressfulness of the mothers' circumstances changed or there were changes in caretaking arrangements, the quality of the infant-mother attachment, as assessed in the Strange Situation, tended to change accordingly. Another question concerns the differential origins of perceived effectance and trust. When the infant consistently elicits mildly aversive or hedonically neutral responses, would one find high perceived effectance and mistrustful (avoidant) social concepts—thus demonstrating that there are indeed two constructs involved, even though they are frequently confused in many naturally occurring circumstances? Experimental research of this nature would advance our understanding of the difference between the avoidant and resistant infants.

Finally, considerable research is needed on the generalization of these concepts. As already noted, infants develop specific expectations of each of their attachment figures, but there has been little research on the manner in which distinctive expectations regarding two or more attachment figures combine to yield a generalized trust or mistrust in others, and how the perceived effectance would differ if the infant had one secure and one insecure attachment for example, rather than two secure relationships. Would an additive or multiplicative process be involved, or would the relationship with the primary attachment figure dominate? These are some of the questions that have yet to be explored in research on the origins of expectations about self and others.

ACKNOWLEDGEMENT

I am grateful to Robert N. Emde, Lewis P. Lipsitt, Ann D. Murray, and Carolyn Rovee-Collier for their comments on earlier drafts of this chapter.

REFERENCES

Abramson, L. Y., Seligman, M. E. P., & Teasdale, J. D. Learned helplessness in humans: Critique and reformulation. *Journal of Abnormal Psychology,* 1978, **87,** 49–74.

Ainsworth, M. D. S. Affective aspects of the attachment of infant to mother: Individual differences and their correlates in maternal behavior. Paper presented to the American Association for the Advancement of Science, Washington, D.C., February 1977.

Ainsworth, M. D. S., Bell, S. M., & Stayton, D. J. Individual differences in the development of some attachment behaviors. *Merrill-Palmer Quarterly,* 1972, **18,** 123–143.

Ainsworth, M. D. S., Bell, S. M., & Stayton, D. J. Infant mother attachment and social development: 'Socialization' as a product of reciprocal responsiveness to signals. In M. P. M. Richards (Ed.), *The integration of a child into a social world.* Cambridge, England: Cambridge University Press, 1974.

Ainsworth, M. D. S., Blehar, M., Waters, E., & Wall, S. N. *Patterns of attachment.* Hillsdale, N.J.: Lawrence Erlbaum Associates, 1978.

Ainsworth, M. D. S. & Wittig, B. A. Attachment and exploratory behavior of one-year-olds in a strange situation. In B. M. Foss (Ed.), *Determinants of infant behavior IV.* London: Methuen, 1969.

Als, H., Tronick, E., & Brazelton, T. B. Analyses of face-to-face interaction in infant-adult dyads. In M. E. Lamb, S. J. Suomi, & G. R. Stephenson (Eds.), *Social interaction analysis: Methodological issues.* Madison: University of Wisconsin Press, 1979.

Arend, R., Gove, F. L., & Sroufe, L. A. Continuity of individual adaptation from infancy to kindergarten: A predictive study of ego-resiliency and curiosity in preschoolers. *Child Development,* 1979, **50,** 950–959.

Aronson, E. & Rosenbloom, S. Space perception in early infancy: Perception within a common auditory-visual space. *Science,* 1971, **172,** 1161–1163.

Bell, S. M. & Ainsworth, M. D. S. Infant crying and maternal responsiveness. *Child Development,* 1972, **43,** 1171–1190.

Berg, W. K. & Berg, K. M. Psychophysiological development in infancy: State, sensory function, and attention. In J. D. Osofsky (Ed.), *Handbook of infant development.* New York: Wiley, 1979.

Bigelow, A. Infants' recognition of mother. Paper presented to the Society for Research in Child Development, New Orleans, March 1977.

Bijou, S. & Baer, D. M. *Child Development* (Vol. 2). New York: Appleton-Century-Crofts, 1965.

Block, J. H. & Block, J. The role of ego-control and ego-resiliency in the organization of behavior. In W. A. Collins (Ed.), *Minnesota symposia on child psychology* (Vol. 11). Hillsdale, N. J.: Lawrence Erlbaum Associates, 1980.

Bornstein, M. H. Perceptual development: Stability and change in feature perception. In M. H. Bornstein & W. Kessen (Eds.), *Psychological development from infancy.* Hillsdale, N.J.: Lawrence Erlbaum Associates, 1979.

Brazelton, T. B. Implications of infant development among the Mayan Indians of Mexico. In P. H. Leiderman, S. R. Tulkin, & A. Rosenfeld (Eds.), *Culture and infancy.* New York: Academic, 1977.

Brazelton, T. B. Implications of infant development among the Mayan Indians of Mexico. In P. H. Leiderman, S. R. Tulkin, & A. Rosenfeld (Eds.), *Culture and infancy.* New York: Academic, 1977.

Brown, C. J. Reactions of infants to their parents' voices. *Infant Behavior and Development,* 1979, **2,** 295–300.

Carpenter, G. C. Mother-stranger discrimination in the early weeks of life. Paper presented to the Society for Research in Child Development, Philadelphia, March 1973.

Carpenter, G. C. Visual regard of moving and stationary faces in early infancy. *Merrill-Palmer Quarterly,* 1974, **20,** 181–194.

Cohen, L. B. & Salapatek, P. (Eds.) *Infant perception: From sensation to cognition* (Vols. I and II). New York: Academic, 1975(a) and (b).

Connell, D. B. *Individual differences in attachment behavior.* Unpublished doctoral dissertation, Syracuse University, 1976.

Davis, J. & Rovee-Collier, C. K. A conditioning analysis of infant long-term memory. Paper presented to the Eastern Psychological Association, Philadelphia, April 1979.

DeCasper, A. J. & Fifer, W. P. Of human bonding: Newborns prefer their mothers' voices. *Science,* 1980, **208,** 1174–1176.

Dweck, C. S. Achievement. In M. E. Lamb (Ed.), *Social and personality development.* New York: Holt, Rinehart & Winston, 1978.

Easterbrooks, M. A. & Lamb, M. E. The relationship between quality of infant-mother attachment and infant competence in initial encounters with peers. *Child Development,* 1979, **50,** 380–387.

Eisenberg, R. B. *Auditory competence in early life: The roots of communicative behavior.* Baltimore: University Park Press, 1976.

Eisenberg, R. B. Stimulus significance as a determinant of infant responses to sound. In E. B. Thoman (Ed.), *Origins of infant social responsiveness.* Hillsdale, N.J.: Lawrence Erlbaum Associates, 1979.

Emde, R. N. & Robinson, J. The first two months: Recent research in developmental psychobiology and the changing view of the newborn. In J. Noshpitz & J. Call (Eds.), *Basic handbook of child psychiatry.* New York: Basic, 1979.

Escalona, S. K. *The roots of individuality: Normal patterns of development in infancy.* Chicago: Aldine, 1968.

Fagen, J. W., Rovee, C. K., & Kaplan, M. E. Psychophysical scaling of stimulus similarity in 3-month-old infants and adults. *Journal of Experimental Child Psychology,* 1976, **22,** 272–281.

Finkelstein, N. W. & Ramey, C. T. Learning to control the environment in infancy. *Child Development,* 1977, **48,** 806–819.

Fogel, A., Diamond, G. R., Langhorst, B. H., & Demos, V. Alteration of infant behavior as a result of "still-face" perturbation of maternal behavior. Paper presented to the Society for Research in Child Development, San Francisco, April 1979.

Frodi, A. M., Lamb, M. E., Leavitt, L. A., & Donovan, W. L. Fathers' and mothers' responses to infant smiles and cries. *Infant Behavior and Development,* 1978, **1,** 181–198.

Frodi, A. M., Lamb, M. E., Leavitt, L. A., Donovan, W. L., Neff, C., & Sherry, D. Fathers' and mothers' responses to the faces and cries of normal and premature infants. *Developmental Psychology,* 1978, **14,** 490–498.

Garcia, J., McGowan, B. K., & Green, K. F. Biological constraints on conditioning. In M. E. P. Seligman & J. L. Hagen (Eds.), *Biological boundaries of learning.* New York: Academic, 1972.

Gekoski, M. *Changes in infant quieting to mother or stranger over the first six months.* Unpublished masters thesis, Rutgers University, 1974.

Goldberg, S. Infant care and growth in urban Zambia. *Human Development,* 1972, **15,** 77–89.

Goldberg, S. Infant development and mother-infant interaction in urban Zambia. In P. H. Leiderman, S. R. Tulkin, & A. Rosenfeld (Eds.), *Culture and infancy.* New York: Academic, 1977.

Haith, M. Visual competence in early infancy. In R. Held, H. Leibowitz, & H. L. Teuber (Eds.), *Handbook of sensory physiology* VIII. Berlin: Springer-Verlag, 1978.

Haith, M. M., Bergman, T., & Moore, M. J. Eye contact and face scanning in early infancy. *Science,* 1977, **198,** 853–855.

Harmon, R. J., Suwalsky, J. D., & Klein, R. P. Infants' preferential response for mother versus an unfamiliar adult. *Journal of the American Academy of Child Psychiatry,* 1979, **18,** 437–449.

Harter, S. Effectance motivation reconsidered: Toward a developmental model. *Human Development,* 1978, **21,** 34–64.

Hinde, R. A. & Stevenson-Hinde, J. (Eds.), *Constraints on learning: Limitations and predispositions.* New York: Academic, 1973.

Konner, M. J. Aspects of the developmental ethology of a foraging people. In N. G. Blurton Jones (Ed.), *Ethological studies of child behavior.* Cambridge, England: Cambridge University Press, 1972.

Konner, M. J. Infancy among the Kalahari desert San. In P. H. Leiderman, S. R. Tulkin, & A. Rosenfeld (Eds.) *Culture and infancy.* New York: Academic, 1977.

Korner, A. F. & Grobstein, R. Visual alertness as related to soothing in neonates: Implications for maternal stimulation and early deprivation. *Child Development,* 1966, **37**, 867–876.

Korner, A. F. & Thoman, E. B. Visual alertness in neonates as evoked by maternal care. *Journal of Experimental Child Psychology,* 1970, **10**, 67–78.

Korner, A. F. & Thoman, E. B. The relative efficacy of contact and vestibular-proprioceptive stimulation in soothing neonates. *Child Development,* 1972, **43**, 443–453.

Lamb, M. E. Qualitative aspects of mother- and father-infant attachments. *Infant Behavior and Development,* 1978, **1**, 265–276.

Lamb, M. E. The development of social expectations in the first year of life. In M. E. Lamb & L. R. Sherrod (Eds.), *Infant social cognition: Empirical and theoretical considerations.* Hillsdale, N.J.: Lawrence Erlbaum Associates, 1981.

Lamb, M. E. & Sherrod, L. R. (Eds.) *Infant social cognition: Empirical and theoretical considerations.* Hillsdale, N.J.: Lawrence Erlbaum Associates, 1981.

Lefcourt, H. *Locus of control: Current trends in theory and research.* Hillsdale, N.J.: Lawrence Erlbaum Associates, 1976.

Lewis, M. & Goldberg, S. Perceptual-cognitive development in infancy: A generalized expectancy model as a function of the mother-infant interaction. *Merrill-Palmer Quarterly,* 1969, **15**, 81–100.

Lieberman, A. F. Preschoolers' competence with a peer: Relations with attachment and peer experience. *Child Development,* 1977, **48**, 1277–1287.

Lipsitt, L. P., Kaye, H., & Bosack, T. N. Enhancement of neonatal sucking through reinforcement. *Journal of Experimental Child Psychology,* 1966, **4**, 163–168.

Little, A. H. *A comparative study of trace and delay conditioning in the human infant.* Unpublished doctoral dissertation, Brown University, 1973.

Macfarlane, A. *The psychology of childbirth.* Cambridge, Mass.: Harvard University Press, 1975.

Main, M. *Exploration, play and cognitive functioning as related to child-mother attachment.* Unpublished doctoral dissertation, Johns Hopkins University, 1973.

Marquis, D. P. Can conditioned reflexes be established in the newborn infant? *Journal of Genetic Psychology,* 1931, **39**, 479–492.

Matas, L., Arend, R. A., & Sroufe, L. A. Continuity of adaptation in the second year: The relationship between quality of attachment and later competence. *Child Development,* 1978, **49**, 547–556.

Maurer, D. & Salapatek, P. Developmental changes in the scanning of faces by young infants. *Child Development,* 1976, **47**, 523–527.

McCall, R. B. The development of intellectual functioning in infancy and the prediction of later IQ. In J. D. Osofsky (Ed.), *Handbook of infant development.* New York: Wiley, 1979. (a)

McCall, R. B. Qualitative transitions in behavioral development in the first three years of life. In M. H. Bornstein & W. Kessen (Eds.), *Psychological development from infancy.* Hillsdale, N.J.: Lawrence Erlbaum Associates, 1979. (b)

McCall, R. B., Eichorn, D. H., & Hogarty, P. S. Transitions in early mental development. *Monographs of the Society for Research in Child Development,* 1977, **42**, whole number 171.

McGurk, H. & Lewis, M. Space perception in early infancy: Perception within a common auditory-visual space? *Science,* 1974, **186**, 649–650.

Mills, M. & Melhuish, E. Recognition of mother's voice in early infancy. *Nature,* 1974, **252**, 123–124.

Moss, H. A. Sex, age and state as determinants of mother-infant interaction. *Merrill-Palmer Quarterly,* 1967, **13**, 19–36.

Murray, A. D. Infant crying as an elicitor of parental behavior: An examination of two models. *Psychological Bulletin,* 1979, **86**, 191–215.

Olson, G. M. The recognition of specific persons. In M. E. Lamb & L. R. Sherrod (Eds.), *Infant social cognition: Empirical and theoretical considerations.* Hillsdale, N.J.: Lawrence Erlbaum Associates, 1981.

Papoušek, H. Conditioned head rotation reflexes in infants in the first months of life. *Acta Paediatrica,* 1961, **50,** 565–576.

Papoušek, H. & Bernstein, P. The functions of conditioning stimulation in human neonates and infants. In A. Ambrose (Ed.), *Stimulation in early infancy.* London: Academic, 1969.

Papoušek, H. & Papoušek, M. Cognitive aspects of preverbal social interactions between human infants and adults. In *Parent-infant interaction.* Amsterdam: Elsevier, 1975.

Pastor, D. L. The quality of mother-infant attachment and its relationship to toddlers' initial sociability with peers. Paper presented at the International Conference on Infant Studies, New Haven, April 1980.

Phares, E. J. *Locus of control in personality.* Morristown, N.J.: General Learning Press, 1976.

Piaget, J. *The origins of intelligence in children* (1936). New York: International Universities Press, 1952.

Piaget, J. *The construction of reality in the child* (1937). New York: Basic, 1954.

Ramey, C. T. & Finkelstein, N. W. Contingent stimulation and infant competence. *Journal of Pediatric Psychology,* 1978, **3,** 89–96.

Riksen-Walraven, M. J. Effects of caregiver behavior on habituation rate and self-efficacy in infants. *International Journal of Behavioral Development,* 1978, **1,** 105–130.

Rotter, J. B. *Social learning and clinical psychology.* Englewood Cliffs, N.J.: Prentice-Hall, 1954.

Rotter, J. B. Generalized expectancies for internal vs. external control of reinforcement. *Psychological Monographs,* 1976, **80,** whole number 609.

Rousseau, J.-J. *Emile* (1762). London: Dent, 1911.

Rovee, C. K. & Fagen, J. W. Extended conditioning and 24-hour retention in infants. *Journal of Experimental Child Psychology,* 1976, **21,** 1–11.

Rovee-Collier, C. K. & Gekoski, M. J. The economics of infancy: A review of conjugate reinforcement. In H. W. Reese & L. P. Lipsitt (Eds.), *Advances in child development and behavior* (Vol. 13). New York: Academic, 1979.

Rovee-Collier, C. K. & Lipsitt, L. P. Learning, adaptation, and memory. In P. M. Stratton (Ed.), *Psychobiology of the human newborn.* New York: Wiley, 1981.

Rovee-Collier, C. K., Sullivan, M. W., Enright, M., Lucas, D., & Fagen, J. W. Reactivation of infant memory. *Science,* 1980, **208,** 1159–1161.

Rudy, J. W. & Cheatle, M. D. Odor-aversion learning in neonatal rats. *Science,* 1977, **198,** 845–846.

Sameroff, A. J. Can conditioned responses be established in the newborn infant: 1971? *Developmental Psychology,* 1971, **5,** 1–12.

Sameroff, A. J. & Cavanaugh, P. Learning in infancy: A developmental perspective. In J. D. Osofsky (Ed.), *Handbook of infant development.* New York: Wiley, 1979.

Sander, L. J. Issues in early mother-child interaction. *Journal of the American Academy of Child Psychiatry,* 1962, **1,** 141–166.

Schaffer, H. R. Acquiring the concept of the dialogue. In M. H. Bornstein & W. Kessen (Eds.), *Psychological development from infancy.* Hillsdale, N.J.: Lawrence Erlbaum Associates, 1979.

Seligman, M. E. P. On the generality of the laws of learning. *Psychological Review,* 1970, **77,** 406–418.

Seligman, M. E. P. *Helplessness.* San Francisco: Freeman, 1975.

Seligman, M. E. P., Maier, S., & Solomon, R. Unpredictable and uncontrollable aversive events. In F. R. Brush (Ed.), *Aversive conditioning and learning.* New York: Academic, 1971.

Sherrod, L. R. Social cognition in infants: Attention to the human face. *Infant Behavior and Development,* 1979, **2,** 279–294.

Sherrod, L. R. Issues in cognitive and perceptual development: The special case of social stimuli. In M. E. Lamb & L. R. Sherrod (Eds.), *Infant social cognition: Empirical and theoretical considerations.* Hillsdale, N.J.: Lawrence Erlbaum Associates, 1981.

Skinner, B. F. On the rate of formation of a conditioned reflex. *Journal of General Psychology,* 1932, **7,** 274–286.

Skinner, B. F. *Science and human behavior.* New York: Macmillan, 1953.

Smith, G. J. & Spear, N. E. Effects of the home environment on withholding behaviors and conditioning in infant and neonatal rats. *Science,* 1978, **202,** 327–329.

Spelke, E. S. & Cortelyou, A. Perceptual aspects of social knowing: Looking and listening in infancy. In M. E. Lamb & L. R. Sherrod (Eds.), *Infant social cognition: Empirical and theoretical considerations.* Hillsdale, N.J.: Lawrence Erlbaum Associates, 1981.

Spelke, E. S. & Owsley, C. J. Intermodal exploration and knowledge in infancy. *Infant Behavior and Development,* 1979, **2,** 13–27.

Sroufe, L. A. & Wunsch, J. The development of laughter in the first year of life. *Child Development,* 1972, **43,** 1326–1344.

Stern, D. *The first relationship.* Cambridge, Mass.: Harvard University Press, 1977.

Strain, B. & Vietze, P. M. Early dialogues: The structure of reciprocal infant-mother vocalization. Paper presented to the Society for Research in Child Development, Denver, March 1975.

Sullivan, M. W., Rovee-Collier, C. K., & Tynes, D. M. A conditioning analysis of infant long-term memory. *Child Development,* 1979, **50,** 152–162.

Suomi, S. J. Contingency, perception, and social development. In M. E. Lamb & L. R. Sherrod (Eds.), *Infant social cognition: Empirical and theoretical considerations.* Hillsdale, N.J.: Lawrence Erlbaum Associates, 1981.

Thoman, E. B., Korner, A. F., & Beason-Williams, L. Modification of responsiveness to maternal vocalization in the neonate. *Child Development,* 1977, **48,** 563–569.

Thompson, R. A., & Lamb, M. E. Quality of attachment and stranger sociability in infancy. Manuscript in preparation.

Thompson, R. A., Lamb, M. E., & Estes, D. Stability of infant-mother attachment and its relationship to changing life circumstances in an unselected middle class sample. Manuscript in preparation.

Tracy, R. L., Farish, G. D., & Bretherton, I. Exploration as related to infant-mother attachment in one-year-olds. Paper presented to the International Conference on Infant Studies, New Haven, Conn., April 1980.

Tronick, E., Als, H., Adamson, L., Wise, S., & Brazelton, T. B. The infant's response to entrapment between contradictory messages in face-to-face interaction. *Journal of the American Academy of Child Psychiatry,* 1978, **17,** 1–13.

Vaughn, B., Egeland, B., Sroufe, L. A., & Waters, E. Individual differences in infant-mother attachment at twelve and eighteen months: Stability and change in families under stress. *Child Development,* 1979, **50,** 971–975.

Vietze, P., Strain, B., & Falsey, S. Contingent responsiveness between mother and infant: Who's reinforcing whom? Paper presented to the Society for Research in Child Development, Denver, March 1975.

Waters, E. The reliability and stability of individual differences in infant-mother attachment. *Child Development,* 1978, **49,** 483–494.

Waters, E., Wippman, J., & Sroufe, L. A. Attachment, positive affect, and competence in the peer group: Two studies in construct validation. *Child Development,* 1979, **50,** 821–829.

Watson, J. S. The development and generalization of contingency awareness in early infancy: Some hypotheses. *Merrill-Palmer Quarterly,* 1966, **12,** 123–135.

Watson, J. S. Cognitive-perceptual development in infancy: Setting for the seventies. *Merrill-Palmer Quarterly,* 1971, **17,** 139–152.

Watson, J. S. Smiling, cooing, and "The Game". *Merrill-Palmer Quarterly,* 1972, **18,** 323–329.

Watson, J. S. Depression and the perception on control in early childhood. In J. G. Schulterbrandt & A. Raskin (Eds.), *Depression in childhood: Diagnosis, treatment, and conceptual models.* New York: Raven, 1977.

Watson, J. S. Perception of contingency as a determinant of social responsiveness. In E. B. Thoman (Ed.), *Origins of the infant's social responsiveness.* Hillsdale, N.J.: Lawrence Erlbaum Associates, 1979.

Watson, J. S. & Ramey, C. T. Reactions to response-contingent stimulation in early infancy. *Merrill-Palmer Quarterly,* 1972, **18,** 219–227.

White, R. W. Motivation reconsidered: The concept of competence. *Psychological Review,* 1959, **66,** 297–323.

Wolff, P. H. The causes, controls, and organization of behavior in the neonate. *Psychological Issues,* 1966, **5,** 1–105.

DIRECT AND INDIRECT INTERACTIONS
IN SOCIAL RELATIONSHIPS

Michael Lewis and Candice Feiring

EDUCATIONAL TESTING SERVICE

Advances in Infancy
Research, Vol. I

Social knowledge and relationships emerge through the child's experiences with people and objects. How children acquire information and how they form relationships is unclear but is usually studied by focusing on the nature of the child's commerce with its environment. In general, models of social interaction, especially in infancy, have tended to be restricted to what has been called direct forms of experience (Bronfenbrenner, 1976; Lewis &

Weinraub, 1976) wherein the child acquires knowledge and forms relationships through its interactions with other people and objects. At least two reasons appear to explain why emphasis has been placed almost exclusively on direct effects. In regard to the first, the influence of the experimental paradigm can be seen. Because the paradigm is concerned with the issue of causality, it is necessary to find specific and manipulatable factors which affect specific outcomes. This cause and effect model focuses attention on direct interactions. The second reason for the failure to examine less direct forms of interaction is the overconcern for studying the dyadic relationship of infant and mother. By focusing attention solely on the mother-child relationship as the primary cause of social and cognitive development, an error only now being corrected, we not only eliminated significant others from consideration in the child's development, but more to the point, only dyadic interactions were studied. The failure to consider more complex interactions restricted our theoretical scope and the consideration of indirect effects. As Bronfenbrenner states (1976):

> In contrast to the conventional dyadic research model, which is limited to assessing the direct effect of two agents on each other, the design of an ecological experiment must take into account the existence in the setting of systems that include three or more elements and hence permit the indirect influence of any one of these on the direct relations taking place between the others, operating as a subsystem. (p. 178)

Certainly information acquisition and the formation of social relationships requires the interaction of the child with the environment. However, relatively little consideration has been given to the types of processes that do not include direct interaction but which influence the nature and form of immediate or future interactions. Children acquire information in a variety of indirect ways which are not necessarily characterized by immediate interaction with people or objects. For example, in observational or imitational learning the child learns about the environment by watching an interaction of another or others but not through direct interaction with the object(s) or person(s) being observed. Children also learn about the environment in a less focused manner (for example, see Hagan & Hale, 1973, for a discussion of incidental learning).

The failure to consider both direct and indirect effects on the child's acquisition of information and formation of social relationships is further exacerbated by the lack of formulations and methods for examining how these two kinds of effects operate separately or in combination to affect socialization. While it has become increasingly clear that both direct and indirect effects need to be considered, relatively little focus on this problem has occurred (see Bronfenbrenner, 1976; Clarke-Stewart, 1978; Lamb, 1976; Lewis & Feiring, 1978; Lewis & Weinraub, 1976; Parke et al., 1979; for exceptions).

In what is to follow, we wish to demonstrate that information about objects and people can be acquired in two general types of interactions, direct and indirect. These two types of interactions can be characterized by the role occupied by the child in gathering information and affecting the interaction. As we shall see, direct types of interaction involve the child immediately and have the quality of being reciprocal while in the indirect types of interaction the child is equally influenced but has no direct or immediate input into the interactions which affect it. In other words, there are some interactions between others (either persons or objects) which do not involve the child but which have an effect on the child's development; these are called indirect effects. On the other hand, there are interactions which involve the child in dyadic interaction and affect its development and these are called direct effects.

I. THE ROLE OF DIRECT AND INDIRECT EFFECTS

A. Direct Effects

Direct effects have been defined as those interactions which represent the effect or influence of one person on the behaviors of another when both are engaged in mutual interaction (Lewis & Weinraub, 1976). In the study of social behavior, direct effects are usually observed in dyadic interactions but could include more than two people as when a teacher instructs a class of students. Direct effects involve information gathered from participation in an interaction with another person or object and always involve the target person as one of the focused participants in the interaction.

Example 1—Direct Effects

The three-month-old infant sitting facing her mother, vocalizes. The mother smiles and vocalizes back. The infant widens her eyes, smiles, and after a pause coos again. Her mother smiles and vocalizes back.

In this example we can see the direct effect of mother on child as well as child on mother. The child's vocalization, which may be random at first, is responded to contingently by her mother. The responsivity of mother to child directly affects the rate of infant vocalization and before long the infant vocalizes in order to produce the maternal response. Besides the direct reinforcement of the vocalization behavior, the child may have learned a number of different social rules, including that people (at least her mother) are responsive, that she can control her environment (a means and ends rule), and that there is turn-taking in social exchanges. The learning of these things occurs as a direct relationship between the behavior of mother and infant, and the variance to be explained and accounted for can be found in the parameters of each of the participants' behavior.

Historically, direct effects in their simplest form, using the mother-infant interaction data, were represented by the role of the mother's behavior on the infant (M→I). The question usually asked was, for example, what is the effect of the mother's vocalization on the infant's vocalization, either concurrently or at some future time. Brazelton, Koslowski, and Mains (1974), Lewis (1972), Stern (1974), and others, by studying the mother-infant interaction, looked at the effects of mother's behavior on the infant's behavior. Since the interactional model has become more dominant (Lewis & Rosenblum, 1974), it is recognized that the interaction is reciprocal and that both mother and child influence each other (M↔I). Nonetheless, the kinds of effects studied are still direct. For example, Stern (1974) has studied the effects of gaze aversion and found that the gaze aversion of one member of the dyad directly affects the gaze pattern of the other. The same direct effects can be studied with people other than the mother, for example, fathers (Brazelton, Yogman, Als, & Tronick 1979), and siblings (Greenbaum & Landau, 1977).

It is also possible to study the direct effect of an interaction at one point in time and relate it to the child's developmental status at a subsequent point. Thus for example, Freedle and Lewis (1977) looked at the mother-infant vocalization pattern when the infant was 12 weeks of age and related it to the dyad's linguistic patterns when the child was two years old. The finding that prelinguistic turn-taking and conversation openings and closings at 12 weeks, as measured in direct interaction, was related to both child's MLU and mother's question asking when the child was two years old, lends support to the study of direct effects as they influence subsequent development.

Interest and focus on the study of direct effects may be found in the infant learning literature, as well, where the process of information acquisition has received considerable attention. At least four types of learning processes in infants and young children have been studied: classical conditioning (Papousek, 1967), instrumental conditioning (Lipsitt, 1963), contingency or conjugate learning (Lewis & Goldberg, 1969; Rovee-Collier & Gekoski, 1979), and habituation (Lewis, Goldberg & Campbell, 1969). Although there is some question as to the developmental course of these different forms of learning, all have been shown to be effective ways for infants at an early age to acquire information from their direct interactions with their environment. Further discussion on the importance of examining direct effects is not necessary since it is commonly recognized that the role of direct interaction and learning has a significant affect on the child's (and parent's) concurrent and subsequent developmental status. It is to the role of indirect effects that attention should be focused.

B.   Indirect Effects

Indirect effect refers to two classes of events. In the first class, indirect effects are those sets of interactions which affect the target person but which occur in the absence of that person. These sets of interactions affect the target person but may best be described as influences which play their role in development as they affect direct effects (or interactions).

More important for the present discussion is the second class of indirect effects, which refers to interactions among members of the system that occur in the presence of the target person even though the interaction is not directed toward or does not involve that person. These kinds of indirect effects are those effects that are based on information which is gathered from sources other than the direct interaction with another person or object. These effects may be the result of observation of another's interaction with persons or objects or may be the result of information gathered from another about the attitudes, behaviors, traits, or actions of a third person.

In the examples to follow these two classes of indirect effects will be presented. The first class, indirect influences, have been discussed in more detail elsewhere, especially as they refer to the role of the father and are presented only to show the various forms of indirect influence (Lewis, Feiring & Weinraub, in press). They included marital satisfaction, support, and arrangement of the environment. The second class, which have to do with phenomena discussed most often under the rubric of identification, observational-, vicarious-, and incidental-learning, imitation, or modeling, will be presented in more detail since it is toward a general theory of these kinds of indirect effects in combination with the direct effects that we are interested in focusing our attention.

1.   *Indirect Influences*

Example 2—Marital Satisfaction—Self Esteem

A husband and wife have gone to dinner at their favorite Indian restaurant and then to a movie. The husband has been especially attentive to the wife and has spoken to her with pride about the precociousness of their one-year-old child. The following day the mother is especially responsive to the child, praising his attempts to walk, smiling and telling him what a smart boy he is.

In this example, the child is being indirectly affected by the father's behavior. The father, in the child's absence, has made the mother feel good about herself as a wife and as a mother. The mother's good feeling about her competence influences her responsiveness to the child in a positive way, making her more likely to praise the child's attempts to master the environment. The mother praises the child's exercise of motor skills which facilitates the child's ability to contact and explore people and things in the environment. Consequently, the child's development of motor and cognitive skills has been indirectly influenced by the father. The child is not present when the husband praises his wife and compliments her on the development of their child. Neither is the father present and praising the child on the following day. However, the father has an indirect effect on the child's development vis-à-vis his support of the mother and the mother's consequent responsiveness to the child. This influence has been discussed in terms of two parameters: marital satisfaction and self esteem. From a marital satisfaction point of view, the parent (either one) will be capable of better parenting if certain other needs are met, in particular, if their adult social relations are satisfactory. The praise of the father for the mother's work in caring for the child also has an effect on maternal self-esteem. If caregiving constitutes an important activity for the mother, her success in this activity serves to foster feelings of competency and high self-esteem which in turn should positively affect the mother-infant interaction. While research has only started to explore such influences, there is some suggestion that they do play an important role.

Of the factors which operate when the child is absent and which indirectly affect the mother-child relationship, the husband-father-wife-mother relationship is most salient. In fact the suggestion has been made that the father's influence on child development is primarily indirect (i.e., mediated by the mother) while the mother's effect is more direct (cf. Clarke-Stewart, 1978; Lamb, 1975; Lewis, Feiring & Weinraub, in press; Lewis & Weinraub, 1976). The indirect effect of the father on the child vis-à-vis the mother's relationship to the child appears to operate through the mother's perception of satisfaction and support in regard to her spouse. The father's support of the mother can be seen in several domains of function—for example, emotional support, financial support, help in completing household duties, support in making child care decisions, etc. However, most of the literature concerns the mother's perception of emotional support.

Research on marital satisfaction indicates a woman's sense of competence as wife and mother is related to the husband's behaviors and perception of his spouse. The findings of Barry (1968, 1970) indicate that healthy marriages are ones in which the husband is supportive of the wife's efforts in her role as mother. Barry found that wives' marital dissatisfaction was related to husbands' being coercive, punitive, and less conciliatory during an experimental interaction. Heath (1976) reports data on the relationship between marital satisfaction as perceived by the mother and paternal behavior. For the wives/mothers in this study, a good father is a person who has the ability to engender supportive relationships between parents and children; the ability to create satisfying adult, parent to parent interactions;

and the ability to make the wife feel adequate as a mother. Feiring (1976) studied the relationship between the mother's perception of how much support she received from the father and maternal involvement and responsivity to the child. The results of this study indicated a positive relationship between maternal ratings of support from the father and ratings of maternal involvement and responsivity to the child. Pedersen (1975) has observed a relationship between the father's esteem for the mother, the amount of tension and conflict in the marriage, and the alertness, irritability, and motor maturity of five-month-old infants. Considered together, the research discussed above suggests that by allaying the mother's frustration and doubts and by making her feel confident, secure, and competent as a wife and mother the father facilitates a responsive mother to child relationship.

Example 3—Support

> Returning from her all day job, a single parent picked up her nine-month-old infant from a day care center. She has yet to do the shopping, clean the laundry, and attend to the child's persistent cough. She is too tired to cook dinner and hopes the child will sleep a bit longer so she will not need to play with her.

Traditionally, fathers influence the direct interactions between child and mother through their sharing of the various tasks that are necessary in the lives of families. Besides the more obvious financial support, adults support one another through the sharing of tasks. The financial burden is currently more equally shared between mother and father, and there has been an increase in the father's sharing of household tasks. While sharing financial and household duties may be important ways a couple supports the family and each other's functioning, a most important support function relative to the role of parenting must be in the ability of two adults to discuss the problem of child care. In Example 3, the child's persistent cough may need attention, and careful discussion with another person on what should be done for the child is an option not easily available to the single parent. The sharing of tasks, responsibilities, information, and philosophies around child care between parents (or other caregivers) is an important indirect influence which has received too little attention, but which nevertheless influences the child's development.

Research documents some of the difficulties experienced by mothers without husbands on a regular basis (cf. Lynn, 1974). Single parent mothers felt psychologically worse and were less goal oriented for themselves or their children than mothers from two-parent families. Single parent mothers were more likely to be dissatisfied with the child's level of work and less likely to be involved in schools or aspire to a college education for their child. Furthermore, mothers whose husbands were temporarily absent on a regular basis led less active social lives, were more concerned with household duties, were more overprotective of the child, and were more likely to be concerned with their child's obedience and manners as compared to happiness and self-actualization.

Example 4—Arranging the Environment

The mother is in her study writing a paper on the tax laws of New York State. In order to keep her two-year-old child occupied, she hands the child some old copies of the *National Geographic*. The child smiles and proceeds to flip the pages of the magazine looking at the pictures, tearing out pages with animals and people that interest him. A week later on a trip to the zoo with his grandparents, the child recognizes the penguins from the pictures in the *National Geographic*.

In this example, the child has learned about its environment not through interaction with its parents but through materials that have been provided by the parent. The mother in this example does not teach the child about the animals pictured in the magazine but arranges the environment so as to make the pictures of penguins available for the child's perusal. Similarly the mother's good relationship with her own parents provides the child with an opportunity to interact with adults other than its parents who are nonetheless very attentive and responsive to its needs. Thus, the mother indirectly affects the child's development by providing opportunities for the child to interact with varied objects and people. Arrangement of the child's physical and social environment is a kind of indirect influence the parent has on the child which does not involve parent-child interaction.

Research indicates that young children spend more of their time interacting with the inanimate as compared to the social environment (cf. Clarke-Stewart, 1973; Wenar, 1972; White, Kaban, Shapiro, & Attonucci, 1976). How the parent arranges the child's inanimate environment represents an indirect influence of the parent on the child vis-à-vis the environment. Positive relationships have been found between the child's cognitive development and the degree to which mothers have arranged the environment so as to permit the child to explore freely without fear of harm to the child or to the environment (cf. Beckwith et al., 1976; Wachs, 1979; Wachs et al., 1967). On the other hand, environments that require close supervision of the child and do not allow for self-initiated exploration have been shown to be negatively related to the child's cognitive competence (cf. Clarke-Stewart, 1973; Elardo et al., 1975; Wenar, 1976; White & Watts, 1973).

In the area of social development, socialization of sex role behavior is related to the parents' arrangement of the child's environment. Room decor is clearly differentiated on the basis of child gender, and as early as the first few months the child is surrounded with toys in keeping with appropriate sex role expectations (Rheingold & Cook, 1975). Children are dressed in conformity to their sex role identity: blue pants for boys, and pink dresses and frills for girls (Brooks & Lewis, 1974). The ways in which the parent organizes and constructs the child's physical environment may be a form of indirect influence as important as the direct social interactions between the parent and child (Mischel, 1970).

The intention of our discussion thus far has been to examine those indirect influences that operate in the child's absence as illustrated in Figure 1. In Figure 1 each cell, A through C, represents a different link in a chain of events that end in a change in the child's developmental status, Cell D. Cell A, the father's support of the mother, affects Cell B, the mother's sense of competence as wife-mother. For the current discussion, the effect of Cell A on B is viewed as a direct one which takes place in the absence of the child. Cell B, the mother's competence, affects Cell C, the mother's behavior toward the child. The effect of Cell B on Cell C has been called a reflexive effect by some (Taylor, 1975) because it denotes within person influences (self-esteem of the mother affects the mother's behavior). The last event in the chain is the direct effect of Cell C, mother's behavior, on Cell D, child's behavior. The kinds of indirect influence we have been discussing involve the indirect influence of Cell A on Cell D as mediated by Cells B and C. Cells A and B take place in the absence of the child, while Cells C and D take place in the child's presence. In this case the mother provides the mechanism whereby the indirect influence of the father on the child operates when the child is not present. Indirect influences that operate when the child is absent may often take this form of persons influencing the child through their interaction with the child's parents.

This class of indirect influences is most broad in that it involves all those factors which have and continue to affect the parent(s) but which do not directly affect the child. A dyadic interaction cannot be understood fully until one can specify the various factors which influence each member separately. Both parent and child enter into an interaction with a set of influences which will have an impact on that interaction. In general, a person's current state, past experience, knowledge, development level, and many more factors must affect a person's interactive interchange with another, and these need to be considered if the meaning and course of the interaction is to be understood.

2. Indirect Effects

The discussion to follow focuses on those indirect effects which occur in the presence of the child. These are effects which the child experiences, but which do not focus on the child and as such have been considered indirect. Indirect forms of information acquisition have been considered under a wide rubric which includes identification, modeling, imitation, and incidental-, vicarious-, and observational-learning. While a distinction between these terms is beyond the scope of this discussion, it should be clear that a discussion of forms other than direct kinds of information acquisition have received considerable attention (see for example, Bandura, 1969, 1973; Freud, 1953;

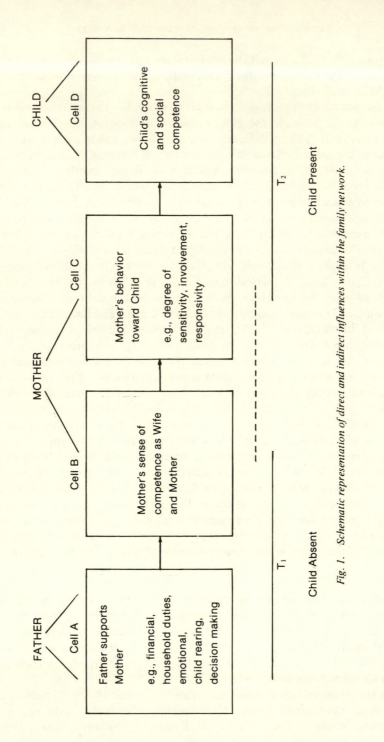

Fig. 1. *Schematic representation of direct and indirect influences within the family network.*

Guillaume, 1971; Hagan & Hale, 1973; Hartup & Coates, 1970; Lewis, 1979b; Parke et al., 1979; Piaget, 1951; Yando et al., 1978). In the examples to follow, each one of these above terms may be appropriate, some less so than others (i.e., incidental-learning), nevertheless the fact that they may play an important role in social interactions and relationships has not been made sufficiently clear in previous analyses of infant social development. A useful framework with which we shall consider these different forms of indirect effects is Bandura's (1973) formulation concerning the three outcomes associated with observational-learning:

1. *modeling effects*—novel behavior learned by observing another;
2. *inhibitory effects*—inhibition of behavior as a result of observing another;
3. *facilitating effects*—behaviors facilitated by observation of another.

Example 5—Modeling or Imitation

The one-year-old infant watches her mother turn the light switch and sees the kitchen light go on. After several trials of observation, she crawls to the wall, stands up, and throws on the switch.

This is an example of imitation learning or modeling. The child has gathered information about her object environment by watching the interaction between her mother and the light switch. This is an indirect effect since her mother did not involve her in the interaction. The direct effect would be a didactic teaching procedure in which the mother, talking to the child, perhaps even taking her hand, would show her how to work the light switch. Although most learning in early development is probably of an indirect type, most emphasis has been placed on the direct effect of didactic teaching and relatively little on imitative or modeling behavior. In Bandura's (1973) terms this is an example of modeling in that the infant acquires a new response pattern through observing a model performing a novel response.

Recently, a large number of studies on infant imitation or modeling behavior have been conducted, although there is also a long history of the study of infant imitation (Baldwin, 1895; Guillaume, 1971; Piaget, 1951). Studies on the developmental course of modeling were originally thought to show that imitative activities do not appear before 6 to 7 months (Guillaume, 1971) although Piaget spoke of imitation as early as the first few months of life even though deferred imitation did not occur until the end of the second year of life. More recent research (Jacobson & Kagan, 1978; Maratos, 1973; Metzoff & Moore, 1977) indicates that imitation occurs by the first month of life. Although the empirical results of very early imitation studies are ambiguous, by the second half of the first year of life most investigators agree that infants are capable of some forms of immediate imitation, especially around visible body movement (Lewis, 1979a).

Example 6—Inhibitory and Disinhibitory Effects

> The two-year-old child has just come into his sister's room and sees his mother
> scolding his five-year-old sister because she has spilled the water color paints on the
> floor and has painted the wall. His mother is quite angry and punishes her by making
> her stay in her room all afternoon. Having witnessed this scene, the two-year-old goes
> quickly into his room to make sure there is no paint on his walls.

In this example, the two-year-old gathers several different pieces of
information about how to behave. This information is acquired in an indirect
form since the interaction occurred between sister and mother. In this indirect
acquisition of information, the child learned not to put paint on the walls and
floor (information about objects). He learned that to do so will make his
mother angry (information about persons). For Bandura (1973), the above
example illustrates an example of inhibitory effects of observing a model; the
occurrence of inhibitory effects of exposure to a model is evidenced when, as a
function of watching an aversive response consequence happen to a model,
the observer shows decrements in the same class of behavior. After having
watched his sister receive punishment for painting the walls, the child is less
likely to attempt to become a painter of murals in his own bedroom. The child
has also acquired information about affects and their expression; that when
angry, it is appropriate to yell and make grimaces, and when sad or
frightened, to cry. Campos and Stenberg (1981) have recently referred to a
process of referencing in discussing emotional development and control.
Although in their formulation the infant references the mother's emotional
behavior in order to gauge what its own emotional response should be, there
is little reason not to extend this phenomena to include others who are
important in the child's life. In the above example, the upset of the older
sibling may be referenced by the younger child and the fearful behavior as
referenced may function to inhibit the child's own behavior. In Example 6, the
mother did not teach the two-year-old directly. She did not show this child
what was wrong, what not to do or how to behave. If she did, this would have
constituted a direct effect. In fact, the mother would not have been upset if the
two-year-old had spilled the paint since she recognized the developmental
limitations the younger child possesses. For this child, the learning of
information about objects, persons, and relationships (including affects) was
acquired indirectly.

Example 7—Facilitative Learning

> The nine-month-old infant sits in her highchair watching her mother and father who
> are sitting at the table at dinner time. Her mother is talking, her father is quiet. Now
> her father talks, her mother is silent. The two parents continue their conversation for
> many minutes. Finally, they pause and look toward the child. She smiles at them and
> begins to babble excitedly. They laugh and talk back to her.

In this example, the infant observes a high frequency event which occurs between these two adult people. Most of this time she can see and hear them talking to one another. Upon reflection, it is clear that conversation between parents is one of the high frequency events that can be observed when paying attention to them; much of the parents' waking, interactive life consists of conversation. The nine-month-old infant has been watching this interaction for many months. Indirectly she has learned that conversation, this activity of sound and gesture, is something people do when they are together. No one has directly taught her either the rule of talking to one another or the specific rules of conversation, such as turn taking. The child's babbling to her parents when they stop their conversation and turn toward her may reflect this indirect learning. While parents, of course, do talk directly to children, it is also the case that they talk among themselves. Indeed, at this dinner table, the distribution of conversation is divided such that more talking takes place between the two adults than between the adults and the infant. While most view the direct effects of talking to the child as instrumental in facilitating language acquisition, there exists the possibility that these indirect effects may also play an important role.

Response facilitating effects of exposure to a model occur in a situation in which the model's responses serve as discriminative stimuli for the observer (Bandura et al., 1966). This discriminative-stimulus function of a model's responses facilitates the occurrence of similar responses in the observer. Thus, in our example, a child's tendency to babble and vocalize may be facilitated by observing the parents talking. Response facilitating effects are considered less novel than the other two effects described above since the child already has the responses in its repertoire. Response facilitating effects may be a most important indirect influence in socialization as a prevalent process for conveying what behaviors are socially acceptable. Another example of response facilitating effects, which we shall discuss in more detail later, involves young children's reactions to strangers. Children's positive social behavior will be directed toward strangers through observation of their mother's positive behavior to the same stranger.

As the foregoing examples and discussion indicate, indirect effects, whether we call them imitation, modeling, identification, vicarious- or observational-learning, are probably of central importance for the development of social knowledge and relationships. It would not be in error to assume that a large degree of culturally appropriate behavior, knowledge, and values are transmitted on the basis of these kinds of indirect effects.

As our examples have been intended to indicate, indirect effects such as modeling can be related to outcomes associated with objects as well as people. While this is certainly the case, our primary focus will be on the role of these effects on social outcomes, more specifically, on the child's behavior toward people. Following the general framework, specific examples of social behavior which are influenced by indirect effects will be given. In both the general and specific cases, we shall attempt to formalize our discussion by the presentation of mathematical formulas. At this point in the development of our understanding of social development, the formulas we present serve mostly a heuristic purpose. They present a means for exploring and organizing the ways in which direct and indirect effects influence children's behavior. We have found the use of these formulas helpful for our conceptualization of ways of partitioning the variance of a child's behavior into its various influences. The formulas to be presented are not intended as mathematical statements about any "real" relationships between variables but rather they describe possible ways in which direct and indirect effects operate in influencing the child's behavior.

The formulas provide statements about only a cross section of time. They are not thought to describe the dynamic and changing aspects of relationships. If we could apply a time change analysis, we would probably find that many of the examples to be discussed probably do not remain stable but change because of the nature of the family structures or systems at different points in time. In general, then, the formulas lack a feedback system wherein a particular outcome serves to affect the direct and indirect effects themselves. Thus, one aspect of outcome which we will not consider in this analysis is the stability of relationships. While others have discussed indirect effects in regard to the mother/father/ child system (Bronfenbrenner, 1976; Feiring & Lewis, 1978; Lamb, 1976; Lewis & Weinraub, 1976), a more general analysis of the role of indirect effects and their relationship to direct effects and outcome requires consideration. In what follows, we will offer a general scheme for understanding both direct and indirect effects and their relationships to one another and to outcome measures.

II.   THE JOINT ROLE OF DIRECT
AND INDIRECT EFFECTS

Relationships are a function of both direct and indirect experiences and, to understand relationships, it is necessary to consider both direct and indirect influences. Toward such an understanding, the following general statement characterized by Formula 1 can be made:

Formula 1: C r Person $= f$ [Direct Effect + Indirect Effect], where
r = relationship and C = child.

In this general case, the child's relationship with person$_A$ is a function of both direct and indirect effects. In all cases to be presented, the influence of direct effects are greater than indirect effects. The indirect effect term always involves two interactions. These are given in Formula 2.

Formula 2: Indirect Effect = $(C \text{ r } Person_B) \times (Person_B \text{ r } Person_A)$.

In this general formula, the two terms refer first to the child's relationship to a third party, another person (person$_B$), and person$_B$'s relationship to person$_A$. The indirect effect involving these two terms state that the child learns about person$_A$ through its (C's) relationship to another (person$_B$) and through the relationship of that other person$_B$ to person$_A$. The indirect effect involving two terms is not additive but reflects some other function. We have chosen to consider them in some interactive way and therefore have considered them multiplicative. That the child has a relationship to person$_B$ who in turn has a relationship to person$_A$, implies an interrelationship which we have called transitivity (see Lewis, Feiring & Weinraub, in press; Lewis & Weinraub, 1976). By this we mean that we learn about persons indirectly to the degree that we have a relationship to the intervening person (person$_B$). Without a relationship to person$_B$, person$_B$'s relationship to person$_A$ will minimally influence the child's relationship to person$_A$.

Utilizing both terms in order to produce a general formula, we have the following:

Formula 3: $C \text{ r } Person_A = f \, m(C \leftrightarrow Person_A) + n[C \text{ r } Person_B \times (Person_B \text{ r } Person_A)]$

In this general formula, the direct term is added to the indirect one made up of two subterms which are multiplicative. In order to assert that direct influences are more powerful than indirect ones, we have given weights m and n for the direct and indirect effects respectively such that, in general, $m > n$.

The heuristics of such a formulation, of course, must determine its use. In the following discussion, we shall consider its utility by looking at two examples: (1) the mother, father, sibling, and child relationship, that is, the nuclear family, and (2) the child's relationship to strangers as it involves the mother's behavior toward the stranger.

A. Indirect Effects Within the Family: Mother, Father, and Child

Within the traditional nuclear family, the child's relationship to the father may be a function of at least three components: (1) the direct interaction of the father and child, (2) the child's relationship with the mother, and (3) the child's observation of the mother-father relationship (or interaction). As we have suggested in the general formula, the child-father relationship can be described as:

Formula 4: $C \text{ r } F = f \ m(F \cdots C) + n[(M \text{ ɪ } C) \times (M \text{ r } F)]$

The utility of such a formulation of the child-father relationship can be examined if we vary the values associated with possible outcomes. Let us, for the moment, assume that the mother-child relationship is positive and examine the types of changes that occur in the child-father behavior outcome when the mother-father and father-child components are varied.

Situation I: Father-child interaction positive, mother-father interaction positive. In Situation I, the relationships between all family members are positive and direct plus indirect effects consequently yield a positive outcome. Assigning positive valences to Formula 4 gives the following result:

Formula 5: $C \text{ r } F = f \ m(F \overset{++}{\leftrightarrow} C) + n[(M \overset{++}{\text{r}} C) \times (M \overset{++}{\text{r}} F)]$

note: $m = 1.0, n = .25$

In applying Formula 4 to Situation I, we have assigned two plus marks (++) to each component of the formula in order to indicate a positive relation. We have also specified that the indirect effect is a multiplicative relationship of $(M \text{ r } C)$ and $(M \text{ r } F)$, an assumption made to indicate that both components of the indirect effect must be more than zero in order for the effect to operate. In addition, we assume that when the child has direct experience with the father, m, the weight for the direct effect of $(F \leftrightarrow C)$ is greater than n, the weight for the indirect effect. In the present instance, given the absence of empirical data, we arbitrarily assign the values of 1.0 and .25 to m and n respectively. Applying the above stipulations to Formula 5 for Situation I yields a three plus positive valence for the child's relationship to the father. The direct effect of the positive behavior between father and child (two plus) is thus enhanced by the positive relationships of the (mother-child) × (mother-father) (.25 × 4 plus = one plus).

Situation II: Father-child positive and mother-father negative. In Situation II, the father-child interaction is positive but the mother-father relationship is negative. Assigning a positive valence to $(F \leftrightarrow C)$ and a negative valence to $(M \text{ r } F)$ gives the following results:

Formula 6: $C \text{ r } F = f \ m(F \overset{++}{\leftrightarrow} C) = n[(M \overset{++}{\text{r}} C) \times (M \overset{--}{\text{r}} F)]$

note: $m = 1.0, n = .25$

Thus, in Situation II, the direct positive effect of $F \leftrightarrow C$ interaction (two plus) is somewhat mitigated by the negative valence of the indirect effect (one minus). Although the positive interaction of father-child remains the strongest determinant of the child's relationship to the father, the degree of the child's relationship is altered due to the indirect influence of the husband and wife's poor relationship. This example suggests that the direct effect determines whether the relationship is positive or negative while the indirect effect contributes to the magnitude of the relationship.

Situation III: Father-child negative and mother-father negative. In Situation III, both the direct effect of $(F \leftrightarrow C)$ and the indirect effect are negative:

$$\text{Formula 7: } C \text{ r } F = f\ m(F \overset{--}{\leftrightarrow} C) + n[(M \overset{++}{\text{r}}\ C) \times (M \overset{-}{\text{r}}\ F)]$$

note: $m = 1.0, n = .25$

Applying Formula 4 to Situation III yields a three minus negative valence for the child's relationship with the father. The resulting negative relationship between father and child is compounded by the negative aspect of both the direct and indirect effects.

Situation IV: Father-child negative and mother-father positive. In Situation IV, the direct effect of $(F \leftrightarrow C)$ is negative while the mother's relationship to the father is positive, thus yielding direct and indirect effects of different valences. These values give the following results:

$$\text{Formula 8: } C \text{ r } F = f\ m(F \overset{--}{\leftrightarrow} C) + n[(M \overset{++}{\text{r}}\ C) \times (M \overset{++}{\text{r}}\ F)]$$

note: $m = 1.0, n = .25$

In Situation IV, the direct negative effect of $F \leftrightarrow C$ (two minus) is somewhat mitigated by the positive valence of the indirect effect (one plus). While the negative interaction of the father to the child remains the strongest determinant of the child's relationship to the father, the degree to which these relationships are negative is lessened by the positive relationship between mother and father.

Situations II-IV in which the mother-child relationship is negative. In all four situations, we have assumed that the child and mother relationship is positive. Consider now the general case when this relationship is negative. The effects of a negative mother-child term on the child-father relationship can be predicted for the various situations just discussed. In Situation II, the positive direct effect of the father-child interaction is summed with another positive term since both indirect valences are negative $(C \text{ r } M)$ and $(M \text{ r } F)$. The addition of both positive terms results in a stronger child-father relationship. This may appear to be counterintuitive until we consider what this type of triadic relationship may produce. Cognitive consistency and balance theory (cf. Heider, 1958; Zajonc, 1968) supply us with the general case which can be stated as follows: An enemy of my enemy is my friend. Thus, two negative indirect effects $(C \text{ r } M)$ and $(M \text{ r } F)$ increases the positive outcome of the child-father relationship.

According to balance theory, this situation would be stable for C and thus not produce any need for change in the existing relationships. Clinically, however, this situation describes a very tense, in fact, unstable family situation. For the child, the negative relationship between its parents as well as its negative relationship with its mother would constitute an extremely negative family environment. It is hard to imagine a positive father-child relationship surviving in such a negative environment without suffering disruption or divorce with the father maintaining custody of the child.

Situation III presents a negative direct effect ($F \nleftrightarrow C$) and two negative indirect terms (C r M) and (M r F). Two negative terms result in a positive indirect effect which should have the effect of reducing the overall negative outcome of the child-father relationship. This situation does not appear likely to occur. However, it may be the case that in a family situation where every interaction is negative, the degree of negative interaction of any specific dyadic relationship is reduced in part because of the lack of contrast effects. This particular situation, which logically follows from our general formula, appears to be the least intuitively appealing situation that is derived.

Situation IV results in a strongly negative child-father relationship. That is, if the direct effect is negative and the indirect effect is also negative because of the multiplication of a positive term (M r F) with a negative term (C r M), the child-father relationship will be highly negative. This family situation seems to describe a mother-father coalition which excludes the child from positive interaction with either father or mother.

The foregoing discussion suggests that our general formula may describe outcomes over wide and varied family circumstance. Clearly, what is needed is a way of testing these predicted outcomes in a more empirical fashion. Before turning to this, however, a particular case of child, mother, father constellation should be considered, that is, the case of the father absent family.

1.   Father Absence

In the situation in which the father is not present, the child does not have experience interacting with the father. Consequently, Formula 4 is reduced to a form in which only indirect effects need to be considered in explaining the child's relationship toward the father:

$$\textit{Formula 9: } C \text{ r } F = f\,[(M \text{ r } F) \times (C \text{ r } F)]$$

It should also be noted that the (M r F) term can no longer denote the child's observation of the mother-father interaction directly but must be comprised of the mother's expression of her attitudes, feelings, etc., concerning the father. In the case of father absence, we explain the child's relationship (i.e., expectations, feelings, attitudes) toward the father as a function of the child's relationship to the mother and the mother's expression of her relationship with the father. Assuming that the child's relationship to the mother is positive, and that the child uses the mother as a credible source of information about the social world, two kinds of situations can occur. In Situation V, the mother's relationship to the father is positive and thus the child's relationship to the father is positive. In Situation VI, the mother's relationship to the father is negative and thus the child's relationship to the father is negative. Assuming that the mother-child relationship is negative, Situations V and VI change their outcomes. In Situation V, two negative terms result in a positive child-father relationship. Again, this prediction fits our common belief that an enemy of an enemy may be a friend. Situation VI results in a negative child-father relationship since a friend of an enemy is an enemy.

Thus, in father absent situations, the major determining factor becomes the indirect effect which involves the child-mother relationship and the child's perception of the mother-father relationship. Assuming that, for the most part, the $(C \ r \ M)$ relationship is positive, the child-father relationship will depend on how the mother presents the parental relationship to her child. The father absence literature has stressed many issues including the child's age at father's absence, the child's sex, and the role identification and moral development of the child. However, our formulation suggests that the child's perception of the mother-father relationship is another important factor.

2. A Case Study

In reviewing the literature concerned with mother, father, and child interactions (no studies look beyond interactions to relationships so that the formulation must center around interactions) we need to determine if, for example, the $(F \leftrightarrow C)$ interaction is effected by the $(F \leftrightarrow M)$ and $(M \leftrightarrow C)$ interactions. The literature to date is rather sparce on this issue. Studies do indicate that the presence of one parent does affect the interaction quantity and quality of the other parent-child interaction (Clarke-Stewart, 1978; Lamb, 1976; Parke & O'Leary, 1975). These studies examine indirect effects in terms of how the functioning of a dyad (M, C) in isolation is changed when this dyad functions as a part of a larger system (i.e., a triad of M, C, F). This kind of indirect effect is a demonstration of the quality of "nonadditivity," a basic characteristic of the social system in which the child is socialized (cf. Buckley, 1967; Feiring & Lewis, 1978). Other studies examine indirect effects in terms of how one dyad $(M \leftrightarrow F)$ affects the functioning of another dyad $(M \leftrightarrow C)$, as in the work on marital satisfaction and its relationship to maternal behavior. By showing that positive maternal satisfaction i.e., a positive husband-wife relationship is also positively related to a positive mother-child relationship there is some support for the notion of indirect influences being important in the mother, father, child relationship (cf. Feiring, 1975; Pedersen, 1975).

There is little work, however, on this subject within the families. In particular, how the $(M \leftrightarrow F)$ affects the $(M \rightarrow C)$ has received the most consideration and demonstrates the heuristics of this formulation. However, the $(M \leftrightarrow F)$ interactions other than marital satisfaction have received no attention, nor has the $(M \leftrightarrow F)$ as it effects the $(C \leftrightarrow F)$ received sufficient consideration. Although there are a few studies, as mentioned, more work needs to be done. How the direct and indirect effects operate in the same situation to influence the child's behavior has not been considered. This is due in part to the fact that the direct effect will be predominant in the interaction and because demonstration of indirect effects rely more heavily on inference processes. However, if one attempts to hold the direct effect constant and manipulate indirect influences, then an examination of both indirect and direct influences in a given interaction can be explored (cf. Feinman & Lewis, 1981; Feiring, Lewis & Starr, 1981; in the discussion to follow). Because of the absence of research data concerning the more specific aspects of our formulation, our approach cannot be demonstrated to be fruitful. However, preliminary data from a study of families can be used to support the merit of our conceptualizations for family research.

Application of Formula 3 to varied family situations has allowed us to explore the manner in which direct and indirect effects may operate within a family. As part of our interest in examining child socialization and family interaction, we have begun to collect data on the vocalization patterns of families at dinner (see Lewis & Feiring, in press). The focus of our observations has been on the vocalization frequencies during dinner of all the family members, and as such we have data on the vocalizations of our three-year-old target children toward their mother, father, and siblings, as well as the vocalization of these people to each other and to the target child. Not all the data have been analyzed as yet. To begin with, we present data from two firstborn children without siblings and their families. In this example, we are interested in predicting the amount of vocalization of the children to their fathers $(C \leftrightarrow F)$. Applying our formula, we obtain:

Formula 10: $C \rightarrow F = f\ m(F \rightarrow C) + n[(M \rightarrow C) \times (M \leftrightarrow F)]$

We see that in order to predict how much vocalization the child does to the father we need to look at how much vocalization the father does to the child, as well as how much vocalization the mother-child and mother-father engage in at the table. For two children we know that the amount of father to child vocalization represents 53 units. The $(F \rightarrow C)$ terms have the same value because we selected two families where this would be the case in order to hold the direct effect constant. The use of only a direct effect analysis would suggest that the vocalization patterns of children should be determined by the pattern of the father; in this case, then, the patterns should be the same. In fact, child 1 vocalizes 44 units to the father while child 2 vocalizes only 18 units. We can account for this difference by examining the indirect effects. However, since we were aware that the mother's vocalization to the child could account for the general vocal fluency of the child, we looked for cases where the $(M \rightarrow C)$ term would be the same or similar. Thus, the indirect effect of $(M \leftrightarrow F)$ would be the most influential. For both children, the indirect term $(M \rightarrow C)$ is the same, 91 units; thus, the only difference between these families was the $(M \leftrightarrow F)$ indirect term. For child 1, this indirect term was 186 units while for child 2, it was 77. Thus, the $(M \leftrightarrow F)$ vocalization pattern was 2½ times as great for child 1 as for child 2, and this appears to account for the children's difference in vocalization frequencies toward their fathers. Thus, controlling for the direct effects by holding them constant we can see how indirect effects play a role in child vocalization patterns. This example is illustrative of our more general theme. The vocalization frequencies of children within the family network will be influenced, first by how much they are spoken to, but also by how much the other members of the family speak to one another.

Although these data are supportive of our theme, more data are necessary. We have collected data on 33 families, varying in family size and social class background. Since number of siblings considerably affects vocalization patterns (Lewis & Feiring in press; Lewis & Kreitzberg, 1979), generalization across these families is not warranted. However, examination of the correlations between various family members may be suggestive of the point we wish to make. The strongest correlation between $(C \rightarrow F)$ vocalization is the direct effect of $(F \rightarrow C)$ vocalization, $(r = .90, p < .01)$. Nevertheless, some indirect effects also show strong correlations; the $(F \leftrightarrow M)$, $(C \rightarrow F)$ correlation is .59 $(p < .01)$ while the $(M \leftrightarrow C)$, $(C \rightarrow F)$ correlation is only .08. Thus, both direct $(F \rightarrow C)$ and indirect $(F \leftrightarrow M)$ effects are related to the child's vocalization to the father. Clearly, more work on the indirect effects within the family are needed. However, this example points to one way in which these effects work and suggests that children's developmental outcomes are a function of both direct and indirect factors.

B. Indirect Effects With Others: Mother, Child, Strangers

The potential array of social objects that influence the child and that are influenced by the child is large and broadens as the child develops. How to make sense of this varied and wide array is one of the more important goals of the child, since it is to this array—including strangers, peers, teachers, etc.—that children must learn to adapt. Beyond interaction with the members of their families, children enter into contact with unfamiliar persons with whom they have little or no experience. Relatively early, children are required to interact with extended family members, friends of the family, peers, and teachers as well as solicitous strangers in places such as shopping centers and supermarkets. The indirect influence of the mother-other relationship on the child's behavior to unfamiliar people is important to explore because, unlike the case of father-child interaction, the child has had little or no previous experience with unfamiliar people. Given the lack of previous interaction with a person, interaction with unfamiliar individuals would seem especially open to indirect influences.

Recall that there are two terms of importance when considering indirect effects and that both terms are interactive: child-mother relationship and the mother-stranger relationship (or interaction). One aspect of the indirect effect that has been given some consideration is the mother-child relationship. However, both need to be discussed and considered when talking about indirect effects. The literature on attachment suggests that the nature of mother-infant relationships—in this case, secure and insecure attachment relationships—have important effects on the infant's concurrent and subsequent relationships with others. In exploring the role of the mother-infant relationship on infant-peer relationships, some researchers have shown a significant correlation between secure attachment and a positive peer relationship (Matas et al., 1978; Waters et al., 1979). Others, however, have viewed the connection between mother-infant and infant-peer relationships as the interplay of two systems rather than one being determined solely by the other (cf. Lewis, 1979b). In either case, the mechanism by which one relationship affects the other is not clearly articulated. Attachment theory suggests the mediating variable to be trait-like, that is, the child's security, ability, and willingness to explore its environment. Lewis and Schaeffer (1981) have suggested that the mother's skills at arranging the environment—getting the child to engage in peer contact—as well as lack of social competence are important variables, while Gunnar (1980) suggests that fearfulness of others may be the result of the infant's inability to control its environment: in this case, the inability to engage peers.

While these different points of view have yet to be reconciled, it is also unclear as to the specific nature of the mechanisms that affect the child's social relationships with others. The young child's use of its mother as a source of information about unfamiliar people is a phenomenon that occurs fairly often, but until recently it received only limited attention (Campos & Stenberg, 1981; Clarke-Stewart, 1978; Lewis & Weinraub, 1976).

Most of the research literature (see for reviews: Lewis & Rosenblum, 1974; Sroufe, 1977) has examined the child's reaction to strangers and several studies have examined the relationship between stranger fear, cognitive capacity, and attachment (cf., Bronson, 1972; Brooks & Lewis, 1976; Lewis, 1980; Lewis & Brooks-Gunn, 1979; Scarr & Salapatek, 1970). The results of these studies have only hinted at a limited relationship between cognition and fear of the strange. Lewis and Brooks-Gunn have shown a relationship between perceptual-cognitive ability, specifically, attention and fear of the strange (Lewis & Brooks, 1974) as well as a relationship between self-permanence and fear (Lewis & Brooks-Gunn, 1979). In general, the relationship between cognitive ability and fear remains unclear. However, two recent studies by Gunnar (Gunnar, 1980; Gunnar-von Gnechten, 1978) indicate that the ability to control a potential fearful event can reduce fearfulness in infants 12 months old. Thus, there is some suggestion that fearfulness may be mediated, in part, by cognitive variables rather than by "behavioral" releasers (Brooks & Lewis, 1976; Campos & Stenberg, 1981).

While fear of the strange has received considerable attention, it is only recently that some investigations have begun to consider that stranger fear is not universal, that large individual differences in the magnitude of fearful behavior are evident and, even more important, that while some infants may be initially frightened of the stranger, children can very quickly become quite friendly toward the stranger, especially if the stranger interacts with them. There are a few studies which have explored the ways in which young children approach unfamiliar persons (cf., Bretherton, 1978; Eckerman & Rheingold, 1974). However, this research did not have as its focus the examination of the indirect influence of the mother on the child's behavior to unfamiliar adults.

Although in most research the mother is present when the child deals with the unfamiliar adult, only two recent studies have varied the mother's behavior to the unknown adult. In general, the mother's role in the child-unfamiliar adult interaction has not been studied. Clarke-Stewart (1978) was interested in how variation in the stranger's affective tone in interaction with the mother affects the child's reaction to the stranger and, in her procedure, had the stranger initiate various interactions. In the sample of 14 thirty-month-old children, it was found that children were equally interested when the stranger interacted in a happy or hostile way with their mother and were equally willing to play with the hostile or happy stranger. Contrary to Clarke-Stewart's expectations, the stranger mood manipulation did not influence the child's reaction to the stranger, although it did affect the child's behavior to its mother. The child's physical contact with the mother was less following her interaction with the hostile stranger and more following the happy interaction. Actually, this finding lends support to the operation of indirect effects in that the child's observation of the mother-stranger interaction, in which the child did not participate or participated minimally, influenced the child's behavior to its mother. A parallel situation which suggests itself here is the influence on the child's behavior to its father (or mother) based on the child's observation of its parents hugging or having a quarrel. Clarke-Stewart's failure to find other indirect effects is difficult to understand. However, the results might have been different had the mother, rather than the stranger, initiated the various types of interactions, if the sample size had been larger, and if more sensitive measures of the child responses had been used.

Feinman and Lewis (1981) observed 87 ten-month-old infants in a standard stranger approach situation. In one set of conditions during the approach of the stranger, mothers were instructed to either speak to the infant about the stranger in a positive or in a neutral manner. Following the stranger approach, the stranger sat down next to the infant but did not attempt to initiate interaction. Measures of amount of smiling to mother and stranger and amount of toy play were obtained. The results indicated that infants whose mothers had spoken positively about the stranger played more with toys and offered a toy more to the stranger than infants whose mothers had spoken in a neutral tone. Since the measure of infant-stranger interaction was obtained after the mother's speech, it cannot be argued that this speech served as a distractor, a situation which could have been the case had the experimenters taken a measure of the infant's behavior during the approach itself. The mother's speech pattern (what she said as well as how she said it) appeared to be used by infants in regulating their behavior to the stranger. At 10 months of age it may be the case that the speech content of the mother played some role, but it is more likely that the tonal qualities of her speech were used by the children in appraising the mother's reaction to the stranger (Scherer, 1974).

Campos (personal communication) reports that infants' behavior on a modified visual cliff can be influenced by maternal behavior. Mothers who exhibited positive, as opposed to fearful, behavior were better able to get their children to cross the visual cliff and to respond with less fear than did the children whose mothers were neutral or fearful.

There is, of course, another set of situations in which the mother's relationship to the stranger may influence the infant's behavior: those situations in which the mother is not present. In these situations, the mother is either busy or absent and cannot interact with the stranger. Under these conditions, the indirect term becomes zero and only the direct term is operative. Since, however, most children have in the past utilized their mother as both a secure base from which to explore and as a basis on which to evaluate persons or objects, her absence in such a situation is doubly upsetting. First, the approach of the stranger is at best neutral, often negative in the experimental paradigm, and second, the absence of the mother may in itself designate a negative situation. Cairns (1972) has suggested that the absence of the mother constitutes an upset because the child has come to associate her with its social context and her absence makes the social context different from what the child has learned to expect. Cairns' analysis shares our belief that part of the importance of the mother is her role as an indirect source of information about the child's environment; when she is absent she cannot act in this capacity. A similar point has recently been made by Lewis (1980) and Campos and Stenberg (1981). In a study showing the effects of mother presence and absence on infants' responses to strangers, children were more frightened of the stranger when the mother was absent than when the mother was present. In fact, the children were not very frightened when the mother was present (Campos, Emde, Gaensbauer, & Henderson, 1975).

III. SOCIAL TRANSITIVITY[1]

In all studies just discussed, the mother may have served as a mediator between child and stranger. It might be the case that witnessing anyone interacting positively as opposed to neutrally or negatively with the stranger would influence the child's subsequent interaction with the stranger. In Formula 3, the indirect term is made up of two components, one having to do with observing an interaction without being a member of that interaction and the other to do with having a prior relationship with one of the participants of that interaction. In all three studies just cited, the second component has not been considered. To do so brings us to the topic of social transitivity.

Young children can use others to form relationships with strangers. The degree to which this "other" shares a relationship with the child would appear to affect the amount and type of relationship the child forms. Thus, for example, if the child sees its mother interact with a stranger, the effect on its relationship to the stranger might be quite different than if the child saw the stranger interact in the same fashion with someone other than the mother. In our formulation, we have indicated this relationship in our indirect effects which always include two terms, one representing the stranger-other and one representing the child-other interaction. We have called the fact that both terms are important in indirect effects "social transitivity" (Lewis & Feiring, 1978; Lewis & Weinraub, 1976). *Social transitivity represents the general case that the degree and magnitude of any indirect effect depends upon the child's relationship to the other$_A$ being mediated by the child's relationship to other$_B$ and other$_B$'s relationship to other$_A$.*

The mother-child case is an example of this social transitivity since the child's relationship toward a stranger is mediated by $(C r M)$ and $(M r S)$. This analysis shares some commonality with the theoretical approaches usually associated with observational learning and cognitive consistency theory. Here also, the relationship or perceived relationship between observer and the other appears to be important in determining the extent to which the observer will imitate the model or like another (Bandura, 1969; Heider, 1958).

While the studies of Clarke-Stewart (1978), and Feinman and Lewis (1981) varied the maternal response to a stranger and the child's subsequent behavior, these studies only employed the condition of mother-stranger interaction and as such do not constitute a test of transitivity. The additional condition that is needed is observation of the effect of someone other than the mother interacting with the stranger. By showing the effect of the child-other relationship *as well as* the other-stranger interaction on the child's interaction

---

[1]The relation between the elements in social transitivity are not bound by logical constraints as in formal transitivity problems.

with the stranger, a test of the notion of social transitivity is obtained. In terms of our general conceptualization, the specific formula concerning child-stranger interactions takes the following form:

Formula 11: $C \text{ r } S = f \, m(S \leftrightarrow C) + n[(O \text{ r } S) \times (O \text{ r } C)]$

All terms in the formula have been discussed before, except that here the direct term $(S \leftrightarrow C)$ has a zero value since the notion of a stranger involves no previous interaction. The O term refers to the other and may be the mother, a sibling or father, or even another stranger. The transitivity term refers to the fact that the $(O \text{ r } C)$ is as important as the $(O \text{ r } S)$ in determining the indirect effect.

A.   Social Transitivity: A Study of the Mother's Role in Infant's Responses to Strangers

Recently, we completed a study (Feiring, Lewis, & Starr, 1981) which examined the indirect effect of the mother's behavior as compared to another's behavior toward a stranger on the child's behavior to that stranger. In this study, we were interested in whether (1) indirect experiences affect the child's behavior toward a stranger, and (2) whether the mother was a more potent purveyor of indirect influences than another person.

Three groups of fifteen-month-old children were exposed to one of three conditions. In Condition I the child observed its mother interacting in a positive way with a stranger$_1$. This positive interaction of three minutes' duration consisted of the mother and stranger$_1$ smiling, laughing, and in general acting in a friendly positive manner toward each other as they discussed such topics as family members, vacations, and movies. During Condition I another stranger$_2$ was in the room, and did not interact with the mother, stranger$_1$, or child, but sat and read a magazine. In Condition II the child observed a stranger$_1$ interacting in a positive way (i.e., laughing, smiling, and acting happy while talking about family members, vacations, and movies) with another stranger$_2$ for three minutes. During the positive stranger$_1$-stranger$_2$ interaction the mother was present in the room and did not interact with either stranger but sat and read a magazine. In Condition III there was no interaction between stranger$_1$ and any other person (i.e., mother or stranger$_2$). Rather, stranger$_1$ sat and read a magazine for three minutes. During Condition III, the mother and other stranger$_2$ were in the room and also sat and read magazines.

For each of the conditions following the stranger$_1$ manipulation, the stranger greeted the child and then attempted to engage the child in play. The mother had been previously instructed not to influence her child's play with the stranger$_1$. The stranger$_1$ called the child by name and then offered the child a toy which she carried in her purse. Coaxing the child to play, the stranger$_1$ sat on the floor and attempted to involve the child in playing with the toys in the room. After 3 minutes of playing with the child, the stranger$_1$ said goodbye and left the room.

We expected that the child's relationship to the person interacting with stranger$_1$ was important in affecting the other indirect component and hence the child's subsequent play with stranger$_1$. Because of this, we hypothesized that there would be more positive behavior from child to stranger$_1$ when the child observed its mother acting in a positive manner to the stranger$_1$, as compared to when the child observed a positive interaction between stranger$_1$ and stranger$_2$. Moreover, we hypothesized that the mother-stranger$_1$ condition would facilitate more positive child-stranger$_1$ interaction than the stranger$_1$ no interaction condition (Condition III). Whether a stranger$_2$ interacting with stranger$_1$ (Condition II) would be different from Condition III, stranger$_1$-no interaction was difficult to predict. Given our formulation, one might expect no difference since the $(S_2 \ r \ C)$ term was essentially zero. However, since stranger$_2$ shares certain commonalities with both mother (she is also an adult female) and child (she is in the same room as the child), the $(S_2 \ r \ C)$ term may not have been zero. If we allow for the $(S_2 \ r \ C)$ term to be slightly positive rather than zero, Condition II should be more positive than Condition III.

In this experiment, one dependent measure was the amount of play behavior that the child was willing to engage in with the stranger$_1$ during the three minutes of play. Our analysis of the data indicated that hardly any negative behavior was directed by the children toward stranger$_1$ in any of the three conditions. However, toy play with the stranger did vary as a function of the three conditions. For the offer and accept toy categories of behavior, we found 7.8 occurrences for Condition I, 6.1 for Condition II, and 4.9 for Condition III. We were also interested in how fast the children were able to make friends. While the level for accept or offer toys remained the same for Conditions II and III, there was a marked increase over the 3-minute time period for Condition I. By the third minute, these differences were significant. Also of interest was the fact that infants in Condition III appeared to show the most wariness toward the stranger during the stranger's initial approach. Thus, the data suggest that in children as young as 15 months of age, indirect effects already play an important role in mediating social interactions. Moreover, that there was some difference, although not significant, between Condition II and Condition III, suggests that at this age the infant may be able to learn some things about strangers through their interaction with one another. However, children need to have some significant relationship with another in order for strong indirect effects to occur, which supports our notion of social transitivity. As we have indicated, it is probably the case that at any age, indirect effects are best facilitated when the person has some

relationship with the other who in turn is interacting with either a third person
or object. While we will not go into detail at this point, it appears reasonable
to assume that the relationship is based on several dimensions, some of which
have been considered by those interested in imitation and modeling
(Bandura, 1969; Lewis, 1979a) and include similarity between oneself and the
other, affective relationship between the self and other, as well as recognition
of the power of the other.

This study of social transitivity, as well as the other studies varying
maternal responsiveness toward strangers, serve to demonstrate the
importance of indirect effects. Together with the indirect effects as seen in
mother, father, and infant research, these studies point to the multifunctional
role of indirect effects in mediating the child's social behavior within the first
year of life. When both direct and indirect effects are available, direct effects
predominate; nevertheless, indirect effects play an important role. In the
absence of direct effects, as in the case of father absence or the approach of a
stranger, indirect effects influence the child's social behavior and knowledge.
From a developmental perspective, direct effects probably operate on the
young organism prior to indirect ones, since indirect effects require cognitive
capacities which may be beyond the child prior to six to eight months of age.
For example, Schaffer (1974) has argued that the ability to compare two
events located in different parts of the child's space is difficult before eight
months of age. If the child needs both to see and to listen to the mother and
watch the stranger at the same time, it may not be able to process all relevant
information. Once the cognitive capacities to profit from indirect effects
emerge, organisms, even infants within the first year of life, utilize indirect
sources of information about the environment.

While in this discussion the mother has been highlighted as the significant
other in terms of social transitivity, we recognize that others in the child's life
may serve this function as well. Fathers, siblings, and even friends may act as
mediators through which indirect effects come to influence the child. In fact,
one might argue that the measure of the significance of a relationship with
another person may be the degree to which that person is able to serve as a
mediator of these effects.

IV. CONCLUSION

As the child's social interactions with various other people become more
relevant for a theory of social development, both singly as in dyadic
interactions or in group of "$N + 2 \ldots$" interactions, the need to consider the
role of indirect effects becomes clear. While the literature on identification,
modeling, imitation, and vicarious-, observational-, and incidental-learning
have already suggested the role of indirect effects, little attempt has been

made to develop a model of social interactions which articulates the impact of both direct and indirect influences. The heuristics of our formulations reside in the focusing on the various components and their joint as well as single influences. The social nexus or the interconnection of the child's social relationships requires conceptualizations which go beyond the stipulation of direct effects and requires that the role of relationships in which the child lacks direct experience be considered. The degree to which the child is imbedded in a social network of many people who know the child and each other is the degree to which such indirect effects must be at work influencing development.

The data and formulation presented here concerning direct and indirect effects makes clear that infant's social, cognitive, and affective experiences are influenced through the interaction of the child with its social world as well as the interaction of the child with significant others who in turn interact with others. Such a scheme of socialization has common sense value and appeal, since learning can take place more effectively when one is able to learn through the experiences of others as well as through direct experience. That children have the capacity to utilize indirect sources of information to direct their behavior and knowledge of the environment, even at early ages, appears reasonable in light of the data and arguments presented here.

REFERENCES

Baldwin, J. M. *Mental development in the child and the race: Methods and processes.* New York: MacMillan, 1895.

Bandura, A. *Aggression: A social learning analysis.* Englewood Cliffs, N.J.: Prentice-Hall, 1973.

Bandura, A. *Principles of behavior modification.* New York: Holt, Rinehart, & Winston, Inc., 1969.

Bandura, A., Grusic, J. E., & Menlove, F. L. Observational learning as a function of symbolization and incentive set. *Child Development,* 1966, **37,** 499–506.

Barry, W. A. *Conflict in marriage: A study of the interactions of newlywed couples in experimentally induced conflicts.* Doctoral dissertation, University of Michigan. Ann Arbor, Mich.: University Microfilms, 1968, 68–13, 273.

Barry, W. A. Marriage research and conflict: An integrative review. *Psychological Bulletin,* 1970, **73**(1), 41–54.

Beckwith, L., Cohen, S. E., Kopp, C. B., Parmelee, A. J., & Marcy, T. Caregiver-infant interaction and early cognitive development in preterm infants. *Child Development,* 1976, **47,** 579–587.

Brazelton, T. B., Koslowski, B., & Main, M. The origins of reciprocity. In M. Lewis & L. Rosenblum (Eds.), *The effect of the infant on its caregiver: The origins of intelligence* (Vol. 1). New York: Wiley, 1974.

Brazelton, T. B., Yogman, M., Als, H., & Tronick, E. The infant as a focus for family reciprocity. In M. Lewis & L. Rosenblum (Eds.), *The child and its family: The genesis of behavior* (Vol 2). New York: Plenum, 1979, 29–43.

Bretherton, I. Making friends with one-year-olds: An experimental study of infant-stranger interactions. *Merrill-Palmer Quarterly,* 1978, **24,** 29–51.

Bretherton, I., & Ainsworth, M. Responses of one-year-olds to a stranger in a stranger situation. In M. Lewis & L. Rosenblum (Eds.), *The origins of fear: The origins of behavior* (Vol. 2). New York: Wiley, 1974, 131–164.

Bronfenbrenner, U. Toward an experimental ecology of human development. *American Psychologist*, 1976, **32**, 513–532.

Bronson, G. W. Infants' reactions to unfamiliar persons and novel objects. *Monographs of the Society for Research in Child Development*, 1972, 37(3, Serial No. 148).

Brooks, J., & Lewis, M. Attachment behavior in thirteen-month-old, opposite-sex twins. *Child Development*, 1974, **45**, 243–247.

Brooks, J., & Lewis, M. Infants' responses to strangers: Midget, adult, and child. *Child Development*, 1976, **47**, 323–332.

Buckley, W. *Sociology and modern systems theory*. Englewood Cliffs, N.J.: Prentice-Hall, 1967.

Cairns, R. B. Attachment and dependency: A psychological and social learning synthesis. In J. L. Gewirtz (Ed.), *Attachment and dependency*. Washington, D.C.: Winston, 1972, 29–80.

Campos, J. J. Personal communication, 1980.

Campos, J. J., Emde, R. N., Gaensbauer, T., & Henderson, C. Cardiac and behavior interrelationships in the reactions of infants to strangers. *Developmental Psychology*, 1975, **11**, 589–601.

Campos, J. J., & Stenberg, C. R. Perception, appraisal and emotion: The onset of social referencing. In M. Lamb & L. Sherrod (Eds.), *Infant social cognition: Empirical and theoretical considerations*. Hillsdale, N.J.: Lawrence Erlbaum Associates, 1981.

Clarke-Stewart, K. A. Recasting the lone stranger. In J. Glick & A. Clarke-Stewart (Eds.), *Studies in social and cognitive development: The development of social understanding* (Vol. 1) New York: Gardner Press, 1978, 109–175.

Clarke-Stewart, K. A. Interactions between mothers and their young children: Characteristics and consequences. *Monographs of the Society for Research in Child Development*, 1973, **38**(6–7, Serial No. 153).

Eckerman, C. O., & Rheingold, H. L. Infant's exploratory responses to toys and to people. *Developmental Psychology*, 1974, **10**, 255–259.

Elardo, R., Bradley, R., & Caldwell, B. The relation of infants' home environments to mental test performance from six to thirty-six months: A longitudinal analysis. *Child Development*, 1975, **46**, 366–478.

Feinman, S., & Lewis, M. Maternal effects on infants' responses to strangers. Paper presented at SRCD meetings, Boston, Mass. April 1981.

Feiring, C. *The effect of the infant and secondary parent on maternal behavior toward a social systems view of attachment*. Doctoral dissertation, University of Pittsburgh, 1975.

Feiring, C. The preliminary development of a social systems model of early infant-mother attachment. Paper presented at the meetings of the Eastern Psychological Association, New York, April 1976.

Feiring, C., & Lewis, M. The child as a member of the family system. *Behavioral Science*, 1978, **23**, 225–233.

Feiring, C., Lewis, M., & Starr, M. Indirect and direct effects on children's reactions to unfamiliar adults. In preparation, 1981.

Freedle, R., & Lewis, M. Prelinguistic conversations. In M. Lewis & L. Rosenblum (Eds.), *Interaction, conversation and the development of language: The origins of behavior* (Vol. 5). New York: Wiley, 1977.

Freud, S. Three essays on the theory of sexuality. In J. Strachey (Ed. & trans.) in collaboration with A. Freud, *The standard edition of the complete psychological works of Sigmund Freud* (Vol. 7). London: The Hogarth Press and the Institute of Psycho-Analysis, 1953. (Originally published, 1905).

Greenbaum, C. W., & Landau, R. Mothers' speech and the early development of vocal behavior: Findings from a cross-cultural observation study. In P. H. Leiderman, S. R. Tulkin, & A. Rosenthal (Eds.), *Culture and infancy: Variations in the human experience.* New York: Academic Press, 1977, 245–270.

Guillaume, D. *Imitation in children.* (E. P. Halperin, trans.) Chicago: University of Chicago Press, 1971. (Originally published, 1926).

Gunnar, M. R. Control, warning signals, and distress in infancy. *Developmental Psychology,* 1980, **16**(4), 281–289.

Gunnar-von Gnechten, M. Changing a frightening toy into a pleasant toy by allowing the infant to control its actions. *Developmental Psychology,* 1978, **14**, 157–162.

Hagen, J., & Hale, G. The development of attention in children. In A. Pick (Ed.), *Minnesota symposia on child psychology* (Vol. 7). Minneapolis: University of Minnesota Press, 1973.

Hartup, W. W., & Coates, B. The role of imitation in childhood socialization. In R. A. Hoppe, G. A. Milton, & E. C. Simmel (Eds.), *Early experiences and the processes of socialization.* New York: Academic Press, 1970.

Heath, D. H. Competent fathers: Their personality and marriage. *Human Development,* 1976, **19**, 26–39.

Heider, F. *The psychology of interpersonal relations.* New York: Wiley, 1958.

Jacobson, S. W., & Kagan, J. Released responses in early infancy: Evidence contradicting selective imitation. Paper presented at the International Conference on Infant Studies, Providence, R.I., March 1978.

Lamb, M. E. Infants, fathers, and mothers: Interaction at 8 months of age in the home and in the laboratory. Paper presented at the meetings of the Eastern Psychological Association, New York, April 1975.

Lamb, M. E. (Ed.) *The role of the father in child development.* New York: Wiley, 1976.

Lewis, M. Issues in the development of fear. In I. L. Kutash & L. B. Schlesinger (Eds.), *Pressure point: Perspectives on stress and anxiety.* San Francisco: Jossey-Bass, 1980.

Lewis, M. Issues in the study of imitation. Paper presented at a symposium on: Imitation in Infancy: What, when, and how; at the meetings of the Society for Research in Child Development, San Francisco, March 1979. Also in Eric's Resources in Education (RIE), #ED 171 394, October 1979. (a)

Lewis, M. The social network: Toward a theory of social development. Fiftieth anniversary invited address at the meetings of the Psychological Association, Philadelphia, April 1979. (b)

Lewis, M. State as an infant-environment interactions: An analysis of mother-infant interaction as a function of sex. *Merrill-Palmer Quarterly,* 1972, **18**, 95–121.

Lewis, M., & Brooks, J. Self, other and fear: Infants' reactions to people. In M. Lewis & L. Rosenblum (Eds.), *The origins of fear: The origins of behavior* (Vol. 2). New York: Wiley, 1974, 195–227.

Lewis, M., & Brooks-Gunn, J. Toward a theory of social cognition: The development of self. In I. Uzgiris (Ed.), *New directions in child development: Social interaction and communication during infancy.* San Francisco: Jossey-Bass, 1979.

Lewis, M., & Feiring, C. Some American families at dinner. Paper presented at a Conference on the Family as a Learning Environment, Educational Testing Service, Princeton, N.J., November-December 1979. To appear in L. Laosa & I. Sigel (Eds.), *The family as a learning environment* (Vol. 1). New York: Plenum, in press.

Lewis, M., & Feiring, C. The child's social world. In R. M. Lerner & G. D. Spanier (Eds.), *Child influences on marital and family interaction: A lifespan perspective.* New York: Academic Press, 1978, 47–69.

Lewis, M., Feiring, C., & Weinraub, M. The father as a member of the child's social network. In M. Lamb (Ed.), *The role of the father in child development* (2nd ed.). New York: Wiley, 1981.

Lewis, M., & Goldberg, S. Perceptual-cognitive development in infancy: A generalized expectancy model as a function of the mother-infant interaction. *Merrill-Palmer Quarterly,* 1969, **15**(1), 81-100.

Lewis, M., Goldberg, S. & Campbell, H. A developmental study of information processing within the first three years of life: Response decrement to redundant signal. *Monographs of the Society for Research in Child Development,* 1969, **34** (9, Serial No. 133).

Lewis, M., & Kreitzberg, V. The effects of birth order and spacing on mother-infant interactions. *Developmental Psychology,* 1979, **15**(6), 617-625.

Lewis, M., & Rosenblum, L. (Eds.) *The origins of fear: The origins of behavior* (Vol. 2). New York: Wiley, 1974.

Lewis, M., & Schaeffer, S. Peer behavior and mother-infant interaction in maltreated children. In M. Lewis & L. Rosenblum (Eds.), *The uncommon child: The genesis of behavior* (Vol. 3). New York: Plenum, 1981.

Lewis, M., & Weinraub, M. The father's role in the infant's social network. In M. Lamb (Ed.), *The role of the father in child development* (Vol. 1). New York: Wiley, 1976, 157-184.

Lipsitt, L. P. Learning in the first year of life. In L. P. Lipsitt & C. C. Spiker (Eds.), *Advances in child development and behavior* (Vol. 1). New York: Academic Press, 1963.

Lynn, D. B. *The father: His role in child development.* Monterey, Calif.: Brooks/Cole Publishing Company, 1974.

Maratos, O. The origin and development of imitation in the first six months of life. Paper presented at the meetings of the British Psychological Association, Liverpool, April 1973.

Matas, L., Ahrend, R. A., & Sroufe, L. A. Continuity of adaptation in the second year: The relationship between quality of attachment and later competence. *Child Development,* 1978, **49**, 547-556.

Metzoff, A. N., & Moore, M. K. Imitation of facial and manual gestures by human neonates. *Science,* 1977, **198**, 75-78.

Mischel, W. Sex typing and socialization. In P. Mussen (Ed.), *Carmichael's manual of child psychology* (Vol. 2). New York: Wiley, 1970.

Papousek, H. Experimental studies of appetitional behavior in human newborns and infants. In H. W. Stevenson, E. H. Hess, & H. L. Rheingold (Eds.), *Early behavior: Comparative and developmental approaches.* New York: Wiley, 1967.

Parke, R. D., & O'Leary, S. Father-mother-infant interaction in the newborn period: Some findings, some observations, and some unresolved issues. In K. Riegel & J. Meacham (Eds.), *The developing individual in a changing world: Social and environmental issues* (Vol. 2). The Hague: Mouton, 1975.

Parke, R. D., Power, T. G., & Gottman, J. M. Conceptualizing and quantifying influence patterns in the family triad. In M. E. Lamb, S. J. Suomi, & G. R. Stephenson (Eds.), *Social interaction analysis.* Madison: Wisconsin University Press, 1979, 231-253.

Pedersen, F. A. Mother, father and infant as an interactive system. Paper presented at the meetings of the American Psychological Association, Chicago, September 1975.

Piaget, J. *Play, dreams, and imitation in childhood.* (C. Gattegno & F. M. Hodgson, trans.) New York: W. W. Norton & Co., Inc., 1951. (Original French edition, 1945).

Rheingold, H. L., & Cook, K. V. The content of boys' and girls' rooms as an index of parents' behavior. *Child Development,* 1975, **46**, 459-563.

Rheingold, H. L., & Eckerman, C. O. Fear of the stranger: A critical examination. In H. W. Reese (Ed.), *Advances in child development and behavior* (Vol. 8). New York: Academic Press, 1973.

Rovee-Collier, C. K., & Gekoski, M. J. The economics of infancy: A review of conjugate reinforcement. In H. W. Reese & L. P. Lipsitt (Eds.), *Advances in child development and behavior* (Vol. 13). New York: Academic Press, 1979.

Scarr, S., & Salapatek, P. Patterns of fear development during infancy. *Merrill-Palmer Quarterly,* 1970, **16**, 53-90.

Schaffer, H. R. Cognitive components of the infant's response to strangeness. In M. Lewis & L. Rosenblum (Eds.), *The origins of fear: The origins of behavior* (Vol. 2). New York: Wiley, 1974.

Scherer, K. Acoustic concomitants of emotional dimensions: Judging affect from synthesized tone sequences. In S. Weitz (Ed.), *Nonverbal communication: Readings with commentary*. New York: Oxford University Press, 1974.

Sroufe, L. A. Wariness of strangers and the study of infant development. *Child Development,* 1977, **48**, 731–746.

Stern, D. N. The goal and structure of mother-infant play. *Journal of the American Academy of Child Psychiatry,* 1974, **13**, 402–421.

Taylor, J. *Systometrics.* Unpublished manuscript, University of Pittsburg, 1975.

Wachs, T. D. Proximal experience and early cognitive-intellectual development: The physical environment. *Merrill-Palmer Quarterly,* 1979, **25**, 3–42.

Wachs, T. D., Uzgiris, J. C., & Hunt, J. McV. Cognitive development in infants of different age levels and from different environmental backgrounds. Paper presented at the meetings of the Society for Research in Child Development, New York, April 1967.

Waters, E., Wippman, A., & Sroufe, L. A. Attachment, Positive Affect, and Competence in the Peer Group: Two studies in construct development. *Child Development,* 1979, **50**, 821–829.

Wenar, C. Executive competence and spontaneous social behavior in one-year-olds. *Child Development,* 1972, **43**, 256–260.

Wenar, C. Executive competence in toddlers: A prospective, observational study. *Genetic Psychology Monographs,* 1976, **93**, 189–285.

White, B. L., Kaban, B., Shapiro, B., & Attonucci, J. Competence and experience. In I. C. Uzgiris & F. Weizmann (Eds.), *The structuring of experience.* New York: Plenum Press, 1976.

White, B. L., & Watts, J. C. *Experience and environment.* Englewood Cliffs, N.J.: Prentice-Hall, 1973.

Yando, R., Seitz, V., & Zigler, E. *Imitation: A developmental perspective.* Hillsdale, N.J.: Lawrence Erlbaum Associates, 1978.

Zajonc, R. B. Cognitive theories in social psychology. In G. Lindzey & E. Aronson (Eds.), *The handbook of social psychology* (Vol. 1). Reading, Mass.: Addison-Wesley, 1968, 320–411.

MUSICAL ELEMENTS IN THE INFANT'S VOCALIZATION: THEIR SIGNIFICANCE FOR COMMUNICATION, COGNITION, AND CREATIVITY

Mechthild Papoušek and Hanuš Papoušek

MAX-PLANCK INSTITUTE FOR PSYCHIATRY, MUNICH, F. R. GERMANY

Advances in Infancy
Research, Vol. I

I. INTRODUCTION

In human beings, vocalizations have developed in two parallel and interdependent directions: the production of musical expressions of emotions from the first spontaneous songs to highly structured artistic vocal music, and the production of verbal symbols from the simplest communicative utterances to abstract symbols in language freeing thought from the constraints of sensory perception and motor action. Whereas verbal communication in many specific variations is considered exclusive to human society, the production of less specific euphonic, melodic sounds with various rhythms and temporal patterns or other musical elements is common to a larger part of animal world.

Along the developmental scale of levels in biological processes (Schneirla, 1965), vocal sounds have been classed either with phasic or with signal levels in the majority of animals (Tavolga, 1970). There they may function as biosocial signals dominated by organic processes or as psychosocial signals resulting from reciprocal stimulations within interactive communication. Only in infrahuman primates, Tavolga admits a primitive symbolic level in agreement with other observers (Altmann, 1967; Darwin, 1872; Washburn, Jay, & Lancaster, 1965). A common evolutionary origin of both singing and verbal language has been discussed speculatively by Jespersen (1922).

Musical elements—pitch, tone, interval, melody, loudness, accent, tempo, and rhythm—or their acoustic correlates—frequency, harmonics, amplitude, and temporal patterns—are matters of a primary interest to musicologists but have not attracted much attention of linguists or phoneticians studying language acquisition. Some of the musical elements have been analysed as prosodic elements substantially contributing to the communicative significance of language (Crystal, 1971, 1973; Kaplan & Kaplan, 1971; Lewis, 1936; Lieberman, 1967). In spite of their atrophy in modern, highly abstract forms of languages (Jespersen, 1922), the intelligibility of language still depends on prosody, albeit perhaps more distinctly in poetry than in the presentation of scientific papers. In two forms of language the part of prosody is particularly strong, namely in the babytalk with which adult caretakers address themselves to infants, and in the infantile vocalization. Both forms play closely interrelated roles in the early ontogeny of vocalization, a process which may typify the ways of the evolution of vocal communication.

Dealing in details with the infant's earliest perception and production of vocal elements which represent musical elements to a musicologist, suprasegmental features to a phonetician, and prosodic or paralinguistic elements to a linguist, we are going to speak of "musical" rather than "prosodic" elements. Thus we want to facilitate our discussion of both linguistic and musicological aspects. For the same purpose our procedures include musical transcription as well.

Crystal (1978) points out difficulties met in the evaluation of preverbal prosody due to its formal and functional heterogenies in adult speech. For instance intonation is a composit of pitch, intensity, and durational aspects (Hadding-Koch & Studdert-Kennedy, 1964). Linguistic stress includes variations in pitch and duration next to the intensity contrast (Lehiste, 1976; Spring & Dale, 1977). On the other hand, even the simple discrimination between statements and questions depends on the entire contour rather than the mere terminal glide (Hadding-Koch & Studdert-Kennedy, 1964). It is also difficult to make linguistic attributions to early preverbal vocalizations.

The development and the role of prosodic elements between the first cry and the first word have remained unexplored even in the recent surveys (Lenneberg & Lenneberg, 1975; Menyuk, 1979); the presyllabic sounds have been viewed as undifferentiated expressions (Carmichael, 1964; Crystal, 1971). Only sporadically in detailed diary studies (Lewis, 1936; Crystal, 1973), prosody has been discussed in relation to preverbal perception and acquisition of language. A more comprehensive picture has recently been sketched by Stark and co-workers in connection with the development of phonological segments (Stark, 1978a,b; Stark et al., 1975; Stark et al., 1978).

The significance of the global prosodic "envelopes" or "matrices" has not escaped the attention of students of cognitive prerequisites of speech acts as of the basic units of linguistic communication (Bruner, 1975; Dore, 1975; Dore et al., 1976). Such a functional approach has substantially elucidated the transition from preverbal communication to one-word speech, but has not yet been applied to earlier stages of development nor to a more detailed analysis of individual prosodic elements. The scattered attempts to study early musical abilities have concerned merely the later ages, typically above 18 months. They will be discussed in Section II.D.

An effective impetus for an increased interest in the earliest musical elements of speech has recently come from following studies:

1. Studies on the infant's perception of speech signals revealing categorical perception of phonetic contrasts in the first two months (Eimas, 1975; Eimas et al., 1971; Eimas & Tartter, 1979; Morse, 1976) have also shown discrimination of prosodic elements (Morse, 1972). This finding is relevant to the question of processing and integration of babytalk where musical elements of speech participate so strongly (Papoušek & Papoušek, 1975, 1979a; Fernald, 1976).
2. Viewed in the context of intuitive parental behaviors babytalk can offer "a peephole to the evolution of human parenting" in relation to language (Papoušek & Papoušek, 1978a, b).
3. Studies of the kinesics of early mother–infant interactions have claimed innate entrainment, i.e., a tendency to synchronize motor activities in the newborn with the rhythm of adult speech (Condon & Sander, 1974). Such a predisposition is also relevant to musical abilities.
4. Early musical vowel-like sounds in infants have been found to be closely related to the infant's fundamental adaptive response system including the regulation of general behavioral states and the activation of basic integrative processes (Papoušek & Papoušek, 1979b).

Yielding to the temptation of observing (and taping ad libidum) an infant as parents intimately familiar with subtle changes in its moods and behaviors, we have followed stimulating examples of other authors, and enriched our research materials with a longterm single-case observation allowing us to illustrate this communication as well. This way, namely, we have been able to collect and interpret records of musical expressions in monologues and dialogues in manners hardly available in usual research practices.

II. PSYCHOBIOLOGICAL ASPECTS
OF MUSICAL ELEMENTS IN VOCALIZATION

Without necessarily being a recapitulationist one can find the similarities between phylogeny and ontogeny interesting. They may help to reveal the most probable mechanisms of differentiation which can sometimes occur only in a limited number of ways in the nature. In such cases as the evolution of languages where paleontology can offer only a modest evidence, developmental and comparative analyses may be important tools in elucidating phyletic relationships (Ploog, 1980; Tavolga, 1970).

A. Musical Elements of Vocalization
and Evolution of Language

The evolvement and interdependence of language and music are phenomena common to all human cultures, and their universality need not to be documented. From the view of parallelism between evolution and ontogeny, it may be more interesting to consider the proportion between biological and cultural determinants. During ontogeny, biological determinants obviously prevail both in the preverbal vocalizations of the infant and in the adult's babytalk addressed to the infant whereas consciously cultivated interventions occur later. The histories of various cultures show a certain dichotomy between intuitive expressions of moods in folksongs or entertainment music, on one hand, and rationally cultivated music on the other. Both language and music become the more formal, ritualized, theoretically elaborate, and abstract the closer they are tied with the pillars of social hierarchies.

The history of Chinese music presents perhaps the best example. According to the earliest literary evidence, the function of music was to sustain the harmony between heaven and earth, and between the male principle, Yon, and the female principle, Yin. The fundamental note itself represented the eternal principle of universe, the five notes of pentatonic scale corresponded to the five elements, along a scale of twelve notes, the fundamental note changed with the twelve months of the year. Each imperial dynasty used to exercise a great care for the correct fundamental note. Already by the first century B.C. an imperial office was established to supervise the absolute pitch of the fundamental note and the musical life in general. Spreading with Buddhism, the Chinese music strongly influenced the music in Japan and other neighbouring countries.

However, the Chinese peasants mostly used work songs—tuning the fundamental note to suit the pitch range of the singers and using rhythms identical with the rhythms of work.

Analogous dichotomies, though perhaps with less striking differences, can be found in the histories of Western music, Islamic music, etc. The history of vocal music documented in literary sources is of course negligibly short in terms of evolution. It is difficult to learn enough about the period prior to the earliest written documents. A look at the last populations more or less untouched by modern civilizations may be of some help. Among the Australian Aborigenes, for instance, music is affected by the totemism which determines the whole sociocultural life. Consequently, only songs traditionally associated with their totems are used by individual clans. Professionals enjoying a prestigeous status contribute to the oral transmission of traditions and legends of the tribe. The other major function, i.e., dealing with the gods and spirits, requires an exact performance of the age-old chant to achieve an effective contact. This task is entrusted to one of the most honorable senior members, and his mistakes may be punished severely, even with death. Entertaining songs, on the other hand, are less formal and often composed ad hoc.

Of a special interest with regard to the biological origins of vocal music is their participation in communication. To overcome an increased distance from a recipient the emitter usually increases the loudness and prosody of his verbal messages. This is believed to have led to the appearance of yodeling in the Alps, or yelled-sung communication between shepherds in the Carpathians. Interestingly, where talking drums had overtaken a similar role, such as typically in African populations, the rhythm and tuning of drums have been faithfully adjusted to the features of language and have helped to quickly deliver rather complex messages. There is a fluent transition between the communicative meaning of drum signals and their important role in different kinds of African music. In this comparatively recent art, based entirely on oral traditions, the vocal performance, too, favors lowpitched voices, countless modifications of complex rhythms, and collective rather than individual songs.

One particularly interesting analogy of the above examples are the whistled languages. They have been studied only since the late forties, and found to be used with the same ease and intelligibility as any ordinary speech. They may be based on the tone feature of the corresponding language such as in the Mazateco Indians of Oaxaca, Mexico (Cowan, 1948, in Busnel & Classe,

1976), whose language is a tone language. Or they may be based on sounds corresponding to articulated speech such as in the whistled language (so-called Silbo) in La Gomera, Canary Islands, consistent with a dialect of Spanish which is not a tone language (Busnel & Classe, 1976). Further types of articulated whistled languages were recorded by Busnel around Aas, French Pyrenese, and at Kusköy, Turkey. In general, whistled languages have appeared to be represented in many more parts of the world. Linguistically, the semantic importance of the tone feature found in Mazateco is particularly interesting, since at least here the tone and intonation determine the intelligibility of whistled language even if phonetic contrasts have been eliminated.

Following Darwin's speculations (Darwin, 1877), Jespersen (1922) envisaged the human's protolanguage closer to singing than to speech, as the abundant musical and paralinguistic elements were used for exclamations and unreflected expressions of emotion rather than for the communication of ideas. The emergence of musical elements prior to the linguistic ones during phylogeny has most frequently been discussed in relation to the role of melodic sounds in birds as in a phylogenetically older class (Petrinovich, 1972). Again, systematic studies of the song tradition, for instance in sparrows, have revealed tendencies irresistibly offering comparisons with the development of speech in children.

Marler (1969, 1977) has pointed out several similarities. Both in the human infant and young birds of different species acoustical experience dominates in shaping the structure of vocalization, and, interestingly, the bird species in question have also been found to be more successful in adaptation and survival. A rich variation in "dialects" is another common consequence of learning. Parallel are also the early sensitive period in perceptual learning and the assumptions of a functional auditory feedback (Konishi, 1965) and of a present adult model. The period of latency between perceptual learning and actual vocal production indicates the necessity of long-term auditory memory. On both sides, amorphous sounds (babbling and subsongs) characterize the early developmental stages. Vocal learning is influenced by a lateralization in nervous processes in both cases: by a left hemispheric dominance in man and by a left hypoglossal dominance in some song birds (Nottebohm, 1971, 1972). The other argument that a genetic predisposition directs the attention and learning processes to species specific vocalization has appeared questionable in the light of present research (Kuhl, 1978). In the best imitators among birds, such as some blackbirds and parrots who can imitate even human whistles and speech, an intrinsic motivation for vocal imitation is evident (Marler, 1977).

On the other hand, as a system open to infinite development, human language remains unparalleled both in birds and nonhuman mammals, including those with the highest brain development, namely chimpanzees and dolphins. As to chimpanzees, even strenuous attempts to teach them verbal language (Hayes, 1951; Kellogg, 1968; Kellogg & Kellogg, 1933) have been unsuccessful most probably due to their vocal tract (Lieberman et al., 1972), inability to imitate sounds (Marler, 1977), or to cognitive restraints (Savage-Rumbaugh, 1979). With dolphins, all attempts to establish how far they use their own whistling for communication have failed (Busnel & Classe, 1976), although dolphins have successfully been trained to respond to complex signals of human whistled languages or to imitate musical elements in them (Batteau, 1967, in Busnell & Classe, 1976).

Thus, the vocal production of musical elements like most other "prerequisites of human language do occur isolated in one or another group of animals, but in none do they coincide to permit the explosive development of human language" (Marler, 1969).

B.   Musical Elements and the Early Ontogeny of Language

With regard to the ontogeny of language, the early participation of musical elements and their interrelationship with fundamental regulatory systems deserve an increased attention.

The lower and upper parts of the vocal tract have played uneven roles both in evolution and ontogeny of vocalization. The lower part controlling pitch, timing, and intensity of vocal sounds, and tied to the autonomic system of arousal, is believed to have functioned earlier during infrahuman evolution and to have produced involuntary vocalizations triggered from deep structures of the limbic system of animals (Myers, 1968; Jürgens & Ploog, 1976). The upper vocal tract responsible for differentiation and timing of the phonetic articulation has evolved later with the progressing cortical control of speech sounds in human beings. In the human newborn, the vocal tract is more similar to the infrahuman than to the adult one (Lieberman et al., 1972), but relatively soon becomes controlled by the cortical system of voluntary acts.

The studies of hemispheric lateralization have attributed to the right hemisphere the control of both emotional and musical behaviors (Damásio & Damásio, 1977), crying, laughing, and other nonverbal vocalizations (Kimura, 1964; King & Kimura, 1972), as well as verbal speech involved in song singing (Damásio & Damásio, 1977). So intimate a relationship allows a sensitive communication of emotional states, moods, and attitudes.

Since associative-imaginative thinking and phantasy involved in daydreaming have been attributed to the right hemisphere, too, one could speculate on the relations between subconscious singing, humming, or whistling of melodies and daydreaming or automized routine activities. Analogies of such states may underlie the occurrence of infant monologues in which the musical elements appear rather early (see Section III.B.)

Next to the semantic content, human languages, and partly even whistled languages, may carry extra-linguistic information helping the recipient to identify the emitter's species, sex, age, identity, states of mind and health, spatial localization, sociocultural status, or even some aesthetic and moral qualities. It has been shown that young infants respond differentially to differences in pitch of voice in naturalistic observations (Wolff, 1969), discriminate familiar and unfamiliar voices (Wolff, 1963), at 3 weeks recognize the mother's voice (Mills & Melhuish, 1974), and at 4 months discriminate, girls better than boys, the voices of both parents from strange ones (Brown 1979). According to Bühler and Hetzer (1928) the 3-month-olds discriminate friendly and angry tones of adult speech without additional cues. Next to cry, the infant's earliest vocalizations have commonly been considered as expressions of comfort or discomfort feelings (Stark et al., 1975; Wolff, 1969), eventually resulting from the course of intrinsic integrative processes in learning or problem solving laboratory tests (Papoušek, 1961, 1967).

"Prosodic envelopes" help to discriminate the situational context and various categories of messages, such as informative statements, questions, alarming/soothing signals, or commands. Intonational contours of individual messages may activate either the recipient's orienting responses, exploratory behaviors and approach, or withdrawal and defensive behaviors as the main parts of the fundamental system of adaptive responses (Papoušek & Papoušek, 1975; 1979b). This is particularly evident in the adaptative modification of parental speech to infants, commonly known as babytalk. Not only does the average higher fundamental frequency in the babytalk tell the infant that the parent speaks to him, but adequate melodic modulations either activate the infant's attention and integrative processes, thus optimizing his ability to profit on social interchange, or vice versa, reduce them in order to facilitate his transition to sleep or mitigate his difficulties, thus protecting a necessary recovery. These principles are strikingly manifested in nursery songs which, according to tempo, rhythm, loudness, and rising or falling contours in melody, can either activate the general state and motor activity in the infant, or sooth and lullaby him (Papoušek & Papoušek, 1977b).

It is easy to imagine that during evolution the means of influencing the conspecific's general behavioral state have had a significant adaptive value and affected the survival probability. Hence we can also better understand the reasons why music has been cultivated by the carriers of power, educators, or professional artists, as well as intuitively exploited by people in work songs, lullabies, consolation songs, or entertaining songs. It has been demonstrated in adults that muscle tone and strength decrease during listening to lullabies, but increase during listening to marching songs (Harrer & Harrer, 1977). Monotonous slow rhythmic stimulation alone induces sleep states. In general, though, only little attention in research has been paid to the role of environmental musical elements in the early behavioral development of human infants.

C. The Infant's Earliest Musical Experience: Babytalk

Infants seem to perceive and process auditory stimulation very early. Even newborns differentially respond to variations in frequency, intensity, duration, and temporal or spatial patterning of sounds (Eisenberg, 1976; Stratton & Connolly, 1973). They are particularly sensitive to the frequency range of adult speech (Hutt et al., 1968) and are able to learn discriminative responses to pitch differences in the first months of life (Janoš, 1959; Kasatkin & Levikova, 1935; Papoušek, 1961; Siqueland & Lipsitt, 1966). In 2- to 3-week-olds, the human voice, especially a high pitched one, outweighs other sounds in terms of arresting the infant's cry (Wolff, 1969) and of eliciting smiles (Wolff, 1963). Certain pleasures and annoyances, perhaps fundamental "hedonic mechanisms," are immediately operative in the newborn and have been reported in relation to olfactory or gustatory perception (Lipsitt, 1979; Steiner, 1974) and in the course of integrative processes (Papoušek, 1967). They have not yet been sufficiently analysed, however, in relation to vocal stimulation. Yet, a pure musical tone has been shown to be tolerated by newborns, who aversively respond to noises of comparable sound levels of 85 db (Levarie & Rudolph, 1978). Friedlander (1970) quotes Butterfield's observation that 1-day-olds actively control auditory stimulation through operant sucks and selectively respond to classical, popular, and vocal compositions.

Linguists agree in general that early responsiveness to intonation precedes lexical comprehension and production (Crystal, 1971, 1973; Kaplan & Kaplan, 1971; Lewis, 1936; Menyuk, 1977; Tonkova-Yampol'skaya, 1969; Weir, 1966). The first "phonetically consistent forms" that are believed to play a central role in syntactic and semantic development and to be the first vocal evidence of intention have been found marked by prosodic envelopes (Bruner, 1975; Crystal, 1971, 1978; Dore, 1975; Dore et al., 1976; Halliday, 1979). Earlier diaries of speech development indicate that 5- to 9-month-olds respond to familiar intonation contours with situation-specific behaviors irrespective of lexical content (Kaczmarek, in Weir, 1966; Schäfer, 1922; Stern & Stern, 1928; Tappolet, 1907). Later investigations using habituation paradigms have shown that independent of the meaning of contours, rising and falling intonation can be discriminated at the age of 8 months (Kaplan,

1969) or even at 1 and 2 months (Morse, 1972), location of stress at 1- to 4 months (Spring & Dale, 1977), and the regularity of order in tone sequences or different rhythmic patterns at 3 and 4 months (Demany et al., 1977).

Looking for the most relevant sources of musical stimulation in the infant's life one soon realizes that a very rich source has been provided by the nature in the human voice of conspecific caretakers, particularly in nursery songs (see Section IV.B) and babytalk.

Babytalk toward older infants has been analysed from phonetic and linguistic views in a series of studies (Ferguson, 1964; Garnica, 1977; Golinkoff & Ames, 1979; Phillips, 1973; Remick, 1976; Sachs, 1977; Snow, 1972). To the Papoušeks' and their collaborators, however, babytalk has appeared to be most interesting as a part of intuitive parenting, excellently exemplifying the psychobiological origins of human care for the cognitive growth of the progeny (Papoušek & Papoušek, 1977c; 1978a), and operative toward newborns even in primiparas (Fernald, 1976). Mothers are hardly aware of the changes in their voice and cannot consciously reproduce babytalk in the baby's absence (Fernald, 1976). When talking alternatively to their babies and some adults, the features of the babytalk seem to be elicited almost reflexively; mothers immediately shift registers, sometimes finishing a narrative addressed to adults in babytalk as soon as they turn to infants (Papoušek & Papoušek, 1977b). A sonagraphic illustration in Fig. 1 compares identical German lexical items used in a narrative speech to an adult and in a babytalk. Following features of babytalk deserve particular attention:

1. The structure and syntax of utterances is simple, individual segments are distinct, abbreviated, and often repeated regularly and/or rhythmically with a slow speed and prolonged intersegmental pauses (Garnica, 1977; Phillips, 1973; Snow, 1977). One segment may consist only of a single syllable or a paralinguistic sound. These structural features help the infant to detect regularities in the flow of speech, become familiar with the repeated patterns, predict and recognize them next time—an experience which may elicit signs of pleasure (see Section IV.A).

2. Strongly accentuated prosodic and paralinguistic elements give the babytalk prominent features of musical quality in terms of intonational contours, stress, and rhythmicity (Fernald, 1976; Garnica, 1974). The main fundamental frequency approaches that of the infant's vocalization (Ferguson, 1964), the pitch range is expanded, according to Fernald (1976) the melody is more expressive with frequent repetitive continuous changes of pitch or glides (Figs. 1, 21), prevalence of basic harmonic intervals (thirds, fourths, fifths, and octaves), and sometimes dramatic changes in intensity.

3. Certain patterns of musical elements affect the infant's behavioral state as alarming/soothing signals and allow the parent to control the infant's alertness (Papoušek & Papoušek, 1977b). Rising intonations with a quiet regular rhythm maintain the attention at a level desirable for an enjoyable interchange, and therefore prevail in babytalk during a lively parent–infant interaction. They are sometimes interpreted as question contours although the utterances are not

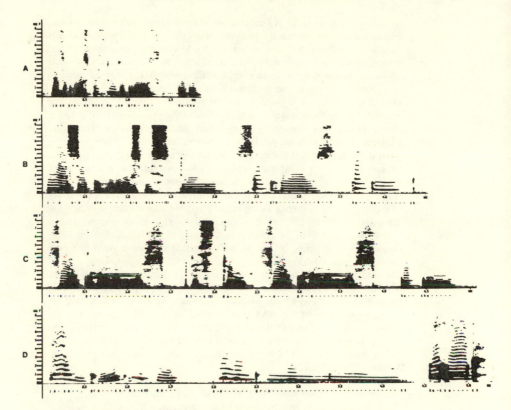

Fig. 1. Sonagrams of babytalk compared to narrative speech. Identical phrases of "Ja, so groβ bist du, so groβ, kuckuck" (in English "Yea, so big are you, so big, cuckoo"), addressed to an adult in a narrative speech by the mother (A), and to a newborn in a babytalk by the mother (B), by the father (C), and by the 2-year-old sibling (D).

necessarily meant as questions (Garnica, 1977; Sachs et al., 1976; Snow, 1977). The tempo and pitch range of the babytalk increase, and pitch contours may rise abruptly, sometimes with "staccato" and/ or increasing intensity ("crescendo") if alertness is to be mobilized in the infant. On the contrary, a slow regular rhythm, continuously decreasing tempo ("ritardando"), prevalence of falling intonation contours with decreasing intensity ("decrescendo") comfort and sooth the infant, eventually lulling him to sleep very much like typical lullabies (Papoušek & Papoušek, 1977b).

4. In babytalk, the parent typically responds to various movements, facial expressions, and vocalizations of the infant, often imitating his behaviors. In such a reciprocal interchange, the infant has the earliest chance to learn that his vocal behavior with certain regularity elicits vocal responses in the parent, and moreover, that the vocalizations on both sides are similar (see Section IV.A).

5. Musical elements of babytalk often represent playful and creative features eliciting further significant integrative processes in the infant (see Section IV.A).

6. Vocal interactions with adults are usually accompanied with signs of joy and pleasure in infants. That raises the question of whether certain musical elements

or linguistic aspects in the babytalk themselves primarily elicit pleasant feelings, trigger some innate hedonic mechanisms, or are tied to some other mechanisms of intrinsic motivation. This question cannot be answered without systematic investigations still missing in the literature. On the other hand, musical elements may gain the dimension of motivational features secondarily, through learning and cognitive processes (see Section IV.A).

7. Didactically seen, it is important that the parent not only adjusts his or her babytalk to the present state and need, but also to every developmental progress of the infant, thus supporting every newly emerging capacity. This gives babytalk signpost features, particularly evident, for instance, when the infant starts producing the first distinct syllables consistently. From that moment on, the parent uses every syllable as a potential core for a future word and teaches the infant to associate the syllable with the corresponding informational content (Papoušek & Papoušek, 1978b). Similarly, the parent may take the opportunity of teaching the baby singing a song as soon as it becomes evident that the baby can imitate a melody. Different functions of the babytalk are consequently set in operation according to the developmental stage of the infant (Bruner, 1975; Garnica, 1977; Phillips, 1973), and with a certain start corresponding to the parent's cognitive advantage.

8. The intuitive features of babytalk indicate an evolutionary similarity in the ontogeny of social communication and suggest innate programs for babytalk. Interviews at the end of our investigations have revealed only a minimal conscious evidence of the form and sense of babytalk in parents. Another evidence might be in the fact that children start using babytalk toward infantile siblings rather early, i.e., between 2 and 4 years of age (Papoušek & Papoušek, 1978b; Sachs, 1977; Sachs & Devin, 1976; Slobin, 1968, in Newport, 1976; Weeks, 1971), (Fig. 1D).

D. Development of Musical Elements in the Infant's Vocalization

The first vocal expression of a newly born child, and also one dominating in the past investigations of early vocalizations, is the *neonatal cry*. The neonatal cry has commonly been described as a rhythmic sequence of segments, each lasting 1.1 to 2.8 s with a fundamental frequency between 250 and 450 cps (Sirviö & Michelsson, 1976; Wasz-Höckert et al., 1968; Wolff, 1969). Auditory discrimination, spectrography, and analysis of temporal aspects have helped to differentiate patterns, such as basic (or hunger) cry, mad cry, pain cry, frustration cry, and fake cry (Wolff, 1969). Murray (1979), on the other hand, found different types of cry to be a mere gradation of intensity characterized by the length of cry, the suddenness of onset, and the sonographic features also used by Truby and Lind (1965), i.e., melodious phonation, dysphonation, and high pitch hyperphonation. The data on the adult's ability to discriminate individual patterns are still controversial, but indicate a major role of experience (Morsbach & Bunting, 1979; Müller et al., 1974; Wasz-Höckert et al., 1964). Intimate caretakers are able to identify their own infant's cry (Murry et al., 1975) and become selectively sensitized so that even a weak cry, unlike other noises, will wake them.

Recently, an improved spectrographic analysis of neonatal cries has allowed an early detection of brain damage, certain anomalies (Sirviö & Michelsson, 1976; Wasz-Höckert et al., 1968), or minor deviations in infants at risk who are otherwise healthy (Zeskind & Lester, 1978).

Only a limited attention has been paid to the early development of musical elements in noncry vocalizations. Sheppard and Lane (1968) collected continuous records of all vocalizations of two infants from 0 to 5 months of age for a computation of fundamental normative measures. The mean fundamental frequencies of 438 Hz and 401 Hz respectively, ranges of pitch and amplitude, and an average duration of utterances of 550 ms were surprisingly stable.

Delack and Fowlow (1978), analyzing nondistress vocalization in nineteen infants from 0 to 12 months in four different situations, found the average fundamental frequency of 355 Hz, the frequency range of 85 to 110 Hz, and a prevalence of rising-falling (undulating) contours to be stable throughout the first year of life. Interestingly, the infant exhibits maximum of vocalization when being alone. Very similar findings have been reported by Laufer and Horii (1977) under both laboratory and home circumstances, however, with special attention to variability.

On the other hand, Keating and Buhr (1978) have found remarkable ranges of fundamental frequencies in six infants at the age of 8 to 36 months, reaching from 30 to 2500 Hz in general, and individually, for instance, from 30 to 1500 Hz, or from 250 Hz to 2500 Hz. Ranges can be divided into three registers. Fry register, around 200 Hz (30 to 250 Hz), usually occurs at the beginning or end of a creaky voiced portion. Most utterances comprise modal register of 150 to 700 Hz. Occasionally, intonation can discontinuously, in older subjects continuously, change into a separate high register—perceptually reminding of "falsetto" in adults.

In three children above 1 year, Weeks (1971) differentiated ten speech registers varying mainly in musical elements. In her comprehensive studies of Russian children from birth to 2 years, Tonkova-Yampol'skaya (1969) found a gradual approximation of comfort intonations to those in adults, whereas discomfort intonations changed very little. In the comfort vocalizations, placid cooing has appeared above 2 months of age, happiness and laughter at 3 months, exclamatory delight at 6 months, requests at 7 months, and questions at 13 months. Unfortunately, measures of variability and reliability have not been published.

Observational and perceptual musicological analyses have not become outdated in the presence of spectrographic and microsegmental quantification of narrower parameters. Pioneered in Bullowa's (1975) sound film techniques, functional and contextual approaches still prevail in the studies of the meaning of vocalizations in naturalistic social communication, and of their functional relation to the cognitive development of children.

Taking vocal utterances as a part of speech acts, Bruner (1975) has differentiated interrogative, vocative, indicative, and demand contours in prosodic envelopes, occurring already at the preverbal level. He has discussed how the infant learns to comprehend intentions conveyed by those patterns and to produce them intentionally as well. In the concept of Dore, Franklin, Miller, and Ramer (1976), the word in the speech act indicates the notion, and the prosodic envelope the intention of the infant. In four 11- to 16-month old infants, Dore has found four classes of context–specific, phonetically consistent forms with rather stable prosodic envelopes for affective, instrumental, indicative, and grouping expressions. In an exhaustive single-case study of an infant from 9 to 12 months, Halliday (1979) has described distinct semantic differences in intonation occurring along an action–reflection continuum leading from instrumental to regulatory, interactional, and personal functions.

The present knowledge of the development of musical elements has not yet allowed either a comprehensive systematic account or a conceptual synthesis. The more appreciated should be the recent attempt of Stark and co-workers (Stark, 1978a, b; Stark et al., 1975; Stark et al., 1978) to fill that gap. They have provided a detailed description of early speech production skills which is based on auditory, phonological, and electroacoustical classifications, including some musical elements. With certain overlaps and considerable individual differences, following sequence of stages has been reported: I—reflexive vocalization (0 to 12 weeks) comprising cry, discomfort and vegetative sounds; II—cooing and laughter (6 to 16 weeks); III—vocal play (16 to 30 weeks), characterized by squealing, growling, yelling, or producing noises; IV—reduplicated babbling (6 to 10 months); V—nonreduplicated babbling (10 to 14 months) including an increasing variety of stress patterns and intonation contours; VI—phonetically consistent forms and single word production (above 10 months).

III. OUR OWN APPROACH:
AN ILLUSTRATIVE SINGLE-CASE STUDY

From our review, we can conclude that the main stream of research has followed the necessary directions of descriptive phenomenology and analytic instrumentation and has reached considerable progress in microanalytic phonetics leaving gaps in the directions of musicologic interests, implication of biological aspects, and relations to the development of integrative competence. The presently increasing interest of behavioral developmentalists in the early social integration of infants has stressed interactionalistic views and improved our understanding of the infant's vocal environment, its biological origin, and significance for cognitive growth.

This may justify our presentation of a pilot observation supposed to serve as a starting point for a longterm investigation on the dyadic infant–adult communication. It is a set of examples relevant to some important topics of our research project and selected from a comprehensive longitudinal observation of our firstborn daughter Tanya.

Such an observation has obvious advantages in our abilities to interpret the context and meaning of vocalizations or record them audiovisually under the most advantageous circumstances. Like many other infants, Tanya between 5:30 and 7:30 A.M. was more advanced by 1 or 2 weeks than Tanya during the rest of the day, or Tanya at the laboratory. Often she exhibited some of the most instructive monologues at unpredictable times of the day.

Our intimate knowledge of her auditory background helped to interpret her musical expressions in detail, although sometimes, only repeated records enabled us to reveal distinct precursors of later performances in their earliest forms. Her auditory background has been particularly rich and musical, since Tanya enjoyed several intimate caretakers fond of music who liked to sing to her at various occasions. Relatively early, rich, and self-oriented verbal competence facilitated the interpretation of her intentions, preferences, interests, and moods.

An observation made under similar circumstances cannot serve as a representation of a normal population, but it may increase the probability of discovering capacities that have been escaping attention in larger, representative samples. An early discovery of new aspects is particularly valuable for projecting further research, particularly if an interactionalistic approach is to be applied.

In our observation, vocalizations were recorded from birth to 16 months with a portable taperecorder Uher Report 4200, and different condensor microphones, either directional or of the Lavalier type. Simultaneous contextual descriptions and comments were either dictated or protocolled in a diary. Following procedures were applied for further analyses of magnetic records: (1) musical transcriptions by two independent musically trained assistants; (2) phonetic transcription with a simplified version of the alphabet of the International Phonetic Association; (3) spectrographic analyses of sounds with a Kay-Sona-Graph Type 6061 A with a frequency range of 85 to 8000 cps, and a narrow bandwidth of 45 cps; (4) automated analysis of temporal structures, fundamental frequency, and of intensity, measured as a function of the amplitude of sound waves on a PDP 11/50 electronic calculator.

It is necessary to mention that Tanya's parents have differed from unexperienced parents of firstborn infants. They both had medical and psychological education specializing in early development, and a very rich experience in the care for infants from preceding research engagements. Knowing that the frequency of initial crying in infants depends significantly on the parents' abilities to respond to precursors of cries (Bell & Ainsworth, 1972), Tanya's parents have typically tried to prevent crying in her and to support noncrying means of communication by principle.

A. Elementary Sounds in
the Infant's Early Vocal Repertoire

On the present level of knowledge, we consider interpretative labels of vocalization, such as reflexive, vegetative, or comfort sounds, as premature. We prefer descriptive terms based upon acoustic parameters primarily, although we are going to speculate on interpretative possibilities in considerations of best fitting conceptual models that may be relevant for further research strategies. For this reason, even our categories remain open to modifications resulting from accumulating evidence to come.

We shall first pay some attention to four sound groups evident in Tanya's early vocalizations: cry, consonant-like sounds, vowel-like sounds, and syllable-like sounds.

Cry corresponded to the descriptions by other authors and was frequent during the first 2 or 3 weeks, particularly during Tanya's stay at the newborn nursery. Although the frequency could not be quantified, it was evident that Tanya often cried for minutes before she was helped and that she responded with cry to other babies' cries. In the presence of parents, the frequency of cries decreased soon, and for her parents it was not difficult to prevent cries signalled by changes in other behaviors or fussy vocal precursors of cries. Firmly closed fists of both hands for more than 20 s, increased alternating flexions and rapid extensions of legs, striking vasodilation in face, or short explosive utterances in fry register belonged to typical precursors of crying.

Tanya's initial crying appeared to vary in intonational contours and rhythm much more than expected according to other authors' data. As shown in Figs. 2 and 3, variations occurred even during individual periods of cries. Partly they seemed to correspond to the general smoothness and coordination of movements in extremities or to the occurrence of jerky movements and the "high frequency and low amplitude tremor" (Prechtl, 1965; Vlach, 1969), (Fig. 3C).

Partly the variations coincided with the parents' appearance and soothing interventions due to their rational attitudes and intuitive urge to intervene. Not even Tanya's father, who as a neonatologist had been exposed to neonatal cries many times a day for many years, could tolerate them without an annoying urge to intervene, thus confirming Ostwald's (1963) aphorism "The cry cries to be turned off." In our unpublished data on intuitive parenting toward newborns, delivered according to Leboyer and passed to mothers immediately, mothers from the beginning unconsciously exhibit two opposing strategies in response to neonatal vocalizations: they respond with quiet, tenderly tonal and melodic, noninterruptive utterances to the slightest signs of noncrying vocalizations, but interrupt crying or even vocal precursors of crying, loudly with rejecting words such as "No, no, don't cry!" and give babies no turns for such vocalizations.

The group of *consonant-like sounds* comprises all voiceless sounds acoustically reminding of consonants and often referred to as vegetative sounds. They seem to be elicited by abrupt changes in breathing and motor activities, or, most distinctly, by oral activities like mouthing, swallowing, licking, sucking, or burping, particularly in the presence of fingers in the oral region. Such sounds may indeed be mere products of responses regulated by the autonomic nervous system. However, sooner or later, having been perceived and associated with consequences within social interchanges, they may gain new features and intrinsically initiate cognitive processing (see Section IV.A). As long as we have no observable parameters indicating at

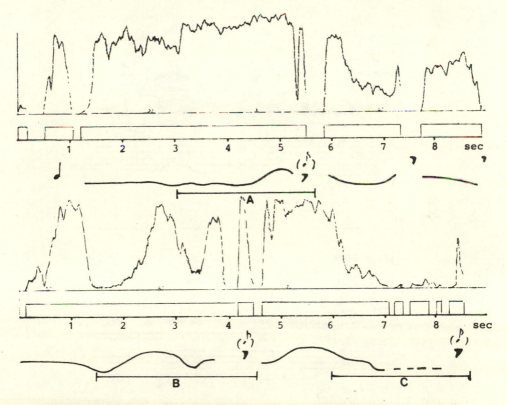

Fig. 2.   Sequence of cries at 1 month. Curves from above: amplitude, duration in seconds, melodic contour in musical transcription (' = inspirium). Sections A, B, and C are shown in sonagrams in Fig. 3.

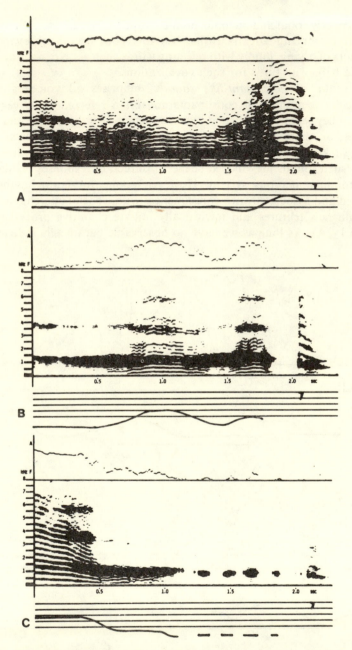

Fig. 3. Sonagrams of sections A, B, and C from the sequence of cries in Fig. 2. Curves from above: amplitude, sonogram, melodic contour in musical transcription.

least in general that corresponding integrative processes are in progress, it is impossible to determine the transition from autonomic to cognitive regulations. However, due to accidental contextual evidence, parents may notice such a transition.

In Tanya's case, the variety of precursors of later linguistically relevant consonants was abundant. During the fourth month, she produced variations which the adult could not imitate at all and which disappeared with the further development of distinct consonants. However, it is not our intention to elaborate on details of phonologic aspects treated much better by phoneticians. To us, it was more important to see how much pleasure could result from her phonological practicing, particularly during interaction with parents, and during vocal plays (Section IV.A).

The *vowel-like sounds* include the initial undifferentiated and nonarticulated *fundamental voicing* which reminds of "æ" or "ə," and may be produced with a closed or slightly opened mouth from the first week of life during quiet waking. It has often been referred to as "cooing" after it had become longer in duration and richer in intonation.

This fundamental voicing is interesting as an indicator of the earliest control of respiration for the sake of vocalization, and as the earliest form of noncry vocalizations modulated in dependence on behavioral states and on the course of integrative processes which the caretaker can interpret as means of communication. Varying in pitch, intensity, and temporal structure (Figs. 4 and 5), the fundamental voicing also functions as the carrier of the first musical elements. Therefore, it will be analysed more closely in Section III.B.

The *syllable-like sounds* consisting of the precursors of consonants and vowels appeared in Tanya during the first month of age, first in the form of "ma," "awa" with transitions to "ava" around two months, "ja" and then "ag," "agr" or "r"-like voiced sounds at 3 months and 3 weeks. However, only at the beginning of the fifth month, an obvious period of reduplicated babbling was started with the syllable "bæ" produced in a new structural pattern typical for syllables. Grouping corresponded to the length of expirium, and the duration of respiratory cycles functioned distinctly as an element of linguistic phrasing. The previously occasional occurrence of syllable-like sounds arrived at a certain turning point in the control of respiration and speech organs enabling an easier production of quickly repeated and morphologically stable syllables (Fig. 6). Every appearance of a new syllable was followed by a 1- to 2-week period of "monomanic" use of that single syllable, during which the preceding syllables were not to hear.

As we are going to explain in Section III.B, the turning point in the linguistic sense simultaneously represented an important turning point in musical capacities allowing to combine new rhythmical sequences with variations in melody and intensity.

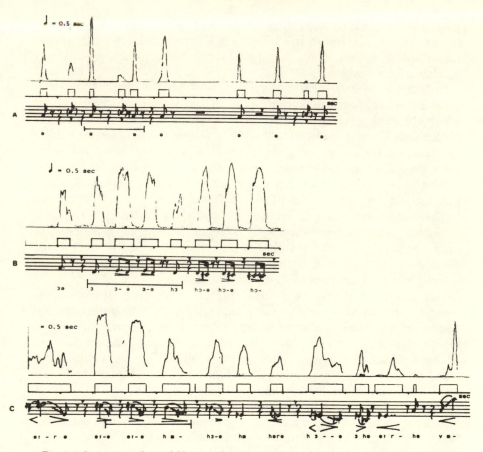

Fig. 4. Sequences of vowel-like sounds: (A) at 4 weeks ($\bar{x}$ = 150 ms; f = 49/min); (B) at 6 weeks ($\bar{x}$ = 306 ms; f = 79/min); (C) at 8 weeks ($\bar{x}$ = 552 ms; f = 54/min). Curves from above: amplitude, duration in seconds, musical transcription. Horizontal abscissae indicate sections shown in sonagrams in Fig. 5.

B. Musical Elements in the Infant's Early Vocal Repertoire

The bare fundamental voicing in the newborn's noncry vocalization acquires the features of musical sounds from the first month on. Musical sounds are characterized by pitch, musical quality, and intensity which, acoustically, correspond to fundamental frequency, composition of upper harmonics, and amplitude of sound waves. These features are perceived as either continuous pitch changes or discrete tones, timbre (sometimes referred to as "tone of voice"), and loudness, respectively. Unlike pitch, the differences

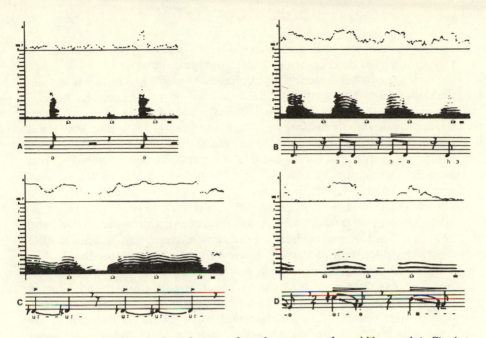

Fig. 5. Sonagrams of indicated sections from the sequences of vowel-like sounds in Fig. 4:
(A) at 4 weeks; (B) at 6 weeks; (C) and (D) at 8 weeks. Curves from above: amplitude, sonagram,
musical transcription.

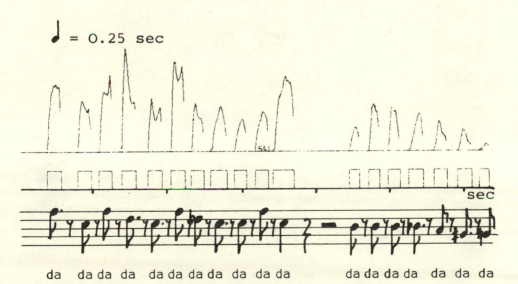

Fig. 6. Syllables (reduplicated babbling) at 11 months. Curves from above: amplitude,
duration in seconds ($\bar{x} = 189{,}7$ ms; $f = 200/min$), musical transcription.

in *musical quality of voice sounds* are difficult to quantify so that we have to rely upon verbal descriptions and spectrographic illustrations.

During the first 2½ months, the vowel-like sounds in Tanya's repertoire developed from brief grating or harsh sounds to longer euphonic musical sounds approximating pure harmoniously voiced tones (Fig. 5). Their musical quality depended largely on age and general behavioral states, but became as differentiated toward the end of the third month as to allow Tanya exhibiting a rather rich variety of tones in dependence on situational context as well. They could be described as cooing, sometimes combined with growling, humming, soft groaning, or brief squeals. Similarly, like other parents in our studies, Tanya's parents also learned to read information on her behavioral states from timbre, musicality, and rhythm of her fundamental voicing without any direct visual contact. For instance, Figs. 4C, 5C, and 5D illustrate tender musical signs of a joyful mood—cooing—produced while Tanya was attentively observing moving birds or her favorite mobile. Another example in Fig. 7 shows cheerful squealing sounds during interactions with parents or during morning monologues at different ages.

In distress situations, the fundamental voicing acquires the form of cry precursors with slight undulation in both fundamental frequency and upper

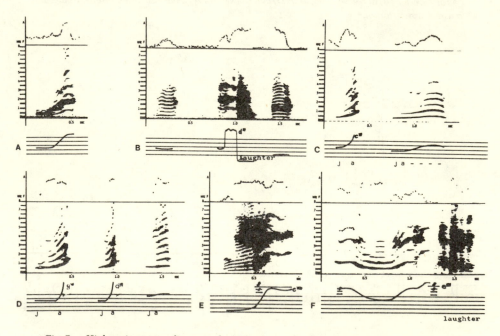

Fig. 7.   High register squealing sounds: (A) at 2 months; (B) at 4 months; (C) and (D) at 11 months; (E) and (F) at 13 months. Curves from above: amplitude, sonagram, musical transcription.

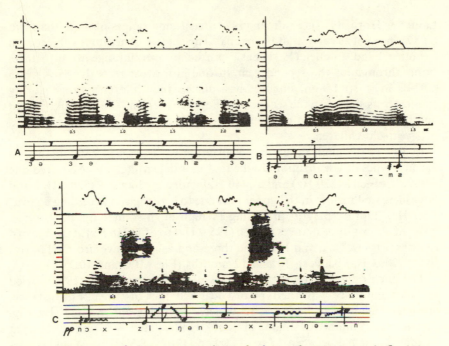

Fig. 8.   *Wailing sounds: (A) precursors of cry in fundamental voicing at 4 weeks (x̄ = 300 ms; f = 90/min); (B) vocative intonation prior to cry at 6 weeks (x̄ = 1.5s); (C) whining tone of voice during sad mood at 15 months. Curves from above: amplitude, sonagram, musical transcription.*

harmonics or with an increased part of irregular noises (Fig. 8) perceived as whining, wailing, or fussy sounds.

Particularly rich variations of timbre during vocal interchanges were elicited while the caretaker was imitating Tanya's utterances and she was responding with eager attempts to match. Not only the length of individual utterances exceeded 5 s, and the pitch range with the variety of melodic contours increased, but also a colorful repertoire of timbre indicating a delightful excitement was displayed. During Tanya's monologues at the age of 4 months, similar expressions occurred as an escalation of an explorative play with new vocal achievements. At the age of 5 months, brief, cheerful, high register squeals were produced when Tanya saw her favorite toys for the first time after a 2-week absence. Further on, they indicated delight with an increasing consistency.

As to the infant's *pitch range*, the data available in the literature are controversial. Some authors (Delack & Fowlow, 1978; Sheppard & Lane, 1968) have reported a moderate range, stable during the first year; others have described remarkable ranges contributing to individual differences among infants or showing a dependence on behavioral states (Keating & Buhr, 1978;

Laufer & Horii, 1977). Fridman (1974) has found ranges of more than two octaves present as early as at the neonatal age in two of her three subjects. On the other hand, Fitchen (1931) has reported an overall range of one octave, stable throughout the second year in one girl. Most recently, McKernon (1979), in a study on singing, has placed the children's range during spontaneous singing in the second year between c' and b', similarly like Jersild and Bienstock (1934) did between d' and a' for correct reproduction of tones in 2-year-old children.

In Tanya, the pitch ranges in vocalization varied considerably both with age and types of vocalization. In the first month her pitch range covered one octave between a (220 Hz) and a' (440 Hz) with a median in e' (329,6 Hz), and later increased mainly in the upper part due to high register squealing up to a" (880 Hz). During playful practising in high pitch sounds the pitch range covered almost three octaves from g (195,9 Hz) to e''' (1318 Hz) at the age of 4 months (Figs. 9, 10A, and 10B), and three-and-a-half octaves from f (174 Hz) to c'''' (2093 Hz) between 10 and 12 months (Figs. 10C and 10D).

The pitch ranges or registers in terms of Keating and Buhr (1978) varied also in accordance with the type of vocal activities in Tanya. For instance, cheerful squeals occurred in the frequencies around or above a" (880 Hz, Fig. 7), whereas spontaneous singing of brief melodic patterns during babbling at 11 months moved between f' (349,2 Hz) and f" (698,5 Hz, Fig. 6), and single-word utterances with speech-like intonation contours at 14 months between a (220 Hz) and a' (440 Hz, Fig. 18). When singing her favorite song ("Der Mond ist aufgegangen") in several transpositions during one monologue at 15 months, Tanya used an overall range from g (195,9 Hz) to a" (880 Hz) with a median of g'-flat (370 Hz) whereby she started the song on several different levels between a-flat and c" (Fig. 16).

Distinct *pitch preferences* concerned a narrow range of Tanya's tones. During the first half-year, the majority of vocal tones clustered around the median of e' (329,6 Hz). Later on the preferential tones were distributed more

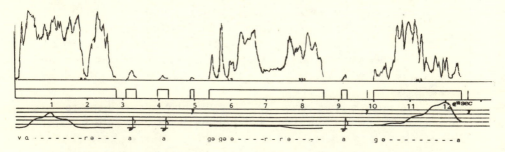

Fig. 9.   Vocal play at 4 months: exploration of pitch range and of duration. Curves from above: amplitude, duration in seconds, musical transcription.

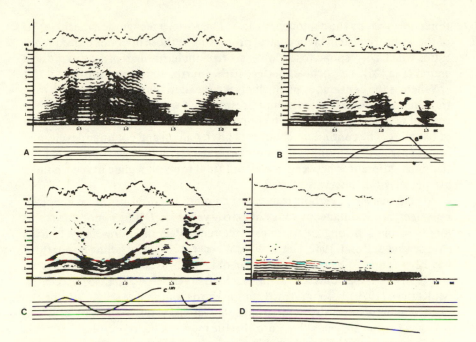

Fig. 10.   Sonagrams of vocal play: exploration of pitch range. (A) and (B) at 4 months; (C) at 12 months (upper pitch range); (D) at 12 months (lower pitch range). Curves from above: amplitude, sonagram, musical transcription.

widely, but not randomly, since 50 percent of 130 tones represented the notes f′, a′, c′, d′, f″ associated with the tonal scale of F-major in one uninterrupted monologue at 11 months. These tones represent the tonic (f′), the dominant (c′), the major triad (f′, a′, c′), and the lyra melodics (a′, c′, d′). At 14 months, 70 percent of 138 tones acounted for a-d′-e′-fis′-a′, corresponding to the scale of D-major and including again the tonic, the dominant, and the major triad next to the subdominant. Obviously, the production of tones during the second half-year of life was influenced by the preference of tones belonging to harmonic series and tonal music. This aspect will be discussed in Section IV.B.

In most cultures including the Western ones, music is based on tone transitions in discrete steps called *intervals*. Although the human auditory system possesses a much higher capability of frequency resolution, scales of discrete tones have been developed, according to Roederer (1975, p. 161/162), because it is "easier for the brain to process, identify, and store a melody that is made up of a time sequence of discrete pitch values bearing a certain relationship to each other, rather than melodies sweeping continuously up and down over all possible frequencies." Relationships of tones are given by their frequency ratio. The pattern recognition mechanisms of the auditory system favor central processing of those intervals or frequency ratios which correspond to the lower six to eight harmonics of a given musical sound (Fig. 26), i.e., octave, perfect fifth, fourth, sixth, and third.

Whereas the continuous pitch changes prevail in the young infant, the tone transitions in discrete steps seem to result from the later achievement in the control of the vocal tract, which approximately coincides with the beginning of babbling. The continuous changes in pitch remain and continue developing in the speech-like intonation contours thereafter, although sometimes even the pitch differences between initial and final tones of a glide in speech units are perceived as intervals as well.

A preference for certain intervals in young children has been reported repeatedly. In spontaneous songs of 2- to 5-year olds, falling minor thirds and major seconds belong to the most frequent intervals followed by fourths (Moorhead & Pond, 1942; Nettl, 1956; Werner, 1917). The falling minor third has been found to be used by 2½-year-olds in phrases like "coal man—coal truck," or by 4-year-olds for teasing each other (Gesell & Ilg, 1943). Recently, McKernon (1979) has confirmed minor thirds and major seconds to be the most common intervals, next to unisons, spontaneously sung by children between 1½ and 2½ years. They are also the most readily reproduced intervals in 3- and 4-year olds (Jersild & Bienstock, 1934). Infants under 1 year have only exceptionally been studied from this view and have been found by Fridman (1974) to be using all possible intervals already at birth as a random outcome of neonatal crying and other vocalizations.

In Tanya's vocalizations between 1 and 16 months of age, practically all mentioned intervals appeared. However, in all age periods, the majority of them was represented by unisons, and seconds (67 percent) followed by fourths, minor thirds, perfect fifths, and octaves. The high incidence of unisons and the smallest intervals, dominating simultaneously with continuous glides and undulating pitch contours during the first months, can be explained with a limited control of the vocal tract. Further development of this control leads to the appearance of reduplicated babbling which then accounts for the prevalence of tone repetitions in unisons or chromatic intervals. At the age of 10 months, for instance, Tanya could alternatively apply a chromatic sequence of five to seven semitones in groups of syllables "ma," "da," "ja," or "ga" (Fig. 6). In all age periods intervals larger than an octave occurred as well, mostly in sudden leaps from one register to another between utterances. Large leaps also occurred within one utterance at 16 months (Fig. 23).

The most frequent intervals in Tanya's spontaneous repertoire (i.e., unisons, seconds, minor thirds, and fourths) constitute a plenty of traditional nursery songs (Fig. 26), and according to musicologists belong to the most frequently sung intervals all over the world (Bernstein, 1976; Nettl, 1956; Orff, 1950).

The beginning of *spontaneous singing of melodic contours* in children above 2 years has been described as simple repetitions of short phrases with descending or undulating contours over a narrow range of two to four tones, with only slight and infrequent variations (Nettl, 1956; Werner, 1917). Moorhead and Pond (1942) distinguished chants and songs in spontaneous musical vocalization. Chant as the most primitive form of musical art is only a heightened speech with a prominent speech-like rhythm and little melodic variation serving the accentuation of most important syllables. Chants are coordinated with motor activities and often performed in groups. Songs, on the other hand, are melodic tunes exhibited by the child for his or her own sake, with a free and flexible rhythm and no apparent tonal center. Revesz (1954) found self-invented melodies bearing some relations to musical structure and tonality only in gifted children at or above 4 years of age.

Little attention has been paid to singing in children under 2 years. McKernon (1979) has reported children between 12 and 18 months to sing in a continuous voice, undulating and gliding irregularly over a narrow pitch range. Even when discrete tones and intervals appeared at 18 months, rudimentary melodic patterns still were irregular, comprised atonal groupings of several tones mixed with glides and spoken utterances, and their rhythm varied. Thus spontaneous songs in 1- to 2-year olds have been considered to lack predictability and memorability in contrast to the structure of conventional songs.

The studies in infants under 1 year have not gone beyond general descriptions of intonation contours. According to Delack and Fowlow (1978) rising–falling contours become increasingly frequent on behalf of falling or rising contours during the first year.

In Tanya, only the first 6 months were characterized by continuous undulating pitch contours in her vocal repertoire. In cries, distinct rising–falling contours were present already at the neonatal age (Figs. 2, 3). In the second and third months falling terminal glides together with voice fading appeared in the vowel-like sounds during quiet waking as if affected by the decrease in expiratory power at the end of expirium (Figs. 4B, 4C, 5B, and 5D). Even her early fundamental voicing was not totally irregular and included elements of melodic and rhythmic structures at least within sequences of repeated sounds (Fig. 4). Not much later, rising contours appeared together with steep glides or leaps over one octave in squealing sounds (Fig. 7). From the fourth month on, quite melodious patterns of intonation were produced during playful vocal practicing. These patterns included even excessive rising–falling contours occasionally covering a wide range of more than two octaves (Figs. 9, 10A, and 10B). These contours, discontinuous and irregular at the beginning, become smooth and continuous with increasing practice (Figs. 10C, 10D). Simultaneously with the production of pitch transitions in discrete steps, Tanya invented the first short melodies (Fig. 11) in the form of hummed sequences of pure musical tones.

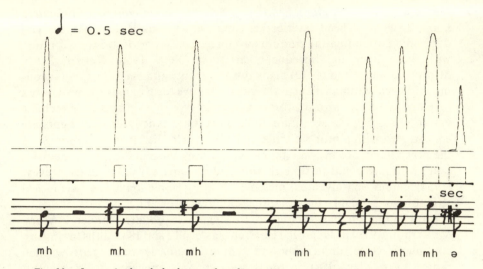

Fig. 11.   Improvised melody, hummed in discrete tones at 7 months. Curves from above: amplitude, duration in seconds, musical transcription.

During the following period of reduplicated babbling a variety of melodic patterns appeared (Fig. 6). In the further development of musical elements two parallel lines become obvious, the speech-like intonation contours accompanying the linguistic differentiation, and the musical melodic contours in imitated, or invented songs.

Little is known on the adoption of *rhythms* in the infant's vocal performance. Fridman (Fridman, 1974; Fridman & Battro, 1977), analyzing the development of rhythmic vocalizations with the help of mere musical notations, has claimed that a variety of "protorhythms" are obvious already in the newborn's vocal expressions. She has considered those protorhythms as "natural rhythmic schemes" underlying the rhythms of both adult speech in various languages, and the classical music. McKernon (1979) has found only little rhythmic organization in the spontaneous songs even in 1- to 2½-year olds. Their songs are irregular and only occasionally show fairly regular beats. Moorhead and Pond (1942) have stressed a prevalence of "free and flexible rhythms" in songs, and pronounced "speech-like rhythms" closely related to motor activities in chants of young children. Nettl (1956) has described the typical pattern of children's songs as a "series of notes of equal length with a final long note."

When learning conventional songs the child only gradually incorporates the rhythmic features of songs (McKernon, 1979; Wing, 1941). This may be related to a general difficulty of the young child to synchronize his singing or movements to a time pattern or beat outside himself (Heinlein, 1929; Jersild & Bienstock, 1935; Wing, 1941), but it contradicts the astonishing finding of

Condon and Sander (1974) that the newborn synchronizes motor activity to the rhythm of adult speech.

The slow assimilation of exogenous rhythms may remind us of the basic difference between unstable biological rhythms in human behaviors and the strictly metrical rhythms and stable tempos which represent a late achievement of technology in the human history. Analogous regular structures are uncommon not only in the physiological regulations of behavior, but also in the infant's naturalistic perceptual environment unless modified technologically. Moreover, the structure of vocalization is so intimately interrelated with breathing that it cannot be inert to changes in behavioral states, or to the course of integrative processes which do strongly influence the rhythm of breathing (Papoušek, 1969; Papoušek & Papoušek, 1979b).

The development of rhythmical patterns in Tanya started with the patterning of fundamental voicing which was fully determined by the parameters of breathing both in the temporal and intonational aspects (Figs. 4, 5). Similarly as in cry, the fundamental voicing sometimes also became saccadic simultaneously with a "high frequency and low amplitude tremor" of extremities, and consisted of several 60 to 100-ms sounds in the rhythm of 5 to 6 per second. The protorhythms in neonatal vocalizations observed by Fridman and Battro (1977) obviously belong to this category. More frequently, however, each sound took a major part of expirium without affecting the respiratory rate.

Fig. 5 illustrates the increasing duration of vowel-like sounds over the first 3 months, from brief "staccato" sounds of about 150 ms to melodic sounds of 550 to 1100 ms. Those sounds frequently appeared in rhythmic sequences of four to eight units, each corresponding to one expirium at a rate of forty to eighty per minute (Fig. 4). Individual sequences were separated from one another by pauses lasting at least one respiratory cycle.

Beginning in the third month and rapidly developing in the fourth month, the control of respiration allowed to prolongate expirium in favor of vocal performance, whereby inspirium segmented the otherwise continuous flow of vocal sounds. At this age the expirium occasionally exceeded 5s (Fig. 9). With a transition from quiet vocalization to a fussy one, the duration of fundamental voicing increased much earlier, i.e., already during the first month (Figs. 8A, 8B), as cry itself lasts 2 or more seconds even in the first days of life; or else due to increased arousal and respiratory rate, the frequency of sounds might increase to 90 per minute.

An articulatory segmentation of one expirium appeared with the earliest syllable-like sounds in the second and third months of age occasionally, and with the development of syllables with increasing frequency above 4 months. A new faster articulatory rhythm appeared within respiratory cycles and served to the future linguistic or musical competences. In the reduplicated

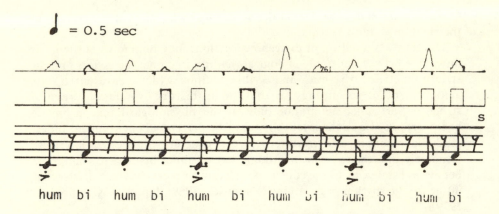

Fig. 12. *Dance-like rhythm (common time) at 13 months. Curves from above: amplitude, duration in seconds, musical transcription.*

babbling, articulatory rhythms became obvious from the fifth month on, in the first musical melodies at seven months (Fig. 11).

Fig. 6 exemplifies the regularity of Tanya's repetitive syllabic patterns exhibited at the age of 10 months, i.e., after several months of frequent practicing. Syllables, grouped by three to eleven at this age, lasted 189.67 ms on average in this sample, the standard error being $s_{\bar{x}} = 11.10$.

At the age of 1 year, Tanya was capable of singing rhythmic sequences and accompanying them with rhythmic movements of extremities or body, and/or with a production of synchronized noises with the help of toys. Fig.12 illustrates a dance-like rhythm recorded at 13 months. A common(four–four) time reminding of the polka or foxtrot rhythm is easy to recognize. Fig. 25 shows how far Tanya was able to adopt the rhythms of nursery songs and reproduce them in repetitive patterns of vocalization with small variations only. When reproducing longer melodies of conventional songs, Tanya slowed down the tempo and interrupted the melodic sequence regularly for inspiratory pauses of 0.5 to 1 s (Fig. 16).

In general, rhythmic patterns appeared quite early, first as by-products of autonomic or other motor behaviors of a rhythmical character, and later as features of vocal products. Rhythmic patterns may reach an astonishing regularity temporarily; in general, however, they remain flexible and vary according to various extrinsic or intrinsic circumstances, calling for a more systematic research. The infant's musical rhythm seems to be closer to folk music or jazz improvisation than to the classical Western music.

C. Imitation and Learning to Sing a Song

The most advanced vocal performance of musical capabilities in children under two years of age is the capability of learning to sing a song. It is a complex phenomenon offering a chance for the study of fundamental integrative processes, such as pattern recognition, concept formation, auditory memory, and vocal imitation, with regard to both the melodic and rhythmic aspects of conventional children's songs which are conveniently simple and repetitive (Moerk, 1972).

The issue of the earliest evidence of *vocal imitation* in infants has attracted a particular attention ever since the studies on facial imitation (Maratos, 1973; Meltzoff & Moore, 1977) reported an evidence of imitation in the first months of life. Papoušek and Papoušek (1977c) have explained in their analysis of intuitive maternal behavior that the mother imitates the newborn's behavior from the first contacts on and makes thus her imitations contingent on the newborn's behavior; hence the interpretation of the infant's earliest nonvocal imitation of facial and oral behavior should consider and experimentally discriminate two alternatives: a true imitation and a "pseudo-imitation" resulting from pure instrumental learning during the generalization phase of instrumental acts. Otherwise, a similar confusion might complicate the analysis of imitative behavior as that caused by the disrespect to pseudoconditioning in the initial studies on early learning in infants. Controversial discussions on the pages of *Science* in 1979 (Anisfeld, 1979; Jacobson & Kagan, 1979; Masters, 1979; Meltzoff & Moore, 1979) confirm the validity of the Papoušeks' warning.

However, Papoušek & Papoušek (1977c) have also pointed out the vocal reciprocal imitation as the earliest chance at which the infant can compare both imitated and imitating products and discover similarities. Therefore, vocal imitation may play a crucial role in the development of imitative capabilities. In studies not yet designed to exclude pseudoimitation, a rudimentary imitation (Lewis, 1936; Stern & Stern, 1928) or tendency to match vocal sounds to those of adults imitating an infant (Wolff, 1969), or those of infants from magnetic tapes (Fridman, 1974), have been reported in infants between 1 and 2 months of age.

The earliest vocal imitation involves perceptual learning (Gibson, 1969) and may be rudimentary due to insufficient development of either integrative capacities, or vocal performance. Later on it develops to the capacity not only to copy a presented model immediately, but also to use the presented models for delayed repetitive practicing.

Due to differences in methods, immediate matching or copying of vocal sounds has been reported to develop at very different ages in infants, in relation to pitch, for instance, at 3 months (Platt, 1933), 3 to 4 months (Fridman, 1974), 13 and 19 months (Wing, 1941), or 24 months (Jersild & Bienstock, 1934). In relation to intervals or short melodies it has been described at 7 months (Fridman, 1974) and 14 months (Wing, 1941).

Delayed imitation as obvious as in the adoption of speech-like intonation contours has been reported in infants above 6 months of age (Bruner, 1975; Dore et al., 1976; Halliday, 1979; Lewis, 1936; Tonkova-Yampol'skaya,

1969), and as singing of tunes at 9½ months (Fridman, 1974), 16 to 24 months (Wing, 1941), and 23 months (Stern, 1924). Gesell and Ilg (1943) discriminated four sequential stages in the adoption of songs: reproduction of phrases, but not on pitch at 2 years; reproduction of parts of songs at 2½ years, of a whole song, but not on pitch at 3 years; and of a whole song correctly from 4 years. There is a general agreement that children first learn a rather general melodic contour of the given tune as a whole (Gesell & Ilg, 1943; McKernon, 1979; Shuter, 1968; Teplov, 1966; Wing, 1941).

According to McKernon's (1979) detailed analysis of the course of song learning in four subjects between 1½ and 2½ years, a portion of the lyrics is adopted and incorporated into spontaneous tunes first. In the next step, short fragments of the melodic sequences stored in memory appear, and are used repeatedly and universally without a specific location. Only later do children develop an "appropriate grasp" of the whole melodic contour, involving recognition and adoption of the basic pattern of the song, and finally reproduce longer, recognizable tunes with correctly sequenced intervals.

Analyzing Tanya's examples of *learning to sing a song* we realized that such an individual analysis can go into many more details and reveal interesting evidence of involved cognitive operations.

At the age of 2 months, Tanya indistinctly matched a pitch or short intonation contour to the typical segments of parental babytalks. At 3½ months, she matched single tones sung to her and played on a piano. Around 4 months, a tendency increased in her to produce longer and unusual combinations of sounds and intonation contours from her repertoire when a parent displayed them first. A distinct turn-taking appeared on her side. She listened very attentively to the parental utterance, and then with signs of pleasure she carried out an equally long utterance, including small parts of equal melodic contours, rhythmic patterns, or consonant-like sounds. She seemed to have perceived the global model, but while copying it she was unable to coordinate all features.

At the age of 8 months, Tanya tried to imitate a new combination of two unequal syllables "ta-ti" (family name for daddy) with an astonishing effort and various strategies: She varied the duration of syllables, escalated intonation contours and/or intensity, and recombined similar syllables (Fig. 13). Such an activation very much resembled the general activation of many kinds of movement during the initial phase of instrumental learning through "trial and error" in infants (Papoušek, 1967); or else, if the articulation was too difficult, Tanya suddenly stopped articulating and hummed repeatedly the appropriate intonation contour.

At 10 months, Tanya rather correctly imitated proto-words and speech-like intonation contours on one hand, and tones, tonal sequences, or short melodies on the other. At the age of 11½ months, she correctly hummed melodies and rhythms of the first phrases of several more complex songs. Fig.

14 illustrates one of Tanya's early attempts to complement her parent in singing a familiar nursery song. Her version of "Hopp, hopp, hopp..." reflects a characteristic portion of lyrics, rhythm, and speed of the last syllables, as well as the global rising and falling melodic contour, but condensed by omitting the most difficult passages.

When hearing a new or a not yet properly adopted song, Tanya listened very attentively, typically asked for several repetitions using the word "noch" ("more" in English), and listened silently, sometimes with lip movements, to all repetitions without decreasing attention. At the age of 13 months, she took a great pleasure in a new version of lyrics in her favorite song "Hopp, hopp,

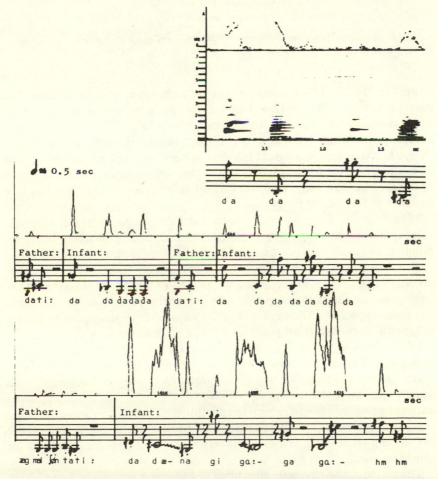

Fig. 13.   Strategies used for imitation of the model word "tati" ("daddy" in English) at 8 months. Curves from above: amplitude, musical transcription. Segment f"—h—g" major—g major is shown in sonagram on the top.

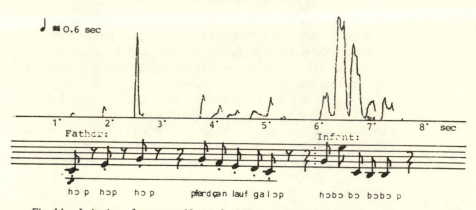

Fig. 14.   *Imitation of a song at 13 months ("Hopp, hopp, hopp, Pferdchen, lauf Galopp"). Curves from above: amplitude, musical transcription.*

hopp." In Fig. 15, Tanya complements her father in the last tone of the first part on correct pitch, invites him for the performance of her perferred onomatopoeic part of the song, and echoes its end herself. Such a complementary turn-taking with a correct tuning in pitch indicated that Tanya had the entire concept of the song at her disposal, and therefore could continue where the father gave turn to her, as well as anticipate the next part of the song or repeat the last contour in an appropriate rhythm bringing it to the correct fundamental note.

Linguistically, Tanya quickly proceeded from a consistent use of single words at 9 months to chaining of words in two- to three-part relations at 13½ months, and to the first grammatical sentences at 14½ months. At this stage, Tanya regularly asked her mother at night to sing several strophs of her favorite lullaby "Der Mond ist aufgegangen" (Fig. 16). At 15 months she learned to sing the melody together with her mother, and incorporated it into her monologues at 15½ months. Fig. 25 shows her spontaneous play with fragments of conventional songs at the age of 16 months.

In the monologue in Fig. 16, Tanya was initially in a sad mood, and encouraged herself in a faint whining tone: "Tanya sad, yes, sing, sing, sing more," before she began to sing. She repeatedly interrupted her singing with similar phrases, first in an equally whining tone. But then her mood improved until she squealed cheerfully between portions of the song. Prior to the taped episode, it had not been exceptional for her to hear words like "Is Tanya sad? Let us sing some song," from caretakers when she had been distressed for some reason.

The melodic and rhythmic structures of that song are simple, whereas the lyrics rather complex, with a vocabulary far exceeding Tanya's linguistic competence at 15 months. Nevertheless, in her reproductions, Tanya did approximate the words of lyrics as well assumedly learning the lyrics with the melody as a whole. Therefore, fragments of the lyrics of any one stroph

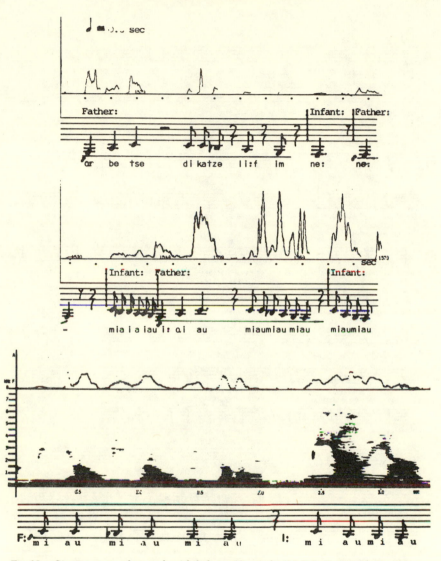

Fig. 15.   *Singing a song alternately with father at 13 months ("A B C, die Katze lief im Schnee, i ei au, miau miau miau"). Curves from above: amplitude, musical transcription. Sonagram of the last section at the bottom.*

appeared in combinations with appropriate melodic fragments. Whenever Tanya was unable to recall the lyrics in one stroph, she substituted them with the correspoding words of another stroph or with humming.

The melody of the lullaby "Der Mond ist aufgegangen" consists of three closely interrelated phrases: I and II are parallel, II being a third higher than I; III is a combination of the first half of II and the second half of I.

Fig. 16. Singing the German song "Der Mond ist aufgegangen...": (A) standard song (I, II, III = phrases of the song; 1, 2, 3 = strophs); (B) alternating with mother at 15 months; (C) in a monologue at 15½ months (7 modulations and transpositions). Corresponding notes are located below the notes of the standard song. Capital letters above notes indicate major keys; small letters, minor keys. Asterisks mark notes sung correctly. The song in the monologue is interrupted first by whining utterances ("Tanya sad, sing, sing more, oh" in English) and by soft squeals toward the end.

Consequently, the half-tone step varies in respect to its position in otherwise identical melodic contours. As the transcript in Fig. 16 shows, Tanya disposed with the entire concept of the whole melody, although she was able to sing only two phrases correctly at a time. She freely transposed the melody to various keys. Whenever she happened to sing a false note, she either used this note as a starting point for a new key, or returned to the initial key after some melodic detour. Interestingly, in the first half of the sample, being still sad, Tanya tended to slip to flat keys, whereas with an improvement of mood the melodies became pure and correct.

Tanya's occasional difficulties in hitting the right note may have been primarily due to an insufficient pitch control in worded reproduction, because they were less frequent in humming. Errors concerned most frequently the fourth notes in any of the three phrases of the song, probably due to confusions between phrases. Another equally appropriate explanation may be in the ambiguity of the fourth notes which represent the sixth and tenth overtones of the harmonic series (see Fig. 26 in Section IV.B) known to be ambiguous tones between two half tones of the tempered scale (Bernstein, 1976).

The rhythmic structure of that song consists of regular tones; only the accentuated syllables are marked with longer notes. Tanya adopted this basic rhythmic pattern and placed the longer notes correctly. On the whole, however, she slowed down the tempo and segmented the tune independently of lyrics with respiratory pauses of 0.5 to 1 s, thus giving the tune a temporal structure of a babytalk.

D. Development of Speech-Like Intonation Contours

The development of speech-like contours parallels that of melodic contours in singing, and cannot be distinguished from it convincingly prior to the infant's transition from babbling to the first lexical items and one-word sentences. However, the speech-like contours must not necessarily be restricted to the lexical content or social context of vocalization. On the contrary, they may abundantly be exhibited in the infant's monologues and in association with any repetitive syllable. This elicits the impression that the infant is practicing prosodic patterns commonly used in its social environment and adopted in "prosodic matrices" similar to the intonational contours of the adults' babytalk. Fig. 17 illustrates several such prosodic envelopes which Tanya used from the age of 7 months with obvious intentions to attract or direct the parent's attention: a melodic high pitch rising contour interpretable as an invitation to mutual play; a horizontal contour with vibrations as a nagging request; and a slowly and fluently falling contour as in a soothing utterance. A high pitch tone with a terminal falling glide as an indicative pattern is shown in Figs. 18 and 19.

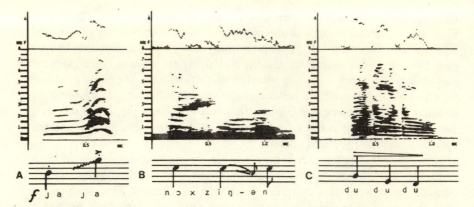

Fig. 17. *Three typical forms of prosodic envelopes between 11 and 15 months: (A) rising contour in an invitation for play; (B) horizontal contour in a nagging request; (C) falling contour in an imitated soothing utterance. Curves from above: amplitude, sonagram, musical transcription.*

Fig. 18. *Speech-like prosodic contours in one-word sentences at 13 months: indicative contours.*

Curves from above: fundamental frequency, amplitude, duration in seconds, musical and phonetic transcriptions.

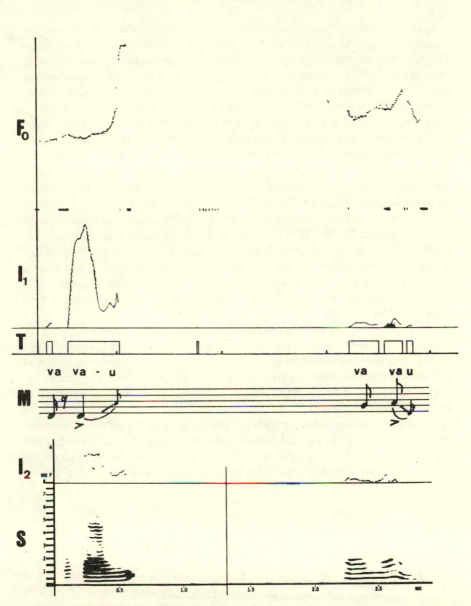

Fig. 19.   Speech-like prosodic contours in one-word sentences at 13 months: interrogative and indicative contours.

Curves from above: fundamental freuqency, amplitude, duration in seconds, musical and phonetic transcriptions, sonagram.

Speech-like prosodic envelopes with sentence-like temporal structures (the "speech-like jargon" or "mimicry of speech" of Sachs, 1977) appeared in Tanya's monologues at the age of 9 months. Those monologues consisted of syllables combined without any detectable semantic relation, as if primarily produced for the sake of imitating the prosody of parental speech. Thus, Tanya would "read a book" from a blank sheet of paper on her own.

Figure 18 shows a collection of Tanya's distinctly articulated one-word sentences extracted from a dialogue with her father at the age fo 13 months. In spite of differences in words and number of syllables the indicative contour alters surprisingly little and mirrors the prosody of the preceding parental sentences. A sequence of interrogative and indicative contours from the same dialogue is given in Fig. 19. Figure 20 shows a monologue in which Tanya, 16 months old, repeatedly imitated the mother's indicative intonation in the German phrase "Schau mal" ("look here" in English) and varied either phonetic or musical features. These and similar prosodic patterns of the infant not only reflect distinct syntactic functions involved in the adult's model sentences, but deliver nonspecific, biologically relevant and physiologically effective messages as we discussed them in Section II.C with respect to the babytalk.

Until the age of 16 months, the speech-like intonation contours used by Tanya still differed from those of a normal adult speech. They beared features of both spoken and sung contours. Their timbre was relatively musical and expressive, and the pitch contour strongly accentuated. Thus, in general, the speech-like intonation contours closely mirrored the features of babytalk of her social environment (Fig. 21).

As to the communicative function of prosodic patterns, a fluent transition was observed from the earliest fundamental voicing, from which the parents learn about the infant's general behavioral state, to the expression of emotional aspects, intentional use of prosodic envelopes for eliciting or

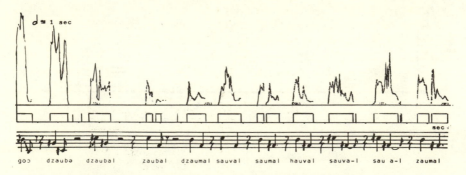

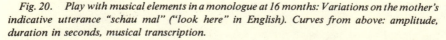

Fig. 20.   *Play with musical elements in a monologue at 16 months: Variations on the mother's indicative utterance "schau mal" ("look here" in English). Curves from above: amplitude, duration in seconds, musical transcription.*

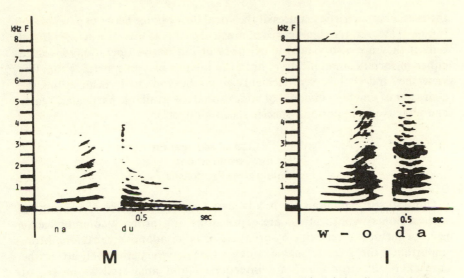

Fig. 21. Sonagrams of comparable prosodic contours in mother's babytalk (M) and infant's monologue (I).

directing the parent's attention, and finally to the delivery of linguistic messages.

Certain patterns maintain the basic features unchanged during the entire period from birth to 16 months. For instance, Tanya's wailing tone during a sad mood at 15 months (Fig. 8C) and envelopes of begging requests, or nagging in distress situations (Fig. 17B) are quite similar to the precursors of cry in the fundamental voicing at one month (Figs. 8A, 8B) or at later ages. A similar continuity was observed in her intentional vocative intonation, angry tones, and also in the melodious signs of good mood or the high pitch squeals accompanying states of cheerful excitement.

Although many more observations are necessary to confirm consistencies or to understand differentiations in the immensely variable repertoire of prosodic patterns, our experience has suggested that such an analysis in individual cases would help to understand their manifold roles in the preverbal communication, assuming that the situational context were taken into consideration as well.

IV. TWO IMPORTANT AVENUES OF DEVELOPMENT

The preceding parts of this communication have demonstrated that the musical elements develop early and interestingly, and, therefore, as a part of the global vocal development deserve a particular attention. They belong to the most characteristic features of the vocal interchange between parents and infant. However, the significance of musical elements becomes evident in full only if they are also viewed as elicitors of integrative operations involved either in social communication, or in the infant's play in general. From this view they indeed represent elements giving interactional vocalizations the character of teaching material or educational toy available particularly early and effective in important, species specific directions.

A. The Significance of Musical Elements for the Development of Integrative Processes

Contradictory opinions can be advocated as to the question of whether the earliest noncry vocalizations are expressions of a primary communicative need or incidental reflexive by-products of other adaptive behaviors. More important is the unquestionable evidence that they very effectively attract the caretakers' attention and are interpreted and answered as means of communication by them in various forms of parenting—innate or learned, general or specific, intuitive or conscious.

The musical elements are usually the earliest to be modulated in the fundamental voicing sounds. Parents soon discriminate these elements adequately, and show it in vocal comments or other caretaking responses. First, they learn to read information on general behavioral states and physiological needs from the infant's vocalizations; later they believe to be informed by the infant how far their behaviors are perceived or anticipated. The musical elements help the parents to evaluate the course of the infant's coping behaviors in various situations, joyful, or problematic and distressing, even if the infant is out of the parents' visual field. The fact that parents take the infant's earliest vocalization as means of communication may certainly reinforce the infant's capacity of using vocalization in communicative sense.

The *parental vocal responsiveness* to the infant's voice is very strong. In a study by Snow (1977), mothers responded to 100 percent of all vocalizations in their 3-month-old babies. Vocal stimulation per se positively reinforces the infant's tendency to vocalize only if combined with a direct visual contact (Bloom, 1975). This effect increases if the stimulation is carried out contingently upon the infant's vocalization, as shown in conditioning experiments (Rheingold et al., 1959). In naturalistic observations (Yarrow et al., 1975), not the total amount, but only the contingent part of maternal vocalization correlated with the infant's overall rate of vocalization. Other authors have stressed similar effects of arousal and affect during simultaneous vocalizations of mothers and infants (Anderson, 1977; Stern et al., 1975). Tanya's vocalization in our observations was most effectively elicited and most joyfully produced if the parental babytalk was contingent on her behavior and carried out with attentive turn-taking. The role of turn-taking has been stressed in several recent studies (Kaye, 1977; Schaffer et al., 1977; Snow, 1977; Stern et al., 1975).

Typically, musical elements in the parental babytalk vary less than other phonetic or lexical features. A limited amount of common prosodic envelopes characterize the most general categories of messages; for instance, the caretaker's intention to calm the infant, to announce him a readiness to help, to confirm presence, to invite him for joyful mutual interaction, to alert him, or to make him aware of a danger. Only in finer details they do bear signs of individual peculiarities. Musical elements help the parent to modulate the infant's behavioral state in accordance with the interactional situation. It is not known how far they can do so per se, but they may signal or accompany other interventions, for instance, changes of body position, tactual, and vestibular–proprioceptive stimulations which have been found effective (Korner & Thoman, 1972).

The consistent presence of musical elements in the babytalk helps the infant to identify the speaker and to understand that the babytalk is addressed to himself (see Section II.C). The consistent appearance gives the musical elements the attributes of *familiarity and predictability* which are potential elicitors of basic cognitive operations. Familiarity alone can become boring, of course, but if counterbalanced with an adequate proportion of novelty it elicits maximum attention (McCall & Kagan, 1967). This is also true about a moderate discrepancy in the auditory stimulation with familiar musical or verbal phrases, varied in melody, rhythm, and timbre (Kinney & Kagan, 1976). Intuitively, parents exploit such a possibility of maintaining the infant's attention aroused whereby they use the affective responses in the infant as a feedback information, according to our observations.

The *contingency* on the infant's behaviors, especially visual, vocal, and facial ones, is another important attribute of musical elements in the babytalk. Contingency can be detected by human newborns already on the first days of life and responded to with an effort to learn how to control contingent events (Papoušek, 1967). Long before infants can explore and manipulate nonsocial environmental events, they can do so in relation to vocal responses in parents.

Basically, the capacity of discovering familiarities, predictabilities, or contingencies is hardly thinkable without categorical perception and storing of information, or without at least simple concept formation. Thus, it is not necessarily overexaggerated to assume that parents deliver a plenty of teaching material in musical elements intrinsically activating and reinforcing cognitive operations in infants from the earliest age. This delivery may be carried out involuntarily, perhaps even innately, and may thus indicate that evolution has favored not only parents responsive to infantile vocalizations, but at first parents responding didactically in favor of the infant's cognitive development (Papoušek & Papoušek, 1978a,b).

Further steps of integration follow soon, and may, among others, also be guided by the functions of musical elements. At the age of 3 to 4 months, the infant is able to conceptualize much more complex relations in the structure of environmental stimulation, and to cope with rules requiring well-coordinated, sequential behaviors (Papoušek & Bernstein, 1969). The parental babytalk also becomes richer and more complex at the same time, adjusted with at least one step start to the level of the infant's cognitive development, and is therefore constantly potent of reinforcing further developmental progress.

The parent's impulsive inclination to imitate the infant's vocal sounds consistently provides the infant with a "biological mirror" or a *"biological echo"* allowing him or her to compare auditory products on both sides, and to learn which motor schemata correspond to the production of the speech sounds just being heard from the parent (Papoušek & Papoušek, 1975). This is an important condition for the development of the *infant's imitative capacity* and hence for the development of both language and self-concept.

With the increasing control of articulation, the infant also pays more attention to the mouth than to the eyes in the parent's face. Later, at the age of the first protowords and words, having asked for a repetition of new utterances or songs, the infant may carry out voiceless articulatory movements while observing the parent's mouth. The parent obviously functions as an instructor, but it would hardly be possible if the infant's imitative capacity were not developed sufficiently.

If the close relationship between the organization of motor acts and the development of the processes of thought has been emphasized in most theories on cognitive development (Bruner, 1966; Piaget, 1952), then the *integration of plans for vocal acts* calls for a closer look, although they are not the easiest responses to observe. However, their products are the earliest post-partum parts of self-perception on one hand, and later means of the species specific level of human thinking on the other. With regard to the early availability and increasing variability of perceivable products in vocal sounds, and particularly to the consistency of social consequences of these products, the integration of plans for the vocal motor acts logically plays a dominant role in cognitive growth. It represents an avenue open for infinite development of the system due to the qualities of vocal symbols that are so easy in terms of production or modification, and so powerful in terms of potential social consequences.

Following Cooley (1912) and Mead (1934), Lewis and Brooks-Gunn (1979) have recently reemphasized that *knowledge of self and other* are dependent upon one another. The implication of this principle is particularly valid with regard to the reciprocal parent–infant imitation of vocal sounds, i.e., in the sphere where, later on, the acquisition of language will enable very powerful expressions of self. Becoming familiar with the vocal production in the other, and hence also in self, is of course a complex process calling for systematic analyses in the future.

Intentionality is another aspect of self which is still a matter of speculation as to definition and criteria, but which has been raised as an urgent issue by psycholinguists with regard to the interpretation of preverbal communication. At present, the assumption has been increasingly advocated that an instrumental act per se gives an evidence of intentionality (Bruner, 1975; Dore, 1975; Papoušek & Papoušek, 1980). An instrumental act, unlike reflexive movements, involves not only efferent and feedback nervous pathways providing an information on the real course of the act in question, but also feedforward "corollary discharge" for associative areas where an ideal course-to-be is designed to achieve a given goal and to serve as a standard for corrections of the act during its course. In his first attempts to analyse voluntary acts in laboratory models, Papoušek (1962) more carefully postulated spontaneous choice from several alternative acts as an additional criterion.

Such assumptions allow us to speak of intentionality in preverbal infants; the more interesting it is to observe that young infants do differently modulate vocalizations during individual stages of learning instrumental acts, and that parents do interpret those vocalizations as expressions of intentions as well.

It is characteristic for the infant's fundamental adaptive response system that an activation of integrative efforts can be perceived as unpleasant before a necessary adaptation is achieved, and, on the other hand, that an achievement of a new adaptation is obviously associated with pleasant feelings. In terms of *intrinsic motivation*, the infant is thus both pushed with unpleasant incongruencies and pulled with the expectation of a pleasure on success to search for solutions in problematic situations, or difficult cognitive operations (Papoušek & Papoušek, 1979b). Seen from this view, the babytalk seems to offer a maximum of situations in which mainly the pleasant experience contributes to the infant's motivation for a vocal communication. The tendency, mostly intuitive, in the parent to be easily intelligible and highly predictable allows the infant to experience the vocal interchange as an increasing amount of pleasant outcomes of integrative processes, while reaching higher and higher levels of integration, including intentional acts and playful or creative activities.

Our explanation of the motivational aspect is based on the best fitting hypothesis and supported both with data from experimental studies on early learning, and with empirical observations of vocal interchanges in infants. One cannot overlook either the infant's joyful affective responses to familiar sounds or the untiring persistence with which the infant vocalizes if left alone. His motivation has been otherwise explained as a primary joy in sound production (Shinn, 1907), in mastery of the vocal tract, and in experiencing new sound patterns (Lewis, 1936; Stark, 1978b).

The significance of musical elements in speech is further determined by their key roles both in the earliest form of reciprocal communication and in the further differentiation of two parallel species specific capacities, language and creativity. These capacities raise the effectivity of integration to a unique level in the animal world. However, one crucial step in their development is still to be explained, namely the *development of play*.

Unlike adults, infants have been shown to vocalize most frequently when they are alone (Delack & Fowlow, 1978; Jones & Moss, 1971). In our observations in Tanya, for instance, we found solitary episodes of soliloquy to appear from the second month of age predominantly in the early morning hours after the night sleep, or prior to falling asleep during the day naps, in connection with attentive observation of a moving mobile, or during her play with objects.

Younger infants have long been believed to produce mere random sequences of sounds during monologues (Kaplan & Kaplan, 1971). According to our experience, a careful analysis can reveal very interesting structures indicating a participation of exploratory learning and playful or creative operations.

According to our concepts (Papoušek & Papoušek, 1977a; 1978a; 1979b), play and creativity are processes of integration on a higher level than simple learning or acquisition of skills. They allow us to reopen simple and seemingly closed concepts acquired on the lower level, examine them from new, unusual aspects, develop them creatively, and thus avoid both the danger of stress from the "unknown" on one hand and the danger of boredom on the "known" on the other. A newborn cannot yet play. First he must become acquainted with many new things and integrate fundamental concepts on them in order to have a chance to reopen and reexamine concepts at all. However, he or she soon begins to be instructed suggestibly by the parent that simple and already familiar concepts can be made surprisingly new, interesting and enjoyable if playfully modified or inventively applied in an unusual context. The musical elements of babytalk give the parent enough opportunities to do with the infant what J.S. Bach did so well with adult listeners in his ingenious variations.

The signs of pleasurable experience observable in infantile monologues strongly contradict the presence of either boredom or the stress from the unknown, and thus suggest that the infant is successfully avoiding both dangers due to his ability for playful operations. The structure of the monologue, on the other hand, confirms the involvement of higher-order cognitive operations enabling the infant to experiment with too familiar concepts, find new modifications, become acquainted with new aspects—in short to reopen the preexisting, seemingly closed, concepts.

At the preverbal stage of *vocal play,* the infant first explores the developing vocal capacities and learns to modify and expand the length of expirium, the pitch range, or the intensity of elementary sounds. Discovery of new sounds, integration of fundamental schemata on sound production, and of concepts concerning the most evident relations between vocal sounds and various behaviors of self or others seem to prevail at the beginning. With the increasing integration of partial functions a higher competence gradually develops which allows more complex operations, such as variations or combinations of previous vocal elements in new patterns eliciting interest in caretakers and pleasant experience in the infant itself.

Nature seems to have provided the infant not only with a powerful intrinsic motivation for playful or creative exploration, but also with a splendid toy in the vocal system offering the richest variety of modulations so early in life.

It would be premature and artificial to suggest any subdivision in this continuous development of the first expressions of play or creative abilities. However, in Tanya's case, we observed periods of acceleration in this process with accumulation of several new signs of progress.

At the age of 2 months and 2 weeks, Tanya started sleeping without interruption between 9 P.M. and 6 P.M. and spending up to 60 min on monologues afterwards. The monologues usually lost the initial joyful character toward the end and signalled hunger and discomfort; but if someone came to help and appeared ready to talk to Tanya, she could enjoy a dialogue for another 15 min very much. Her motivation for interaction outweighed hunger and discomfort. At the same time, the length of expirium increased even above 4 s, and was used for uninterrupted utterances with rich intonation contours. Occasionally, the first precursors of syllables in the forms of "ja-ja-ja" or "agaga" appeared. In dialogues, Tanya was distinctly able to use turn-taking, and attentively waited for the parent's utterance having finished hers. She responded to imitative parental utterances with happily relaxed face, and joyful short utterances before taking her turn, and exhibiting a long utterance with a facial expression of concentration and effort while looking at the parent's eyes.

From 4 months on the monologues began to include repetitive segments followed with a modified repetition, and then with facial signs of pleasure. Modifications concerned melodic, temporal or intensity features in musical elements (Figs. 9, 10), i.e., still those features that are presumably functions of the lower vocal tract, but serving now for the exhibition of voluntary vocal acts probably of cortical origin which allow playful processing, reopening, and recombining of global concepts.

With the appearance of distinct syllables (Fig. 6) and periods of reduplicated or nonreduplicated babbling (in terms of Stark, 1978b), i.e., with the development of the cortical control over the upper vocal tract necessary for syllabic articulation, the repertoire of vocal play expands to new dimensions. Syllabic sequences are sung in short structured melodies with distinct patterns of rhythm and accent. Typically, such song fragments are repeated and playfully modified as a whole, whereby all the inherent features, i.e., syllabic articulation, melody, rhythm, or intensity, are varied simultaneously while one of them is emphasized more than the others.

Several examples of Tanya's vocal play from the babbling period illustrate the increasing richness of play repertoire. Figure 22 demonstrates her monologue at the age of 16 months in which short syllabic patterns are musically varied in combination with a few different melodic fragments, one of them suddenly being repeated ten times with minimal variations and then

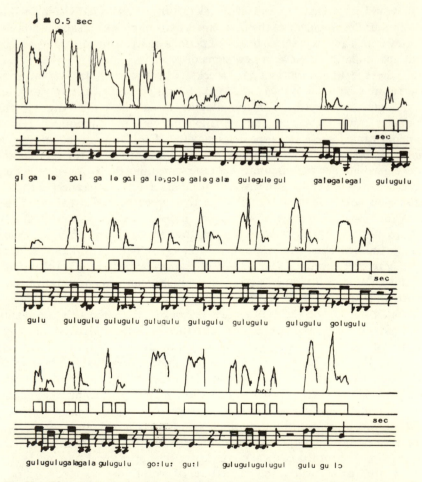

Fig. 22.   Play with various musical elements at 16 months. Curves from above: amplitude, duration in seconds, musical transcription.

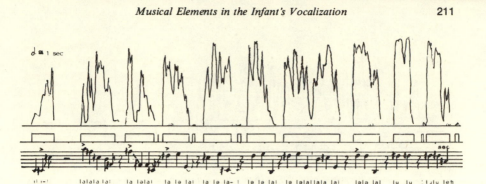

Fig. 23.   *Play with musical elements at 16 months: discrete leaps from high to low registers. Curves from above: amplitude, duration in seconds, musical transcription.*

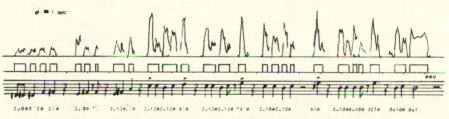

Fig. 24.   *Play with musical elements at 16 months: variations of interrogative contours. Curves from above: amplitude, duration in seconds, musical transcription.*

applied in a new melodic contour. Patterns of shifts in registers are exemplified in Fig. 23 with leaps from a high melodic register to a low one over up to one-and-a-half octaves. In Fig. 24, variations of melodic phrases with a consistent final rise are carried out in a long sequence as if practicing playfully the typical interrogative and attention-eliciting contours, respectively. In addition, the final note is marked by an accent and preceded by an attention-capturing pause. Interestingly, analogous structural modifications had been used in the parent's vocal games prior to Tanya's monologue.

Figure 20 shows Tanya's attempt in ten steps to approximate the correct articulation and intonation of a model phrase frequently used by the mother. Marked variations are exhibited in the overall intensity, but only moderate ones in stress and temporal patterns. Finally, in Fig. 25 it is mainly the melody of a popular nursery song which is playfully varied through half-tone modulations and led to its tonic or fundamental note c′, whereas the rhythmic pattern is strikingly regular.

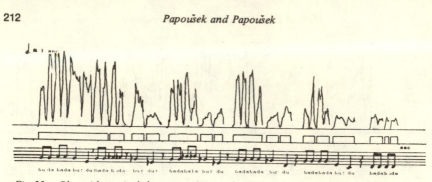

Fig. 25. Play with musical elements at 16 months: Variations on the melody of nursery songs given in Fig. 26. Curves from above: amplitude, duration in seconds, musical transcription.

B. The Significance of Musical Elements for the Infant's Musical Creativity

The increasing involvement of spontaneous and learned songs in vocal plays of older infants raises the question of the development of musical creativity. When listening to such melodic plays one does have an impression of an abundant flow of improvisation and creation of new sound patterns or combinations of musical elements. In the same way, of course, one could see elementary scientific operations, experimenting and testing, in vocal play. The amount of discrepancy between individual interpretations depends on the observer's theoretical views of play, arts, and sciences. In our opinion, all three of them have a common root in the preverbal infant's capacity to go beyond the seemingly finished form of a concept on the way from the "unknown" to the "known" (Section IV.A), in spite of the strong human inclination to integrate closed concepts on unknown things as fast as possible (Papoušek &Papoušek, 1978a). Only much later on, this common capacity, due to complex determinants, develops to specific capacities interpretable in terms of different arts or sciences.

The degree to which musical elements may be represented in playful activities is individually different and facilitates the further development of future musical arts in different degrees. As early as 1917, Werner has drawn attention to the creative improvisations in spontaneous singing of children aged 2 to 5 years. Lewis (1936) considered babbling as a rudimentary form of art and as a beginning of the aesthetic use of language which may reinstate emotional experience and its expression and convey "aesthetic emotion" resulting from the "joy of manipulating spoken sounds."

Examining those aspects of vocal play which might be precursors of the main functions of musical art, we have paid attention to the question of how far early vocal play or spontaneous singing help to communicate emotional experience, to induce musical sensations, and to reach a relief from distress or unpleasant moods. In the musical theories, various formal principles of harmony make it possible to construct compositions, the musical structure of which may symbolize the composer's emotional experience and evoke analogous ones in the listener. Those principles of harmony are based on different, culturally specific scales and may thus be applied in a seemingly enormous variety of communicative ways. We have to ask, of course, how far a preverbal infant, not aware of the knowledge of musical theories, still can use similar principles in spontaneous creative singing.

Tanya's example has convincingly demonstrated that, in her spontaneous singing, musical models were incorporated which had been offered to her in the babytalk (Fig. 19) or traditional songs for children (Fig. 25). The high incidence of harmonic intervals in the babytalk was mentioned in Section II.C.

Analyses of nursery songs (Bernstein, 1976; Orff, 1950) have shown that those of the oldest tradition and highest popularity are composed of typical sequences of either two tones (falling minor third as in calls, teasing rhymes, or "cuckoo calls"), three tones (lyra melodics, see Fig. 26), or four to five tones (pentatonic melodics). In stimulating Harvard lectures on the "Unanswered Question" of musical art, Bernstein (1976) has explained that both the tonal scales in Western traditional polyphony, and the serial twelve-tone music or other scales in other cultures are derived from the fundamental harmonic scale which, therefore, represents an innate, biologically determined universality. This view has been shared with him in recent theories on pitch perception and on the physical properties of the human auditory system (Roederer, 1975).

The harmonic scale and six examples of German popular nursery songs in Fig. 26 may help to follow the derivation of the main prototype of songs from the harmonic scale. The fundamental note (No. 1 in Fig. 26) represents the tonic, and its first different overtone (No. 2 in Fig. 26), the dominant. Together with the second different overtone (No. 4 in Fig. 26), tonic and dominant make up the major triad. Adding the third and fourth different overtones (No's. 6 and 8 in Fig. 26) we obtain the pentatonic scales. The sixth (No. 6 in Fig. 26), tenth, and still higher overtones (not given in Fig. 26), respectively, are ambiguous tones in terms of the Western scales, but regular tones in scales of other cultures. Below the harmonic scale in Fig. 26, six examples demonstrate nursery songs consisting only of the three tones included in the lyra melodics. All of them repeat various sequences of the first, second, and third different overtones of the tonic (Nos. 2, 4, and 6 in Fig. 26).

Thus, the fundamental elements of musical compositions seem to have the same biologically determined roots as those of intuitively composed nursery songs, naturally selected calls, babytalks, and also spontaneously preferred melodies in the preverbal vocal plays. Consequently, it was not too surprising, occasionally, to detect in Tanya's musical improvisations a short piece of music corresponding to the formal principles of harmony (Fig. 27), although no relation to prior musical stimulations could be found.

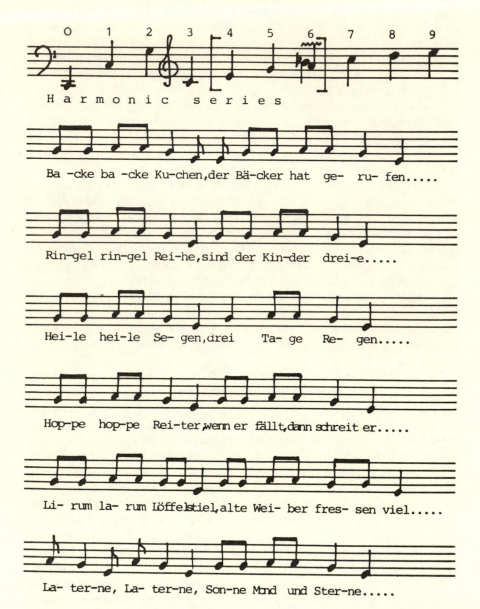

Fig. 26. Relation of nursery songs to the harmonic series. Top: harmonic series with fundamental note C and the first nine overtones. Brackets indicate the three tones of lyra melodics common to six traditional German nursery songs given below.

Fig. 27.   Play with musical elements at 16 months: an improvised song.

An interesting example (Fig. 27) was recorded at Tanya's age of 16 months. Noteworthy is the structure of Tanya's invention, basically a repetition and free modification of two phrases—A and B—resulting in a sequence of "A-B-B_1B_2-B_3-A_1." The tonal center of the melody is a' which is not only the lowest tone on which the melody ends, but the fundamental tone of the key A-major to which the melody fits surprisingly well. The rhythm is certainly not metric but moves in a steady, somewhat flexible pace, regularly interrupted by pauses of similar length.

The way for expressing, communicating, or sharing moods and emotional experience musically seems to be paved by coincidence of the infant's predispositions and environmental guidance present both in parenting and in cultural traditions.

To understand the effectiveness of musical elements, we also have to consider their nonspecific relational properties, i.e., intrinsic invariants, which result from the subjective processing of a musical experience, influence the general behavioral states, and initiate various cognitive operations. We have discussed these aspects in relation to the fundamental adaptive response system (Section IV.A), others with regard to the psychophysics of music (Roederer, 1975). For instance, one of the typical strategies of musical compositions is to introduce and repeat a phrase until it becomes predictable, and at that moment to surprise with a variation which arouses attention and elicits a pleasant degree of excitement.

At Tanya's age of 15 months, a chance helped us to tape an unusual monologue in which Tanya verbally confirmed that she was able of using singing intentionally for a relief of distress (Fig. 16, see Section III.C). Probably, the preceding performances of that song by the mother, or Tanya's own vocal play with parts of the song had been associated with pleasant feelings so consciously that Tanya could count on their effectiveness at the time of a sad mood and really evoked them with the help of singing. At the same time, the changing way of singing did correspond to an improvement in Tanya's mood.

V. CONCLUSION

Our attempt to take a closer look at the roles and early development of musical elements in vocalizations has been motivated by many an interest. That corresponds to the fact that musical elements do not develop as a solitary phenomenon, but as a part of global behaviors in the context of social interaction, and, therefore, may be viewed from different aspects.

One aspect concerns the biological roots of behaviors involved in parent–infant interactions—communicative behaviors in particular. Musical elements have a rich and interesting history of evolvement, although not easy to reveal. Next to comparative biological approaches and cross-cultural studies, a detailed analysis of their ontogeny helps to reconstruct their evolution. Unfortunately, not enough studies have paid attention to the developmental period between the first neonatal cry and the first word.

Another aspect has to do with the fundamental regulation of behavior in the infant. Musical elements are both by-products of major changes in behavioral states, and means of influence on behavioral states. This is true not only about the level of autonomic arousal and emotions, but also about the interrelation between musical elements and cognitive integration, another relevant—and neglected—aspect. In this light musical elements appear to be a rich learning material, no matter whether delivered to the infant in the caretaker's babytalk or generated by the infant itself.

Yet another aspect bears upon the potential precursors of musical arts, a view which has lead us to speculations on the substance of arts and to the hypothesis on common roots of arts and science in the playful cognitive operations with the fundamental, seemingly finished concepts.

This communciation includes experience from our previous studies on early learning and cognition, a survey of literature, and materials from pilot observations. The most informative part of the pilot materials has been a detailed single-case study of musical elements in our first-born daughter. That study alone has brought enough to share with a broader community of readers. Yet to us this communication is a basis for next explorations rather than a final report, and its timely discussion might be a valuable contribution to them.

The main profit of our attempt seems to be the finding that a close look at musical elements in each individual case together with a good understanding of their context does provide a very interesting information, relevant to all mentioned aspects. Further on, our present experience suggests that the importance of modern audiovisual records of behavior, spectrographic, and partially computerized digital analyses of vocal sounds do not yet outdate traditional musicological methods including subjective evaluation and musical transcription. A more detailed digital microanalysis, hopefully available in the near future, will certainly improve our methodological approach but will hardly eliminate the present methods.

ACKNOWLEDGEMENTS

The authors' research has been supported generously by the foundations "Stifterverband für die Deutsche Wissenschaft", "Deutsche Forschungs-gemeinschaft", and "Stiftung Volkswagenwerk". We are much indebted to Prof. Hans G. Tillmann, Head of the Department of Phonetics at the University of Munich, for allowing us to use his facilities, and to Prof. Detlev Ploog, the Director of Max-Planck Institute for Psychiatry who has significantly influenced the biological and developmental approaches to psychiatry. We wish to dedicate this manuscript to Detlev Ploog's 60th birthday.

Special debts are acknowledged to Gerhard W. Sandner, who carried out the electronic processing of our tapes, and to Uwe Jürgens, who allowed us to use his sonagraphic equipment. We thank also Angelika Weinmann for musical transcriptions, Dagmar Ellgring, Angelika Fischer, Alexa Kabiersch, Karin Malchert, and Veronika Stroh for their enormous technical and secretarial help with processing data and preparation of manuscript.

REFERENCES

Altmann, S. A. (Ed.) *Social communication among primates.* Chicago: University of Chicago Press, 1967.

Anderson, B. J. The emergence of conversational behavior. *Journal of Communication,* 1977, **27,** 85–91.

Anisfeld, M. Interpreting 'imitative' responses in early infancy. *Science,* 1979, **205,** 214–215.

Bell, S. M., & Ainsworth, M. D. S. Infant crying and maternal responsiveness. *Child Development,* 1972, **43,** 1171–1190.

Bernstein, L. *The unanswered question.* The Charles Eliot Norton Lectures, 1973. Cambridge, Mass.: Harvard University Press, 1976.

Bloom, K. Social elicitation of infant vocal behavior. *Journal of Experimental Child Psychology,* 1975, **20,** 51–58.

Brown, C. J. Reactions of infants to their parents' voices. *Infant Behavior and Development,* 1979, **2,** 295–300.

Bruner, J. S. On cognitive growth. I, II. In J. S. Bruner, R. R. Olver, & P. M. Greenfield (Eds.), *Studies in cognitive growth.* New York: Wiley, 1966.

Bruner, J. S. The ontogenesis of speech acts. *Journal of Child Language,* 1975, **2,** 1–19.

Bühler, C., & Hetzer, H. Das erste Verständnis für Ausdruck im ersten Lebensjahr. *Zeitschrift für Psychologie,* 1928, **197,** 50–61.

Bullowa, M. When infant and adult communicate, how do they synchronize their behaviors? In A. Kendon, R. N. Harris, & M. R. Key (Eds.), *Organization of behavior in face-to-face interaction.* The Hague: Mouton, 1975.

Busnel, R. G., & Classe, A. *Whistled languages.* Berlin: Springer, 1976.

Carmichael, L. The early growth of language capacity in the individual. In E. H. Lenneberg (Ed.), *New directions in the study of language.* Cambridge, Mass.: M.I.T. Press, 1964.

Condon, W. S., & Sander, L. S. Neonate movement is synchronized with adult speech: Interactional participation and language acquisition. *Science,* 1974, **183,** 99–101.

Cooley, C. H. *Human nature and the social order.* New York: Scribner's, 1912.

Crystal, D. Prosodic systems and language acquisition. In P. R. Léon, G. Faure, & A. Rigault (Eds.), *Prosodic feature analysis.* Studia Phonetica (Vol. 3). Montréal: Didier, 1971.

Crystal, D. Non-segmental phonology in language acquisition: A review of the issues. *Lingua,* 1973, **32,** 1–45.

Crystal, D. The analysis of intonation in young children. In F. D. Minifie & L. L. Lloyd (Eds.), *Communicative and cognitive abilities: Early behavioral assessment.* Baltimore, Md.: University Park Press, 1978.

Damásio, A. R., & Damásio, H. Musical faculty and cerebral dominance. In M. Critchley & R. A. Henson (Eds.), *Music and brain.* London: W. Heinemann Medical Books, 1977.

Darwin, C. *The expression of the emotions in man and animals.* London: John Murray, 1872.

Darwin, C. A biographical sketch of an infant. *Mind,* 1877, **2,** 285–294.

Delack, J. B., & Fowlow, P. J. The ontogenesis of differential vocalization: Development of prosodic contrastivity during the first year of life. In N. Waterson & C. Snow (Eds.), *The development of communication.* New York: Wiley, 1978.

Demany, L., McKenzie, B., & Vurpillot, E. Rhythm perception in early infancy. *Nature,* 1977, **266,** 718–719.

Dore, J. Holophrases, speech acts and language universals. *Journal of Child Language,* 1975, **2,** 21–40.

Dore, J., Franklin, M. B., Miller, R. T., & Ramer, A. L. H. Transitional phenomena in early language acquisition. *Journal of Child Language,* 1976, **3,** 13–28.

Eimas, P. D. Speech perception in early infancy. In L. B. Cohen & P. Salapatek (Eds.), *Infant perception: From sensation to cognition* (Vol. 2): *Perception of space, speech and sound.* New York: Academic Press, 1975.

Eimas, P. D., Siqueland, E. R., Jusczyk, P. W., & Vigorito, J. Speech perception in infants. *Science,* 1971, **171,** 303–306.

Eimas, P. D., & Tartter, V. C. On the development of speech perception: Mechanisms and analogies. In H. W. Reese & L. P. Lipsitt (Eds.), *Advances in child development and behavior* (Vol. 13). New York: Academic Press, 1979.

Eisenberg, R. B. *Auditory competence in early life: The roots of communicative behavior.* Baltimore, Md.: University Park Press, 1976.

Ferguson, C. A. Baby talk in six languages. *American Anthropologist,* 1964, **66,** 103–114.

Fernald, A. *The mother's speech to the newborn.* Paper presented at the Max-Planck Institute for Psychiatry, Munich, 1976.

Fitchen, M. Speech and music development of a one-year-old child. *Child Development,* 1931, **2,** 324–326.

Fridman, R. *Los comienzos de la conducta musical.* Biblioteca de Psicologia Evolutiva Serie 2 (Vol. 13). Buenos Aires: Paidos, 1974.

Fridman, R., & Battro, A. M. Vocal rhythms in the newborn. The first day of life. *Estudos Cognitivos,* 1977, **2,** 25–30.

Friedlander, B. Z. Receptive language development in infancy: Issues and problems. *Merrill-Palmer Quarterly,* 1970, **16,** 7–51.

Garnica, O. K. *Some characteristics of prosodic input to young children.* Doctoral dissertation, Stanford University, 1974.

Garnica, O. K. Some prosodic and paralinguistic features of speech to young children. In C. E. Snow & C. A. Ferguson (Eds.), *Talking to children: Language input and acquisition.* Cambridge: Cambridge University Press, 1977.

Gesell, A., & Ilg, F. *The infant and child in the culture of today.* London: Hamilton, 1943.

Gibson, E. J. *Principles of perceptual learning and development.* New York: Appleton-Century-Crofts, 1969.

Golinkoff, R. M., & Ames, G. J. A comparison of father's and mother's speech with their young children. *Child Development,* 1979, **50,** 28-32.

Hadding-Koch, K., & Studdert-Kennedy, M. An experimental study of some intonation contours. *Phonetica,* 1964, **11,** 175-185.

Halliday, M. A. K. One child's protolanguage. In M. Bullowa (Ed.), *Before speech: The beginning of interpersonal communication.* Cambridge: Cambridge University Press, 1979.

Harrer, G., & Harrer, H. Music, emotion and autonomic function. In M. Critchley & R. A. Henson (Eds.), *Music and brain.* London: W. Heinemann Medical Books, 1977.

Hayes, C. *The ape in our house.* New York: Harper, 1951.

Heinlein, C. P. A new method of studying the rhythmic responses of children. *Journal of Genetic Psychology,* 1929, **36,** 205-228.

Hutt, S. J., Hutt, C., Lenard, H. G., Bernuth, H. V., & Muntjewerff, W. J. Auditory responsitivity in the human neonate. *Nature,* 1968, **218,** 888-890.

Jacobson, S. W., & Kagan, J. Interpreting "imitative" responses in early infancy. *Science,* 1979, **205,** 215-217.

Janoš, O. Development of higher nervous activity in premature infants. *Pavlov Journal of Higher Nervous Activity.* 1959, **9,** 760-767.

Jersild, A. T., & Bienstock, S. F. A study of the development of children's ability to sing. *Journal of Educational Psychology,* 1934, **25,** 481-503.

Jersild, A. T., & Bienstock, S. F. *The development of rhythm in young children.* Child Development Monograph 22. Columbia: Teachers' College, 1935.

Jespersen, O. *Language: Its nature, development, and origin.* London: George Allen and Unwin, 1922.

Jones, S. J., & Moss, H. A. Age, state and maternal behavior associated with infant vocalizations. *Child Development,* 1971, **42,** 1039-1051.

Jürgens, U., & Ploog, D. Zur Evolution der Stimme. *Archiv für Psychiatrie und Nervenkrankheiten.* 1976, **222,** 117-137.

Kaplan, E. L. *The role of intonation in the acquisition of language.* Unpublished doctoral dissertation, Cornell University, 1969.

Kaplan, E. L., & Kaplan, G. The prelinguistic child. In J. Eliot (Ed.), *Human development and cognitive processes.* New York: Holt, Rinehart & Winston, 1971.

Kasatkin, N. I., & Levikova, A. M. On the development of early conditioned reflexes and their differentiations in infants. *Journal of General Psychology,* 1935, **12,** 416-435.

Kaye, K. Toward the origin of dialogue. In H. R. Schaffer (Ed.), *Studies in mother-infant interaction.* London: Academic Press, 1977.

Keating, P., & Buhr, R. Fundamental frequency in the speech of infants and children. *Journal of the Acoustical Society of America,* 1978, **63,** 567-571.

Kellogg, W. N. Communication and language in the home-raised chimpanzee. *Science,* 1968, **162,** 423-427.

Kellogg, W. N., & Kellogg, L. A. *The ape and the child.* New York: McGraw-Hill, 1933.

Kimura, D. Left-right differences in the perception of melodies. *Quarterly Journal of Experimental Psychology,* 1964, **16,** 355-358.

King, F. L., & Kimura, D. Left-ear superiority in dichotic perception of vocal nonverbal sounds. *Canadian Journal of Psychology,* 1972, **26,** 111-116.

Kinney, D. K., & Kagan, J. Infant attention to auditory discrepancy. *Child Development,* 1976, **47,** 155–164.

Konishi, M. The role of auditory feedback in the control of vocalization in the white-crowned sparrow. *Zeitschrift für Tierpsychologie,* 1965, **22,** 770–783.

Korner, A. F., & Thoman, E. B. The relative efficacy of contact and vestibular-proprioceptive stimulation in soothing neonates. *Child Development,* 1972, **43,** 443–453.

Kuhl, P. K. Predispositions for the perception of speech-sound categories: A species-specific phenomenon? In F. D. Minifie & L. L. Lloyd (Eds.), *Communicative and cognitive abilities: Early behavioral assessment.* Baltimore, Md.: University Park Press, 1978.

Laufer, M. Z., & Horii, Y. Fundamental frequency characteristics of infant non-distress vocalization during the first twenty-four weeks. *Journal of Child Language,* 1977, **4,** 171–184.

Lehiste, I. Suprasegmental features of speech. In N. J. Lass (Ed.), *Contemporary issues in experimental phonetics.* New York: Academic Press, 1976.

Lenneberg, E. H., & Lenneberg, E. (Eds.), Foundations of language development: A multidisciplinary approach (Vol. 1 and 2). New York: Academic Press, 1975.

Levarie, S., & Rudolph, N. Can newborn infants distinguish between tone and noise? *Perceptual and Motor Skills,* 1978, **47,** 1123–1126.

Lewis, M. M. *Infant speech: A study of the beginnings of language.* New York: Harcourt Brace, 1936.

Lewis, M., & Brooks-Gunn, J. Toward a theory of social cognition: The development of self. In J. C. Užgiris (Ed.), *Social interaction and communication during infancy.* San Francisco: Jossey-Bass, 1979.

Lieberman, P. *Intonation, perception, and language.* Cambridge, Mass.: M.I.T. Press, 1967.

Lieberman, P., Crelin, E. S., & Klatt, D. H. Phonetic ability and related anatomy of the newborn and adult human, Neanderthal man, and the chimpanzee. *American Anthropologist,* 1972, **74,** 287–307.

Lipsitt, L. P. The pleasures and annoyances of infants: Approach and avoidance behavior. In E. B. Thoman (Ed.), *The origins of the infant's social responsiveness.* Hillsdale, N.J.: Lawrence Erlbaum, 1979.

Maratos, O. *The origin and development of imitation in the first six months of life.* Ph. D. Thesis, University of Geneva, 1973.

Marler, P. Animals and man: Communication and its development. In J. D. Roslansky (Ed.), *Communication.* A Discussion at the Nobel Conference. Amsterdam: North Holland Publishing Company, 1969.

Marler, P. The evolution of communication. In T. A. Sebeok (Ed.), *How animals communicate.* London: Indiana University Press, 1977.

Masters, J. C. Interpreting 'imitative' responses in early infancy. *Science,* 1979, **205,** 215.

McCall, R. B., & Kagan, J. Attention in the infant: Effects of complexity, contour, perimeter, and familiarity. *Child Development,* 1967, **38,** 939–952.

McKernon, P. E. The development of first songs in young children. In H. Gardner & D. Wolf (Eds.), *Early symbolization.* New directions for child development (Vol. 3). San Francisco: Jossey-Bass, 1979.

Mead, G. H. *Mind, self and society: From the standpoint of a social behaviorist.* Chicago: University of Chicago Press, 1934.

Meltzoff, A. N., & Moore, M. K. Imitation of facial and manual gestures by human neonates. *Science,* 1977, **198,** 75–78.

Meltzoff, A. N., & Moore, M. K. Interpreting 'imitative' responses in early infancy. *Science,* 1979, **205,** 217–219.

Menyuk, P. *Language and maturation.* Cambridge, Mass.: M.I.T. Press, 1977.

Menyuk, P. Methods used to measure linguistic competence during the first five years of life. In R. B. Kearsley & J. E. Sigel (Eds.), *Infants at risk: Assessment of cognitive functioning.* Hillsdale, N.J.: Lawrence Erlbaum, 1979.

Mills, M., & Melhuish, E. Recognition of mother's voice in early infancy. *Science,* 1974, **252,** 123-124.

Moerk, E. Principles of interaction in language learning. *Merrill-Palmer Quarterly,* 1972, **18,** 229-257.

Moorhead, G. E., & Pond, D. *The music of young children: II General Observations.* Pillsbury Foundation Study, 1942.

Morsbach, G., & Bunting, C. Maternal recognition of their neonates' cries. *Developmental Medicine and Child Neurology,* 1979, **21,** 178-185.

Morse, P. A. The discrimination of speech and nonspeech stimuli in early infancy. *Journal of Experimental Child Psychology,* 1972, **14,** 477-492.

Morse, P. A. Speech perception in the human infant and rhesus monkey. *Annals of the New York Academy of Sciences,* 1976, **280,** 694-707.

Müller, E., Hollien, H., & Murry, T. Perceptual responses to infant crying: Identification of cry types. *Journal of Child Language,* 1974, **1,** 89-95.

Murray, A. D. Infant crying as an elicitor of parental behavior: An examination of two models. *Psychological Bulletin,* 1979, **86,** 191-215.

Murry, T., Hollien, H., & Müller, E. Perceptual responses to infant crying: Maternal recognition and sex judgments. *Journal of Child Language,* 1975, **2,** 199-204.

Myers, R. Neurology of social communication in primates. *Proceedings of the Second International Congress of Primatology,* 1968, **3,** 1-9.

Nettl, B. Infant musical development and primitive music. *Southwestern Journal of Anthropology,* 1956, **12,** 87-91.

Newport, E. L. Motherese: The speech of mothers to young children. In N. J. Castellan, Jr., D. B. Pisoni, & G. R. Potts (Eds.), *Cognitive Theory* (Vol. 2). Hillsdale, N.J.: Lawrence Erlbaum, 1976.

Nottebohm, F. Neural lateralization of vocal control in a passerine bird. I. Song. *Journal of Experimental Zoology,* 1971, **177,** 229-262.

Nottebohm, F. Neural lateralization of vocal control in a passerine bird. II. Subsongs, calls, and a theory of vocal learning. *Journal of Experimental Zoology,* 1972, **179,** 35-50.

Orff, C. *Orff-Schulwerk-Musik für Kinder* (Vol. 1). Mainz: B. Schott's Söhne, 1950.

Ostwald, P. F. *Soundmaking: The acoustic communication of emotion.* Springfield, Ill.: Charles C. Thomas, 1963.

Papoušek, H. *Conditioned motor nutritive reflexes in infants.* (In Czech), Thomayerova Sbirka, the whole No. 409. Prague: Státní zdravotnické nakladatelství, 1961.

Papoušek, H. On the development of the so-called voluntary movements in the earliest stages of the child's development. (In Czech), *Československá Pediatrie,* 1962, **17,** 588-591.

Papoušek, H. Experimental studies of appetitional behavior in human newborns and infants. In H. W. Stevenson, E. H. Hess & H. L. Rheingold (Eds.), *Early behavior: Comparative and developmental approaches.* New York: Wiley, 1967.

Papoušek, H. Individual variability in learned responses in human infants. In R. J. Robinson (Ed.), *Brain and early behavior.* London: Academic Press, 1969.

Papoušek, H. Verhaltensweisen der Mutter und des Neugeborenen unmittelbar nach der Geburt. *Archives of Gynecology,* 1979, **228,** 26-32.

Papoušek, H., & Bernstein, P. The functions of conditioning stimulation in human neonates and infants. In A. Ambrose (Ed.), *Stimulation in early infancy.* London: Academic Press, 1969.

Papoušek, H., & Papoušek, M. Cognitive aspects of preverbal social interaction between human infants and adults. In M. O'Connor (Ed.), *Parent-infant interaction.* Amsterdam: Elsevier, 1975.

Papoušek, H., & Papoušek, M. Das Spiel in der Frühentwicklung des Kindes. *Supplement Pädiatrische Praxis,* 1977, **18,** 17-32. (a)

Papoušek, H., & Papoušek, M. *The first musical experience of the child, its biological and psychological significance.* Invited paper presented at the Symposium of the Herbert von

Karajan's Institute on Experimental Psychology of Music in Salzburg, Austria, on April 12, 1977. (b)

Papoušek, H., & Papoušek, M. Mothering and the cognitive headstart: Psychobiological considerations. In H. R. Schaffer (Ed.), *Studies in mother-infant-interaction.* London: Academic Press, 1977. (c)

Papoušek, H., & Papoušek, M. Interdisciplinary parallels in studies of early human behavior: From physical to cognitive needs, from attachment to dyadic education. *International Journal of Behavioral Development,* 1978, **1**, 37–49. (a)

Papoušek, H., & Papoušek, M. *Biological aspects of parent-infant communication in man.* Invited Address at the International Conference on Infant Studies in Providence, R. I., on March 10–12, 1978. (b)

Papoušek, H., & Papoušek, M. Early ontogeny of human social interaction: Its biological roots and social dimensions. In M. v. Cranach, K. Foppa, W. Lepenies, & D. Ploog (Eds.), *Human ethology.* London: Cambridge University Press, 1979. (a)

Papoušek H., & Papoušek, M. The infant's fundamental adaptive response system in social interaction. In E. B. Thoman (Ed.), *Origins of the infant's social responsiveness.* Hillsdale, N.J.: Lawrence Erlbaum, 1979. (b)

Papoušek, H., & Papoušek, M. How human is the human newborn, and what else is to be done. In K. Bloom (Ed.), *Prospective issues in infant research.* Hillsdale, N.J.: Lawrence Erlbaum, 1980.

Petrinovich, L. Psychobiological mechanisms in language development. In C. Newton & A. H. Riesen (Eds.), *Advances in psychobiology* (Vol. 1). New York: Wiley, 1972.

Phillips, J. Syntax and vocabulary of mother's speech to young children: Age and sex comparisons. *Child Development,* 1973, **44**, 182–185.

Piaget, J. *The origins of intelligence in children.* New York: International University Press, 1952.

Platt, W. Temperament and disposition revealed in young children's music. *Character and Personality.* 1933, **2**, 246–251.

Ploog, D. Soziobiologie der Primaten. In K. P. Kisker, J.-E. Meyer, C. Müller & E. Strömgren (Eds.), *Psychiatrie der Gegenwart,* Vol. 1/2, 2nd edit. Berlin: Springer-Verlag, 1980.

Prechtl, H. F. R. Prognostic value of neurological signs in the newborn infant. *Proceedings of the Royal Society of Medicine,* 1965, **58**, 3.

Remick, H. Maternal speech to children during language acquisition. In W. von Raffler-Engel & Y. Lebrun (Eds.), *Babytalk and infant speech.* Lisse, Netherlands, Swets and Zeitlinger, 1976.

Revesz, G. *Introduction to the psychology of music.* Norman: University of Oklahoma Press, 1954.

Rheingold, H. L., Gewirtz, J. L., & Ross, H. W. Social conditioning of vocalizations in the infant. *Journal of Comparative and Physiological Psychology,* 1959, **52**, 68–73.

Roederer, J. G. *Introduction to the physics and psychophysics of music* (2nd ed.). New York: Springer, 1975.

Sachs, J. The adaptive significance of linguistic input to prelinguistic infants. In C. E. Snow & C. A. Ferguson (Eds.), *Talking to children: Language input and acquisition.* Cambridge: Cambridge University Press, 1977.

Sachs, J., Brown, R., & Salerno, R. A. Adults' speech to children. In W. von Raffler-Engel & Y. Lebrun (Eds.), *Babytalk and infant speech.* Lisse, Netherlands: Swets and Zeitlinger, 1976.

Sachs, J., & Devin, J. Young children's use of age-appropriate speech styles. *Journal of Child Language,* 1976, **3**, 81–98.

Savage-Rumbaugh, E. S. Symbolic communication—its origins and early development in the chimpanzee. In H. Gardner & D. Wolf (Eds.), *Early symbolization.* New directions for child development (Vol. 3). San Francisco: Jossey-Bass, 1979.

Schäfer, P. Beobachtungen und Versuche an einem Kinde. *Zeitschrift für Pädagogische Psychologie,* 1922, **23**.

Schaffer, H. R., Collis, G. M., & Parsons, G. Vocal interchange and visual regard in verbal and pre-verbal children. In H. R. Schaffer (Ed.), *Studies in mother–infant interaction.* London: Academic Press, 1977.

Schneirla, T. C. Aspects of stimulation and organization in approach/withdrawal processes underlying vertebrate behavioral development. In D. S. Lehrman, R. Hinde, & E. Shaw (Eds.), *Advances in the studies of behavioral development* (Vol. 1). New York: Academic Press, 1965.

Sheppard, W. C., & Lane, H. L. Development of the prosodic features of infant vocalization. *Journal of Speech and Hearing Research,* 1968, **11**, 94–108.

Shinn, M. W. The development of the senses in the first three years of childhood. University of California Publications in Education (Vol. 4), 1907.

Shuter, R. *The psychology of musical ability.* London: Methuen, 1968.

Siqueland, E. R., & Lipsitt, L. P. Conditioned headturning in human newborns. *Journal of Experimental Child Psychology,* 1966, **3**, 356–376.

Sirviö, P., & Michelsson, K. Sound-spectrographic cry analysis of normal and abnormal newborn infants. A review and a recommendation for standardization of the cry characteristics. *Folia Phoniatrica,* 1976, **28**, 161–173.

Snow, C. E. Mothers' speech to children learning language. *Child Development,* 1972, **43**, 549–565.

Snow, C. E. The development of conversation between mothers and babies. *Journal of Child Language,* 1977, **4**, 1–22.

Spring, D. R., & Dale, P. S. Discrimination of linguistic stress in early infancy. *Journal of Speech and Hearing Research,* 1977, **20**, 224–232.

Stark, R. E. Features of infant sounds: The emergence of cooing. *Journal of Child Language,* 1978, **5**, 379–390. (a)

Stark, R. E. *Stages of speech development in the first year of life.* Paper presented at the NICHD Conference on Child Phonology: Perception, Production and Deviation, Bethesda, Md., May 1978. (b)

Stark, R. E., Rose, S. N., & Benson, P. J. Classification of infant vocalization. *British Journal of Disorders of Communication,* 1978, **13**, 41–47.

Stark, R. E., Rose, S. N., & McLagen, M. Features of infant sounds: The first eight weeks of life. *Journal of Child Language,* 1975, **2**, 205–221.

Steiner, J. E. Innate, discriminative human facial expressions to taste and smell stimulation. *Annals of the New York Academy of Sciences,* 1974, **237**, 229–233.

Stern, C., & Stern, W. *Die Kindersprache* (4th ed.). Leipzig: Barth, 1928.

Stern, D. N., Jaffe, J., Beebe, B., & Bennett, S. L. Vocalizing in unison and in alternation: Two modes of communication within the mother-infant dyad. *Annals of the New York Academy of Sciences.* 1975, **263**, 89–100.

Stern, W. The psychology of early childhood up to the sixth year of age. New York: Holt, 1924.

Stratton, P., & Connolly, K. Discrimination by newborns of the intensity, frequency and temporal characteristics of auditory stimuli. *British Journal of Psychology,* 1973, **64**, 219–232.

Tappolet, E. *Die Sprache des Kindes.* Basel, 1907.

Tavolga, W. N. Levels of interaction in animal communication. In L. R. Aronson, E. Tobach, D. S. Lehrman, & J. S. Rosenblatt (Eds.), *Development and evolution of behavior: Essays in memory of T. C. Schneirla.* San Francisco: Freeman, 1970.

Teplov, B. M. *Psychologie des aptitudes musicales.* Paris: Presses Universitaires de France, 1966.

Tonkova-Yampol'skaya, R. V. Development of speech intonation in infants during the first two years of life. *Soviet Psychology,* 1969, **7**, 48–54.

Truby, H., & Lind, J. Cry sounds of the newborn infant. *Acta Paediatrica Scandinavica,* 1965, **163**, 7–59.

Vlach, V. *Nepodmíněné novorozenecké reflexy*. Unconditioned reflexes in the newborn. (In Czech), Hálkova Sbírka, the whole No. 15. Praha: Státní zdravotnické nakladatelství, 1969.

Washburn, S. L., Jay, P. C., & Lancaster, J. B. Field studies of Old World monkeys and apes. *Science*, 1965. **150**, 1541–1547.

Wasz-Höckert, O., Lind, J., Vuorenkoski, V., Partanen, T., & Valanne, E. *The infant cry. A spectrographic and auditory analysis*. London: Heinemann, 1968.

Wasz-Höckert, O., Partanen, T. J., Vuorenkoski, V., Valanne, E., & Michelsson, K. The identification of some specific meanings in newborn and infant vocalization. *Experientia*, 1964, **20**, 154.

Weeks, T. E. Speech registers in young children. *Child Development*, 1971, **42**, 1119–1131.

Weir, R. H. Some questions on the child's learning of phonology. In F. Smith & G. A. Miller (Eds.), *The genesis of language. A psycholinguistic approach*. Cambridge, Mass.: M.I.T. Press, 1966.

Werner, H. *Die melodische Erfindung im frühen Kindesalter*. Eine entwicklungspsychologische Untersuchung. Sitzungsberichte 182 (4). Wien: Kaiserliche Akademie der Wissenschaften, 1917.

Wing, H. D. *Musical ability and appreciation*. Ph.D. Thesis, London University, 1941.

Wolff, P. H. Observations on the early development of smiling. In B. M. Foss (Ed.), *Determinants of infant behaviour II*. London: Methuen, 1963.

Wolff, P. H. The natural history of crying and other vocalizations in infancy. In B. M. Foss (Ed.), *Determinants of infant behaviour IV*. London: Methuen, 1969.

Yarrow, L. J., Rubenstein, J. L., & Pedersen, F. A. *Infant and environment: Early cognitive and motivational development*. New York: Wiley, 1975.

Zeskind, P. S., & Lester, B. M. Acoustic features and auditory perceptions of the cries of newborns with prenatal and perinatal complications. *Child Development*, 1978, **49**, 580–589.

THE RETRIEVAL OF MEMORY IN EARLY INFANCY*

Carolyn K. Rovee-Collier and Jeffrey W. Fagen

RUTGERS UNIVERSITY

Advances in Infancy
Research, Vol. I

*The research described in this chapter has been supported by Grant Nos. MH32307 and 24711 from the National Institute of Mental Health to the senior author. We are particularly grateful to Byron A. Campbell and Norman E. Spear, whose research provided the impetus for our own and whose criticisms and suggestions have sharpened our theoretical and methodological focus. In addition, we thank David C. Riccio and Kenneth L. Hoving for providing us with copies of unpublished materials. Finally, we gratefully acknowledge the untiring efforts of the many students, both graduate and undergraduate, who have contributed to our research.

I.   AN OVERVIEW OF INFANT
MEMORY RESEARCH

Over the past decade, research on infant memory has been shaped almost exclusively by models of adult verbal learning and memory and has reflected the traditional assumptions of a dual memory store (Estes, 1976). Investigators have focused on encoding, storage, and factors (e.g., interference) which presumably disrupt memory processing or degrade memory (Cohen & Gelber, 1975; Fagan, 1977; Olson, 1976; Werner & Perlmutter, 1979). The assumption that information resides briefly (30 sec or less) in a short-term store prior to transfer into a relatively permanent long-term store has justified the widespread use of brief (2–8 min) single sessions in studies of long-term retention and has encouraged investigators to describe retention failures in terms of memory deficits arising from the permanent loss of information during either encoding, short-term storage, or transfer.

Measurement of retention in this research has been indirect, inferred from indices of infant attention (Werner & Perlmutter, 1979). This practice has reflected varying degrees of commitment to Sokolov's (1963) model of habituation of the orienting reflex. Presumably, an organism constructs an internal representation (an "engram") of a stimulus during repeated encounters with it; the amount of attention is inversely related to the completeness of the engram. A retention test, administered after one or more exposures of a given stimulus (S_1), involves the simultaneous (paired-comparison paradigm) or successive (habituation/discrimination paradigm) presentation of a novel stimulus (S_2). Retention ("recognition") of S_1 is *inferred* from the relatively greater attention allocated to S_2 i.e., from the extent to which the infant does *not* attend to S_1. Paradoxically, this analysis terminates with response to S_2; it provides no mechanism by which to measure whether the infant can use the information "recognized" in S_1. When carried to a logical conclusion, this model describes the processing and storage of stimulus attributes to to which an infant will systematically *not* attend in the future. It is difficult to conceptualize the evolutionary advantage of such a memory system. We concur with Bruner (1964) that "the most important thing about memory is not storage of past experience, but rather the retrieval of what is relevant in some usable form . . ." (p. 2). Recently, it has been argued that the construct of memory processing is not applicable to situations which simply involve altered attention. Spear (1973) described the effect of novel cues which elicit orienting responses as distracting attention from effective (familiar) retrieval cues, and Jeffrey (1976) proposed that the infant's response-to-novelty is a simple perceptual processing strategy, devoid of memorial implications.

In this chapter, we describe an alternative approach to the study of infant memory and the research which it has inspired. We focus on the retrieval of memory and factors which promote retention, and we discuss forgetting as a retrieval failure rather than as a memory deficit. Finally, we provide evidence for a mechanism by which infants demonstrate the cumulative effects of prior experiences and also by which early experiences may influence later behavior.

II. BASIC CONCEPTS

A. What Is Memory?

The term "memory," as used here, refers to a multidimensional collection of attributes, each of which represents a characteristic of an event which the organism noticed. These attributes are hypothetical representations and functionally independent (Spear, 1978), and hence may be forgotten at different rates. They may include aspects of both the external and internal environments, responses, etc. and may be differentially coded as a result of various factors known to affect attention (cue salience, biological predispositions, etc.). The working hypothesis of our research is that memories are permanent; that is, they neither decay nor are lost.

B. Memory Retrieval

Memory retrieval, like memory storage, is a hypothetical process. An attribute of memory is extracted from storage or "retrieved" when a subject "notices an event sufficiently similar to that event represented by the attribute" (Spear, 1976, p. 35). Once aroused (i.e., noticed), any of the memory attributes may promote the arousal of others. The more attributes of the same memory that are noticed, the greater the probability that the target attribute measured by the experimenter will be retrieved. The behavioral evidence from which retrieval is inferred constitutes *retention* and is typically obtained in recognition, recall, or transfer tasks.

A large proportion of memory attributes represent contextual cues. To the extent that the retention test context differs from the context of the original experience, the number of effective retrieval cues will be reduced and the probability of retrieval diminished. In addition to obvious alterations in the physical environment of the test setting, contextual variation can arise from (1) sensory and physiological changes associated with learning or aging; (2) rhythmic changes in the internal or external environment; (3) the acquisition of other memories with attributes which are common to the memory containing the target attribute (i.e., interference); (4) changes in idiosyncratic response patterns that immediately precede retention testing; and (5) aspects of the reinforcer and its consequences (Spear, 1973). If changes in contextual cues contribute to apparent memory deficits by impeding retrieval, then the provision of contextual cues which were present during the original experience should facilitate retrieval. The cuing role of contextual cues has recently assumed major theoretical significance in memory research with animals (Campbell & Spear, 1972; Medin, 1976; Spear, 1971) and human adults (Jenkins, 1974; Tulving, 1972; Underwood, 1969).

III. A LEARNING ANALYSIS OF INFANT MEMORY

A. The Relation Between Learning and Memory

Given the vast amount of learning which infants acquire in the first year of life, it is apparent that they must have an efficient means by which to code and retrieve information. Without this, early experiences, which are hypothesized to play such a critical role in development, would have little lasting import. Not only must infants learn the correlations between environmental events, but they must also learn the correlations between their own responses and the consequences of those responses. However, because evidence of learning can only be obtained *ex post facto,* in terms of a behavioral change tests of learning are also tests of memory. The logical relation between learning and memory has been succinctly characterized by Bolles (1976):

> Without some long-term memory of what is learned, there would be little learning evident in the animal kingdom and there would be little reason for animals being able to learn.... It should also be noted that were it not for learning, that is, for acquired associations between events, animals would have nothing to remember. (p. 22)

In fact, the frequency with which animal researchers use naive animals reflects the popular bias that animals other than elephants may not readily forget. This bias is not unfounded. Remarkable retention for specific acquisitions has been exhibited after periods of months and even years (Liddell, James, & Anderson, 1934; Skinner, 1938).

There has been little correspondence between the findings and models of human and animal memory research. However, we believe that there is a natural affinity between conditioning analyses of infant memory (Rovee & Fagen, 1976; Sullivan, Rovee-Collier, & Tynes, 1979) and animal memory paradigms. In both, subjects trained in a highly distinctive setting are asked to reproduce the acquired response in the same setting at a later point in time. In essence, the experimental context provides the cues for the production of the conditioned response in a fashion analogous to the cued-recall tests of verbal learning. In addition, because infants and animals are nonverbal, the experimenter must provide instructions to the subject as to the nature of the task through the way in which the experimental environment is structured. The anticipatory production of a conditioned response under these circumstances requires that the organism not only *recognize* the contextual cue but also *use* the information which it conveys as the basis for response.

The disinterest of infant memory researchers in conditioning procedures probably reflects the view that infant learning is unstable or difficult to obtain, or that conditioning paradigms are cumbersome (Atkinson & Braddick, 1976). In a recent review, Cohen and Gelber (1975) described conditioning procedures as too complex and inefficient to index infant memory. If visual attention procedures, which consume only a few minutes of a single session, yielded the same information as conditioning procedures, which might evolve lengthy multiple sessions, then the more time-consuming approach would be unwarranted. However, these two procedures lead to different conclusions regarding infant memory, and only the conditioning analysis yields a direct index of retention.

B. The Research Paradigm

1. Mobile Conjugate Reinforcement

In all of our studies, infants learn to produce movement (the reinforcement) in an overhead crib mobile by means of foot-kicks. A ribbon connected from the infant's ankle to a suspension hook from which the mobile hangs (Fig. 1) permits the infant to draw and release the suspension bar, thereby moving the mobile in a manner commensurate with the vigor and rate of response. This procedure produces rapid acquisition and high, stable response rates not attributable to behavioral arousal (cf. Rovee-Collier & Gekoski, 1979). Because the frequency and intensity of the reinforcing stimulation are determined from moment to moment by each infant, the paradigm permits lengthy and multiple sessions with minimal attrition.

2. Measurement of Retention

The procedure for measuring retention across sessions resulted from the resolution of three major problems: (1) the need to obtain measures prior to the reinstatement of reinforcement so that the extremely rapid acquisition characteristic of the mobile conjugate reinforcement paradigm, and especially of older infants (Gekoski, 1977), would not obscure "pure retention"; (2) the need for an index of retention immediately following training as a standard for the assessment of long-term retention; and (3) the need to maintain a high degree of similarity between the contexts of immediate and long-term retention tests. We thus assessed retention during periods in which no reinforcement contingencies were present (i.e., extinction) at the end of each training session and, again, at the outset of each subsequent session. This procedure reflects the fact that large numbers of responses continue to be emitted for relatively long periods in the absence of

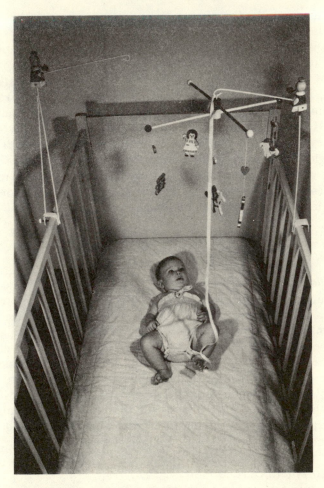

Fig. 1.   The experimental arrangement in the mobile conjugate reinforcement paradigm. A 12-week-old is shown during a reinforcement phase. During retention testing (nonreinforcement phases), the mobile is hung from the mobile stand at the left, but the ankle ribbon remains in its current position. (Photographed by Breck P. Kent.)

reward while remaining under strict control of the prior reinforcement contingencies (Guttman, 1956).

Our basic procedure is illustrated in Fig. 2. During Phases 1 and 3, the mobile is visually available but is suspended from a mobile stand to which the ankle ribbon is not attached (Fig. 1); kicks during these phases do not produce mobile movement. In Sesesion 1, the pretraining baseline response rate is obtained in Phase 1; in all subsequent sessions, Phase 1 is a *long-term retention test,* and the characteristics of the nonmoving mobile are retrieval

RETENTION PARADIGM

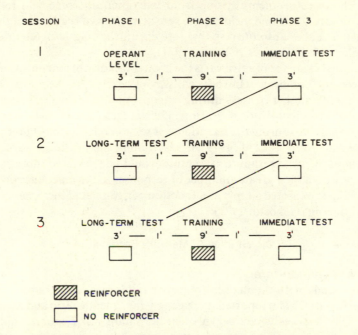

Fig. 2. *The standard retention paradigm. Sessions 1 and 2 are separated by 24 hours; Sessions 2 and 3 are separated by intervals ranging from 1–28 days, depending upon the study. In studies with a reactivation treatment, the priming event is presented 24 hours prior to Session 3. Each session involves a 9-min reinforcement phase preceded and followed by a 3-min nonreinforcement phase. Approximately 1 min intervenes between phases, during which time the mobile is positioned on the appropriate suspension hook. Performance during each long-term retention test is assessed in relation to performance during the procedurally identical immediate retention test of the preceding session (diagonal lines). During retention tests the mobile is visually present but is nonmoving; its components serve as retrieval cues.*

cues (Rovee-Collier & Capatides, 1979). Performance during the long-term retention test is assessed in relation to performance in Phase 3 of the preceding session (the *immediate retention test*), which is procedurally identical to Phase 1.

Sessions 1 and 2 are always separated by 24 hours, but the interval between Sessions 2 and 3 varies, depending upon the study. The change in response rate from the immediate retention test of one session to the long-term retention test of the next session is expressed as a *retention ratio* for each infant (Sullivan et al., 1979). This ratio is of the form B/A, with B the rate during the long-term test, and A the rate during the immediate test. Ratios of ≥ 1.00 indicate no forgetting over the retention interval, and < 1.00 indicates the fraction of conditioned responding which persisted after a given interval. Ratios eliminate problems arising from individual differences in response level or reward value and yield a more sensitive index of the effect of the text interval than either absolute response rate during the long-term retention test or simple *A–B* differences (Church, 1971).

Additional evidence of retrieval is the greater rapidity of reacquisition once reinforcement has been reintroduced. *Savings ratios* of the form *D–C/C* (*D* = the total number of kicks during reacquisition; *C* = the total number of footkicks during acquisition in Session 1) reflect the extent of each infant's net gain in responding during the retention test session relative to his pretraining response rate (Sullivan et al., 1979). If past training has facilitated subsequent acquisition, then the response asymptote would be recovered more rapidly, and there would be a greater number of responses in the reacquisition phase than would be expected simply as a function of age-related increases in speed of conditioning (Gekoski, 1977).

C.   Studies of Memory Retrieval

1.   *The Retention Interval*

In a pilot study with the mobile conjugate reinforcement paradigm, Smith (cited in Lipsitt, 1971), reported increasingly rapid acquisition and extinction across daily sessions which began when her infant was 2 months old. This spurred our initial attempt to assess the extent of response carry-over from one daily conditioning session to the next (Rovee & Fagen, 1976). We found that the number of conditioned footkicks of 3-month-olds increased linearly during succesive daily long-term retention tests and reflected the training level measured in each of the preceding immediate retention tests (Fig. 3). This was the first clear demonstration of long-term (24-hour) retention of acquired associations involving a "cued-recall" task. The daily increase in responding during Phase 1, when the mobile was present but could not be activated by footkicks, could result only from memory retrieval, not from relearning. Moreover, the daily increase in total responding during reacquisition demonstrated the cumulative advantage of past training. Although this study antedated our use of retention and savings ratios, we have subsequently confirmed that individual retention was veridically reflected in the group data.

The maximum retention interval over which training effects persist was investigated by Sullivan et al. (1979). Three-month-olds received two training sessions spaced apart by 24 hours and a third session (Fig. 2) after 48, 72, 96, 120, 144, 192, or 336 hours. Only infants tested after 336 hours showed significant forgetting: Their long-term retention test performance was indistinguishable from their pretraining baseline performance (Session 1). Also, these infants did not exhibit more rapid reacquisition. The data indicate

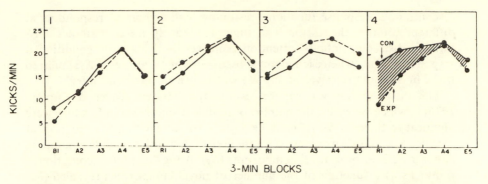

Fig. 3. *Conditioning curves of 3-month-olds over four consecutive training sessions spaced by 24 hours each. During Sessions 1–3, all infants received the "same" mobile model; during Session 4, infants in the control group (CON) were tested with the original mobile, but infants in the experimental group (EXP) were tested with a different model. The decrement in performance attributable to the altered test context is indicated by diagonal lines. Note the high level of retention during each successive long-term retention test (R1) relative to performance during the immediate retention test (E5) of the preceding session. B indicates baseline; A indicates acquisition phases. (Redrawn from Rovee & Fagen, 1976.)*

that the forgetting function of a newly acquired memory, expressed in terms of retention ratios, declines gradually over time since training. Retention ratios remain relatively high (i.e., .80–1.00) for 4–5 days, decline to .50–.70 after 7–8 days, and fall to values consistent with operant level (.30–.40) after 14 days. The latter values are obtained even after retention intervals of 28–35 days, providing evidence that infants do not become more active during Phase 1 with age.

2. The Test Context

In the preceding studies, infants were tested in an experimental context identical to the training context except that the reinforcement contingency was not in effect. That is, the same crib mobile which signalled reinforcement during training was presented as a retrieval cue during the immediate and the long-term retention tests. When retention is assessed in a context which differs from that of the original experience, this constitutes a generalization test, with the number of common attributes in the two contexts determining the probability of retrieval.

Our original retention study (Rovee & Fagen, 1976) had included a group of infants who had been trained for three consecutive days with one mobile (S_1) and tested in the fourth daily session with a second mobile model (S_2). Instead of exhibiting the characteristic response carryover typical of the infants tested with S_1, these infants exhibited little or no responding during the long-term retention test (Phase 1) of Session 4. Although reattainment of asymptote appeared to be gradual (Fig. 3), in fact individual infants produced discontinuous response functions, resuming high and stable responding at different points in the session. This suggested that the novel attributes of S_2 initially distracted infants' attention from retrieval cues for conditioned responding. Only when each infant subsequently noticed cues in S_2 similar to those in S_1 could retrieval occur. We will return to this point later.

This interpretation was supported in a study (Fagen, Rovee, & Kaplan, 1976) in which we varied the number of mobile components in S_2 which were identical to those in S_1. After three days of training with a five-component mobile (S_1), infants were tested on the fourth day with a mobile containing either 0, 1, 2, 3, or 4 novel components (S_2). A log–log plot of conditioned footkicks as a function of the number of novel components revealed that long-term retention test performance was described by a power function with a slope of $-.90$ ($r^2 = .87$). Interestingly, looking at S_2 was greater than at S_1, but attention was not differentiated with respect to the number of novel elements. Given the robust attentional response to novelty of 3-month-olds, we think that increasing the number of novel components in S_2 increased the distraction time and thus the time required by infants to notice the familiar objects which were the effective retrieval cues.

This study highlights the differences between measures of retention used in "visual recognition memory" paradigms and those used in conditioning analyses. According to Sokolovian-based interpretations, increased attention to the novel S_2 implies that the infant must have retrieved information (attributes) corresponding to the previously exposed S_1. This implication is never subjected to direct test. We argue, however, that attention to novel attributes can never result in retrieval; retrieval or memory processing can only occur when attributes corresponding to stored memory attributes are noticed. Once this occurs, a renewal of conditioned responding (i.e., the target attribute) is predicted. Visual recognition paradigms do not predict what will occur once the infant has stopped attending to the novel aspects of S_2. Moreover, because of the exclusive reliance on attention measures, there is no way of ascertaining whether the infant has noticed familiar cues in the test context because there is no overt or distinctive response to index this. The infant has no opportunity to demonstrate that retrieval has occurred; such is not the case in a conditioning analysis of memory. Thus, although the response-to-novelty indexes the detection of contextual change, this alone is not sufficient for the inference of retention.

Finally, two recently completed studies have provided some insights into the functional organization of infant memory and the temporal parameters of such organization. These studies address the problem of what constitutes the effective retrieval cues when all components of the test mobile are novel. Under such circumstances, could the infant ever demonstrate generalization? Would retrieval be precluded by the lack of previously noticed (familiar) cues? The fact that infants do produce previously conditioned responses in completely altered test contexts (Rovee & Fagen, 1976) led us to speculate as to the organization of infant memories. The notion that information can be coded in terms of both general or prototypic features and specific visual details is not new in either the adult (Loftus & Kallman, 1979) or developmental (Williams, Fryer, & Aiken, 1977) memory literature. One way in which infants could respond appropriately in an altered test context would be through the detection of prototypic cues which correspond to coded memory attributes. Because the ability to classify stimuli on the basis of both general features and specific details is invariant from preschool age through adulthood (Williams et al., 1977), it seemed highly plausible that young infants might also organize visual information along these dimensions. Following the suggestion that general features are accessible to retrieval for longer periods of time than are specific visual details (Hasher & Griffin, 1978), we sought to differentiate these classes of retrieval cues on a temporal basis through exploitation of the response-to-novelty phenomenon (Rovee-Collier & Sullivan, 1980).

Three-month-olds were trained with S_1 for two sessions and, in a third session, half again received S_1 (control groups) and half, a completely different mobile (S_2). The third session occurred after retention intervals of 24, 48, 72, or 96 hours (see Fig. 4). The typical response carry-over from Session 1 to Session 2 can be seen in the curves of all infants and, from Session 2 to Session 3, in the curves of those who received the "same" mobile in the third session. As before (Fagen et al., 1976; Rovee & Fagen, 1976), presentation of a "different" model (S_2) impaired performance in Session 3. However, as the length of the retention interval increased, infants tested with S_2 exhibited increasingly greater savings until, after a retention interval of 96 hours, their Session 3 performance in the novel test context was indistinguishable from that of infants in the 96-hour control group tested with S_1.

That infants tested with a physically different S_2 could show complete generalization suggests the retrieval of attributes corresponding to features defining the general class "mobile." The increase in savings as a function of the length of the retention interval suggests that general attributes are accessible for lengthier periods or are learned better than specific attributes. Thus, infants can exhibit positive transfer through noticing prototypic features in the contemporary context which match or are identical to stored memory attributes. These data suggest that the robust retention ratios obtained by Sullivan et al. (1979) after intervals of 6–8 days reflected retrieval of prototypic cues rather than of details associated with the specific training mobile.

If attributes representing both general features and specific details comprise the memory of an event, can infants selectively retrieve only one type of cue? Can they learn to notice only attributes which represent general

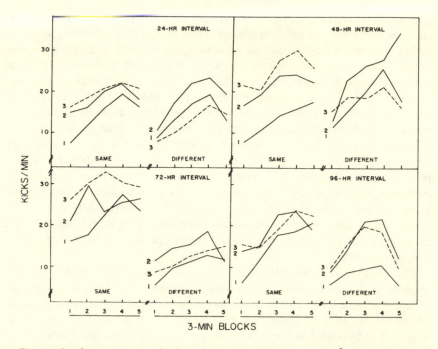

Fig. 4.   Conditioning curves of independent groups of infants receiving the "same" mobile for three consecutive sessions or the "same" mobile for two sessions only and a "different" mobile in Session 3 (dashed line). Blocks 1 and 5 in each session are nonreinforcement phases; Blocks 2–4 are reinforcement phases. The interval between Sessions 1–2 was always 24 hours; the interval between Session 2–3 varied from 24–96 hours, as indicated in each panel. Note the within-group pattern of response over sessions. (From Rovee-Collier & Sullivan, 1980.)

features and to ignore specific details? Morrongiello and Gekoski (1978) trained 10-week-old infants for four days, as before (Rovee & Fagen, 1976), but in some (Group ABCA) or all (Group ABCD) sessions the mobile was novel. A control group (Group AAAA) was trained with the same mobile in every session. If these infants learned to ignore the novel attributes of the training stimuli and to respond to the invariant general features of the training stimuli, the response cessation associated with the introduction of novel stimuli would be eliminated, and generalized responding to the novel mobile would be predicted. The results were robust and revealed some startling insights into how 10-week-olds organize the world. None of the original predictions were confirmed: Conditioned responding of all groups was equivalent in all training sessions (Fig. 5, top panels), and idiosyncratic attentional differences among groups at the outset of training disappeared as training progressed, (Fig. 5, bottom panels) in spite of the fact that familiarization differences between groups became increasingly greater over sessions. All groups showed positive transfer from problem to problem over

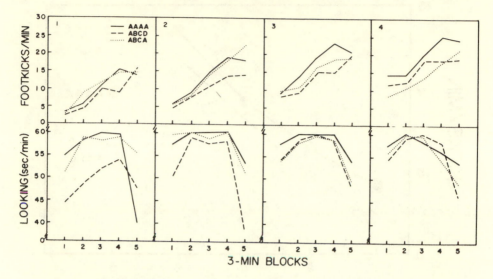

Fig. 5.   Changes in responses within and between four sessions spaced by 24 hours. Infants received either the Session 1 mobile for all sessions (Group AAAA), a different mobile in every session (Group ABCD), or a different mobile in each of the first three sessions but the Session 1 mobile in Session 4 (Group ABCA). Blocks 1 and 5 are nonreinforcement phases; Blocks 2–4 are reinforcement phases. Footkick rates (top panels) and seconds of visual attention (bottom panels) are averaged within minutes and expressed in 3-min blocks. (From Morrongiello & Gekoski, 1978.)

successive sessions, whether retention was tested in the same or an altered context. Also, the performance of all groups continued to exceed the pretraining (Session 1) level during a retention test with the Session 2 mobile during a fifth session at least seven days after the completion of training. The fact that some infants who received the Session 1 mobile in Session 4 (ABCA) actually showed a response reduction during the initial long-term retention test in Session 4 is evidence that a single day of training is sufficient to permit infants to notice the details of the training stimulus: Clearly, they must have noticed the specific details of the Session 1 mobile in order to respond differentially to it 72 hours later in spite of the fact that they had viewed other mobiles (B, C) in the intervening sessions (Fig. 6). Thus, although they can detect physical differences between mobiles, when the response–reinforcer contingency remains unchanged and the physical differences do not acquire differential signal value, infants ignore these novel attributes and use general features as the basis of retrieval.

These data, when considered cojointly with previous data collected in our laboratory, suggest that two successive encounters with a different exemplar is sufficient for the abstraction of general features as the principal attributes by which an event will be represented, even though memory attributes

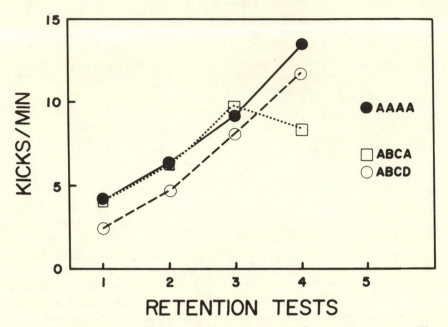

Fig. 6. *Performance of three groups f infants over successive long-term retention tests (Phase 1) of five sessions; Session 1 performance actually reflects operant level. The interval between Tests 1–4 was 24 hours; the interval between Tests 4–5 was either 7 (AAAA, ABCA) or 12 (ABCD) days. (From Morrongiello & Gekoski, 1978.)*

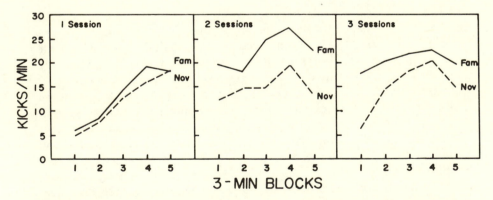

Fig. 7. *A composite showing the effect of introducing a novel (NOV) mobile as a function of the number of previous training sessions with an alternative model (one, two, or three prior sessions). The difference in conditioned footkicking between infants continuing to receive the same mobile (FAM) and those receiving the novel one is significant in the first (nonreinforced) block, only when two or more sessions with an alternative model have been experienced (middle and right panels). Blocks 1 and 5 are nonreinforcement phases; Blocks 2–4 are reinforcement phases.*

corresponding to specific details remain relatively accessible during the same time period. As shown in Fig. 7, retrieval deficits accompany the introduction of S_2 at the outset of a session following three (Rovee & Fagen, 1976, right panel) and two (Rovee-Collier & Sullivan, 1980, middle panel) prior encounters with S_1, but no deficit occurs after just a single prior encounter (Morrongiello & Gekoski, 1978, left panel), in spite of the fact that the specific details of S_1 can be discriminated at that point. Thus the higher-order organization of memory attributes occurs during or after a second encounter and may reflect an automatic frequency-processing mechanism (Hasher & Zacks, 1979). This type of organizational system for processing memories is highly efficient and adaptive. It permits infants to respond appropriately to the multiple variations of recurring stimuli while simultaneously permitting appropriate, differential response to those stimuli which remain invariant over successive encounters. Moreover, the differential accessibility of the two types of memory attributes as a function of increasing time-since-last-encounter ensures that infants will produce a response reflecting retrieval of abstracted features to less frequently encountered stimuli. This system reduces to a "manageable" amount the large amount of information which must be kept relatively accessible for retrieval. Taken together, the preceding studies (Morrongiello & Gekoski, 1978; Rovee-Collier & Sullivan, 1980) demonstrate that infants can produce generalized responses based on retrieval of abstracted features of different stimuli in two ways: (1) by "forgetting" the distinctive details over time; and (2) by selectively noticing only those attributes which represent abstracted features (i.e., by ignoring attributes which correspond to specific visual details). These two strategies, available to infants as young as 10 weeks old, may in fact be invariant over the course of development (Olson, 1976; Werner & Perlmutter, 1979).

3. Age Differences in Retention

It is generally assumed that younger organisms learned more slowly and forget more rapidly than do older organisms. For example, Gekoski (1977) tested infants longitudinally between 9 and 15 weeks of age and obtained age-related differences in learning: Only one-half of the infants tested at 9 weeks exhibited reliable conditioning in a single session. Those who did learn were slower to exceed operant level, attained a relatively low asymptote of conditioning, and continued to increase responding in extinction. In contrast, at 12 weeks, all learned rapidly within one session, achieved a higher level of conditioning, and did not increase responding once reinforcement was withdrawn. These trends were even more exaggerated when infants were retested at 15 weeks of age.

Davis and Rovee-Collier (1979) confirmed a part of Gekoski's original observations in a group of 8-week-olds. Surprisingly, however, when retention was assessed 14 days after the completion of training, the cued-recall performance of the 8-week-olds was superior to that of infants initially trained at 12 weeks of age. Although their 24-hour retention ratios were comparable to those of 12-week-olds (Sullivan et al., 1979), their 336-hour retention ratio was .60, equivalent to the 7–8 day retention ratios of the older infants.

We can only speculate as to whether infants at 8 and 12 weeks of age are noticing the same kinds (or numbers) of attributes during training and/or the long-term retention test. Since storage and retrieval factors cannot be measured independently, this problem must remain unresolved for the moment.

IV.   REACTIVATION OF MEMORY

A.   The Role of Contextual Cues

Our assumptions that memory is relatively permanent and that forgetting reflects only a retrieval failure have led us to seek means by which memory attributes which are *available* in storage can be made more *accessible* for retrieval. Among the factors which influence retrieval are real or perceived differences in the training and test contexts (cf. Section II, B). These differences result from the manipulation of conditions at the time of retention testing: (1) the introduction of novel cues can increase unlearned exploratory behaviors which may interfere with the measurement of retention; (2) when noticed, novel cues may arouse attributes associated with memories not containing the target attribute, thereby impeding retrieval of the target attribute; and (3) the fewer the number of contextual cues present during original learning, the smaller may be the probability that the target attribute will be aroused (Spear, 1976).

One way to alleviate forgetting, therefore, is to make the cues noticed during testing as similar as possible to those noticed during original training. A second way is through *prior cuing* (Spear, 1973, 1976; Spear & Parsons, 1976), or the presentation of "reminders" (isolated aspects of the original context) prior to the retention test. The effect of this manipulation can be either to establish an internal state similar to that which accompanied original learning and which persists after the cue has been withdrawn, or to "prime" or "recycle" the memory so that it is more accessible during the subsequent retention test. The effectiveness of prior cuing was originally suggested by Campbell and Jaynes (1966), who addressed the paradox of memory deficits in immature organisms for whom the effects of early experience are so critical. Attributing the superior retention of adults to a greater opportunity for intermittent reexposure to the conditons of original training, they proposed *reinstatement* as the mechanism by which access to early memories could be maintained over relatively lengthy intervals. Reinstatement can occur only if an organism has been previously trained and reencounters some of the original conditions of training. Only the training (without the reencounters) or only the reencounters (without prior training) will be insufficient for retention over extended intervals. Reinstatement-like facilitation of retrieval can also occur when the organism has been exposed to only a fractional component of the original training context (the CS, the US, the original apparatus, etc.) prior to retention testing (Spear & Parsons, 1976).

Spear (1973) described the prior cuing procedure as *reactivation,* emphasizing the hypothetical process of priming stored memory attributes, as distinguished from the empirical terminology of Campbell and Jaynes (1966), who described the procedural "reinstatement" of a former context. Considerable evidence of facilitation of retention by means of prior cuing procedures had been obtained with animals (Campbell & Jaynes, 1966, 1969; for review, see Riccio & Haroutunian, 1979; Spear, 1971, 1973, 1976, 1978) and young children (Hoving & Choi, 1972; Hoving, Coates, Bertucci, & Riccio, 1972). In Section IV, C, we will describe the use of reactivation procedures with human infants.

B. Prototypic Experiments with Animals

In their original study, Campbell and Jaynes (1966) used a classical aversive conditioning procedure, administering footshock (US) in the black compartment (CS) of a two-chamber apparatus. Two groups of rats received a total of thirty footshocks at approximately 25 days of age; in the course of the procedure, rats were placed in the nonshock white chamber for a period corresponding to the time spent in the shock chamber. A third group was treated identically but received no shock in the black compartment. One, two, and three weeks later, one of the two shock groups and the nonshock group were returned briefly to each compartment, receiving a single shock in the black chamber. The second shock group received the same treatment but received no shock in subsequent weeks. Four weeks following original training and one week after the last "reinstatement" trial, animals were placed singly in the black compartment for one hour. The door between the two compartments was open throughout this period, and no shocks were administered. The amount of time each animal spent in the "safe" white compartment indexed the extent of the animal's "fear" of the black compartment. The results demonstrated that animals who had been shocked repeatedly in the black compartment four weeks earlier and who had also received periodic reexposure (reinstatement) to the shock in the black chamber in the intervening weeks spent more than 60% of the final test session on the white side. Animals with prior repetitive shock experience only (no intervening reexposure to shock) and animals with no prior CS + US pairings but with intervening exposure to shock only demonstrated no fear of the black compartment, remaining on the black side (where they were placed) for 80% to 90% of the test session. This demonstration was unequivocal evidence of the efficacy of reinstatement in *maintaining* an early learned response (a fear CR) at a high level throughout an interval in which it would otherwise have been forgotten.

The reactivation experiments of Spear and Parsons (1976) have involved the presentation of only a single "reminder" during the retention interval. Animals receive Pavlovian fear conditioning with a footshock (US) and light or tone (CS) in a distinctively painted (black or white) compartment. A partition separates the shock compartment from an adjacent chamber in which shock is never administered. During training, animals are not permitted to escape, but during testing the partition is lowered so that the animal can hurdle the partition into the second compartment and terminate the CS. The US is never presented during the retention test.

Rats of all ages forget this task rapidly, showing no signs of retention after 28 days. However, if rats are placed in a neutral apparatus and given a single presentation of the US 24 hours prior to the 28-day retention test, forgetting is significantly alleviated, and retention is at a level comparable to 24-hour retention. Control groups receivinag either no US presentation after training (*no-reactivation group*) or the US presentation without prior conditioning experience (*no-prior-learning group*) do not escape into the second compartment when the CS is turned on during the retention test. Thus the alleviation of forgetting is neither artifactual nor a result of new learning.

Spear and Parsons (1976) tested the retention of preweanling rats (16 days of age), weanling rats (22–24 days), and adult rats (60–80 days) at various intervals (3 min, 1 day, 7 days, 14 days, 28 days) following fear conditioning. The retention of adults and weanlings was excellent after 1 day and poor after 28 days, but preweanlings showed poor retention after just 1 day. Similarly, a reminder presented 24 hours prior to testing at 28 days significantly alleviated the forgetting of adults and weanlings but not of preweanlings. A reinstatement procedure in which the US was presented on six distributed occasions produced comparable age effects. However, both reactivation and reinstatement procedures alleviated forgetting significantly if preweanlings were tested 7 days after original learning, when their retention level was comparable to that of older organisms 28 days after training.

C. Reactivation Experiments with Human Infants

Some researchers have suggested that the memory systems which operate across phylogeny must be qualitatively different (Medin, 1967; Roberts & Grant, 1976), just as others have proposed that ontogenetic systems might differ (Bruner, 1964; Campbell & Coulter, 1976; Piaget, 1952). One possibility is that the different types of tasks encountered across phyletic lines and in the course of development require different types of representation. However, it seems theoretically cumbersome, if not extravagant, to posit a different memory system for every task accomplished by every species at every age. A more parsimonious and potentially fruitful approach is to seek a unifying set of principles by which to relate learning and memory differences within and across phylogeny and ontogeny. The experiments which follow constitute our progress toward this goal. Our working assumptions are simple: (1) memory is permanent; (2) context influences retrieval; and (3) accessibility of memory attributes is facilitated by cuing procedures. We do not assume a dual memory store.

In all studies, we trained and tested infants in their home cribs using the mobile conjugate reinforcement procedure (Section III, B-1). Unless otherwise specified, they received two consecutive daily training sessions and a procedurally identical third retention test session after a given interval had elapsed (see Fig. 2). Infants in the experimental group received a reactivation treatment prior to the third session but after the source of forgetting had occurred. Except when the interval between the reactivation treatment and subsequent retention testing (Session 3) was the independent variable, the reactivation treatment was administered 24 hours prior to Session 3. We used a 3-min noncontingent exposure to the reinforcer as the reactivation treatment. The choice of the reinforcer as the reminder was based on two factors: (1) it has been reported to be a particularly potent reactivating agent for animals (Riccio & Haroutunian, 1979; Spear & Parsons, 1976), and (2) cues noticed during the reactivation treatment must be identical to those noticed during original training. Because attention is typically asymptotic during reinforcement periods when the mobile is moving but diminishes when it is not, reactivation with the moving mobile maximized the probability that effective retrieval cues would be noticed.

Because of individual differences during training in footkick levels and hence in the degree of mobile movement which different infants saw, each infant was exposed to a rate of mobile movement which corresponded to his own footkick rate in the final 3 min of acquisition in Session 2. The ankle ribbon was not attached to the infant's ankle during the reactivation treatment but was draped over the crib side-rail where it was drawn and released by the experimenter, hidden from view, who also simulated the typical "burst" pattern of conjugate mobile movement. To preclude new learning during the reactivation procedure, infants were placed in an infant seat within the crib (see Fig. 8). This had the effect of redistributing the infant's weight in a way that minimized footkicks and generally constrained bodily activity. Actual counts of footkicks during the reactivation treatment ranged from 0–2 per min for infants reactivated at 14 weeks of age (Sullivan,

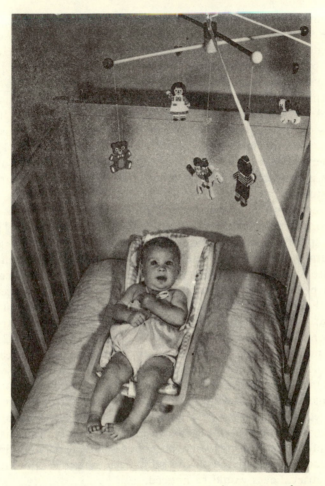

Fig. 8.   *An infant receiving a reactivation treatment 24 hours prior to long-term retention testing of a response acquired several weeks earlier. The ankle ribbon is draped over the crib rail where it is drawn and released by the experimenter, hidden from view. Not shown is the second mobile stand, affixed to the left crib rail as during original training (cf. Fig. 1). (Photographed by Breck P. Kent.)*

1980); moreover, those "kicks" which did occur were topographically different from conditioned footkicks (Rovee-Collier, Morrongiello, Aron, & Kupersmidt, 1978) and primarily consisted of squirms, bilateral extensions, or unidirectional side excursions.

The initial study was a portion of Sullivan's doctoral dissertation (Sullivan, 1980). In view of her findings that 12-week-olds did not exhibit evidence of retention following a 14-day retention interval (Sullivan et al., 1979), Sullivan decided to attempt to alleviate their forgetting by administering a reactivation treatment 24 hours prior to their 14-day retention test. Two groups of infants were trained, but only one of these (the *reactivation group*) received a reexposure to the moving crib mobile 13 days later; the other group (*no-reactivation group*) received no reminder prior to retention testing. A third group (the *familiarization/reactivation control group*) received a procedure identical to that of the two training groups during Sessions 1 and 2 except that infants in this group were removed from their cribs during the reinforcement phase of each session, and thus were familiarized with the nonmoving mobile but were not trained. This group received a "reactivation" treatment 13 days later, and was tested on Day 14 in a session identical to that of the other two groups. (For this group, then, Session 3 was the first training session.) The initial activity level of this control group did not change except during Session 3, when the response-reinforcer contingency was introduced for the first time. On Day 14, their conditioning performance was indistinguishable from the initial (Session 1) performance of infants in the no-reactivation control group (Fig. 9), who showed no evidence of retention in the 14-day test. Thus infants do not simply become more active in the presence of a nonmoving mobile over the period of the retention interval (2 weeks), nor do they show familiarity reactions in the form of excitement or enhanced general bodily activity, including increased footkicks, to a stimulus which they had viewed 2 weeks earlier in a nonmoving condition or even 24 hours earlier in a moving condition. The no-reactivation group also exhibited their original operant level during the 2-week long-term retention test, providing additional confirmation of the fact that infants do not simply show increased activity over a 2-week period in this context and that prior familiarity with the mobile *even with training* is insufficient to promote evidence of cued recall 2 weeks later. The inhibitory-like effect produced by 3 min of response-contingent mobile movement, which actually could be conceptualized as a self-produced "reminder" in Session 3 (no-reactivation group, Fig. 9), appears to be a genuine phenomenon and may reflect some of the temporal properties of the retrieval process. In fact, in this group several infants were observed to fuss and emit periodic cries during the final two-thirds of Session 3. This is most unusual behavior in the mobile conjugate reinforcement paradigm, particularly during a reinforcement phase. The characteristic learning curve of the familiarization/reactivation control group in that session further implicates aspects of the retrieval process in this phenomenon.

The effectiveness of a reactivation treatment in alleviating infant forgetting is summarized in Fig. 10. Although reactivation and no-reactivation groups did not differ in either original acquisition or 24-hour retention, their performance 14 days after training was different. Specifically, the reactivation groups evidenced little or no forgetting during the long-term retention test of Session 3 (Block 1), but the no-reactivation groups evidenced no retention, performing at a rate equivalent to their original operant level.

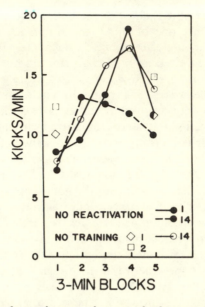

Fig. 9.   *Performance of control groups who received either no training prior to "retention" testing 14 days following Session 2 or who were trained but received no reactivation treatment prior to testing 14 days following training (Session 2). Mean kicks per min during Sessions 1 (open diamonds) and 2 (open squares), and familiarization with the nonmoving mobile (Blocks 1, 5) are indicated for the no-prior-training group, as is the Session 3 performance of this group (open circles). Session 3 actually constituted their first training day. Their performance in Session 3 was comparable to the Session 1 training curve of the no reactivation control group (filled circles vs. open circles, solid lines). The Session 3 performance of the latter group (filled circles, dashed line) 14 days after training is also shown. (From Sullivan, 1980.)*

We have recently repeated the reminder procedure, administering the reactivation treatment 27 days following the completion of training and 24 hours prior to a long-term retention test (Rovee-Collier, Sullivan, Enright, Lucas, & Fagen, 1980). The results of this study are summarized in the bottom row of curves, Fig. 10. Again, the two groups did not differ in measures of 24-hour retention, but after a 28-day retention interval only the reactivation group remembered the contingency. These findings are consistent with those of Spear and Parsons (1976): A reactivation treatment is also effective in alleviating the forgetting of conditioned responding of 11-week-old human infants after a period of 28 days. When one considers that infants received contingency training for only 9 min in each of two sessions and that 6 min of each session comprised nonreinforcement phases, the effectiveness of the treatment is still more remarkable. Moreover, we must recall that a period of 4 weeks is almost one-third the lifetime of an infant of this age!

Recently, we have questioned the resilience of the reactivation treatment. Does the reactivation treatment facilitate access to stored memory attributes

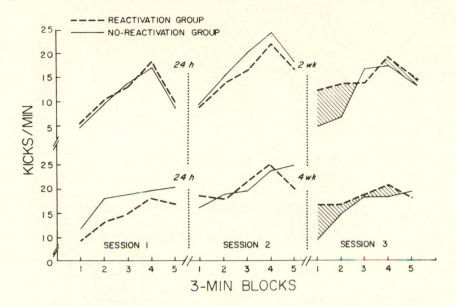

Fig. 10.   A composite showing the conditioning and retention performance of infants who received a reactivation treatment 24 hours prior to Session 3 (dashed line) in relation to the performance of a control group who received no reactivation treatment between the final training session (Session 2) and the long-term retention test (Block 1) of Session 3. Note that infants who did not receive a reminder began Session 3 at operant level (Block 1, Session 1), whereas those who received a reminder were performing the conditioned response at a level consistent with that of the immediate retention test (Block 5) of Session 2. (From Rovee-Collier et al., 1980.)

for only a brief period? Over what interval might performance during a cued-recall test continue to reflect the facilitating effects of a reminder? Lucas (1979) extended the original findings of Sullivan (1980) by administering a reactivation treatment to infants 13 days after training and testing for evidence of retention either 3, 6, 9, or 15 days later. (This corresponded to 16, 19, 22, or 28 days, respectively, following original training.) The forgetting function following a reactivation treatment was identical to the forgetting function following original training. Figure 11 presents a composite of the data we have now collected from independent groups of 11- to 13-week-olds ($N \geq 5$ per group) who were trained for two sessions and tested in a temporally distant third session following either a reactivation treatment administered 13 days after training (dotted line) or simply time passage with no interpolated priming event (solid line). Also shown in Fig. 11 is the 28-day retention ratio of infants who had received a reactivation treatment 27 days after training (Rovee-Collier et al., 1980).

These data demonstrate that a brief reminder can facilitate access to stored memory attributes for periods extending over several days. Moreover, the

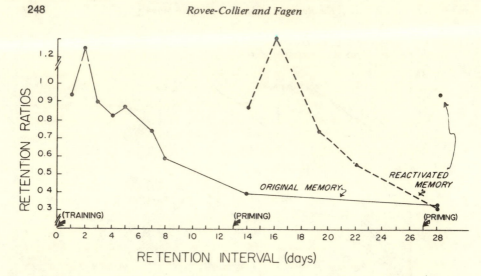

Fig. 11.   *A composite summarizing the data of a number of studies conducted with the procedure of Fig. 2. Retention ratios reflect the fraction of Session 2 immediate retention test performance which was exhibited during the initial 3-min cued-recall long-term retention test of a temporally distant third session. The retention interval between training and subsequent testing is indicated on the x-axis. The forgetting curves of infants who received no reactivation treatment between training and testing (solid lines) describe the temporal course of the newly acquired or "original memory"; the forgetting curves of infants who received a priming event 13 days following training (dashed lines) indicate the forgetting curve of the "reactivated memory". Note that priming (i.e., a reactivation treatment) which follows training by as long as 27 days can arrest forgetting and return performance to a level equivalent to that observed during the immediate retention test at the conclusion of training. Each point represents independent groups of at least five infants; data of 115 infants are represented in this figure.*

reminder is *as effective as original training* in producing retrieval access to memory attributes. Finally, the data enhance our suspicions regarding the special importance of the 48–72 hour period following original training or a reactivation treatment (Morrongiello & Gekoski, 1978; Rovee-Collier & Sullivan, 1980). The elevation in the retention index to a value > 1.00 may reflect some underlying organizational process such as the abstraction of prototypic cues which, after 48–72 hours, become the principal memory attributes that are subsequently aroused and noticed.

These data raise important questions regarding the kind of attributes which are "reactivated" by the priming event. Yengo, Fagen, and Enright (1980) asked whether a reactivation treatment with a discriminative stimulus ($S +$) would arouse or activate the memory attributes associated only with that stimulus, or whether such a treatment would have a generalized effect on responding during the cued-recall test. Also, would exposure to $S-$ (a nonmoving mobile) be as effective in reactivating stored memory attributes as exposure to $S +$? They used a behavioral contrast paradigm during training to achieve reliable and relatively rapid differences in response to $S+$ and $S-$ (Rovee-Collier & Capatides, 1979), and administered a reactivation treatment with either $S+$ or $S-20$ days later, 24 hours prior to the long-term retention test. The $S+$ and $S-$ were unique color/pattern cues on the mobile objects. As expected, both prior training *and* a particular reminder were necessary for the alleviation of forgetting which was subsequently observed. The presentation of $S-$ as a reminder was no more effective in alleviating forgetting than no reactivating stimulus at all. During the long-term retention test, infants reactivated with $S-$ and infants in the no-reactivation group exhibited performance consistent with their pretraining levels. However, infants reactivated with $S+$ had retention ratios averaging 0.89 when tested with $S+$ during the long-term cued-recall test, whereas performance to $S-$ remained low. The significantly greater level of responding to $S+$ on the part of the reactivation group primed with $S+$, relative to infants with no prior training who were tested with the $S+$ mobile model, can be described as the *memory component* (cf. Spear & Parsons, 1976). Note that simply presenting a reinforcer for 3 min, 24 hours prior to retention testing, does not have a generalized arousal effect with respect to *all* stored memory attributes. Rather, the attributes of $S-$ and $S+$ become differentially accessible, possibly as a result of decreased attention during training to cues which are negatively correlated with reward. Second, it is important to note that a nonmoving mobile, presented after an interval in which we know the specific details of the mobile have been forgotten, does not enhance conditioned responding to either the same or a different model 24 hours later, if that nonmoving model has previously been associated with withdrawal of reinforcement. This again emphasizes the importance of the training, priming, and test context.

Finally, it should be noted that the reactivation treatment procedure is also effective with younger infants. Davis (1980) used the standard training procedure with 8-week-olds and administered the reactivation treatment 17 days after the conclusion of training. Long-term tests of cued-recall were given 24 hours later (18 days after training), when infants who received no reminder exhibited no evidence of retention (Davis & Rovee-Collier, 1979). In contrast to the performance of a control group which received no reactivation treatment, the reactivation group showed little evidence of forgetting during the long-term retention test, responding at a rate 1.6 times above operant level which was equivalent to 24-hour retention performance. The low level of performance of an age-control group with no prior training excluded a simple maturational interpretation of these data.

D. Theoretical Significance

These results support a distinction between the *availablity* and *accessibility* of stored information and suggest that failures to observe evidence of retention in young infants are more parsimoniously discussed in terms of *retrieval failures* than as memory deficits. Clearly, when the course of forgetting is arrested and reversed by the provision of contextual cues which were present during original training, it is no longer possible to speak with certainty about the loss of information from storage. We think that procedures which improve accessibility to important retrieval cues will radically alter current views of infant memory. In addition, evidence of the sort which we have described challenges theorists whose memory constructs require semantic processing to broaden their constructs to incorporate the full range of data on human memory processing. Similarly, students of development must begin to recognize the limitations of theories of memory which either ignore or deny the representational capacities of the prelinguistic infant. Whereas the *manner* of representation may change ontogenetically, i.e., coding based on language may become the preferred or principal form of memory processing in the older infant or child, the *fact* of representation in the very young infant is indisputable.

Even more important, the present results permit an answer to two central developmental questions: (1) How do very young infants *accumulate* learning acquired during the infancy period? (2) How do the effects of their early experiences influence their later behavior? The second question reflects the paradox (Campbell & Jaynes, 1966) of the theoretical importance attributed to early experiences in spite of the extensive literature documenting infantile amnesia. We think that the mechanism which Campbell and Jaynes proposed as a resolution to the paradox, *reinstatement*, is the logical answer to the first question as well. We have demonstrated that reinstatement "works" with human infants. An occasional reencounter with stimuli which are either identical or highly similar to stimuli which were present (and noticed) during original training is clearly effective in maintaining conditioned responding at a high level after an interval of such length that the response would otherwise be forgotten. This mechanism, then, permits future behavior to "build" upon past experiences.

Particularly surprising is the precision with which the mechanism operates after extended intervals. The reactivation of stored memory attributes by means of a prior cuing procedure can restore conditioned responding (the target memory attribute) to the high level it attained immediately posttraining, with no indication that any forgetting had occurred in the interim. Moreover, retention of a reactivated memory follows the same temporal course as retention of a newly acquired memory. It is not far fetched to envision numerous encounters with highly similar aspects of a given event over the days and weeks following its initial occurrence. Each encounter would return conditioned responding to its previous level or, at least, to a level commensurate with the temporal interval between the encounter and the cued production of the conditioned response. Also, new contextual cues noticed during each subsequent reencounter and response production become stored as additional memory attributes, thereby increasing the number of potential effective retrieval cues.

As time passes, increasing numbers of generalized stimuli may function as retrieval cues (Campbell & Randall, 1976; Rovee-Collier & Sullivan, 1980).

Because this account assumes that memories are permanent, i.e., are always available, the role of a mechanism such as reinstatement is to increase response efficiency. It would be uneconomical for the organism to maintain ready access to all memories which had ever been processed. In addition to probable metabolic costs, the sorting task which would be required prior to response would be time consuming and inefficient. More frequently retrieved attributes are likely to be more readily accessible than those retrieved more rarely, etc. Reinstatement provides a means by which the organism can maintain selective access to certain memories while not being simultaneously encumbered by the requirement that all memories of a particular age be equally accessible. Although it is obviously useful to remember, it is also adaptive under many circumstances to forget.

V. SUMMARY AND CONCLUSIONS

Other than the program of research described in this chapter, there have been no systematic studies of the influence of context on infant retention (Olson, 1976). Research based on the Sokolovian (1963) model of the orienting reflex has been the major source of information regarding infant "recognition memory," but this has yielded only implicit indices of retention. In addition, in the conventional visual attention paradigms, retention tests are conducted in altered contexts. Under such circumstances it could be argued that the novel test cues *distract* the infant from the effective (previously noticed or familiar) cues in the situation which would facilitate retrieval. From our perspective, these paradigms tell us much about the infant's ability to detect stimulus change but do not address the problem of how the infant can retrieve and use stored information.

We have proposed a learning analysis as an alternative approach to the study of infant memory. This approach yields a highly sensitive and direct index of retention as well as direct evidence of the manner in which past experiences influence future performance. The data obtained from conditioning analyses of infant memory correspond closely to data which have been obtained in animal memory studies which also involve the use of conditioning procedures (Campbell & Coulter, 1976; Spear & Parsons, 1976). Thus a learning approach offers a potentially fruitful means by which to expand our knowledge and understanding of memory processing in very young infants and also to bridge the gap between human adult and animal memory research.

We have argued that infants retrieve memories of past events through encounters with contextual cues which were previously noticed, and we have demonstrated that manipulation of these cues can alleviate forgetting after quite lengthy retention intervals. Our findings challenge interpretations which presume loss of information from storage and confirm the suggestion of Campbell and Jaynes (1966) that reinstatement is a potent mechanism by which the effects of early experiences persist to influence behavior after relatively lengthy time periods. The lesson we have learned is clear: It *is* possible to teach new dogs old tricks!

REFERENCES

Atkinson, H., & Braddick, O. Stereotypic discrimination in infants. *Perception,* 1976, **5,** 29–38.

Bolles, R. C. Some relationships between learning and memory. In D. L. Medin, W. A. Roberts, & R. T. Davis (Eds.), *Processes of animal memory.* Hillsdale, N.J.: Lawrence Erlbaum Associates, 1976.

Bruner, J. The course of cognitive growth. *American Psychologist,* 1964, **19,** 1–15.

Campbell, B. A., Coulter, X. Neural and psychological processes underlying the development of learning and memory. In T. J. Tighe & R. N. Leaton (Eds.), *Habituation.* Hillsdale, N.J.: Lawrence Erlbaum Associates, 1976.

Campbell, B. A., & Jaynes, J. Reinstatement. *Psychological Review,* 1966, **73,** 478–480.

Campbell, B. A., & Jaynes, J. Effect of duration of reinstatement on retention of a visual discrimination learned in infancy. *Developmental Psychology,* 1969, **1,** 71–74.

Campbell, B. A., & Randall, P. K. The effects of reinstatement stimulus conditions on the maintenance of long-term memory. *Developmental Psychobiology,* 1976, **9,** 325–334.

Campbell, B. A., & Spear, N. E. Ontogeny of memory. *Psychological Review,* 1972, **79,** 215–236.

Church, R. M. Aversive behavior. In J. W. Kling & L. A. Riggs (Eds.), *Woodworth & Schlosberg's experimental psychology* (3rd ed.). New York: Holt, Rinehart, & Winston, 1972.

Cohen, L. B., & Gelber, E. R. Infant visual memory. In L. Cohen & P. Salapatek (Eds.), *Infant perception: From sensation to cognition* (Vol. 1). New York: Academic Press, 1975.

Davis, J. *Alleviated forgetting in 8-week-old infants.* Paper presented at the meeting of the Eastern Psychological Association, Hartford, Conn., April 1980.

Davis, J., & Rovee-Collier, C. K. A conditioning analysis of long-term memory in 8-week-old infants. Paper presented at the meeting of the Eastern Psychological Association, Philadelphia, April 1979.

Estes, W. K. Introduction to Volume 4. In W. K. Estes (Ed.), *Handbook of learning and cognitive process* (Vol. 4). Hillsdale, N. J.: Lawrence Erlbaum Associates, 1976.

Fagan, J. F., III. Infant recognition memory: Studies in forgetting. *Child Development,* 1977, **48,** 68–78.

Fagen, J. W., Rovee, C. K., & Kaplan, M. G. Psychophysical scaling of stimulus similarity in 3-month-old infants and adults. *Journal of Experimental Child Psychology,* 1976, **22,** 272–281.

Gekoski, M. J. Visual attention and operant conditioning in infancy: A second look (Doctoral dissertation, Rutgers University, 1977). *Dissertation Abstracts International,* 1977, **38,** 875B (University Microfilms No. 77-17, 533).

Guttman, N. The pigeon and the spectrum and other perplexities. *Psychological Reports,* 1956, **2,** 449-460.

Hasher, L., & Griffin, M. Reconstructive and reproductive processes in memory. *Journal of Experimental Psychology: Human Learning and Memory,* 1978, **4,** 318-330.

Hasher, L., & Zacks, R. T. Automatic and effortful processes in memory. *Journal of Experimental Psychology: General,* 1979, **108,** 356-388.

Hoving, K. L., & Choi, K. Some necessary conditions for producing reinstatement effects in children. *Developmental Psychology,* 1972, **7,** 214-217.

Hoving, K. L., Coates, L., Bertucci, M., & Riccio, D. C. Reinstatement effects in children. *Developmental Psychology,* 1972, **6,** 426-429.

Jeffrey, W. E. Habituation as a mechanism for perceptual development. In T. J. Tighe & R. N. Leaton (Eds.), *Habituation.* Hillsdale, N. J.: Lawrence Erlbaum Associates, 1976.

Jenkins, J. J. Remember that old theory of memory: Well, forget it! *American Psychologist,* 1974, **29,** 785-795.

Liddell, H. S., James, W. T., & Anderson, O. P. The comparative physiology of the conditioned motor reflex based on experiments with the pig, sheep, goat, and rabbit, *Comparative Psychology Monographs,* 1934, **11,** No. 1.

Lipsitt, L. P. Infant learning: The blooming, buzzing confusion revisited. In M. E. Meyer (Ed.), *Second western symposium on learning: Early learning.* Bellingham, Wash.: Western Washington State College, 1971.

Loftus, G. R., & Kallman, H. J. Encoding and use of detail information in picture recognition. *Journal of Experimental Psychology: Human Learning and Memory,* 1979, **5,** 197-211.

Lucas, D. A. *Alleviated forgetting in 3-month-old infants.* Paper presented at the meeting of the Eastern Psychological Association, Philadelphia, April 1979.

Mactutus, C. F., Riccio, D. C., & Ferek, J. M. Retrograde amnesia for old (reactivated) memory: Some anomalous characteristics. *Science,* 1979, **204,** 1319-1320.

Medin, D. L. Animal models and memory models. In D. L. Medin, W. A. Roberts, & R. T. Davis (Eds.). *Processes of animal memory.* Hillsdale, N.J.: Lawrence Erlbaum Associates, 1976.

Morrongiello, B. A., and Gekoski, M. J. Familiarization of novelty: The effect of changing visual cues on infant conditioning and retention. Paper presented at the meeting of the Eastern Psychological Association, Washington, D. C., March 1978.

Olson, G. M. An information-processing analysis of visual memory and habituation in infants. In T. J. Tighe & R. N. Leaton (Eds.), *Habituation.* Hillsdale, N.J.: Lawrence Erlbaum Associates, 1976.

Piaget, J. *Origins of intelligence in children.* New York: International Universities Press, 1952.

Riccio, D. C., & Haroutunian, V. Some approaches to the alleviation of ontogenetic memory deficits. In B. A. Campbell & N. E. Spear (Eds.), *Ontogeny of learning and memory.* Hillsdale, N. J.: Lawrence Erlbaum Associates, 1979.

Roberts, W. A., & Grant, D. S. Studies of short-term memory in the pigeon using the delayed matching to sample procedure. In D. L. Medin, W. A. Roberts, & R. T. Davis (Eds.), *Processes of animal memory.* Hillsdale, N.J.: Lawrence Erlbaum Associates, 1976.

Rovee, C. K., Fagen, J. W. Extended conditioning and 24-hr retention in infants. *Journal of Experimental Child Psychology,* 1976, **21,** 1-11.

Rovee-Collier, C. K., Sullivan, M. W., Enright, M., Lucas, D., & Fagen, J. W. Reactivation of infant memory. *Science,* 1980, **208,** 1159-1161.

Rovee-Collier, C. K., & Capatides, J. B. Positive behavioral contrast in 3-month-old infants on multiple conjugate reinforcement schedules. *Journal of the Experimental Analysis of Behavior,* 1979, **32,** 15-27.

Rovee-Collier, C. K., & Gekoski, M. J. The economics of infancy: A review of conjugate reinforcement. In H. W. Reese & L. P. Lipsitt (Eds.), *Advances in child development and behavior* (Vol. 13). New York: Academic Press, 1979.

Rovee-Collier, C. K., Morrongiello, B. A., Aron, M., & Kupersmidt, J. Topographical response differentiation in three-month-old infants. *Infant Behavior & Development*, 1978, **1**, 323–333.

Rovee-Collier, C. K., & Sullivan, M. W. Organization of infant memory. *Journal of Experimental Psychology: Human Learning and Memory*, 1980, **6**, 798–807.

Skinner, B. F. *The behavior of organisms.* New York: Appleton-Century Crofts, 1938.

Sokolov, E. N. *Perception and the conditioned reflex.* New York: Macmillan, 1963.

Spear, N. E. Forgetting as a retrieval failure. In W. K. Honig & P. H. R. James (Eds.), *Animal memory.* New York: Academic Press, 1971.

Spear, N. E. Retrieval of memory in animals. *Psychological Review*, 1973, **80**, 163–194.

Spear, N. E. Retrieval of memories. In W. K. Estes (Ed.), *Handbook of learning and cognitive processes* (Vol. 4). Hillsdale, N.J.: Lawrence Erlbaum Associates, 1976.

Spear, N. E. *The processing of memories: Forgetting and retention.* Hillsdale, N.J.: Lawrence Erlbaum Associates, 1978.

Spear, N. E., & Parsons, P. J. Analysis of a reactivation treatment: Ontogenetic determinants of alleviated forgetting. In D. L. Medin, W. A. Roberts, & R. T. Davis (Eds.), *Processes of animal memory.* Hillsdale, N.J.: Lawrence Erlbaum Associates, 1976.

Sullivan, M. W. Infant memory in a learning paradigm: Long-term retention and alleviated forgetting (Doctoral dissertation;, Rutgers University, 1980). *Dissertation Abstracts International*, 1980, **40**, 5059B (University Microfilms No. 80–8923)

Sullivan, M. W., Rovee-Collier, C. K., & Tynes, D. M. A conditioning analysis of infant long-term memory. *Child Development*, 1979, 50, 152–162.

Tulving, E. Episodic and semantic memory. In E. Tulving & W. Donaldson (Eds.), *Organization of memory.* New York: Academic Press, 1972.

Underwood, B. J. Attributes of memory. *Psychological Review*, 1969, **76**, 559–573.

Werner, J. S., & Perlmutter, M. Development of visual memory in infants. In H. W. Reese & L. P. Lipsitt (Eds.), *Advances in child development and behavior* (Vol. 14). New York: Academic Press, 1979.

Williams, T. M., Fryer, M. L., & Aiken, L. S. Development of visual pattern classification in preschool children: Prototypes and distinctive features. *Developmental Psychology*, 1977, **13**, 577–584.

Yengo, L. A., Fagen, J. W., & Enright, M. The effect of reactivation on infant memory of a learned discrimination. Paper presented at the meeting of the Eastern Psychological Association, Hartford, Conn., April 1980.

NAME INDEX

Abramson, L. Y., 114, *121*
Adamson, L. *100,* 112, *126*
Adkinson, C. D., 12, *36*
Adler-Stoller, S., 80, *96*
Ahrend, R. A., *160*
Aiken, L. S., 235, *254*
Ainsworth, M. D. S., 108, 111, 116,
  117, 118, *121, 122, 158,* 178, *217*
Als, H., 75, *96, 100,* 108, 112, *122,*
  126, 132, *157*
Altman, S. A., 164, *217*
Ames, E. W., 21, *40*
Ames, G. J., 172, *219*
Anderson, B. J., *217*
Anderson, O. P., 228, 253
Ainsfeld, M., *217*
Anscombe, G. E. M., 42, 54, *56*
Antinucci, F., 53, *56*
Appelbaum, M. I., 21, *39*
Arend, R. A., 119, *122, 124*
Aristotle, 14
Aron, M., 244, *254*
Aronson, E., 110, *122*
Atkinson, H., 220, *252*
Attonucci, J., 136, *161*
Austin, G. A., 29, *37*
Axelrod, J., 91, *96*

Babiri, C., *98*
Bach, J. S., 208
Baer, D. M., 10, *122*
Bakeman, R., 58, 87, *96, 97*
Baldwin, J. M., 139, *157*
Barry, W. A., 134, *157*
Bartoshuk, A. K., 84, 94, *96*
Battro, A. M., 190, 191, *218*
Baumel, M. H., 3, *39*
Beare, A. C., 6, *37*
Beason-Williams, L., 106, *126*
Beckwith, L., 58, *97,* 136, *157*
Beebe, B. A., 74, *96, 223*
Bell, S. M., 108, 111, 116, *121, 122,*
  178, *217*

Bennett, S. L., *223*
Benson, P. J., *223*
Berg, K. M., 84, 94, *96,* 109, 110,
  122
Berg, W. K., 12, *36,* 109, 110, *122*
Bergman, T., 106, *123*
Berkeley, G., 33, *37*
Berlin, B., 36, *37*
Berlyne, D. E., 21, *37*
Bernstein, N. A., *56*
Bernstein, P., 105, *125,* 188, 199,
  206, 213, *217, 221*
Bertucci, M., 241, *253*
Bienstock, S. F., 186, 188, 190, 193,
  219
Bigelow, A., 107, *122*
Bijou, S., 105, *122*
Birns, B., 86, *96*
Blehar, M., 116, *122*
Block, J., 119, *122*
Block, J. H., 119, *122*
Bloom, K., 204, *217*
Boehmer, A., 35, *39*
Bohrer, R. E., 60, *99*
Bolles, R. C., 228, *252*
Bornstein, M. H., 2, 3, 5, 6, 7, 8, 9,
  10, 12, 14, 16, 17, 18, 19, 23, 24,
  25, 26, 28, 29, 34, 36, *37, 39, 40,*
  102, *122*
Bosack, T. N., 103, *124*
Bourne, L. E., 29, 32, *37*
Bower, T. G. R., 11, *37*
Boynton, R. M., 12, 14, 17, *37*
Braddick, O., 229, *252*
Bradley, R., *158*
Brazelton, T. B., 61, 62, 63, 67, 75,
  82, 86, 87, 93, *96, 97, 100,* 108,
  112, *122, 126,* 132, 157
Bretherton, I., 119, *126,* 151, *157,*
  158
Bridger, W. H., 87, *99*
Bromwich, R., 58, *97*
Bronfenbrenner, U., 129, 130, 142,
  158

SUBJECT INDEX